Leavenworth Paper *Number 22*

Moving the Enemy: Operational Art in the Chinese PLA's Huai Hai Campaign

by Dr. Gary J. Bjorge

Combat Studies Institute Press
Fort Leavenworth, Kansas

Published by Books Express Publishing
Copyright © Books Express, 2010
ISBN 978-1-907521-21-8
To purchase copies at discounted prices please contact
info@books-express.com

Contents

Chapter	Page
Figures	v
Maps	v
Tables	vi
Preface	vii
Introduction	1
Significance of the Huai Hai Campaign	1
The Huai Hai Campaign and Operational Art	2
The Haui Hai Campaign and Sunzi's *The Art of War*	5
Organization of the Study	7
1. Historical Background of the Huai Hai Campaign	11
Background Chronology	11
Building Rural Base Areas and Military Forces	16
Developing Military Leaders	24
Transforming the PLA	35
Communist Strategy From the Time of Japan's Surrender to Summer 1948	41
2. The Emergence of the Huai Hai Campaign Vision and Plan	49
Su Yu Plants the Seed of the Huai Hai Campaign	50
Communist Strategic Thinking, Summer 1948	53
Prelude to the Huai Hai Campaign—the ECFA Captures Jinan	54
Su Yu Proposes the Huai Hai Campaign	55
The Huai Hai Campaign Plan Evolves	59
The CPFA's Increasing Role in the Campaign	61
The ECFA Prepares for the Huai Hai Campaign	70
PLA Doctrine, Sunzi's *The Art of War*, and Su Yu's Campaign Design	72
The Final ECFA Campaign Plan	76
3. Nationalist Strategy During Summer and Early Fall 1948	85
The August Strategy Session in Nanjing	85
Du Yuming Seeks the Initiative	86
He Yingqin and Gu Zhutong Develop an Active Defense Concept	88
Reconsidering He Yingqin and Gu Zhutong's Plan	89
Nationalist Indecision	90

Chapter	Page
The Nationalists Decide to Defend Xuzhou	92
4. The Physical Setting of the Huai Hai Campaign and a Comparison of the Opposing Forces	97
The Physical Environment of the Huai Hai Campaign Area	97
Comparing Nationalist and Communist Political and Economic Strengths	99
Quantitative Comparison of Military Forces	102
Qualitative Comparison of Military Forces	112
5. The Huai Hai Campaign Begins	123
The Nationalists Start to Redeploy	123
The Third Pacification Area Defects	129
Encircling the Seventh Army	131
Nationalist Efforts to Retrieve the Situation	139
6. Expanding Campaign Objectives	149
Su Yu's Strategic and Operational Analysis	150
Campaign Visions of 9-23 November	152
The CPFA Occupies the Central Position	155
Su Yu's Sunzian Vision for Shaping the Campaign	158
Su Yu Attempts to Execute His Plan	163
Nationalist Moves on the Southern Front	169
PLA Commanders Debate Alternative Courses of Action	172
The Seventh Army's Final Destruction	178
7. Contesting the Central Position	185
Nationalist Strategy to Retake the Central Position	187
Communist Strategy to Hold the Central Position	189
Liu Bocheng's Sunzian Plan for Attacking the Twelfth Army	193
Encircling the Twelfth Army	197
Intimidating the Sixth and Eighth Armies	201
Holding the Line on the Northern Front	202
Communist Visions and Operational Concepts, 27 November-1 December	205
The Nationalists Decide to Abandon Xuzhou	212
Encircling Du Yuming's Army Group	215
The Nationalists Advance Again on the Southern Front	221
The Hard Fight to Destroy the Twelfth Army	223

Chapter	Page
8. End Moves in the Campaign	247
Nationalist Planning to Save Du Yuming's Army Group	247
An Operational Pause for Strategic Purposes	249
The CMC and General Front Committee Look Ahead	250
The Political Offensive Against Du Yuming's Army Group	252
The ECFA and CPFA Make Ready to Resume Combat	256
Du Yuming's Preparations to Break Out	257
Destroying Du Yuming's Army Group	257
Conclusion	267
Epilogue	267
The Haui Hai Campaign as Operational Art	268
The Huai Hai Campaign and Sunzi's *The Art of War*	268
Glossary	271
List of Names and Positions	273

Figures

Chapter 2
Su Yu's Proposal to the CMC to Undertake the Huai Hai Campaign 56

Chapter 4
1. Communist Military and Political Organization Down to the Regional Level, Summer-Fall 1948 101
2. PLA Organization for the Huai Hai Campaign 105
3. PLA Infantry Division Organization, Autumn 1948 106
4. Nationalist Military Organization During the Huai Hai Campaign 109
5. Nationalist Infantry Division Organization, Autumn 1948 110

Maps

Chapter 1
Political Map of Eastern China, 1928 17

Chapter 2
1. Location of Forces, 5 November 1948 69
2. Huai Hai Campaign Plan of Attack According to ECFA Order Issued 4 November 1948 75

Chapter 4
Communist Military Districts and Subdistricts in the Area of the Huai Hai Campaign 104

Chapter 5
1. Planned Seventh Army Redeployment, 6-9 November 1948 125

	Page
2. The ECFA's Plan to Encircle the Seventh Army, 8 November 1948	132
3. Encirclement of the Seventh Army	136

Chapter 6
- 1. The CPFA Seizes the Central Position 156
- 2. Su Yu's Initial Plan to Cut Off the Second Army/Thirteenth Army Relief Force 159

Chapter 7
- 1. Holding the Central Position 190
- 2. Encirclement of the Twelfth Army 198
- 3. Pursuing Du Yuming's Army Group 216
- 4. The CPFA's Deployment for the 6 December General Attack Against the Twelfth Army 228

Chapter 8
- The ECFA's Plan for Attacking Du Yuming's Army Group, 5 January 1948 259

Tables

Chapter 4
- 1. Concurrent Appointments That CCP Central China Bureau Members Held, Summer-Fall 1948 102
- 2. ECFA Divisional Weapons 107
- 3. CPFA Divisional Weapons 107
- 4. Nationalist Army Divisional Weapons 111
- 5. Nationalist Aircraft Available for Use During the Huai Hai Campaign 113
- 6. Selected PLA Logistics Statistics for the Entire Huai Hai Campaign 115

Preface

The genesis of this book lies so many years in the past that it is hard to imagine that it is actually being published. In 1986, as a member of the Research Committee in the Combat Studies Institute (CSI) at the U.S. Army Command and General Staff College (CGSC), I was tasked to study the Huai Hai Campaign as an example of large-unit maneuver. As part of that assignment, I asked for, and was granted, an invitation from the Chinese Academy of Military Science (AMS) to visit China to conduct research on the campaign. I was able to meet with military historians at AMS and the Military Museum in Beijing. I met with former Nationalist commanders such as Huang Wei, who commanded the Nationalist Twelfth Army during the campaign. I also traveled to Xuzhou, the main city in the campaign area and the site of the Huai Hai Campaign Memorial and Memorial Museum. While in Xuzhou, I visited the Nianzhuangxu area where the Nationalist Seventh Army was encircled and destroyed. I also met with former veterans of the campaign. This visit to China was of immense benefit to my research.

In early 1989, as I was writing my manuscript, an unexpected research opportunity arose when the Taiwan Armed Forces University invited me to come to Taiwan to meet with military historians and study the campaign. This I did in late April, and thanks to the arrangements made for me at the behest of General Lo Pen-li, President, Armed Forces University, I acquired additional valuable material and developed new perspectives on the campaign. Then my research and writing ended when, during summer 1989, the CSI research committee was abolished and all CSI staff members were assigned as full-time classroom teachers.

While teaching, conducting small research projects was possible, but writing on a topic as large as the Huai Hai Campaign was not. For several years my Huai Hai Campaign material sat on shelves at home while I pursued other projects such as writing a short study of Merrill's Marauders in northern Burma. In 1998 I became involved in an effort to develop a military history exchange program between the U.S. Army and the Chinese army. As a result of that involvement, I visited Xuzhou, China, again and went to all of the Huai Hai Campaign's major battlefields. This rekindled my desire to complete my manuscript, but it did not solve the problem of not having the time to devote to the effort. In fall 2001 the Director, CSI, selected me to participate in CSI's Wagner Research Fellowship Program. This not only gave me time to refine my research work and write, but the Director, CSI, also supported me taking another research trip to China. In November 2001 I returned to Xuzhou for the third time and spent two weeks conducting research at the Huai Hai Campaign Memorial. There I had a desk in the office of the Memorial's historian and was able, daily, to ask questions and more deeply understand how Chinese military historians view the campaign and the generals who led it.

The time the Wagner Fellowship Program gave me and my present position on a recently established research and publication team have made it possible for me to complete my manuscript. But I could never have done this without the support, encouragement, and assistance of many people. First, I wish to express my appreciation to Colonel (COL) Lawyn Edwards, the current director, CSI, for selecting me to be a Wagner Fellow; for believing in the value of this project; and for getting me to China in 2001. I would like to thank the former director, CSI, COL Jerry Morelock, for supporting my involvement in military history exchange activities with the Chinese army and for being the senior officer on the delegation that went to Xuzhou in fall 1998. I must also thank my current immediate supervisor, Lieutenant Colonel

Kevin Farrell, for his patience and support beyond the call of duty. For their assistance in my research, I wish to specifically thank Zhou Hongyan, AMS's expert on the Huai Hai Campaign; Yu Shijing, former director of the Huai Hai Campaign Memorial Musem; Fu Jijun, historian, Huai Hai Campaign Memorial; and Zhou Liping, deputy director, Huai Hai Campaign Memorial Museum. For their commitment to excellence, I wish to thank the two editors who worked on this book, Patricia Whitten, who edited the text and did layout, and Robin Kern who did the maps. For her understanding and patience as she deciphered my handwriting, I wish to thank my typist, Virginia Wright. The patience and support of my wife Nancy and daughter Joanne were also of immeasurable importance.

The material I have used in my research has been almost exclusively written in the Chinese language. I have translated that material myself and assume responsibility for all errors in translation that may have occurred. However, I would like to give the reader some confidence that what he is reading is an accurate translation by saying that I have spent years studying Chinese and have received complimentary reviews on my published translations of Chinese literature. I hope readers find what appears on the pages of this work to be interesting and even stimulating. I know that has been my reaction to learning more about the Huai Hai Campaign throughout the considerable period that its study has been part of my life.

Introduction

Those who excel in war move the enemy and are not moved by the enemy.
—Sunzi, *The Art of War*

Forcing the enemy to react is the essence of seizing and retaining the initiative.
—FM 3-0, *Operations*, 2001

Significance of the Huai Hai Campaign

Among the numerous wars of the 20th century, one of the largest and most significant was the Chinese civil war of 1946-1949 fought between the armies of the Nationalist government of China led by President Jiang Jieshi (Chiang Kai-shek) and Communist armies under the leadership of Chinese Communist Party (CCP) Chairman Mao Zedong (Mao Tse-tung).[1] During this war, military forces numbering in the millions fought across the vast space of China in a struggle that ended with the Nationalist government taking refuge on the island province of Taiwan and the Communists establishing the People's Republic of China (PRC) on 1 October 1949. For China this meant a radical new direction in economic, political, and social development. Externally, the result was a major alteration of world power bloc equations and new challenges for US policymakers.

The subject of this study, the Huai Hai Campaign, was the largest and most decisive campaign of the Chinese civil war. Beginning on 6 November 1948 and ending on 10 January 1949, this campaign was first conceived by Communist generals as an effort to push aside Nationalist forces positioned along the Long-Hai railroad east of Xuzhou and link together the Communist-controlled areas in Shandong and Jiangsu provinces.[2] Such a result, it was determined, would facilitate the mobilization of men and materiel in Jiangsu and create a situation favorable for further operations against Nationalist forces north of the Yangzi (Yangtze) River in eastern China. After the campaign began, however, Communist commanders, taking advantage of battlefield victories and Nationalist command decisions, decided to extend operations and attempt to destroy all Nationalist armies in this crucial area in one great campaign. The result was a smashing victory. Communist forces destroyed five Nationalist armies totaling around one-half million men, captured immense quantities of weapons and ammunition, and advanced into positions that directly threatened the Nationalist capital of Nanjing and the economic heartland of Nationalist China in the lower Yangzi Valley. With this defeat, the Nationalist government lost whatever chance it might have had of resisting a Communist thrust into southern China.

By virtue of its magnitude (more than one million combatants), duration, and strategic impact, the Huai Hai Campaign ranks as one of the major campaigns in world military history. The campaign is also important as the classic example of the type of fighting that Mao envisioned as the final stage of revolutionary war, the time when insurgent forces would concentrate and engage government forces in large-scale mobile operations. The Communist People's Liberation Army (PLA) committed more troops to the Huai Hai Campaign than it did to any other campaign it had fought before or has fought since. CCP organizations in Henan, Hebei, Jiangsu, Anhui and Shandong provinces mobilized approximately 5 million civilian laborers to move supplies to support PLA combat units. In villages throughout the Communist-controlled areas in eastern and central China, hundreds of thousands of women were organized to sew heavy cotton uniform jackets, make shoes, grind grain, and perform other tasks that aided the war effort. This was Mao's "people's war" carried out on a grand scale, a powerful example of what a large revolutionary army could accomplish with the support of the masses.

The Huai Hai Campaign and Operational Art

The Huai Hai Campaign could be studied as an example of a people's war or as part of the Maoist model for revolutionary war. This work, however, treats the campaign as an example of warfare at the operational level and focuses on the planning and execution of large-scale operations by PLA commanders; in other words, how the PLA commanders practiced what US Army doctrine describes as operational art. It will further validate the importance of operational art as a doctrinal concept, both in theory and in practice, and also increase the reader's understanding of the professional knowledge and skill of the PLA officer corps.

The concept of the operational level of war was introduced into U.S. Army doctrinal literature in the 1982 edition of Field Manual (FM) 100-5, *Operations*:

> The operational level of war uses available military resources to attain strategic goals within a theater of war. Most simply, it is the theory of larger unit operations. It also involves planning and conducting campaigns. Campaigns are sustained operations designed to defeat an enemy force in a specified space and time with simultaneous and sequential battles. The disposition of forces, selection of objectives, and actions taken to weaken or to outmaneuver the enemy all set the terms of the next battle and exploit tactical gains. They are all part of the operational level of war. In AirLand Battle doctrine, this level includes the marshalling of forces and logistical support, providing direction to ground and air maneuver, applying conventional and nuclear fires in depth, and employing unconventional and psychological warfare.[3]

The 1986 edition of this FM introduced the term "operational art" to describe the effective use of military force at the operational level:

> Operational art is the employment of military forces to attain strategic goals in a theater of war or theater of operations through the design, organization, and conduct of campaigns and major operations. A campaign is a series of joint actions designed to attain a strategic objective in a theater of war. Simultaneous campaigns may take place when the theater of war contains more than one theater of operations. Sequential campaigns in a single theater occur when a large force changes or secures its original goals or when the conditions of the conflict change. . . . A major operation comprises the coordinated actions of large forces in a single phase of a campaign or in a critical battle. Major operations decide the course of campaigns.
>
> Operational art thus involves fundamental decisions about when and where to fight and whether to accept or decline battle. Its essence is the identification of the enemy's operational center-of-gravity—his source of strength or balance—and the concentration of superior combat power against that point to achieve a decisive success. . . . No particular echelon of command is solely or uniquely concerned with operational art, but theater commanders and their chief subordinates usually plan and direct campaigns. Army groups and armies normally design the major ground operations of a campaign. And corps and

divisions normally execute those major ground operations. Operational art requires broad vision, the ability to anticipate, a careful understanding of the relationship of means to ends, and effective joint and combined cooperation. Reduced to its essentials, operational art requires the commander to answer three questions:

(1) What military condition must be produced in the theater of war or operations to achieve the strategic goal?
(2) What sequence of actions is most likely to produce that condition?
(3) How should the resources of the force be applied to accomplish that sequence of actions?[4]

The 1993 version of FM 100-5 basically repeated what the 1986 edition had said about the operational level of war and operational art. FM 3-0, *Operations*, published in June 2001, delved deeper into the mental demands placed upon an operational commander, refined the questions that operational art requires a commander to answer, and added a fourth question to the three questions listed in the 1986 and 1993 editions of FM 100-5:

2-5. The operational level of war is the level at which campaigns and major operations are conducted and sustained to accomplish strategic objectives within theaters or areas of operations (AOs). It links the tactical employment of forces to strategic objectives. The focus at this level is on operational art—the use of military forces to achieve strategic goals through the design, organization, integration, and conduct of theater strategies, campaigns, major operations, and battles. A campaign is a related series of military operations aimed at accomplishing a strategic or operational objective within a given time and space. . . . Operational art determines when, where, and for what purpose major forces are employed to influence the enemy disposition before combat. It governs the deployment of those forces, their commitment to or withdrawal from battle, and the arrangement of battles and major operations to achieve operational and strategic objectives.

2-6. Operational art helps commanders use resources efficiently and effectively to achieve strategic objectives. It includes employing military forces and arranging their efforts in time, space, and purpose. Operational art helps commanders understand the conditions for victory before seeking battle. It provides a framework to assist commanders in ordering their thoughts when designing campaigns and major operations. Without operational art, war would be a set of disconnected engagements with relative attrition the only measure of success. Operational art requires commanders who can visualize, anticipate, create, and seize opportunities. It is practiced not only by JFCs [joint force commanders] but also by their senior staff officers and subordinate commanders.

2-7. Operations usually imply broader dimensions of time and space than tactics; the strategic orientation at the operational level requires commanders to look beyond the immediate situation. While tactical commanders fight the current battle, operational commanders look deeper in time, space, and events. They seek to shape the possibilities of upcoming events in advance to create the most favorable conditions possible for subordinate commanders, whose tactical activities execute the campaign. Likewise, operational commanders anticipate the results of battles and engagements, and prepare to exploit them to obtain the greatest strategic advantage.

2-8. Operational commanders continually communicate with their strategic superiors to obtain direction and ensure common understanding of events. Mutual confidence and communications among commanders and staffs allow the flexibility to adapt to tactical circumstances as they develop. Tactical results influence the conduct of campaigns through a complex interaction of operational and tactical dynamics. Operational commanders create the conditions for the conduct of battles and engagements, while the results of battles and engagements shape the conduct of the campaign. In this regard, commanders exploit tactical victories to gain strategic advantage, or even to reverse the strategic effect of tactical losses.

2-9. Operational art is translated into operation plans through operational design. A well-designed plan and successfully executed operation shape the situation for tactical actions. Executed skillfully, a good plan increases the chances of tactical success. It does this by creating advantages for friendly forces and disadvantages for the enemy. A flexible plan gives tactical commanders freedom to seize opportunities or react effectively to unforeseen enemy actions and capabilities. Flexible execution maintains the operational initiative and maximizes tactical opportunities.

2-10. Without tactical success, a campaign cannot achieve its operational goals. An essential element of operational art, therefore, is the ability to recognize what is possible at the tactical level and design a plan that maximizes chances for the success in battles and engagements that ultimately produces the desired operational end state. Without a coherent operational design to link tactical successes, battles and engagements waste precious resources on fights that do not lead to operational goals. A thorough understanding of what is possible tactically, and the ability to create conditions that increase the chances of tactical success, are important attributes of an operational commander. Tactical commanders must understand the operational context within which battles and engagements are fought as well. This understanding allows them to seize opportunities (both foreseen and unforeseen) that contribute to achieving operational goals or defeating enemy initiatives that threaten those goals. Operational commanders require experience at both the operational and tactical levels. From this experience, they gain the instincts and intuition, as well as the knowledge that underlie an understanding of the interrelation of tactical and operational possibilities and needs.

2-11. Among many considerations, operational art requires commanders to answer the following questions:

- What military (or related political and social) conditions must be produced in the operational area to achieve the strategic goal (ends)?
  - What sequence of actions is most likely to produce that condition (ways)?

- How should resources be applied to accomplish that sequence of actions (means)?
- What are the likely costs or risks in performing that sequence of actions (risk management)?[5]

As this lengthy excerpt from FM 3-0 indicates, operational art is now an essential element in U.S. Army warfighting doctrine. It is viewed as a way to bring coherence to military action, linking tactical ways and means to operational ways and means so that resources are used efficiently.[6] It ensures that operations are directed toward achieving a strategic objective by requiring commanders to "continually communicate with their strategic superiors to obtain direction and ensure common understanding of events."[7] Operational art asks commanders to look ahead in time, space, and events and to try to "shape the possibilities of upcoming events in advance to create the most favorable conditions possible for subordinate commanders."[8] It requires that commanders "recognize what is possible at the tactical level and design a plan that maximizes chances for the success in battles and engagements that ultimately produces the desired operational end state."[9] Operational art has become an indispensable framework for organizing a commander's thoughts as he analyzes a situation; visualizes what may be possible; and then plans, prepares, executes, and assesses operations designed to achieve strategic goals.

This study uses US Army doctrine on operational art as presented in FM 3-0 as the basis for analyzing and assessing PLA generalship during the Huai Hai Campaign. Certainly, the great victory the PLA won in this campaign was a "desired operational end state" that contributed greatly to achieving Communist strategic objectives. By destroying five Nationalist armies, the PLA caused the military, social, economic, and political situation to shift dramatically in favor of the Communists. If results are a measure of effectiveness, the PLA commanders were indeed excellent practitioners of operational art.

Some may question the relevancy of the operational art practiced during the Huai Hai Campaign to current U.S. Army thinking about operational art. By present-day standards, the battlefields of the Huai Hai Campaign were unsophisticated. The forces the PLA employed did not have the air assets, the precision-guided munitions, the seamless communication architecture, and the other products of advanced technology that are available to the U.S. Army today. But as the doctrinal statements on operational art contained in FM 3-0 indicate, operational art is not about technology. It is about human thought—the mental process in which an operational-level commander decides on a course of action after evaluating information, considering many factors, and answering the four questions listed in paragraph 2-11 of FM 3-0. The instincts and intuition that are part of this process are not found in integrated circuits. The ability to visualize, anticipate, create, and seize opportunities does not reside in a computer data base. Because operational art is neither a product of technology nor dependent on it, the operational art of the Huai Hai Campaign will always be worth studying. In fact, as the U.S. Army continues to refine its thinking about operational-level warfare and operational art, the sophisticated practice of operational art by generals whose education and experience lie outside the so-called Western military tradition should be of special interest.

The Huai Hai Campaign and Sunzi's *The Art of War*

In addition to examining the Huai Hai Campaign in terms of "operational art as described in FM 3-0, this study also examines the campaign from the perspective of the military thought contained in Sunzi's *The Art of War*. This ancient Chinese military classic, probably written sometime during 400 to 320 B.C., clearly belongs to a non-Western military tradition. Furthermore, Chinese military historians have shown that the theories and principles contained in this work greatly influenced Mao, who played a significant role in planning and executing the Huai Hai Campaign, and also his generals in the field.[10] Dr. Tan Yiqing, a researcher in the Academy of Military Science's Department of Strategic Studies, has written the following about how Sunzi's ideas helped shape Mao's thinking about war and how to conduct it effectively:

> The primary source of Mao Zedong's military thought was the practical experience of the Chinese revolutionary war . . . [but he] also drew upon China's splendid ancient military heritage, most notably the essence of Sunzi's *The Art of War*. If one does not understand what Mao Zedong's military thought inherited from Sunzi's *The Art of War*, it will be impossible to understand its deep grounding in history, and it will also be very hard to explain the unique Chinese characteristics inherent in Mao's strategy and tactics.[11]
>
> Mao Zedong not only put Sunzi's theories about war into practice, he used the fine quintessence of Sunzi's thought to create strategic theories that fit the specific conditions of China's revolutionary war, pushing Sunzi into a new age.[12]

Non-Chinese students of Chinese military thought and military history have also established this link. Samuel B. Griffith's translation of *The Art of War* contains a chapter on Sunzi's influence on Mao and PLA commanders. Robert B. Rigg, a US Army attaché in China from 1945 to 1948, makes this statement in his 1951 book, *Red China's Fighting Hordes*: "The impact of Sun Tzu goes beyond his influence on Mao and Mao's direction of the PLA; it extends down to the combat action and reaction of many generals, and even of some battalion commanders. It provides the spirit, if not the letter of guidance."[13]

The distinctly Chinese origin of *The Art of War* and its enduring and profound impact on Chinese military thought for more than 2,000 years give this work special value as a framework for analyzing the Huai Hai Campaign. First, it provides a Chinese theoretical basis for explaining the decisions PLA commanders made. Second, it establishes a Chinese standard for evaluating the practice of operational art during the campaign. Third, it provides a basis for assessing whether or not there might be an operational art with Chinese characteristics. Finally, and perhaps most important, looking at the Huai Hai Campaign from the perspective of this work with ancient Chinese roots is a useful way to examine the universality of certain fundamental principles of war and tenets of military operations. Sunzi is not quoted in US Army doctrinal manuals, including FM 3-0, because he writes about a Chinese way of war. *The Art of War* has been integrated into U.S. Army doctrine and has become a part of U.S. Army officer education because the ideas it contains about war and the psychology of those who wage it transcend any specific space or time.

As indicated by the passage from *The Art of War* that appears at the beginning of this introduction and the short excerpt from that passage that is used in the title of this work, "Moving the Enemy," Sunzi emphasized the importance of initiative and freedom of action. His statement that knowing oneself and one's enemy ensures victory while not knowing about either ensures defeat expresses the critical value he placed on information. *The Art of War* addresses the need to effectively combine sustaining, shaping, and decisive operations to accomplish missions and achieve desired results. Sunzi, simply speaking, understood "the fundamentals of full spectrum operations" as expressed in FM 3-0 and advocated what has become known as operational art. Looking at the Huai Hai Campaign through the lens of his ideas not only provides a Chinese perspective for assessing the campaign, it also provides a way to probe more deeply into the basic nature of operational art.

Organization of the Study

The Huai Hai Campaign was long and very complex. For more than 2 months the East China Field Army (ECFA) and the Central Plains Field Army (CPFA) coordinated operations across a large theater of operations against Nationalist forces that, at one point in the campaign, consisted of seven armies. Most of the major operations the ECFA and CPFA executed were offensive, but both field armies also carried out defensive operations aimed at creating opportunities for subsequent attacks.[14] At any given time, each of them was simultaneously conducting both decisive and shaping operations within their own areas of responsibility while providing shaping support for the other field army.[15] This helped make it possible for the field armies to take turns conducting the main effort for the campaign. During the campaign, both the ECFA and the CPFA continually carried out large sustainment operations that may have actually been the operations that decided the outcome.[16]

In Chinese histories of the campaign, a certain amount of order is brought to what was a very fluid situation by dividing the campaign into three sequential phases, each centered on a battle of annihilation against surrounded pockets of Nationalist forces. In this organizational scheme, phase one focuses on the ECFA destroying the Nationalist Seventh Army; phase two focuses on destroying the Nationalist Twelfth Army; and phase three primarily involves destroying the Nationalist Second, Thirteenth, and Sixteenth Armies. This is the standard approach Chinese military historians use when they describe or analyze the campaign. The exhibits explaining the development of the campaign in the Huai Hai Campaign Memorial Museum in Xuzhou are also organized according to these three phases.

Dividing the campaign this way does reflect what happened in a general way. However, it is an organizational framework formed by looking back at what occurred. The three phases were not envisioned during the planning for the campaign, and even three weeks into the campaign they had not yet taken shape. This study, instead of looking at the campaign in three phases, looks at it as two major offensives—the first by the ECFA and the second by the CPFA—and the subsequent exploitation of the opportunities that these two offensives created for both armies.

The first offensive that the ECFA launched in the Huai Hai Campaign on 6 November 1948 sought to destroy the Nationalist Seventh Army as a step toward achieving other objectives. It was conducted as the main effort in what later came to be called the "little" Huai Hai Campaign. The second offensive that the CPFA carried out from 12 to 16 November resulted in capturing Suxian and cutting the rail line connecting Xuzhou with Bengbu, thereby isolating the Nationalist Second, Thirteenth, and Sixteenth Armies in Xuzhou. It was the first major operation of the "big" Huai Hai Campaign, and it placed the CPFA in the central position of the area of operations. Viewed at the time as a shaping operation in support of the ECFA's main effort east of Xuzhou, it set the stage for a series of battles in which the central position was defended and the conditions for a great decisive victory were created. Employing these two field armies in these two major operations and their sequels over a period of several weeks was operational art on a grand scale. Thinking of the campaign as three sequential phases that were set to follow one another in a natural order would mute the command artistry that emerged in response to a very fluid situation.

Chapter 1 places the campaign in its historical context with a short chronology of events before the campaign, an examination of the growth of Communist capabilities between 1927 and 1948, and a review of Communist strategies during the civil war before the campaign. Chapter 2 examines the emergence of the operational vision that led to the proposal for the Huai Hai Campaign and describes the development of the Huai Hai Campaign plan. Chapter 3 describes Nationalist strategy in summer and fall 1948. Chapter 4 describes the area of operations and the opposing forces. Chapter 5 examines the start of the campaign, the encirclement of the Seventh Army, and Nationalist efforts to retrieve the situation. Chapter 6 examines Su Yu's proposal to expand the campaign, describes the CPFA's seizure of the central position, and discusses the process in which PLA commanders decided on what course to take in developing the campaign. Chapter 7 looks at the CPFA-ECFA efforts to hold the central position against Nationalist attacks. Chapter 8 discusses the battle in which the ECFA destroys the last encircled pocket of Nationalist forces and ends the campaign. The conclusion reviews what the campaign accomplished, analyzes the command decisions that were made, and relates the conduct of the campaign to the concept of operational art.

Notes

1. This study uses the pinyin romanization system to represent the pronunciation of Chinese characters. Pinyin was developed for use in the People's Republic of China, and during the 1980s, it was adopted by the Library of Congress, the Board of Geographic Names, the news media, and other organizations for use in the United States, supplanting the Wade-Giles romanization system and a number of common nonstandard romanizations based on regional dialects. When this happened, Peking became Beijing; MaoTse-tung became Mao Zedong; Sun Tzu became Sunzi; Canton became Guangzhou; and Chu Teh, People's Liberation Army chief of staff in 1948, became Zhu De. Changing romanization systems has created confusion because many readers of books about China and Chinese people are unaware of this change. In the text, the previously used common romanization of the names of these two leaders is presented in parentheses to help readers make the connection between the pinyin romanization and a romanization that may be familiar to them. This practice will be followed throughout the study wherever the name of an important person or place first appears.

2. At the time of the Huai Hai Campaign, there were few railroads in China, and they were known by the province, city, or other geographic feature at each end. The Long-Hai railroad was the east-west rail line running from the sea (hai) near Haizhou to Gansu (single character name: Long) Province. It was also common practice to refer to a segment of a railroad by the towns (cities) at each end of the segment. For example, the Xu-Beng railroad would be that portion of the Jin-Pu (Tianjin-Jiangpu) railroad lying between Xuzhou and Bengbu.

3. US Army Field Manual (FM) 100-5, *Operations* (Washington, DC: US Government Printing Office [GPO], August 1982), 2-3.

4. FM 100-5, *Operations* (Washington, DC: GPO, May 1986), 10.

5. FM 3-0, *Operations* (Washington, DC: GPO, June 2001), paragraphs 2-2 to 2-5.

6. Ibid., paragraphs 2-6 and 2-10.

7. Ibid., paragraph 2-8.

8. Ibid., paragraph 2-7.

9. Ibid., paragraph 2-10.

10. Tan Yiqing, "*Mao Zedong junshi sixiang yu Sunzi bingfa*" [Mao Zedong's Military Thought and Sunzi's *The Art of War*], *Junshi Lishi* [Military History], 1999, No. 1, 17.

11. Ibid., 18.

12. Ibid., 19.

13. Robert B. Rigg, *Red China's Fighting Hordes* (Harrisburg, PA: The Military Service Publishing Co., 1951), 49.

14. FM 3-0 defines a major operation as "a series of tactical actions (battles, engagements, strikes) conducted by various combat forces of a single or several services, coordinated in time and place, to accomplish operational and sometimes strategic objectives in an operational area.," 2-3.

15. FM 3-0 defines decisive and shaping operations as follows: "*Decisive operations* are those that directly accomplish the task assigned by the higher headquarters. Decisive operations conclusively determine the outcome of major operations, battles, and engagements." "*Shaping operations* at any echelon create and preserve conditions for the success of the decisive operation. . . . They support the decisive operation by affecting enemy capabilities and forces or by influencing enemy decisions," 4-23.

16. FM 3-0 defines sustaining operations as "operations at any echelon that enable shaping and

decisive operations by providing combat service support, rear area and base security, movement control, terrain management, and infrastructure development," 4-24.

Chapter One

Historical Background of the Huai Hai Campaign

War is a matter of vital importance to a state. It is the place where death or life is decided. It is the path leading to either survival or extinction. It must be carefully examined.
—Sunzi, *The Art of War*

All the issues between two hostile armies depend on war for their solution, and China's survival or extinction depends on her victory or defeat in the present war. Hence our study of military theory, of strategy and tactics and of army political work brooks not a moment's delay.
—Mao Zedong, *Problems of War and Strategy*

Operational art is the conduct of campaigns and major operations to achieve strategic objectives. As such, it requires that three basic elements be present: forces of sufficient size and capability; resources to sustain those forces in the field; and competent commanders who can plan and conduct operations successfully at the operational level. This chapter describes how the Communists created and developed these three essential components of operational-level warfare during the two decades before the Huai Hai Campaign. The first section contains a short chronology that places these events in a historical context. The next section describes Mao's thoughts on how to build Communist strength in China, the Communists' use of rural bases to mobilize peasant support and increase the size of their military forces, the dramatic growth in Communist power during the War of Resistance Against Japan, and the effect of the land reform program on Communist efforts to organize the countryside during the civil war with the Nationalists. Section three presents biographical information on the primary leaders of the field armies committed to the Huai Hai Campaign and analyzes various factors that contributed to their ability to practice operational art. Section four discusses actions the Communists took to transform their military forces and ready them for large-scale battles with Nationalist armies. The last section describes Communist military strategy from the time of the Japanese surrender in 1945 to summer 1948. This material provides a basis for understanding the military-politico-economic-social environment in which the Huai Hai Campaign was fought and command decisions that were made during the campaign.

Background Chronology

China, during the first decades of the 20th century, was a country in turmoil politically, economically, and socially. After the collapse of the Qing (Ch'ing) Dynasty in 1911, political organizations like Sun Yat-sen's Nationalist Party (Guomindang [GMD]/Kuomintang) vied for power with warlords while foreign imperialist powers extended their influence across the country. In July 1921, the CCP was founded, and with the help of the Communist International (Comintern) in Moscow, it soon joined in an alliance with Sun and the GMD. This alliance, however, was not based on a common vision of China's future. There were always serious differences between the leaders of these two parties, and eventually those differences brought millions of Chinese to the battlefields of the Huai Hai Campaign where one-quarter million of them died. The following chronology briefly lays out the Communist-Nationalist relationship from 1922 to 1948:

1922	The Comintern, believing that the GMD represents the mainstream of Chinese nationalism and can be used to foment revolution in China, sends an agent, Adolf Joffe, to China to work out a basis for CCP-GMD cooperation. He meets with Sun Yat-sen, and Sun agrees to a policy of "alliance with Soviets; admission of the Communists."
1923	Sun's supporters drive warlord Chen Jiongming from Guangzhou (Canton). In February, Sun arrives in Guangzhou from Shanghai and establishes a new government with himself as the leader. A formal GMD-CCP alliance is established. Soviet advisers arrive in Guangzhou to help Sun reorganize the GMD and establish a party army. Sun sends Jiang Jieshi to the Soviet Union to study the Soviet military system.
1924	The Soviet Union helps the GMD establish a military academy at Huangpu (Whampoa) near Guangzhou to train an officer corps for a GMD army. Many Soviet officers are on the faculty. CCP members are appointed to important administrative positions within the Huangpu Military Academy and attend as students.
1925	Sun Yat-sen dies. Wang Jingwei becomes the new president of the GMD (Nationalist) government in Guangzhou. Jiang Jieshi, founder and superintendent of the Huangpu Military Academy, wields military control.
1926	Jiang Jieshi is named commander in chief of the National Revolutionary Army, a force of nearly 100,000 troops. In July, he leads this army northward (the Northern Expedition) to attack the northern warlords. In the fall, the Nationalists capture several major cities in the Yangzi River valley.
1927	Jiang Jieshi's forces capture Shanghai in late March. In April, Jiang orders a purge of Communists in areas under his control. The CCP-GMD alliance begins to crumble. On 1 August, Communist-led units at Nanchang revolt and fighting between Communists and Nationalists spreads across southern China. In September, Mao Zedong leads an unsuccessful peasant uprising in Hunan province. In December, the Communists seize Guangzhou, but can only hold it for three days. The year ends with Mao and other Communists seeking refuge in remote mountain areas.
1928	Early in the year, Mao Zedong and Zhu De combine forces and establish a base area in the Jinggang (Chingkang) Mountains of Jiangxi province. They form the Fourth Red Army, with Zhu as the commander and Mao as the political adviser. In July, the CCP holds its Sixth Party Congress in Moscow. The Congress recognizes Mao's organizational work among the peasants and his rural, base-building efforts but emphasizes the importance of organizing the urban proletariat. The CCP headquarters remains underground in Shanghai. On 10 October, a new national government headed by Jiang Jieshi and dominated by the GMD is established in Nanjing (Nan [south] jing [capital]). Bei (north) jing (capital) is renamed Bei (north) ping (peace) as it will remain until 1949.
1929	Mao and Zhu fight to defend and expand their bases against Nationalist

	attacks. They move most of their forces into southern Jiangxi.
1930	Li Lisan emerges as the leader of the CCP in Shanghai. Acting on the advice of the Comintern, Li prepares plans for armed insurrections in key Chinese cities to advance the development of the Chinese Revolution. He regards Mao's strategy of gradually organizing the peasantry and creating rural base areas to encircle the cities as "extremely erroneous... localism and conservatism characteristic of the peasant mentality." The Li Lisan policy of using the Red army to support urban uprisings proves disastrous and, late in 1930, Li is removed from his leadership position. Mao characterizes Li's ideas as "leftist adventurism." Mao and Zhu establish a Soviet government in southern Jiangxi with Ruijin as the capital.
1930-1932	Jiang Jieshi carries out four "encircle and exterminate" campaigns to try to destroy the Communist base area in Jiangxi. All fail with heavy losses. In September 1931, Japan invades northeastern China (Manchuria).
October 1933	Jiang Jieshi begins his fifth campaign to exterminate the Communists.
October 1934	The Communists are forced to abandon their Jiangxi base. Around 100,000 troops and government officials begin what will become known as the Long March, a 6,000-mile trek that will end a year later in northern China. A small number of troops, including some commanded by Chen Yi and Su Yu, is left behind to divert GMD attention from the main body. Mao is out of favor within the CCP.
January 1935	At an expanded session of the CCP Political Bureau held while the retreating Communists are pausing in the small Guizhou city of Zunyi, Mao and his supporters regain control of the CCP. From this point, Mao is the party's leader in setting political and military strategy.
October 1935	The Long March ends as the survivors reach northern Shaanxi province. The Japanese extend their control farther into northern China.
1936	Jiang Jieshi continues to adhere to a policy of defeating the Communists before dealing with the Japanese threat. In December, he flies to Xi'an, the capital of Shaanxi to push his field commanders to attack the Communists with greater vigor. The generals in Xi'an want to fight the Japanese instead of their fellow Chinese. They arrest Jiang and force him to agree to a united front with the Communists against the Japanese. After he agrees, he is allowed to return to Nanjing.
1937	In February a Communist delegation arrives in Nanjing, and formal negotiations on Communist-Nationalist military collaboration begin. Negotiations proceed very slowly until the Japanese attack Chinese forces outside Beiping on 8 July (the Marco Polo Bridge Incident), and the fighting escalates into full-scale war with Japan.
22 August	The Nationalists and Communists agree that the main Communist forces in Shaanxi will be brought into the organization of the national army under the name Eighth Route Army.

12 October	The Nationalist government announces that all Communist army units and guerrillas in Henan, Hubei, Hunan, Guangdong, Jiangxi, Fujian, Zhejiang, and Anhui will be reorganized as the New Fourth Army of the national army and will operate along the Yangzi River. Japanese forces capture large areas during the latter part of year, including Shanghai and the capital city of Nanjing.
1938	Japanese advances continue. They capture China's main ports and most major cities in eastern China.
1939-1940	Attrition warfare between the Chinese and Japanese with little change in positions on the ground.
	The Communists focus on self-development and expansion and establish local governments that are not subservient to the Nationalist government in Chongqing (Chungking). Nationalist suspicion of Communist intentions grows. Scattered fighting breaks out between GMD and CCP forces. In May 1939, the Nationalists institute a blockade of the Communist-controlled area in Shaanxi.
1941	On 4 January, Nationalist units attack the New Fourth Army headquarters force (9,000 soldiers) and destroy it. On 17 January, the Nationalists announce the dissolution of the New Fourth Army due to its failure to follow orders. The GMD-CCP united front is shattered.
	Japan attacks Pearl Harbor.
1942-1945	Both Mao Zedong and Jiang Jieshi believe that the United States will defeat Japan. Both prepare for a postwar CCP-GMD struggle for power.
	The Communists take the leading role in organizing peasant resistance to Japanese occupation in eastern and northern China. They establish many base areas behind Japanese lines and dramatically increase the size of their military forces.
1945	
8 August	The USSR enters the war against Japan.
9 August	Mao announces that the time is right for a general CCP offensive.
10 August	Zhu De, as commander in chief of Communist forces, orders Communist units to seize Japanese occupied towns and cities.
11 August	Jiang Jieshi orders Communist forces to remain in their current positions and await further orders.
11 August	The Communists ignore Jiang's order to stay in place. Lin Biao (Lin Piao) leads the first elements of what will become a 100,000-man force into northeast China. The Russians quickly overrun Japanese forces in that area and facilitate Communist movements. They also turn over large quantities of captured Japanese arms to the Communists.
14 August	Japan surrenders.

15 August	Jiang Jieshi orders the commander, Japanese forces in China, to hold his current positions and await further instructions.
23 August	Jiang Jieshi orders Japanese army units in China to defend their positions, keep lines of communication open, and await the arrival of Nationalist troops.
September–December	The Soviet Union refuses permission for Nationalist forces to enter northeast China. This gives the Communists time to establish control of the area and increase their armed strength there. Soon after the Japanese surrender, the United States lands 50,000 marines in Japanese-occupied areas. During the autumn, the United States helps move one-half million Nationalist troops from southwest China to eastern and northern China. Fighting between Nationalist and Communist forces occurs across China as both sides strive to gain control of areas the Japanese formerly occupied.

In November President Harry S. Truman appoints General George C. Marshall as a special presidential ambassador to China. His mission is to help negotiate a peaceful political solution to the CCP-GMD conflict. Marshall arrives in China in late December. |

1946

January	The Soviets finally allow Nationalist units to enter northeast China. US officers are concerned about an overextension of Nationalist forces as Jiang Jieshi deploys nearly 500,000 of his best troops to the area.
April	Heavy fighting between Nationalist and Communists troops breaks out in northeastern China.
July	Jiang Jieshi launches a major offensive against Communist forces, and a countrywide civil war begins.
Summer and Fall	Nationalist forces push Communists out of many of their base areas that were established during the war against Japan in Jiangsu, Henan, Anhui, and Shandong provinces. Communists are on the strategic defensive trying to destroy isolated Nationalist units when the tactical situation is favorable.

1947

6 January	President Truman recalls Marshall.
March	Nationalists capture the Communist capital of Yan'an.

By the end of the first year of the civil war, the Communists lose control of more than 120,000 square miles and 18 million people. However, the Nationalists overextend themselves while the Communists build up their forces.

In late June the Communists launch a major counterstroke in central China. Liu Bocheng and Deng Xiaoping lead four corps through the Nationalist defense line along the Yellow River northeast of Kaifeng. In August this force marches 300 miles to the south and begins establishing base areas |

	in the Dabie Mountains. This causes the Nationalists to redeploy forces, relieving pressure against Communist forces in Shandong and elsewhere. Despite a major Nationalist effort to destroy the Liu-Deng forces, the Communists retain a foothold in the Dabie Mountains. This thrust to the Dabie Mountains marks a shift in the war's strategic balance, with the Communists beginning to assume the strategic offensive.
1948	Communist forces win several important battles in Henan and other areas of central and eastern China during the spring and summer. As the civil war enters its third year, the Communists clearly hold the initiative.

Building Rural Base Areas and Military Forces

At the end of 1927, the future of the Communist revolution in China looked bleak. The Nanchang Uprising in August had failed, the Hunan Autumn Harvest Uprising in September had collapsed, and the Guangzhou Uprising in December had been crushed. The CCP leadership was in disarray, and what military forces were loyal to the party were scattered across remote areas of China. Mao Zedong, however, did not abandon his commitment to the revolution or lose faith in the Communists' ability to eventually prevail. In late 1927 he led a small group of followers into the Jinggang Mountains along the Hunan-Jiangxi border and began to implement his strategy for gaining victory:

- Using the military forces that were available to mobilize and organize the peasantry and set up a rural base.
- Relying on that rural base to expand the military so it could defend the rural base.
- Improving the military to the point at which it could extend its area of operations and either expand the base area or start new base areas.

Building a rural base and increasing military force structure was a difficult process. In a report to the CCP Central Committee in Shanghai made in November 1928 Mao wrote: "Wherever the Red Army goes, the masses are cold and aloof, and only after our propaganda do they slowly move into action. Whatever enemy units we face, there are hardly any cases of mutiny or desertion to our side and we have to fight it out. . . .We have an acute sense of our isolation which we keep hoping will end."[1] Gradually, however, because so many people living in the countryside had grievances against the existing political and economic order, Mao and his political cadres were able to change the cold aloofness of the peasants and others to support. Where there was fertile ground for changing attitudes, Mao exploited every opportunity. In the report just quoted, he described one Communist action that gained widespread approval: "The landlords imposed very heavy taxes and levies on the people; the Pacification Guards of Suichuan levied five toll charges along the seventy-*li* road from Huangao to Tsaolin, no farm produce being exempt. We crushed the Pacification Guards and abolished these tolls, thus winning the support of all the peasants as well as the small and middle merchants."[2]

Small actions such as this; a moderate land reform program; and the establishment of a measure of democracy in the township, district, and county governments that were set up under party guidance enabled the Communists to consolidate power and establish their base in the Jinggang Mountains. However, even a modest step like crushing the Pacification Guards of Suichuan required an armed force. In addition, the Nationalist government and regional

Political map of eastern China, 1928.

warlords were not happy with the existence of such a base. During 1928 they launched a series of attacks against it. Mao wrote: "How to deal with the enemy, how to fight, has become the central problem in our daily life. An independent regime must be an armed one. Wherever such an area is located, it will be immediately occupied by the enemy if armed forces are lacking or inadequate."[3]

The problem was how to create and maintain an effective armed force of sufficient strength in a poor rural area with little surplus wealth. Only so much money could be obtained by confiscating the property of "local tyrants." Taxes could not be higher than they had been before the Red army arrived; to gain peasant support, taxes had to be less. Mao's solution to this challenge was a three-tier organizational structure. In addition to the regular Red army, two irregular military organizations, the Red Guards and "insurrectionary detachments," were established. The important point was that both irregular forces would provide military capability while allowing their members to continue normal productive labor. The Red Guards, organized by county, were the better trained and equipped of the two. Their commanders had generally completed a training course with the Red Army, and their soldiers had a number of five-round rifles to go along with spears, knives, and other simple weapons. Their main mission, using the principle of dispersion, was to combat the local regional warlords' security forces and the local landlords' levies.[4]

The insurrectionary detachments, organized by township, were armed only with spears and a few shotguns. Their task was to "suppress counter-revolution, protect the township government, and assist the Red Army and Red Guards in battle when the enemy appeared."[5]

Whatever the capabilities of these irregular formations, as Mao acknowledged, they were no substitute for the combat power of regular units:

> The existence of a regular Red Army of adequate strength is a necessary condition for the existence of Red political power. If we have local Red Guards only, but no regular Red Army then we cannot cope with the regular White forces, but only with the landlords' levies. Therefore even when the masses of workers and peasants are active, it is definitely impossible to create an independent regime, let alone an independent regime which is durable and grows daily, unless we have regular forces of adequate strength.[6]

Mao continually sought both durability and growth by using his army. The ability to defend the Jinggang Mountain base was important because the base served as a haven for the Red army. He emphasized this point in a November 1928 report: "All the strategic passes in the mountains are fortified [and] our bedding and clothing workshops, ordnance department and regimental rear offices are all here. . . . Provided we have adequate supplies, the enemy can never break in."[7] Expansion, however, not defense, was Mao's objective, and to move along that path, Mao gave the Red army two major nonoperational missions: "promot[ing] the development of the local Party organization with the help of the army Party organization and promot[ing] the development of the local armed forces."[8] Mao's vision was that after an initial period of Red army assistance, local political and military organizations would "gradually reduce the extent to which local work [was] dependent on the assistance of Red Army personnel, so that the border area [would] have its own personnel to take charge of the work *and even provide personnel for the Red Army and the expanded territory of the independent regime* [author's italics]."[9] Mao believed that by moving forward step by step "small Red areas . . . [would] continue to expand and gradually approach the goal of seizing political power throughout the country."[10]

The CCP leaders who were based in Shanghai recognized Mao's success in developing an independent Communist base in a relatively remote rural area of China, but they did not agree with his strategy or methods. His reliance on peasants as a source of revolutionary energy ran counter to orthodox Marxist ideology that viewed the urban industrial worker as the key element in a Communist revolution. Mao wanted to rely on the mass base he had established in the countryside and then "gradually enlarge the Red army by the use of correct tactics, fighting no battle unless we can win it and capture arms and men."[11] The orthodox Communists advocated using the peasant-based Red Army that Mao and Zhu De had established in large offensives that would capture cities and bring large numbers of urban workers into the revolutionary movement. They also wanted him to fight more positional battles and deepen the class struggle in the countryside. Where Mao counseled patience, these other party leaders pushed for bold action in pursuit of quick results.

During 1934 the power struggle between Mao and his opponents within the CCP intensified. In July, Mao was placed under house arrest and barred from party meetings.[12] However, in October, when the Communists were forced to abandon the Jiangxi base area in the face of Jiang Jieshi's massive fifth encircle and exterminate campaign, Mao was allowed to join the flight to the west. Had he not been allowed to do so, the course of the Communist revolution in China might have been much different. As it was, three months later, at an expanded session of the CCP Political Bureau held in mid-January in Zunyi, a small city of 50,000 in eastern Guizhou, Mao and his supporters regained control of the CCP. Building and gradually expanding rural bases was once again the guiding concept of the CCP and its army. Protracted war became CCP strategy. In October 1935 the remnants of the Communist force that had departed southern Jiangxi a year earlier reached northern Shaanxi.[13] The 6,000-mile Long March was over, but the challenges facing the Communists were enormous. Jiang Jieshi, confident because his forces had destroyed the Jiangxi Soviet, pressed ahead with efforts to eradicate this new base area in Shaanxi and the scattered guerrilla units still fighting in southern China.

At this critical moment, Japanese aggression against China intervened to give the Communists a much-needed respite. In December 1936 Jiang Jieshi flew to Xi'an, the headquarters of his forces fighting the Communists in northern Shaanxi. His purpose was to urge them on to greater efforts, but he ended up being seized by officers who wanted to fight the Japanese instead of their fellow Chinese. As part of the terms for his release, Jiang agreed to work with the Communists to resist Japan. The anti-Communist campaign ended, and in February 1937, a Communist delegation arrived in the Chinese capital, Nanjing, for the start of formed negotiations aimed at establishing a Nationalist-Communist united front against Japan.

After several months, with Japan and China in open warfare following a Japanese attack on Chinese forces outside Beiping, agreements on military collaboration were finally reached. On 22 August 1937 the Nationalist government announced that the main Communist military force in Shaanxi province would be reorganized, and it became the Eighth Route Army of the National Revolutionary Army.[14] On 12 October the government announced that all Red Army units and guerrillas in the eight provinces of Henan, Hubei, Hunan, Guangdong, Jiangxi, Fujian, Zhejiang, and Anhui were to be reorganized as the New Fourth Army of the National Revolutionary Army.[15] This force was to be subordinate to the Nationalist third war zone and operate along the Yangzi River. All across China the united front gave the Communists new legitimacy as patriotic fighters against a foreign enemy, a temporary reduction in overt Nationalist hostility, and fresh opportunities for growth and expansion. As the following excerpts from a speech Mao gave at the National Conference of the CCP in May 1937 indicate, the CCP was sure to take advantage of this new situation:

> A great revolution requires a great party and many first-rate cadres to guide it. . . . Our Party organizations must be extended all over the country and we must purposefully train tens of thousands of cadre and hundreds of first-rate leaders.[16]

> If we succeed in bringing millions upon millions of the masses under our leadership . . . our revolutionary task can be speedily fulfilled.[17]

The two field armies that fought together during the Huai Hai Campaign, the ECFA and the CPFA, and the politico-military organizations that supported them were outgrowths of Mao Zedong's base-building strategy and the opportunities presented by the War of Resistance Against Japan. During this 8-year-long war, wherever Communist military forces were present to provide security, bases with CCP bureaus and CCP-dominated governments were quickly set up. As these bases expanded and the organizational work among the peasants developed, the Communists dramatically increased their military strength using the three-tier model that Mao had developed in the Jinggang Mountains.

The magnitude of this increase in strength can be seen clearly by looking at what happened in eastern and central China during the war. The New Fourth Army, which eventually became the ECFA, consisted of only 10,000 soldiers in four detachments located in the mid-Yangzi River valley when it was established on 25 December 1937.[18] During 1938-1941, its main area of operations shifted northeastward to those parts of Jiangsu and Anhui that lay north of the Yangzi River, and several base areas were established. By the time Japan surrendered in 1945, the New Fourth Army had grown to 118,000 regulars, 100,000 guerrillas, and 525,000 self-defense forces.[19] Similar success was achieved to the north and west of the New Fourth Army area of operations. There the Eighth Route Army's 115th and 129th Divisions came out of the Shaanxi base to build bases and create forces in Shaanxi, Hebei, Henan, and Shandong.

Eventually, most of the forces the 115th Division established would become part of the New Fourth Army, while forces that the 129th Division created became the main elements of the CPFA. The 115th Division, which in 1937 had a total strength of around 15,000, in late 1938 sent part of a regiment into eastern Hebei (Ji) and western Shandong (Lu) to establish the Ji-Lu border region base.[20] It then expanded its activities over most of Shandong. By August 1945, Communist strength in what had become the Shandong military region base stood at 270,000 regulars and more than 500,000 self-defense forces.[21] The 129th Division, which in 1937 had about 13,000 soldiers, in 1937 and 1938 sent approximately 9,000 soldiers into Shaanxi (Jin), Hebei (Ji), and Henan (Yu) to set up the Jin-Ji-Yu border region base. In July 1941, reflecting the 129th Division's activity in southwestern Shandong, the Jin-Ji-Lu-Yu border region government was established. In August 1945 the 129th Division, or the Liu-Deng army (named after division commander Liu Bocheng and political commissar Deng Xiaoping), as it was popularly called, controlled 300,000 regulars and 400,000 local militia.[22] The Jin-Ji-Lu-Yu military region that Liu also commanded at the time, with Deng again assisting as political commissar, covered 110,000 square miles and had a population of 24 million.[23]

The Communists were able to make such impressive strides in organizing and mobilizing those living in the countryside because of the psychological environment the Japanese army's brutal behavior created. Chalmers A. Johnson, in his book *Peasant Nationalism and Communist Power: the Emergence of Revolutionary China, 1937-1945*, concludes that "The importance of [Japanese army mopping up] campaigns to the growth and entrenchment of the Communist movement cannot be overstated."[24] In his opinion, the peasant mobilization that the Communists carried out was "a process that was *initiated* by the Japanese invasion and by the conditions of rural anarchy following the evacuation of local elites."[25] "The Communists," he notes, "were the beneficiaries and not the main source of this mobilization; their contribution was the organization of the mobilized peasants, the establishments of rear-area bases, and the leadership of effective guerrilla warfare against the Japanese."[26] So critical was the Japanese army's involvement in the process that, according to Johnson, "as a general rule, the Communists were not able to establish guerrilla bases in regions that had no direct experience with the Japanese Army."[27] Suzanne Pepper, in her book *Civil War in China: The Political Struggle, 1945-1949*, makes the same point: "The anti-Japanese resistance mobilized the manpower and the CCP provided the leadership" necessary for building the rural bases.[28]

During the war against Japan, the Communists did not attempt to initiate class struggle in rural villages. There was no need to stir up a mass movement to build support for them when Japanese army depredations were producing this effect. Not wanting to weaken their position as leaders of all Chinese people in the fight against Japan, the Communists implemented a modest rent-reduction/interest-reduction program that did not drastically threaten anyone's economic livelihood. They emphasized political indoctrination, building political structures, and developing mass organizations, all of which supported their goals of mobilizing resources for the war effort and increasing the size of the military forces they controlled. What emerged over time was a broad range of civilian and military organizations designed to fight what Mao Zedong referred to as "people's war." The following excerpt from Mao's report to the CCP's Seventh National Congress in April 1945 shows the breadth and depth of Communist organizational efforts, especially in the military area:

> [Our] army is powerful because all its members have a discipline based on political consciousness; they have come together and they fight not for the private interests of a few individuals or a narrow clique, but for the interests of the broad masses and of the whole nation. The sole purpose of this army is to stand firmly with the Chinese people and to serve them whole-heartedly.
>
> Furthermore, this army is powerful because it has the people's self-defence corps and the militia—the vast armed organizations of the masses—fighting in co-ordination with it. In the Liberated Areas of China all men and women, from youth to middle age, are organized in the people's anti-Japanese self-defence corps on a voluntary and democratic basis and without giving up their work in production. The cream of the self-defence corps, except for those who join the army or the guerrilla units, is brought into the militia. Without the co-operation of these armed forces of the masses it would be impossible to defeat the enemy.

Finally, this army is powerful because of its division into two parts, the main forces and the regional forces, with the former available for operations in any region whenever necessary and the latter concentrating on defending their own localities and attacking the enemy there in co-operation with the local militia and the self-defence corps. This division of labour has won the whole-hearted support of the people. Without this correct division of labor—if, for example, attention were paid only to the role of the main forces while that of the regional forces were neglected—it would likewise be impossible to defeat the enemy in the conditions obtaining in China's Liberated Areas. Under the regional forces, numerous armed working teams have been organized, which are well trained and hence better qualified for military, political and mass work; they penetrate into the rearmost areas behind the enemy lines, strike at the enemy and arouse the masses, . . . thus giving support to the frontal military operations of the various Liberated Areas. In all this they have achieved great success.

Under the leadership of their democratic governments, all the anti-Japanese people in the Liberated Areas of China are called upon to join organizations of workers, peasants, youth and women, and cultural, professional and other organizations, which will whole-heartedly perform various tasks in support of the armed forces. These tasks are not limited to rallying the people to join the army, transporting grain for it, caring for soldiers' families and helping the troops in meeting their material needs. They also include mobilizing the guerrilla units, militia and self-defence corps to make widespread raids and lay land mines against the enemy, gather intelligence about him, comb out traitors and spies, transport and protect the wounded and take a direct part in the army's operations. At the same time, the people in all the Liberated Areas are enthusiastically taking up various kinds of political, economic, cultural and health work. The most important thing in this connection is to mobilize everybody for the production of grain and other necessities and to ensure that all government institutions and schools, except in special cases, devote their free time to production for their own support in order to supplement the self-sufficiency production campaigns of the army and the people and thus help to create a great upsurge of production to sustain the protracted War of Resistance. In a word, everything for the front, everything for the defeat of the Japanese aggressors and for the liberation of the Chinese People—this is the general slogan, the general policy for the whole army and the whole people in the Liberated Areas of China. Such is a real people's war.[29]

The idea for a people's war did not originate during the War of Resistance Against Japan. It was always at the heart of Mao's view on how the Communists would gain power in China. It was the concept behind his first base-building efforts in the Jinggang Mountains. It was behind his decisions in 1938 to send Eighth Route Army units behind enemy lines to build bases. When Mao spoke to the CCP Central Committee in November 1938 about using the army to "create Party organizations . . . create cadres, create schools, create culture, create mass movements," he was expressing a vision of a people's war.[30] During the war with Japan, because of favorable conditions for mobilizing peasant support, a people's war did develop to a very high level.

After the end of the War of Resistance Against Japan, the Communists moved away from their moderate position to implement a "land to the tiller" land reform program. In April 1945 Mao explained why implementing such a policy during the war against Japan would have been improper:

> The Communist Party has made a major concession in the anti-Japanese war by changing the policy of 'land to the tiller' to one of reducing rent and interest. This concession is a correct one, for it helped bring the Kuomintang [GMD] into the war against Japan and lessened the resistance of the landlords in the Liberated Areas to our mobilization of the peasants for war.[31]

However, with that war over and an all-out civil war with the Nationalists looming, these were no longer valid reasons for not moving forward with land reform. In Mao's view, a different war called for different means to mobilize support for it. Codified in the "Directive on the Land Question" the CCP Central Committee issued on 4 May 1946, the land reform "mass movement" rolled across areas under Communist control while the war against the Nationalists was being fought.

Implementing land reform was a crude, complex process. Mass meetings at which peasants were encouraged to "settle accounts" with the ruling elite were convened. Land was confiscated and redistributed to the poor as "struggle fruits." With emotions running high, many owner-cultivators, independent craftsmen, and even professionals became "struggle objects." Agricultural production dropped, at least temporarily.[32] Some industrial and commercial activities were disrupted by cadres that labeled the industrial and commercial holdings of landlords and rich peasants as "disguised wealth" and confiscated them for redistribution as part of land reform.[33] With the revolutionary zeal of many cadre leading to such excess, the party was forced to take corrective action.

Mao Zedong addressed this problem in an inner-party circular he drafted for the CCP Central Committee meeting held in September 1948 in Xibaipo, a small village in Hebei:

> [T]he Party has in the past year overcome, and is continuing to overcome, some 'Left' mistakes which accompanied the large-scale mobilization of the peasant masses in the struggles to solve the land problem; these were the partial but fairly numerous encroachments on the interests of the middle peasants, the damage done to some private industrial and commercial enterprises and the overstepping in some places of certain lines of demarcation in the policy for suppressing counter-revolutions.[34]

Despite its negative side effects, taken as a whole, the land reform program did contribute to Communist efforts to mobilize human and materiel resources for the war with the Nationalists. As Suzanne Pepper explains in her excellent study of the Communist land reform program, land reform's contribution did not come directly in the form of large numbers of inspired poor young peasants rushing into the army to defend their families' new land. "It took more than that image," she notes, "to overcome the peasant's innate reluctance to join the army, and to leave a new-won plot of land."[35] Pepper does not dispute Mao Zedong's statement that during the first two years of the civil war 1,600,000 peasants who obtained land joined the People's Liberation Army (PLA).[36] But she considers those enlistments to be more the product of an all-encompassing organizational structure than the result of spontaneous enthusiasm. Land reform, to paraphrase her view, was valuable to the CCP because it first required and then facilitated both creating and strengthening organizations that served the Communists in many ways:

> The construction of [a new village power structure] was the real fulfillment of land reform as the 'mother of all other work.' Peasants who participated most actively in the multifeatured accusation movement provided new recruits for the Communist Party and new village leadership. Recipients of land and property added their numbers to the peasant associations and other village organizations. This was the institutional structure, manned by the peasants themselves, that the Communists could then rely on to assume responsibility for collecting the grain tax, organizing military transport teams, and exerting social pressure on reluctant peasants during the [army] recruiting drives.[37]

During the planning for the Huai Hai Campaign, the existence of institutional structures that could mobilize resources to support military operations was a major factor affecting the decisions that were made. Twenty years earlier Mao had felt an "acute sense of isolation" in his small base in the Jinggang Mountains. As the third year of the civil war was beginning, the Communists controlled one-quarter of China's total area and 168,000,000 people.[38] From June 1946 to June 1948, the PLA had grown from 1,200,000 to 2,800,000.[39] The base building and army building strategies used over some 20 years had borne much fruit. Conditions were now ripe to conduct larger offensives than any that had been executed before.

Developing Military Leaders

Concurrent with developing Communist military forces came developing those who led those forces. This section examines the background of seven primary leaders of the Huai Hai Campaign. Five were members of the Huai Hai Campaign General Front Committee that the CCP Central Military Commission (CMC) established on 16 November 1948 to ensure unity of effort between the ECFA and the CPFA, and two were the chiefs of staff of those field armies. Among these leaders, there are those who made a name for themselves as commanders and those who gained prominence as political commissars. Some had experience in both positions.

The political commissar, or "party representative," system was brought into the Nationalist army by the Russian advisers who came in 1924 to help establish the Huangpu (Whampoa) Military Academy and build a GMD army. Originally, the purpose of the system, which assigned a party representative—in the Nationalist army, a GMD party representative; in the PLA, a CCP representative—to the headquarters of units down to company level, was to ensure the loyalty and political reliability of the officer corps. Gradually, the work of the commissars evolved, and they assumed responsibility for a wide range of tasks that was militarily significant but did not bear directly on commanding combat troops in action. That remained the commander's province.

The political commissar's major responsibility was acting as liaison with local CCP organs and organizing civilian support for military forces. Commissars thus became involved in recruitment and logistics operations because successful mobilization of peasants was necessary to obtain supplies and form transportation teams. Other tasks the commissars performed included "consoling the wounded, indoctrinating prisoners of war, explaining the political purpose of a particular battle, providing recreation, [and] giving lectures on political objectives."[40] In some ways, the commissars were like chaplains in the U.S. Army, working to ensure the psychological well being and good morale of their soldiers. They also helped commanders address the civil considerations factor when doing a mission, enemy, terrain and weather, troops and support available, time available, and civil considerations (METT-TC) analysis. Sometimes there was tension between commanders and commissars over areas of responsibility, but when the men in these positions worked well together, they could produce a highly synergistic effect. At the time of the Huai Hai Campaign, Liu Bocheng and Deng Xiaoping, probably the most successful commander-commissar team in the history of the PLA, had been working together for more than 10 years.

The five members of the Huai Hai Campaign General Front Committee were Chen Yi, Liu Bocheng, Su Yu, Tan Zhenlin and Deng Xiaoping. Liu, Chen, and Deng formed the committee's standing committee with Deng serving as secretary.[41] In keeping with the Chinese practice of assigning multiple responsibilities to single individuals, at the time of the campaign, these men also held the following positions:

- Chen Yi—commander, ECFA; commander, East China Military Region (ECMR); political commissar, ECFA; deputy commander, Central Plains Military Region (CPMR); and deputy commander, CPFA.[42]
- Liu Bocheng—commander, CPMR, and commander, CPFA.[43]
- Su Yu—acting commander, ECFA, and acting political commissar, ECMR.[44]
- Tan Zhenlin—deputy political commissar, ECFA, and political commissar, Shandong army.[45]
- Deng Xiaoping—political commissar, CPMR, and political commissar, CPFA.[46]
- Li Da, chief of staff of the CPFA—chief of staff, CPMR.[47]
- Chen Shiju had the single position of chief of staff, ECFA.[48]

Brief chronologies of these leaders are presented to show how extensive their experiences were, how many of them had shared common experiences and had even worked together for long periods of time, and the steps they took as they advanced within the ranks of the CCP political and/or military leadership. By the time of the Huai Hai Campaign, they all had records of achievement that inspired confidence in each other's abilities. They had all endured hardships that proved their personal commitment to the common cause. They clearly knew their profession and how to work together.

Liu Bocheng was the oldest of these men and had the most military education:

1892	Born in Sichuan Province.
1911	Graduates from military school in Chengdu, the Sichuan capital, and becomes a junior officer in the provincial warlord's army.
1913	While serving as a brigade commander is wounded and loses an eye. Later will earn the nickname, "one-eyed dragon."
Early 1920s	Becomes involved in Nationalist/Communist agitation for political change.
1926	Joins the CCP. Is commander of a unit in the GMD's Northern Expedition.

1927	Joins the planning for the Communist's Nanchang Uprising against Jiang Jieshi. Is chief-of-staff of the Revolutionary Committee which the Communists set up after taking Nanchang. Joins the southward flight from Nanchang after the Nationalists attack in force. Makes his way to Hong Kong. Requests to go to the Soviet Union to study. Leaves for Moscow as the year is ending.
1928-1930	For two and one-half years, attends military schools in Moscow; first an advanced infantry academy and then the Frunze (Red army) Academy.
1930	Returns to Shanghai, China, in the summer and becomes a staff officer assisting the CCP Central Committee's Military Affairs Council. Helps plan Li Lisan's offensives to capture major industrial cities and takes part in the attack on Changsha. After the Li Lisan offensives fail, joins the Zhu De-Mao Zedong army.
1931-1934	Does army staff work for the Zhu-Mao army in southern Jiangxi as it fights against a series of encircle and exterminate campaigns mounted by the Nationalists. Serves as president of the Red army school.
1934-1935	On the Long March, serves concurrently as chief of staff of the Central Revolutionary Military Council and the Zhu-Mao First Front Army.
1937	Receives command of one of the Eighth Route Army's three divisions, the 129th.
1937-1945	Commands the 129th Division as it builds the Shanxi (Jin)-Hebei (Ji)-Shandong (Lu)-Henan (Yu) Resist Japan Base Area. Works hand in hand with his political commissar, Deng Xiaoping. Stays in the field for almost the entire eight-year war against Japan. Goes to Yen'an for the CCP Seventh Party Congress held April-June 1945 and is elected to the CCP Central Committee. On 20 August 1945 the Jin-Ji-Lu-Yu Military Region is established. Liu is named commander and Deng the political commissar.
1945-1948	Commands progressively larger forces in progressively larger operations against the Nationalists. In many of these operations coordinates his actions with those of Chen Yi's forces. On 14 July 1946, the 129th Division is redesignated the Jin-Ji-Lu-Yu Field Army with Liu and Deng staying on as commander and political commissar respectively. On 9 May 1948, this field army is renamed the CPFA when a new CPMR is established. Liu and Deng continue in place.[49]

Deng Xiaoping had no formal military education. As a student he developed an interest in political mobilization and organization. He continued to pursue this interest in political work and became the consummate political commissar:

1904	Born in Sichuan.
1920	Early in the year, goes to France to participate in a work-study program.
1920-1925	Becomes politically active and joins the Chinese Socialist Youth League. Works on the staff of a league publication. Meets Chen Yi. Joins the CCP in 1924.

1926	Leaves France and goes to Moscow where he studies for several months.
August	Goes to Xi'an to work in the Political Department of the Sun Yat-sen Military and Political Academy set up to train officers in Feng Yuxiang's army. This was at a time when Feng, the warlord controlling much of northwest China, was cooperating with the Communists and the USSR.
Mid-1927	Feng purges the Communists and Deng goes to Shanghai. Works in the CCP apparatus there for the next 2 years.
Mid-1929	CCP sends him to Guangxi province to help establish a rural revolutionary base. Becomes the political commissar of the army that is formed there.
1930	The Guangxi Communist force moves north to help the Zhu-Mao army attack Changsha, but the offensive collapses while they are en route. The force goes to Jiangxi and is incorporated into the forces led by Mao Zedong and Zhu De.
1930-1934	Stays in the Communist base area in Jiangxi. Edits a Red army newspaper and lectures on CCP history at the Red army academy.
1934-1935	On the Long March, serves in the political department of the First Army Corps.
1936	Becomes deputy political commissar, First Army Corps.
1937	Serves as the assistant to the director of the General Political Department in the newly established Eighth Route Army.
1938-1948	On 18 January 1938, becomes the political commissar, 129th Division. From this point throughout the Huai Hai Campaign and beyond, works as Liu Bocheng's political commissar. Is elected to the CCP Central Committee at the CCP Seventh Party Congress held in Yen'an in April-June 1945.[50]

Chen Yi's early life was similar to Deng Xiaoping's. Born in Sichuan, as were Liu Bocheng and Deng Xiaoping, he studied in France and became involved in Communist political education activities in China in the mid-1920s. After joining Mao Zedong in the Jinggang Mountains following the failure of the Nanchang Uprising, he turned toward a career as a military commander, not a political commissar. Unlike Liu Bocheng, he did not receive a formal advanced military education, but as the chronology shows, he held many important military positions during the years leading up to the Huai Hai Campaign.

1901	Born in Sichuan.
1919	During the summer arrives in France to take part in a work-study program.
1922	In October is deported from France for political agitation and returns to China.
1923	Joins both the GMD and CCP.
1923-1924	Is active in Marxist-oriented student organizations in Beijing.
1926	Goes to Guangzhou and joins the staff of the Huangpu Military Academy's political department. Serves as the GMD political commissar in a regiment in the GMD's Northern Expedition.

1927	The regiment Chen is in participates in the Communist Nanchang Uprising. Is involved in planning the uprising. After the uprising fails, he goes south with the troops under Zhu De's command. In early 1928 this force joins with Mao Zedong's force in the Jinggang Mountains. Chen serves under Mao as head of the Zhu-Mao army's political department.
1930	Receives command of the 12th Division.
1931	When the Chinese Soviet Republic is declared in November 1931, Chen is elected to the republic's highest political body, the Central Executive Committee.
1931-1934	Commands the Jiangxi Military District and the XXII Corps during the Nationalist's third and fourth encircle and exterminate campaigns.
1934	Is left behind in Jiangxi when the Long March begins. His mission is to command a rear guard for the Communist force that moves west out of Jiangxi.
1935-1937	Leads small bands of Communist guerrillas struggling to survive in the mountainous area along the Hunan-Jiangxi-Guangdong border area. Is out of contact with the CCP Central Committee for two and one-half years. After Japanese aggression leads to GMD-CCP military collaboration, the Communist guerrillas in southern China are organized as the New Fourth Army under the command of Ye Ting. Chen is designated commander of one of this army's four detachments, the 1st Detachment.
1938	Chen's detachment conducts operations in southern Anhui and then moves east to the mountainous area south of Nanjing in southern Jiangsu.
1939	In November Chen is designated commander of the South Jiangsu Command with three detachments under his control.
1940	Moves forces north of the Yangzi River and establishes his headquarters in north central Jiangsu at Yencheng. This force is designated the North Jiangsu Command. The Nationalist high command orders all New Fourth Army units to move north of the Yangzi River.
1941	In January, Nationalist troops attack the New Fourth Army headquarters unit as it is preparing to cross the Yangzi River from southern to northern Anhui and imprison the army's commander, Ye Ting. Chen is named the acting commander of the New Fourth Army. The New Fourth Army is extensively reorganized. Seven divisions are created out of the former detachments and other units that had been established. His 1st Detachment becomes the 1st Division under the command of Su Yu.
1941-1944	Chen commands the New Fourth Army in the field.
1944	Goes to Yen'an and stays there for several months. Helps make preparations for the CCP Seventh Party Congress, held April-June 1945. Serves on the congress presidium and is elected to the CCP Central Committee.
1945	After the CCP Seventh Party Congress, returns to Jiangsu to command the New Fourth Army in the field. In October, after Shandong military region

	commander Luo Runghuan leads 60,000 Shandong troops to Northeast China, Chen's New Fourth Army takes charge of the Shandong military region and the troops remaining there.
1946	On 7 January an organizational change formalizes the New Fourth Army's assumption of command over the Shandong Military Region. In April the commander of the New Fourth Army, Ye Ting, is killed in a plane crash shortly after his release from prison. Chen formally becomes the New Fourth Army commander.
1946-1947	Chen leads the New Fourth Army in many campaigns and battles with the Nationalists, sometimes working in concert with Liu Bocheng's forces. On 21 January 1947 the New Fourth Army and Shandong military region command become the East China Military Region (ECMR) and the East China Field Army (ECFA). Chen is designated the commander of the ECMR and ECFA and also the political commissar, ECFA. Su Yu is designated deputy commander, ECFA.
1948	Chen leads the ECFA in campaigns and battles, sometimes coordinating movements with Liu Bocheng's forces. On 9 May the Central Plains Military Region (CPMR) and Central Plains Field Army (CPFA) are established. The CCP CMC asks Chen to leave Shandong and to go to Henan to help Liu Bocheng and Deng Xiaoping carry out political mobilization and military development work in this new military region. Chen retains his positions as commander and political commissar, ECMR and ECFA. Su Yu is named the acting commander and acting political commissar, ECFA.[51]

Su Yu can be considered one of Chen Yi's protégés. Several times he held positions under Chen, including his positions during the Huai Hai Campaign. However, Su's role in planning and executing the Huai Hai Campaign was greater than Chen Yi's, a fact that may illustrate what some have said is his superiority over Chen as an operational-level commander. Like Chen Yi, Su did not receive a formal military education, but as the chronology indicates, he had more than two decades of rich military experiences before the Huai Hai Campaign:

1908	Born in Hunan.
1926	Su joins the Communist Youth League while a normal school student. Excited by the revolutionary ferment about him, becomes a political instructor in a unit under Ye Ting's command during the Northern Expedition.
1927	Joins the Communist Party. Is with Ye Ting's forces that participate in the Nanchang Uprising. Comes to the attention of Zhu De and Chen Yi during the uprising and moves south with their forces after the uprising fails.
1928	Is with the Zhu-Chen forces that link up with Mao Zedong's forces in the Jinggang Mountains. Becomes a company commander.
1931	Assumes command of the 64th Division in Chen Yi's XXII Corps.
1933	Becomes chief of staff of the newly formed VII Corps commanded by Xun Huaizhou.

1934	In July, as the Nationalists' fifth encircle and exterminate campaign is compressing the Communist's Jiangxi base area, the VII Corps and X Corps are sent on a mission designed to draw Nationalist forces away from southern Jiangxi. For political purposes, the force is called the "Red Army Vanguard Moving North to Resist Japan." After several months of maneuvering and fighting in southern Anhui, the Nationalists scatter the force in early 1935.
1935-1937	Su leads a few hundred soldiers from the Red Army Vanguard in guerrilla warfare against the Nationalists in the area along the borders of Fujian, Jiangxi, and Zhejiang. For three years he is out of touch with the CCP Central Committee in Shaanxi.
1938	After the New Fourth Army is established, Su's guerrillas became part of this army's 2d Detachment. Su is designated the detachment's deputy commander. The detachment's area of operations is those parts of Anhui and Jiangsu that lie south of the Yangzi River.
1939	The 2d Detachment is attached to Chen Yi's South Jiangsu Command and continues anti-Japanese operations.
1940	2d Detachment units begin operating north of the Yangzi River in central Jiangsu.
1941	Becomes commander of the 1st Division in the reorganized New Fourth Army (see Chen Yi's chronology). Receives command of the Central Jiangsu Military District.
1942-1943	Conducts anti-Japanese operations and base-building activities.
1944	At the CCP Seventh Party Congress is elected as an alternate member of the CCP Central Committee. On 18 April the Japanese launch the Ichi-Go offensive to consolidate their holdings in eastern China, capture U.S. air bases, and create a secure land line of communication to their southern army in Southeast Asia. As the Japanese advance, Nationalist troops withdraw to the west creating, in the CCP leaders' view, an opening for Communist penetration. Looking ahead, the CCP Central Committee decides that a move into this area will "establish conditions for the future capture of the large cities of Nanjing, Shanghai, and Hangzhou."[52] To pursue this opportunity, on 27 September 1944 a directive is issued to the New Fourth Army specifying that Su Yu lead his 1st Division south across the Yangzi River.[53] This he does on 27 December 1944.
1945	On 13 January Su establishes the Jiangsu-Zhejiang Military District with himself as the commander.[54] After planning how to deploy his troops, he begins extending the area under Communist control by establishing various military subdistricts and building a new Jiangsu-Zhejiang-Anhui base area. This activity quickly attracts the attention of the Nationalist third war zone commander, and he begins launching attacks to thwart Su's efforts. Su's smaller force overcomes these attacks using surprise and maneuver. In June Su wins his greatest victory to date when in the Tianmu Mountain Campaign

	his force of 21,000 defeats 66,000 Nationalist troops.[55] In September, as the result of agreements reached in CCP-GMD negotiations in Chongqing, Su and his 1st Division are recalled to central Jiangsu. Su is made commander of a 50,000-man force called the Central China Field Army.
1946	In July and August leads a brilliant campaign against Nationalist forces moving north into central Jiangsu following the outbreak of full-scale civil war, then withdraws to the north.
1947	On 21 January becomes the deputy commander, ECFA, when it is established.
1947-1948	Commands progressively larger forces in progressively larger operations against the Nationalists.[56]

Tan Zhenlin's career contains many of the same experiences as Chen Yi's and Su Yu's. Born in Hunan in 1902, he joined the CCP in 1926 and participated in the Autumn Harvest Uprisings in Hunan that Mao Zedong directed. After the uprisings were put down, he went with Mao to the Jinggang Mountains. During the next several years he rose steadily within the Communist military and political structure in Jiangxi and Fujian. Like Chen and Su, he did not go on the Long March but spent from 1934 to 1937 organizing peasants and conducting guerrilla operations in Jiangxi and Fujian. In 1938 he became the commander and political commissar of the New Fourth Army's 3d Detachment. In 1941, when the New Fourth Army was reorganized, he was named commander and political commissar of the 6th Division. He held this military command until 1946. Tan was elected as a member of the CCP Central Committee at the Seventh Party Congress that took place April–June 1945, and he was given increasingly important commissarial positions during the civil war. When the ECFA was established on 21 January 1947, he was named deputy political commissar. In March 1948, when part of the ECFA was designated the Shandong army, he was made that army's political commissar.[57]

The chiefs of staff of the CPFA and the ECFA, Li Da and Chen Shiju respectively, shared certain experiences with the five other leaders previously discussed. Both were with Mao Zedong in the Jinggang Mountains during winter 1927-1928. Both served in the Jiangxi base area. Both were on the Long March. But unlike the other five, neither of them, apparently, ever served as a political commissar. Li was a staff officer during the Long March and then served as Liu Bocheng's chief of staff from the time the 129th Division was created in 1937 through the Huai Hai Campaign and beyond. He had become friends with Liu while studying at the Frunze Military Academy in Moscow, and Liu had great respect for his talents as a planner.[58] Chen did not have the military education that Li Da had, but he did study at the Anti-Japanese Military and Political Academy in Yan'an before becoming the chief of staff of a brigade in Lin Biao's 115th Division in 1937. In 1938 he was promoted to division chief of staff, and in 1939 he moved with the division into Shandong. During the war he exercised command at times, but when Chen Yi assumed control of Communist forces in Shandong in 1945, he served as his chief of staff. In 1947 he was named chief of staff of the ECFA.[59]

These brief biographical sketches show that a common attribute of all these leaders as they approached the time of the Huai Hai Campaign was a wealth of experience in warfare. Military education was important to the Communists. They established military schools wherever they could to give officers of all ranks an opportunity to study military history, military theory, and principles of operation. But, as the following excerpt from a lecture given by Mao Zedong to officers attending the Red army colleges in northern Shaanxi indicates, the Communists viewed personal experience as the best teacher. Reading and studying war on paper had their utility; however, experience coupled with thoughtful reflection on the meaning or significance of that experience was the surest path to mastering the art of war. Since our chief method of learning warfare is through fighting, Mao told his officers, people who do not attend military schools can learn warfare and civilians can quickly become soldiers. This was possible because, according to Mao, experience was at the heart of the "process of knowing":

> This process of knowing is extremely important; without . . . a long period of experience, it would be difficult to understand and grasp the laws of an entire war. Neither a beginner nor person who fights only on paper can become a really able high-ranking commander; only one who has learned through actual fighting in war can do so.
>
> All military laws and military theories which are in the nature of principles are the experience of past wars summed up by people in former days or in our own times. We should seriously study these lessons, paid for in blood, which are a heritage of past wars. That is one point. But there is another. We should put these conclusions to the test of our own experience assimilating what is useful, rejecting what is useless, and adding what is specifically our own. The latter is very important, for otherwise we cannot direct a war.
>
> Reading is learning, but applying is also learning and the more important kind of learning at that. Our chief method is to learn warfare through warfare. A person who has had no opportunity to go to school can also learn warfare—he can learn through fighting in war. A revolutionary war is a mass undertaking; it is often not a matter of first learning and then doing, but of doing and then learning, for doing is itself learning. There is a gap between the ordinary civilian and the soldier, but it is no Great Wall, and it can be quickly closed, and the way to close it is to take part in revolution, in war. By saying that it is not easy to learn and to apply, we mean that it is hard to learn thoroughly and to apply skillfully. By saying that civilians can very quickly become soldiers, we mean that it is not difficult to cross the threshold. To put the two statements together, we may cite the Chinese adage, 'Nothing in the world is difficult for one who sets his mind to it.' To cross the threshold is not difficult, and mastery, too, is possible provided one sets one's mind to the task and is good at learning.[60]

The issue of how much experience and formal military education contribute to developing a successful operational-level commander is worth raising here because Su Yu did not have any formal military education while Liu Bocheng had a great deal. Liu graduated from a *military school* and became a *junior officer* 15 years before Su Yu was caught up in the revolutionary fervor brought to Hunan by the GMD Northern Expedition and left *normal school* to become a *political instructor* in the Nationalist army. While Liu studied at an infantry school and the Frunze Academy in Moscow, Su was learning war through war in Jiangxi. Yet, as time went by, Su Yu proved his abilities as a commander and by the time of the Huai Hai Campaign was widely recognized as one of the PLA's most competent generals. Despite his lack of military schooling, he had basically "caught up" with Liu and was the acting commander of an army much larger than Liu's CPFA. Su's experiences, it seems, had more than compensated for what he had missed by not being a student in a classroom setting.

Interestingly, FM 3-0 reflects Mao Zedong's emphasis on the role of experience in developing the qualities that make a successful operational-level commander. No mention is made in the manual of a "genius factor" creating operational commanders who can "visualize, anticipate, create, and seize opportunities." No mention is made of an officer education system producing competent practitioners of operational art. Rather, this doctrinal manual refers simply to the benefits experience produces: "Operational commanders require experience at both the operational and tactical levels. From this experience, they gain the instincts and intuition, as well as the knowledge, that underlie an understanding of the interrelation of tactical and operational possibilities and needs."[61]

Whatever, the reasons for the emergence of Su Yu and Liu Bocheng as excellent generals, the PLA was fortunate to have them in positions of command during the Huai Hai Campaign. There is a Chinese saying that *Qian jun yi de, yi jiang nan qiu* ("One thousand armies can easily be raised, but a general is hard to find"). In the case of this campaign, the PLA had found two. As Robert Rigg's assessments of their talents show, both Su and Liu clearly possessed the instincts, intuition, and knowledge needed to practice operational art. Rigg had this to say about Su Yu:

> Su Yu is the Reds' military darling of daring, who has a reputation for producing troops out of his cap. He has long served under General Chen Yi, and a measure of Chen's military reputation results from Su's efforts as a staff officer and commander as well. General Su has more than the ordinary Chinese Red general's skills in handling artillery. He seems to like the heavy guns. From a given bolt of military manpower Su can cut, trim, fit, and sew together an excellent battle garment with a minimum of waste. Organizationally he achieves the maximum combat effectiveness with a given number of men. Tactically he is a chance-taker, who has been lucky in his gambling.

> Certain of the Chinese Red militarists regard Su Yu as a more skillful field commander than Chen Yi. Lacking any formal military education, Su can skillfully handle large bodies of soldiers in combat. Su commanded the forces which took the strongly fortified and pillbox-studded city of Tsinan [Jinan] in eight days during September 1948. The Reds had long hesitated to try to take fortified Tsinan, with its reported garrison of 100,000.

> Whether Su persuaded the higher command to let him take it or not, is unknown. However, the attack marked the significant transition in Red tactics from mobile to positional assault, and undoubtedly the command selection for the attack was seriously weighed beforehand by the Red General Staff. . . . If one could conveniently label this officer with one title, it would be 'trouble shooter.'[62]

Rigg wrote this about Liu Bocheng:

> Few generals pause to place in poetry their thoughts on tactics and strategy. The one-eyed Liu enjoys that distinction, and this verse of his reveals a portion of his basic concept:

> *When you keep men and lose land*
> *The land can be retaken.*
> *If you keep land and lose soldiers*
> *You lose both.*

During the latter half of the China Civil War, Liu was criticized for the loss of some of the towns he had taken. His rebuttal was that 'I traded seventeen empty cities for 60,000 of Chiang Kai-Shek's soldiers.' The Nationalist generals on Formosa today rate Liu as Red China's Number One general; but what is more important, the Peking Red hierarchy regards Liu as their top best.

A realist who is terrain conscious, insofar as commanding heights are concerned, Liu Po-cheng places little value on holding military real-estate for the holding's sake. Late blooming, in the field of Red military poppies, Liu rose in public stature after 1946. In terms of campaign talent he shows great originality and should be ranked ahead of Lin Piao [Lin Biao]. Liu has originality; he is daring, but calculating.

Liu was the originator of the 'take away' competition for American arms in the China Civil War. Liu sets his units in competition with each other, using the catch phrase, 'Which outfit can capture the most American arms?' Thereafter Liu's staff officers busied themselves at compiling trophy lists. He spurs his troops by such competitive measures.

Liu's command post is always in a village, or in a cluster of far houses, but never in a large town or city. If the term "field soldier" were applied to only one general in the PLA, this man would rate the title.

Practitioner of mobile war, Liu is one of the most militarily elusive and wily field army commanders in China today. He is also one whose personal past is least known. His main imprint on the field of combat is visible in the China Civil War, not during World War II against the Japanese. Here is a man to be seriously reckoned with in combat. He has been surrounded many more times than written history records, yet he has escaped, not as an individual but as an army commander—with his troops intact, but dispersed. The 'One-eyed Dragon' holds no fear of encirclement; his opponent should never brag until he has closed the bag.

A Party member since 1926, he was Moscow-schooled (1928-1931) at a Red Army military academy and subsequently became Chief of Staff to Chu Teh.

He is adept at devising his own strategy to meet changing military situations. He ably demonstrated this when, in 1947, under considerable Nationalist pressure, he led his six columns (armies) into the Tapieh [Dabie] Mountains and established a threatening base of operations that forced quite a re-adjustment in Nationalist strategy. To this day the answer has never been satisfactorily given as to just how he managed logistically to support his fast moving columns during this period, for about one year. He is obviously adept at 'living off the land.' In terms of the mobility of the campaigns, he might be called 'China's Patton.'[63]

Transforming the PLA

While years of experience were giving the commanders who played leading roles in the Huai Hai Campaign the knowledge, instincts, and intuition to direct large regular forces at the operational level, the PLA was growing and being transformed into the conventional armies that they directed in that campaign. As noted earlier, while fighting in the Jinggang Mountains in 1928, Mao Zedong had stated clearly that without a regular Red army it would be impossible to preserve Communist political power in a base area and expand. Perhaps even more important, Mao believed that the regular forces should be continually improved with better weapons, better communications equipment, and better staff work. They should, in other words, undergo a continual process of transformation and growth that would eventually make them equal to, if not superior than, any enemy they might face.

In late 1936, with the Red army deeply involved in defending the Communist base in northern Shaanxi against Nationalist attacks, Mao presented his vision of the PLA of the future to officers at the Red army college in Yan'an. He spoke of the need for the army to change its organization and introduce new technology into the force. The goal was to increase combat effectiveness, gain the ability to conduct large-scale operations, and overcome the limitations imposed on them by their existing circumstances:

> As the Red Army reaches a higher stage, we must gradually and consciously. . . . make the Red Army more centralized, more unified, more disciplined and more thorough in its work—in short, more regular in character. In the directing of operations we should also gradually and consciously reduce such guerrilla characteristics as are no longer required at a higher stage. Refusal to make progress in this respect and obstinate adherence to the old state are impermissible and harmful, and are detrimental to large-scale operations.

> We are now on the eve of a new stage with respect to the Red Army's technical equipment and organization. We must be prepared to go over to this new stage. Not to prepare ourselves would be wrong and harmful to our future warfare. In the future, when the technical and organizational conditions in the Red Army have changed and the building of the Red Army has entered a new stage, its operational directions and battle lines will become more stable; there will be more positional warfare; the fluidity of the war, of our territory and of our construction work will be greatly reduced and finally disappear; and we will no longer be handicapped by present limitations, such as the enemy's superiority and his strongly entrenched positions.[64]

Soon after this speech was made, the outbreak of war with Japan affected PLA force structure and operations. During the War of Resistance Against Japan, there was a renewed emphasis on having regular forces disperse to carry out guerrilla operations and build rural bases behind Japanese lines. But even as this change in strategy and employment of forces was occurring, Mao strove to keep "regularization" and transformation before the army leadership. In May 1938, in an article that was actually written to justify the new focus on guerrilla warfare, he reminded his readers that they should continually work to turn guerrilla units into regular units capable of conducting mobile operations:

> [T]he development of guerrilla warfare into mobile warfare means . . . the

gradual formation, in the midst of widespread guerrilla warfare, of a main force capable of conducting mobile warfare, a force around which there must still be numerous guerrilla units carrying on extensive guerrilla operations. These guerrilla units are powerful auxiliaries to the main force and serve as inexhaustible reserves for its continuous growth.

To raise the quality of the guerrilla units it is imperative to raise their political and organizational level and improve their equipment, military technique, tactics and discipline, so that they gradually pattern themselves on the regular forces and shed their guerrilla ways. Politically, it is imperative to get both the commanders and the fighters to realize the necessity of raising the guerrilla units to the level of the regular forces, to encourage them to strive toward this end and to guarantee its attainment by means of political work. Organizationally, it is imperative gradually to fulfill all the requirements of a regular formation in the following respects—military and political organs, staff and working methods, a regular supply system, a medical service, etc. In the matter of equipment, it is imperative to acquire better and more varied weapons and increase the supply of the necessary communications equipment. In the matter of military technique and tactics, it is imperative to raise the guerrilla units to the level required of a regular formation. In the matter of discipline, it is imperative to raise the level so that uniform standards are observed, every order is executed without fail and all slackness is eliminated. To accomplish all these tasks requires a prolonged effort, and it cannot be done overnight; but that is the direction in which we must develop. Only thus can a main force be built up in each guerrilla base area and mobile warfare emerge for more effective attacks on the enemy. Where detachments or cadres have been sent in by the regular forces, the goal can be achieved more easily. Hence all the regular forces have the responsibility of helping the guerrilla units to develop into regular units.[65]

A speech Mao gave to the CCP Central Committee on 6 November 1938 also referred to the importance of regular forces fighting regular warfare. Yes, Mao told his audience, the regular Communist army had dispersed and was conducting guerrilla operations. However, he reminded them, this army was not a guerrilla army in "its sense of organization or to its discipline."[66] In those important aspects it remained a regular army and once the strategic situation in the war changed it would fully become one again. Mao's "objective force" continued to be a regular army capable of conducting conventional operations: "If we take the war as a whole, therefore, regular warfare is primary and guerrilla warfare supplementary. Unless we understand this, unless we recognize that regular warfare will decide the final outcome of the war, and unless we pay attention to building a regular army and to studying and directing regular warfare, we shall be unable to defeat Japan."[67]

During the war against Japan, the PLA took numerous steps to improve its performance. There was political education, physical training, individual marksmanship training, and unit training in tactics and techniques.[68] There were activities designed to "change the individual habits . . . of soldiers and inculcate the habits of collective life."[69] Strict discipline was enforced. Adherence to basic rules of sanitation and personal hygiene such as eating cooked food and boiling water was required.⁷⁰ Staff work was improved.⁷¹ The ability of units from the Eighth Route Army and the New Fourth Army to cooperate with one another and coordinate their actions was developed and enhanced. Cooperation between the three tiers of the military force structure (main forces, local forces, and militia and self-defense forces) was strengthened.⁷² Efforts were made to integrate captured artillery into certain units and operations.⁷³

A concerted effort was also made to improve the supply situation for all units in the Communist force structure. Blockades against the Communist base areas imposed by the Japanese army, the Chinese puppet government the Japanese established, and the Nationalist army created serious supply problems in the Communist-controlled areas. However, as PLA Commander in Chief Zhu De noted in April 1945, by capturing weapons from the enemy (from September 1937 to March 1945 PLA regular and guerrilla forces captured 1,028 mortars and artillery pieces, more than 7,700 machine guns, and more than 430,000 rifles and carbines⁷⁴) and practicing self-sufficiency, the Communists were not only able to survive but they also prospered. Zhu De's report to the CCP's Seventh National Congress contained the following description of Communist accomplishments in this regard:

> For several years the most difficult problem facing us in the Liberated Areas has been obtaining equipment and military supplies. We are solving this in several ways. First, we arm ourselves with weapons seized from the enemy. For several years now we have relied on this method of strengthening our forces and maintaining our fighting power. Second, we make use of locally obtainable materials. The abundance of coal, iron and metal obtained from dismantled railway tracks in north China has greatly facilitated our manufacture of arms; this is how the greater part of the militia forces have been able to engage in mine-laying on an increasing scale. Third, we have set up small-scale ordnance factories by assembling odds and ends of equipment captured from the Japanese and puppet troops. Fourth, we disperse and camouflage these factories, which often become the target of enemy 'mopping-up' campaigns. Greater armed protection must be provided for them so that ammunition can be produced without interruption to supply the front. As far as medical supplies go, we use both traditional Chinese and Western medicines. We manufacture only a small part of the medicines we use; the main sources of supply are purchase and seizure from the enemy.⁷⁵

All of these measures improved the PLA's ability to conduct guerrilla operations and contributed to PLA regularization. They were valuable steps along the path of army transformation. In spring 1945, however, there was still much to do to prepare the army for large-scale mobile operations. In his report to the Seventh National Congress, Zhu laid out eight major military tasks that, when accomplished, would position the army to meet the challenges that lay ahead:

> (1) We must expand the Liberated areas.
> (2) We must expand the people's forces.
> (3) We have to intensify the training of our existing forces—the regular troops, local forces and the militia and self-defence forces—in preparation for the counter-offensive. To prepare our main forces for mobile warfare, we must ensure that they are steadily toughened and provided the experience of

properly planned concentrated attacks on the enemy. We must also see that the militia get their training. They should learn various methods of detonation so that they can use them in the greatest number of ways.

(4) We must improve technical skills. Strategic counter-offensive calls for modern equipment. From now on we must improve our technical skills so that we can handle such equipment when the opportunity arises. We have already captured some pieces of artillery. We must learn about gunnery and the tactics of modern warfare.

(5) We must strengthen our command system. We must improve our staff work to make it equal to the task of commanding our troops under present conditions and at the same time get it ready for an expansion of the war. We must make better preparations for a great counter-offensive.... In our political task we have a new duty: to make proper arrangements to deal with the present situation and to work out far-sighted plans for the changes the future will bring. The work of the rear service must be strengthened in regard to supplies, health care, ordnance, and so forth. It should meet both current war needs and prepare to meet the needs of the future counter-offensive. Then we shall not be caught napping when the time of great need comes. We shall in the future need highly qualified personnel in vast numbers for our commands, and we should not hesitate to send large numbers of our best cadres into the army.

(6) We must prepare a material base from which to launch the general counter-offensive. The whole army should be mobilized for productive work and mobilized to practice economy and lay in stocks of food and materials. In collecting the materials required for our counter-offensive we have to rely on our own efforts. And when the time comes for concentrated operations, we should be fully prepared for every exigency.

(7) We must take better care of the families of anti-Japanese fighters. We must improve pension services for the wounded and the families of those killed in action, and we must make better arrangements for the disabled and demobilized soldiers.

(8) In order to promote all this work and fulfill all these tasks, there must be complete unity within the Eighth Route Army, the New Fourth Army and the other armed forces of the people.[76]

Zhu stated that fulfilling these tasks was essential because the war situation as a whole was changing and that a different army was required. He reminded the assembled CCP leaders of Mao's statement made seven years earlier about the need for army transformation and asked them to prepare for change:

All these military tasks that will confront the Liberated Areas from now on, in other words, the central strategic task for which we must be prepared, correspond, generally speaking, to what Comrade Mao Zedong said in the early period of the War of Resistance: that the Eighth Route and New Fourth Armies had to be prepared for a strategic change from guerrilla warfare to regular warfare in the later period of the war. It is now time for us to be prepared to make this change, step by step, in our practical work. All personnel in the army should be prepared to make fundamental changes in their outlook and in their practical work, so they will be ready for the general counter-offensive against the Japanese aggressors.[77]

During the very month of Zhu's report to the CCP National Congress, the PLA moved forward on implementing the fourth task that he had mentioned by taking steps to establish an artillery school in Yan'an. The school was officially opened on 1 August (the anniversary of the Nanchang Uprising and the birthday of the PLA) with a ceremony that included practice firing mortars. Zhu attended, and was impressed by what he saw and heard in discussions with members of the school staff. On 6 August he sent a letter to the CCP Central Committee explaining the need for greater firepower in PLA combat units and describing how that firepower could be increased. He also addressed the broader need to have a manufacturing base and repair facilities to support artillery:

> 1. In battles against enemy and puppet troops and troops of the diehard clique of the Kuomintang [GMD], our fighters often encounter pillboxes and temporary earthworks common in mobile warfare, which keep them from gaining victory.
> 2. During the year ahead, we should provide each full-strength regiment with a mortar battery and each under-strength regiment with a mortar platoon in order to better cope with the enemy.
> 3. Artillery units should be organized by leaders at all levels as a first step in building our army for the present stage. In the future, our army should have all types of artillery, beginning with mortars.
> 4. To organize artillery units, it is necessary first to define the tasks of our munitions factories at the front and in the rear. As we see it, what these factories are actually doing now is repairing weapons and manufacturing ammunition. They should be able to repair all kinds of artillery, machine-guns and rifles, and also to manufacture more mortar shells, which will help us destroy the enemy's pillboxes.[78]

Zhu De's inclusion of Nationalist forces among the enemies that the better PLA artillery would be bombarding is worthy of note because the scale of Nationalist-Communist fighting had been increasing in 1945 as the Nationalists had tried to retard the growth and expansion of Communist military activity. Soon, fighting the Nationalists would be the PLA's only concern. On 6 August the United States dropped an atomic bomb on Hiroshima. Two days later the Soviet Union entered the war against Japan. On 9 August the United States dropped another atomic bomb, this time on Nagasaki. On 14 August the Japanese emperor announced Japan's surrender. This sudden turn of events meant that the general counteroffensive against Japan that the PLA had been preparing for would not occur as envisioned. What did occur was a frantic competition between the Communists and Nationalists to seize as much of the territory the Japanese occupied as they could before the other side reached it. This led to more battles between them and helped set the stage for the outbreak of full-scale civil war the following year.

While the threat changed with Japan's surrender, the strategic policy of army transformation did not. During the first part of 1945 there had been a steady shift away from guerrilla warfare against Japanese forces to regular warfare against them. After Japan's surrender change continued, only now it was part of a shift "from regular warfare against Japan to regular warfare against an internal opponent" as the Communists worked to enhance their ability to conduct large-scale conventional operations.[79]

On 20 August 1945 the CCP CMC took action to regularize army organization and establish large maneuver forces. Each military region was directed to quickly organize 50 to 60 percent of its forces into a large field army with the remainder going into a local army. The divisions in the field army were to be "triangular," with three regiments per division, three battalions per regiment, and three companies per battalion. Each company was to have a heavy machine gun platoon. Division size was not to exceed 7,000 soldiers, and companies were not to have more than 142 soldiers. Each military region was responsible for supplying the field army it created and for replacing soldier casualties. To ensure the ability of each military region to meet the second of these two requirements, each was directed to mobilize new recruits numbering one-third of the current troop strength in the region. However, the military regions were also told that the number of men taken from production could not exceed 2 percent of the region's total population.[80]

On 22 August an important policy statement on regularization appeared in the form of an editorial in the *Dazhong Ribao* (*Masses Daily*). The editorial reiterated the decision of the CCP's Seventh National Congress to move toward regular war with its centralized direction and greater concentration of forces. It focused especially on the problems that supporting large maneuver forces would create for rear area organizations, exhorting them to get ready for what lay ahead: "If one day the situation suddenly changes and you are asked to immediately ensure the ability of a large army to conduct operations, it will be very difficult to respond in a short period of time."[81]

On 21 September the CCP Central Committee clarified several points regarding the employment, command relationships, and logistics support of the large field armies that were to be established. From that day forward, these armies were to be employed under the CMC's direction and were not to be considered part of a military region's order of battle. They were to be ready to conduct operations outside their military regions at any time. However, soldier replacement remained the responsibility of the military region in which the field army had been formed. Furthermore, when such a main force was positioned in its "home" military region, that military region would provide its supplies.[82]

These directives, Zhu De's report to the CCP's Seventh Party Congress, and his letter on firepower all indicate the intentions of the Communist leadership in 1945 to push ahead with army transformation. The PLA truly was, to again quote Mao's speech of 1936, "on the eve of a new stage with respect to [its] technical equipment and organization."[83] During 1945 to 1948, the pace of transformation would accelerate as more and more Nationalist weapons and Nationalist soldiers with the technical skills to use them were captured and incorporated into the PLA. At the same time, the staffs, communications infrastructure, logistics systems, and other elements needed to support large-scale regular operations were being improved. The end result was armies like the CPFA and ECFA. In 1936 Mao had spoken of a time in the future when the PLA would "no longer be handicapped by present limitations, such as the enemy's superiority and his strongly entrenched positions."[84] By the time of the Huai Hai Campaign, that future had arrived.

Communist Strategy From the Time of Japan's Surrender to Summer 1948

On 13 August 1945, with Japan's surrender, in his words, a "foregone conclusion," Mao Zedong laid out CCP policy for the coming months.[85] He emphasized two points: the need to keep the Nationalists from moving into all of the areas formerly under Japanese occupation and the need to prepare for civil war. War with the Nationalists, in Mao's view, was a virtual certainty:

> The entry of the Soviet Union into the war has decided Japan's surrender and the situation in China is entering a new period. Between the War of Resistance and the new period there is a transitional stage. The struggle during this transitional stage is to oppose Chiang Kai-shek's usurpation of the fruits of victory in the War of Resistance. Chiang Kai-shek wants to launch a country-wide civil war and his policy is set; we must be prepared for this. No matter when this country-wide civil war breaks out, we must be well prepared. If it comes early, say, tomorrow morning, we should also be prepared. That is point one. In the present international and domestic situation it is possible that for a time the civil war may be kept restricted in scale and localized. That is point two. Point one is what we should prepare for, point two is what has existed for a long time. In short, we must be prepared. Being prepared, we shall be able to deal properly with all kinds of complicated situations.[86]

Days before Mao's speech and Japan's surrender, the CCP-GMD competition for the "fruits of victory" had already begun. On 10 August Zhu De issued an order to all Communist forces directing them to begin demanding the surrender of Japanese and puppet troops in their areas. On 11 August he sent out orders for a general offensive to seize territory from the Japanese. That same day, Jiang Jieshi ordered the Communist forces to stay in place and await further orders. Mao rejected Jiang's order in a telegram sent on 13 August. Furthermore, in a statement prepared on 13 August for distribution by the New China News Agency, Mao had harsh words for Jiang: "Even before the enemy's actual surrender, Chiang Kai-shek, China's fascist ringleader, autocrat, and traitor to the people had the audacity to 'order' the anti-Japanese forces in the Liberated Areas to 'stay where they are, pending further orders', that is, to tie their own hands and let the enemy attack them."[87]

The day after Japan announced its surrender on 14 August, Zhu De issued an order to Yasuji Okamura, commander in chief of Japanese forces in China, demanding that he surrender all of his soldiers, except for those surrounded by GMD troops, to PLA units. Jiang Jiehshi, on the other hand, sent out an order that day directing Okamura to maintain order and protect supplies until he told him to do otherwise. On 23 August the Nationalist high command ordered Okamura to have Japanese forces defend their positions, keep lines of communication open, and await the arrival of GMD troops. The effect of this order was to place Japanese troops in a supporting role for Nationalist movement.

With both Communist and Nationalist forces rushing to take control of as much Japanese-occupied land as possible, fighting between them became common. Over the next several months their battles increased in both frequency and intensity. However, domestic considerations and international influence kept what was, to use Mao's words, a civil war that was "restricted in scale and localized" from turning into a full-scale civil war.

For the Communists, August 1945-July 1946 was a time of both consolidation and growth. Even though they were much stronger militarily than they had ever been, their forces were still markedly inferior to Nationalist forces in size and weaponry. In August 1945 the Communists had 1.2 million regulars, while the Nationalist army had 4.4 million soldiers.[88] This disparity led the Communists to adopt a cautious strategy that initially emphasized expansion where they would not come into contact with Nationalist forces. This strategy, known as "develop toward the north, defend in the south," was promulgated by the CCP Central Committee on 19 September 1945.[89] It took advantage of the Soviet Red army's presence in northern and northeastern China and the Soviet refusal to allow Nationalist forces into the area. For several months of fall 1945, the troops from Shandong and elsewhere that were rushed to northeastern China in accordance with this strategy were able to freely organize new base areas and prepare to fight against the Nationalists when they came.

This "develop to the north, defend in the south" strategy provided the basis for shifting the main elements of the New Fourth Army from Jiangsu into Shandong. It also underlaid a concession Mao Zedong made during his face-to-face negotiations with Jiang Jieshi from 28 August to 10 October 1945. In these negotiations, Mao agreed to abandon eight base areas scattered across southern China in Guangdong, Hunan, Hubei, southern Henan, southern and central Anhui, southern Jiangsu, and Zhejiang. If not conceded, they were sure to be attacked, Mao explained upon his return to Yen'an. Furthermore, taking a long view of the struggle with the Nationalists and showing his understanding of nonmilitary factors that were part of the equation, he stated that by abandoning those base areas voluntarily, the Communists appeared to be reasonable compromisers and would gain favor in the court of public opinion: "It is a great pity to concede these eight areas, but it is better to do so. . . . Why should we concede these areas? Because . . . so long as we are there, they [the Nationalists] will . . . fight for those places at all costs. Our concession on this point will help frustrate the Kuomintang's [GMD's] plot for civil war and win us the sympathy of the numerous middle elements at home and abroad."[90]

The decision to abandon these base areas had significance for the Huai Hai Campaign because it brought Su Yu and his 1st Division back to central Jiangsu. He had taken his division south across the Yangzi River on 27 December 1944 and since that time had been engaged in establishing the Su-Zhe (Jiangsu-Zhejiang) Military District and conducting military operations. Upon his return to central Jiangsu in November 1945, his division, in accordance with the policy of creating large regular maneuver forces, was incorporated into the newly organized 50,000-man Central China Field Army, and he was made the army commander.[91]

General Marshall, President Truman's special ambassador, arrived in China in late December 1945 to try his hand at mediating the GMD-CCP dispute. A number of agreements were reached and documents were signed. Cease-fires were ordered, but on fundamental issues, the two sides remained far apart. In the spring, fighting in the northeast became extremely intense. Finally, in June 1946, Jiang Jieshi decided to force Communist concessions with a massive offensive. "It was first necessary," he told Marshall, "to deal harshly with the Communists, and later, after two or three months, to adopt a generous attitude."[92] By that time, according to Jiang, "the Communists would appeal for a settlement and would be willing to make the compromises necessary for a settlement."[93] In July all-out civil war began.

The latter half of 1946 and the first half of 1947 witnessed a series of Nationalist victories. In eastern and central China, many Communist base areas were overrun. By spring 1947 all county seats in Jiangsu were under Nationalist control.[94] Nationalist forces had occupied the areas south of the Yellow River that had formerly been under Communist control and were pushing deep into Shandong. In March 1947 Nationalist forces took the Communist capital, Yen'an. By the end of the first year of civil war, the Communists had lost control over 120,000 square miles and 18 million people.[95]

The problem for the Nationalists was that their advances had been gained at a high cost in men and materiel and had not achieved any decisive results. They had been unable to reach many of the Communist base areas in Shandong, Hebei, Shanxi, and northern Henan. They had failed to destroy any sizable Communist force. At the end of the first year of civil war, their offensive was reaching a culmination point while the Communists were gathering strength for a counterstroke.

Communist strategy was to eliminate Nationalist units steadily while preserving its own forces. The tactic of choice was to concentrate an absolutely superior force, encircle a Nationalist unit, and annihilate that unit. The goal was to achieve Sunzi's dual ideal of "winning a battle and becoming stronger."[96] As Mao stated in a directive to the CMC on 16 September 1946:

> Only complete annihilation can deal the most telling blows to the enemy, for when we wipe out one regiment he will have one regiment less, and when we wipe out one brigade, he will have one brigade less. . . . Only complete annihilation can replenish our own forces to the greatest possible extent. It is now not only the main source of our arms and ammunition, but also an important part of our manpower.[97]

In summer 1947 the Nationalists were stretched to the limit with few reserves. During the previous year their troop strength had declined from 4.3 million to 3.73 million.[98] Communist troop strength had risen from 1.27 million to 1.95 million.[99] The Communists felt that the time had come to seize the initiative and change the shape of the war. In June, with Nationalist forces attacking in the east into central Shandong and in the west into northern Shaanxi, the CCP Central Committee ordered Liu Bocheng and Deng Xiaoping to break through the Nationalist defense line along the Yellow River northeast of Kaifeng and move into Nationalist-held southwestern Shandong. On the night of June 30, after intense artillery fire destroyed a portion of the Nationalist defenses, the Liu-Deng force of 120,000 successfully completed the river crossing and began its campaign. After a series of successful battles, in late July, it received orders from the CMC directing it to drop its logistics line of communication with its Shandong base area and march to the Dabie Mountains 300 miles away in southwestern Anhui.[100] There it would mobilize the masses and build new rural bases in a strategic area close to the Yangzi River and the major cities of Wuhan and Nanjing.

The Liu-Deng army's deep thrust exemplified the CCP's strategy for the second year of the civil war. As laid out in a Central Committee directive dated 1 September 1947 that Mao Zedong drafted, that strategy placed great emphasis on having large armies end their reliance on base areas and advance into Nationalist territories. There they would establish new bases and force the Nationalist forces to disperse. This would increase the possibilities for the Communists to destroy them piecemeal through mobile operations:

> In the second year of fighting, our army's basic task is to launch a country-wide counter-offensive, that is, to use our main forces to fight our way to exterior

lines, carry the war into the Kuomingtang areas, wipe out large numbers of the enemy on the exterior lines and completely wreck the Kuomintang's [GMD's] counter-revolutionary strategy, which is, on the contrary, to continue to carry the war into the Liberated Areas, further damage and drain our manpower and material resources and make it impossible for us to hold out very long.

Our army will of course meet many difficulties in carrying out the policy of fighting on exterior lines and bringing the war into the Kuomintang [GMD] areas. For it takes time to build new bases in the Kuomintang [GMD] areas and we can build stable bases only when we have wiped out large numbers of the enemy in many back-and-forth mobile operations, aroused the masses, distributed land, established our political power and built up the people's armed forces. Until then, there will be quite a few difficulties. But they can and must be overcome. For the enemy will be forced to spread out even more, and vast territories will be available to our army as battlefields for mobile operations, and so we will be able to wage mobile warfare.[101]

The Liu-Deng army began its march from southwestern Shandong to the Dabie Mountains on 7 August, and on 27 August, the last units crossed the Huai River and entered the mountains.[102] This was the opening round in a struggle to control the central plain of China that lasted until the Huai Hai Campaign was over. The central plains, the area bounded roughly by the Yellow River in the north, the Yangzi River in the south, the Grand Canal in the east, and the Han River and Funiu mountains on the west, has been an important area in wars since antiquity. Control of that area was key to controlling China. Jiang Jieshi saw the danger posed by the Liu-Deng move into the Dabie Mountains and quickly concentrated 33 divisions to attack them. But this redeployment weakened Nationalist forces elsewhere.

While Liu and Deng avoided destruction by using a mobile defense on interior lines, Chen Yi and Su Yu sent part of their army from Shandong into northeastern Henan and attacked Nationalist positions there. Unable to meet all of the new challenges simultaneously, the Nationalists began to lose the initiative. During the first half of 1948, Chen Yi and Su Yu increased their coordination with units from Liu-Deng's army as the Communists fought a series of successful campaigns in central and eastern Henan. By the end of July, the Communists had created conditions for peasant mobilization in large swaths across eastern Henan, northern Anhui, northern Jiangsu, and southern Shandong. The Nationalists, on the other hand, were increasingly concentrating their large maneuver units in the cities and towns along the three main railroads in the area and the Grand Canal. After two years of civil war they still possessed significant military power in east central China, but their options for employing that power in the pursuit of operational-level victories were diminishing.

Notes

1. Mao Zedong, "The Struggle in the Chingkang Mountains," *Selected Works of Mao Tse-tung* (hereafter cited as *SWM*), vol. 1 (Peking: Foreign Languages Press, 1967), 97-98.

2. Ibid., 98.

3. Ibid., 80.

4. Ibid., 84-85.

5. Ibid., 84.

6. Mao Zedong, "Why Is It That Red Political Power Can Exist in China?" *SWM*, vol. 1, 66.

7. Mao Zedong, "The Struggle in the Chingkang Mountains," *SWM*, vol. 1, 86-87.

8. Ibid., 76.

9. Mao Zedong, "Why Is It That Red Political Power Can Exist in China?" *SWM*, vol. 1, 69.

10. Ibid., 66.

11. Mao Zedong, "The Struggle in the Chingkang Mountains," *SWM*, vol. 1, 101.

12. Immanuel C.Y. Hsu, *The Rise of Modern China*, 2d ed. (New York: Oxford University Press, 1975), 674.

13. Harrison E. Salisbury, *The Long March: The Untold Story* (New York: Harper & Row, 1985), 119-26.

14. Zhongguo renmin jiefangjun lishi cidian bianweihui [Committee for Editing the Historical Dictionary of the Chinese People's Liberation Army], ed., *Zhongguo renmin jiefangjun lishi cidian* [Historical Dictionary of the Chinese People's Liberation Army] (Beijing: Junshi kexue chubanshe, 1990), 7.

15. Ibid., 597.

16. Mao Zedong, "Win the Masses in Their Millions for the Anti-Japanese National United Front," *SWM*, vol. 1, 291.

17. Ibid., 293.

18. Committee for Editing the Historical Dictionary of the Chinese People's Liberation Army, 597.

19. William W. Whitson with Chen-hsia Huang, *The Chinese High Command: A History of Communist Military Politics, 1927-71* (New York: Praeger Publishers, 1973), 224.

20. Committee for Editing the Historical Dictionary of the Chinese People's Liberation Army, 13.

21. Whitson and Huang, 228.

22. Committee for Editing the Historical Dictionary of the Chinese People's Liberation Army, 15.

23. Ibid.

24. Chalmers A. Johnson, *Peasant Nationalism and Communist Power: The Emergence of Revolutionary China, 1937-1945* (Stanford, CA: Stanford University Press, 1962), 49.

25. Ibid.

26. Ibid.

27. Ibid., 146.

28. Suzanne Pepper, *Civil War in China: The Political Struggle, 1945-1949* (Berkeley, CA: University of California Press, 1980), 276.

29. Mao Zedong, "On Coalition Government," *SWM*, vol. 3, 214-17.

30. Mao Zedong, "Problems of War and Strategy," *SWM*, vol. 2, 224-25.

31. Mao Zedong, "On Coalition Government," *SWM*, vol. 3, 248.

32. Pepper, 310.

33. Mao Zedong, "On Some Important Problems of the Party's Present Policy." *SWM*, vol. 4, 183.

34. Mao Zedong, "On the September Meeting—Circular of the Central Committee of the Communist Party of China," vol. 4, 270-71.

35. Pepper, 311.

36. Ibid.

37. Ibid.

38. Mao Zedong, "On the September Meeting—Circular of the Central Committee of the Communist Party of China," *SWM*, vol. 4, 270.

39. Ibid., 269.

40. Whitson and Huang, 440.

41. Zhonggong zhongyang dangshi ziliao zhengji weiyuanhui [Chinese Communist Party Central Committee's Committee for the Collection of Party Historical Material], ed., *Huaihai zhanyi* [The Huai Hai Campaign] (hereafter cited as *HHZY*) (Beijing: Zhonggong dangshi ziliao chubanshe, 1988), vol. 1, 325.

42. Ibid., 50.

43. Ibid.

44. Ibid., 47.

45. Ibid., 52.

46. Ibid., 71.

47. Ibid., 50.

48. Ibid., 108.

49. The biographical information in this chronology of Liu Bocheng's life is taken from *Biographic Dictionary of Chinese Communism, 1921-1965*, Donald W. Klein and Anne B. Clark, eds. (Cambridge, MA: Harvard University Press, 1971), vol. 1, 611-14.

50. The biographical information in this chronology of Deng Xiaoping's life is taken from Ibid., vol. 2, 819-22.

51. The biographical information in this chronology of Chen Yi's life is taken from Ibid., vol. 1, 104-110.

52. *Zongguo renmin jiefangjun zhanshi* [A History of the Wars of the Chinese Peoples' Liberation Army], Junshi kexueyuan lishi yanjiubu [Historical Research Department of the Academy of Military Science], ed., vol. 2 (Beijing: Junshi kexue chubanshe, 1987), 435.

53. Ibid.

54. Ibid.

55. Ibid., 437-38.

56. The biographical information in this chronology of Su Yu's life is taken from *Biographic Dic-

tionary of Chinese Communism, 1921-1965, vol. 2, 774-76 unless otherwise indicated.

57. The biographical information on Tan Zhenlin contained in this paragraph is taken from Ibid., vol. 2, 796-99.

58. Whitson and Huang, 210.

59. *Biographic Dictionary of Chinese Communism, 1921-1965,* vol. 1, 134-35.

60. Mao Zedong, "Problems of Strategy in China's Revolutionary War," *SWM*, vol. 1, 189-90.

61. US Army, Field Manual 3-0, *Operations* (Washington, DC: US Government Printing Office, June 2001), 2-4. See paragraph 2-10 on page 5 of this work.

62. Robert B. Rigg, *Red China's Fighting Hordes* (Harrisburg, PA: The Military Service Publishing Co., 1951), 33-34.

63. Ibid., 31-33.

64. Mao Zedong, "Problems of Strategy in China's Revolutionary War," *SWM*, vol. 1, 243-44.

65. Mao Zedong, "Problems of Strategy in Guerrilla War Against Japan," *SWM*, vol. 2, 108-109.

66. Mao Zedong, "Problems of War and Strategy," *SWM*, vol. 2, 228.

67. Ibid., 229-30.

68. Zhu De, "Training and Leading Troops," *Selected Works of Zhu De* (Beijing: Foreign Languages Press, 1986), 109, hereafter cited as *SWZD*.

69. Ibid.

70. Ibid., 112.

71. Zhu De, "The Battle Front in the Liberated Areas," *SWZD*, 178.

72. Ibid.

73. Ibid., 186.

74. Ibid., 154.

75. Ibid., 178-79.

76. Ibid., 185-87.

77. Ibid., 188.

78. Zhu De, "Views on Setting Up Mortar Units and on Armament Production," *SWZD*, 196.

79. Committee for Editing the Historical Dictionary of the Chinese People's Liberation Army, 429.

80. *Zhongguo renmin jiefangjun shijian renwu lu* [A Record of Chinese People's Liberation Army Events and People], Shao Weizheng, Wang Jin, and Liu Jianjing, eds. (Shanghai: Renmin chubanshe, 1988), 6.

81. *Ibid.*, 6-7.

82. *Ibid.*, 11-12.

83. Mao Zedong, "Problems of Strategy in China's Revolutionary War," *SWM*, vol. 1, 244.

84. Ibid.

85. Mao Zedong, "The Situation and Our Policy After the Victory in the War of Resistance Against Japan," *SWM*, vol. 4, 11.

86. Ibid., 22.

87. Mao Zedong, "Chiang Kai-shek is Provoking Civil War," *SWM*, vol. 4, 27.

88. Deng Maomao, *Deng Xiaoping: My Father* (New York: Basic Books, 1995), 357.

89. *Xinsijun shijian renwu lu* [A Record of New Fourth Army Events and People] Wang Fuji, ed., (Shanghai: Renmen chubanshe, 1988), 540.

90. Mao Zedong, "On the Chungking Negotiations," *SWM*, vol. 4, 56-57.

91. *A Record of New Fourth Army Events and People*, 542.

92. Hsu, 755.

93. Ibid.

94. Pepper, 299.

95. Hsu, 758.

96. Sunzi, *The Art of War*, Samuel B. Griffith, trans. (New York: Oxford University Press, 1963), 76.

97. Mao Zedong, "Concentrate a Superior Force to Destroy the Enemy Forces One by One," *SWM*, vol. 4, 104.

98. Hsu, 759.

99. Ibid.

100. Deng Maomao, 398.

101. Mao Zedong, "Strategy for the Second Year of the War of Liberation," *SWM*, vol. 4, 141-42.

102. Deng Maomao, 405.

Chapter Two

The Emergence of the Huai Hai Campaign Vision and Plan

Strategy is the art and science of developing and employing armed forces and other instruments of national power in a synchronized fashion to secure national or multinational objectives.
— FM 3-0, *Operations*, 2001

Why is it necessary for the commander of a campaign or a tactical operation to understand the laws of strategy to some degree? Because an understanding of the whole facilitates the handling of the part, and because the part is subordinate to the whole.
— Mao Zedong, *Problems of Strategy in China's Revolutionary War*

There are roads not to be taken, armies not to be attacked, cities not to be assaulted, ground not to be contested, and orders from the sovereign not to be accepted.
— Sunzi, *The Art of War*

The preceding chapter described the ways in which, during 1927-1948, the Communists created a powerful military instrument of power by developing capable forces and competent commanders. It examined the creation of the political, social, and economic foundation that supported Communist armies in the field. It discussed the different military strategies that were employed as changes occurred in the overall strategic situation. In summary, the chapter showed how the Communists grew in strength during the two decades before the Huai Hai Campaign so that a campaign like Huai Hai could be envisioned.

What happened in the years leading up to 1948 did not mean that the Huai Hai Campaign or a campaign like it was destined to occur. In fact, Central Military Commission (CMC) strategy in late 1947 and early 1948 was taking the flow of operations down a path that, if followed, would have made it impossible to carry out a campaign as large as the Huai Hai Campaign in the central plains area. At the time the CMC, impressed by the results achieved by the Liu-Deng army's move from Shandong to the Dabie Mountains, wanted to send more forces into Nationalist-controlled areas to compel them to disperse their armies even farther. Such action was seen as a way to weaken the Nationalists' ability to launch offensives into Communist base areas and to provide more opportunities to isolate and annihilate Nationalist units. The concept was to build on the momentum established by Liu-Deng's first "strategic leap forward," as it was called, by carrying out an even more ambitious, second strategic leap.[1] This leap would be dispatching a large body of troops from Chen Yi's East China Field Army (ECFA) deep into the area south of the Yangzi River to create more threats for the Nationalists to deal with.

If this strategic concept had been implemented, there would have been no Huai Hai Campaign as we now know it. There would have been other campaigns that would probably have produced the same effect—expelling Nationalist forces from the central plains and opening the Yangzi River valley to Communist penetration. However, there is reason to believe that that result would not have come as quickly as it did if Su Yu had quietly accepted an order he received from the CMC on 27 January 1948 directing him to lead three of the ECFA's best columns, the 1st, 4th, and 6th, across the Yangzi River to conduct mobile operations in the Hunan-Jiangxi-Zhejiang-Fujian area.[2]

Su Yu Plants the Seed of the Huai Hai Campaign

Su Yu did not approve of this concept of operations because he saw it as dispersing ECFA strength with uncertain results. The CMC estimate on 27 January 1948 was that by sending a force of three columns—70,000 to 80,000 soldiers—into the Hunan-Jiangxi area it would compel the Nationalists to pull between 20 and 30 divisions (from a total force of 80 divisions) away from the central plains and redeploy them south of the Yangzi River.[3] Su was not so sure that this would happen. His answers to the questions posed by operational art to operational commanders pointed toward a different course of action—concentrating Communist forces in the central plains area to conduct mobile operations there.

On 22 January 1948 Su Yu had sent a message to the CMC suggesting this very approach. After describing Nationalist advantages and People's Liberation Army (PLA) weaknesses that were making it difficult for Communist forces to achieve objectives, or achieve them as quickly as they wished, he stated:

> Because of these reasons, I propose that from now on for a period of time the three armies (Liu-Deng, Chen-Xie, and Ours) adopt the 'suddenly concentrate—suddenly disperse' operational method in an attempt to achieve the relatively complete destruction of a large Nationalist army. If the ECFA did not need to undertake the responsibility of attacking Nationalist units arriving to aid the force under attack, our troop strength is sufficient to do this now. If we have the timely support of neighboring military region forces to attack Nationalist reinforcements or tie them down, it is very likely that we can destroy a large army.
>
> Once the battle of annihilation in an area is over, and the enemy concentrates forces there, we can then disperse or move to a different area. In general, whichever area offers a good opportunity for wiping out the enemy is the area where we'll concentrate our forces.
>
> If we can fight two or three battles of annihilation like this, then there will probably be a change in the situation. Please let us know if my limited understanding is correct. If you feel that this proposal can be implemented, then please have Liu Bocheng and Deng Xiaoping exercise over-all command.[4]

The CMC's response to this message was the 27 January message mentioned previously. After receiving it, Su and his staff prepared options for crossing the Yangzi for the CMC to consider. On 31 January these options were sent to the CMC with a request for its guidance. Su candidly presented the difficulties to be encountered, no matter which option was selected, but he did not express opposition to the concept of making this deep thrust into Nationalist territory.

As part of his preparation to implement the CMC's 27 January directive, in March, Su Yu brought the three columns that would be going south of the Yangzi out of Shandong and moved them across the Yellow River to Puyang County in northeastern Henan province to train, gather supplies, and study how to best accomplish their mission. Their official unit designation was the First Army of the Southeast Field Army. Su was the commander and political commissar of the First Army and the deputy commander, Southeast Field Army that Chen Yi commanded.[5]

Creating this field army headquarters established the organizational structure for easily expanding this force in the future.

Su Yu understood the benefits to be gained by the forthcoming operation, but as the training progressed and he considered the problems the force faced, the more convinced he was that sending these columns across the Yangzi at this time was a mistake. The river crossing itself was a major challenge. Since a force of that size could not cross the Yangzi River in one night, the next day it was likely to be attacked by Nationalist aircraft and gunboats with considerable losses. Another problem was that when fighting from place to place over a long distance, it would need to establish a number of small guerrilla bases along the way to provide havens for sick and wounded soldiers. Su estimated that leaving a regiment here and there to meet this requirement would reduce his force by half or more before it reached its objective.[6]

Operating in new areas without a reliable rear base of supply posed more difficulties that Su knew all too well from his experiences in 1934 with the "Red Army Vanguard." Furthermore, as he considered the terrain in the area, terrain that he was very familiar with because he had commanded forces fighting there for several years, he concluded that because it was unsuitable for large-scale maneuver warfare, it was highly unlikely that the Nationalists would shift powerful, highly mobile units like the V Corps or the XVIII Corps from the central plains to this area.[7] To Su, the situation was obvious. The three columns of the First Army, Southeast Field Army, were about to be sent on a risky, difficult, high-cost mission that would net little in return. He believed that this force would contribute much more to the war effort by staying with the ECFA and fighting on the central plains. His challenge now was to convince his superiors that they should change their directive and let this happen.

In early April Su Yu brought up his concerns and ideas to Chen Yi, who recently had come from Communist central headquarters and had the latest information on strategic thinking there. Chen thought Su's analysis had merit.[8] Shortly afterward, when Li Xiannian, deputy commander, Jin-Ji-Lu-Yu Field Army, paid a visit to Puyang, Su Yu shared his thoughts with him and found that Li, too, agreed with his analysis.[9] Thus emboldened, Su proceeded to send messages to Liu Bocheng, Deng Xiaoping, and others soliciting their views. When they all informed Su that they also felt that the time was not ripe for crossing the Yangzi River and that they would prefer to concentrate forces and fight in the central plains, Su Yu decided to express his concerns and suggestions directly to the CMC.[10]

Su Yu presented his views in a lengthy message he sent to the CMC on 18 April. In another illustration of his competence as an operational-level commander, his analysis addressed not only the military conditions that this "strategic leap" south of the Yangzi River would produce but also the economic, social, and political conditions that would result. Su Yu's argument that the military benefits to be gained by forcing the Nationalists to send troops south of the Yangzi might not outweigh the opportunities that would be lost on the central plains if the ECFA voluntarily dispersed probably gave CMC members pause. But what was likely of greater concern to them was his assertion that such a military move would have serious negative effects economically, socially, and politically.

As the following excerpt from this message indicates, drawing on his own extensive experience of leading troops in the area, Su Yu was issuing a clear warning to his superiors at the strategic level. The military operations they were asking him to carry out would force him to confiscate food from the peasants. This would create deep resentment and harm the Communists' efforts to carry out their political program in the area far into the future:

> For large armies moving into new areas, the most serious issue is the problem of food. When we and the enemy are locked in a seesaw struggle, both sides must search for large amounts of food, which creates a situation where we are competing with the people for food. (In newly liberated areas it is very difficult for local work to provide food for a large army.) If every company every day asks for food from the masses (because of circumstances, it is very hard to do overall planning) and therefore infringes upon the interests of the masses, this will influence the mobilization of the masses. I remember being in the Tianmu Mountains in 1945 with fewer than 20,000 troops. We controlled an area nearly 150 kilometers by 150 kilometers for only three months and left the people impoverished. During the period when the fighting was most intense (the Xiaofeng battle) we even took almost all of the food belonging to the poor peasants and farm laborers. Up to the present time, the people in that area still carry deeply felt negative feelings about those events.
>
> In taking a force of 100,000 into the mountains south of the Yangzi, crossing the river will definitely be extremely difficult. (So long as we are able to cross the river, the other military difficulties can be easily overcome.) But the resupply of food is a long-term serious problem. Going south of the Yangzi now will no doubt cause the enemy to redeploy more troops, will sow confusion deep in the enemy's rear, and will advance the war situation. However, the large armies of both sides will be fighting seesaw battles, and taking food directly from the people, and as before, this will give us trouble (Those new areas will soon become liberated areas, but taking food from the people will hinder arousing the masses.) and be an extremely large obstacle to arousing the masses in the new areas. This [food] problem can be said to be the key to whether or not, after our army has crossed the Yangzi, we can accomplish the mission given us by the CMC.[11]

The CMC responded to Su Yu's message with a request sent on 21 April for a face-to-face meeting with Chen Yi and Su Yu to discuss Su's ideas. In early May Chen and Su traveled to Fuping, a small town in the Taihang Mountains northwest of Shijiazhuang and there met with Mao Zedong, Liu Shaoqi, Zhou Enlai, Zhu De, Ren Bishi, and others.[12] After considering Su's presentation, the CMC agreed with his logic. Plans were changed. The 1st, 4th, and 6th columns were not to be sent south of the Yangzi River. Communist forces were to be concentrated on the central plains between the Yellow River and the Huai River to fight large battles of annihilation against the Nationalists there.[13] At this time the CMC also decided that Chen Yi should leave Shandong for Henan province to help promote political organization and mobilization work in the new Central Plains Military Region (CPMR). To replace Chen, Su Yu was appointed acting commander and acting political officer of the ECFA.[14]

Su Yu was gratified and relieved that the CMC had accepted his proposal, but he also felt pressure to show that his vision had been correct. This he did in a series of battles during the summer, the most notable of which was the Eastern Henan Campaign that lasted from 17 June to 6 July. During this campaign the ECFA cooperated effectively with the Central Plains Field

Army (CPFA), and Su made good use of the three columns that had not gone south. Victory in the Eastern Henan Campaign, during which the Nationalists suffered 90,000 casualties, coupled with the capture of Yanzhou, a move that isolated Jinan, the capital of Shandong, made it possible for Su Yu to attack Jinan on 14 September. After only 10 days of fighting, Jinan fell on the 24th. Before the fighting had completely ended, Su Yu's proposal for a new campaign, the Huai Hai Campaign, was on its way to the CMC.

Communist Strategic Thinking, Summer 1948

In large measure, Communist military strategy for the third year of the civil war was the same as it had been during the first two years—operations designed to steadily eliminate Nationalist units and soldiers. Estimating that the civil war would last a total of five years, in a meeting held in September 1948, the CCP Central Committee laid out an attrition road map for reaching victory:

> In the light of our successes in the past two years' fighting and of the general situation as between the enemy and ourselves, the meeting convened by the Central Committee considered it fully possible to build a People's Liberation Army of five million in a period of about five years (beginning from July 1946), to wipe out a total of some 500 brigades (divisions) of the enemy's regular forces (an average of about 100 brigades a year), to wipe out a total of some 7,500,000 men of his regular and irregular forces and of the special arms (an average of about 1,500,000 men a year) and to overthrow the reactionary rule of the Kuomintang [GMD] completely.[15]

Specific guidance on how many divisions (brigades) each field army should destroy during the third year of the war was issued. The following excerpt from a message sent to the Northeast Field Army on 7 September 1948 contains ECFA and CPFA goals:

> We are prepared to bring about the fundamental overthrow of the Kuomintang in about five years, counting from July 1946. This is possible. Our objective can be attained provided we destroy about 100 brigades of Kuomintang [GMD] regular troops every year, or some 500 brigades over the five years. In the past two years our army has annihilated a total of 191 brigades of enemy regulars, an average of 95 1/2 brigades a year or nearly 8 brigades a month. In the next three years it is required that our army should wipe out 300 or more brigades of enemy regulars. Between July this year and June next year we expect to destroy some 115 brigades of enemy regulars. This total is apportioned among our various field armies and armies. The Eastern China Field Army is required to wipe out about 40 brigades (including the 7 already wiped out in July) and capture Tsinan [Jinan] and a number of large, medium and small cities in northern Kiangsu [Jiangsu], eastern Honan [Henan] and northern Anhwei [Anhui]. The Central Plains Field Army is required to wipe out about 14 brigades (including the 2 brigades wiped out in July) and capture a number of cities in the provinces of Hupeh [Hubei], Honan [Henan] and Anhwei.[16]

Another aspect of strategy at this time was the CCP Central Committee's decision that during the third year of the civil war "the whole of the People's Liberation Army will continue to operate north of the Yangzi River and in northern China and the Northeast."[17] This agreement with Su Yu's operational vision also meant that more attention would be given to the central plains. During the months following the Liu-Deng army's move to the Dabie Mountains, there had been steady improvement in the Communist position in the central plains. In April part of the Jin-Ji-Lu-Yu Field Army, with the support of ECFA troops, captured the important city of Loyang in western Henan. In May the three columns that Su Yu had been readying for a thrust south across the Yangzi River were ordered to move into Henan where they played a major role in making the Eastern Henan Campaign a success. During this campaign the ECFA and CPFA (the renamed Jin-Ji-Lu-Yu Army) joined forces to fight a series of battles in which the Communists captured the Henan provincial capital, Kaifeng, on 22 June and held it for four days. While achieving these battlefield victories, the Communists also improved their organizational structure in the central plains by establishing the CPMR and CPFA on 9 May 1948.

As summer 1948 was drawing to a close, however, the Communist leaders still did not feel they had gained absolute superiority in the central plains. There was great optimism about the way the war was progressing. At that time, the Communists were in control of 25 percent of China's territory with a population of 168,000,000 (35 percent of China's total population).[18] They had a substantial capacity for producing war materials and the proven ability to acquire and transport the supplies and food that large maneuver units needed. Yet, as Zhu De stated at a military briefing at PLA headquarters on 23 August 1948, there were still two major areas of concern. One was the need to ensure that the one-half million Nationalist troops in northeast China were bottled up there. "If [Jiang Jieshi's] troops are allowed to come south . . . to reinforce those in either north or central China," Zhu said, "that will add much to our trouble."[19] The other was the presence of large Nationalist armies in the central plains. Zhu did not yet feel the PLA was prepared for a decisive battle with those forces, but he knew that such a battle would greatly affect the outcome of the civil war: "The Central Plains battlefield has been the scene of decisive battles. Since ancient times, those who have triumphed in the Central Plains have become the final victors."[20]

Prelude to the Huai Hai Campaign—the ECFA Captures Jinan

Close on the heels of the Eastern Henan Campaign, which ended on 6 July, the CMC decided that the ECFA should begin thinking about attacking the largest cities in its area of operation—Jinan, the capital of Shandong, and Xuzhou, the major railroad junction where the Jin-Pu line and the Long-Hai line crossed. On 14 July the CMC sent a message to Su Yu suggesting that he prepare to attack Jinan: "If during August or September you take Jinan, then . . . in October the entire army could move south . . . to fight several large battles and seize the possibility of taking Xuzhou in the winter or in the spring."[21]

After Su Yu advised the CMC that his forces would need some time to rest, reorganize, replenish, and redeploy before attacking Jinan, an August attack was ruled out. The ECFA finally did launch its attack on 14 September. On 24 September the city fell.

Su Yu had calculated that taking Jinan would require about 20 days.[22] There were more than 100,000 Nationalist troops in and around the city, and the prepared defensive positions were strong. This would be a major test of his army's ability to fight positional warfare. As events turned out, the fighting lasted only half as long as expected, and casualties were well below the estimates. Su Yu had a reputation for looking ahead to his next battle even as his forces were engaged in fighting. In keeping with this style of generalship, as soon as the outcome of the fight for Jinan became clear, he began staff work on how to take his next objective—Xuzhou.[23]

Su Yu Proposes the Huai Hai Campaign

To start the staff planning process, Su Yu presented his own ideas on how to approach this challenge. He was familiar with the area, having commanded forces in Jiangsu, Henan, and Shandong for many years. He was familiar with the enemy, having fought the Nationalist armies that were located in and around Xuzhou on several previous occasions. Given the strength of the Nationalist forces close to Xuzhou, he viewed a direct attack from the north as being too difficult. He preferred to first isolate Xuzhou using operational-level maneuver and then attack.

Su Yu saw this operational maneuver taking two possible forms. One possibility was to move southwest across the Long-Hai railroad and join forces with the CPFA to conduct large-scale operations on the broad plain bounded on the north by the Long-Hai railroad and on the west by the Ping-Han (Bei<u>ping</u>-Wu<u>han</u>) railroad. Defeating Nationalist forces in this area, he felt, could lead to the strategic encirclement of Xuzhou from the west. The second alternative was for the ECFA alone to conduct a series of operations that would capture territory east and southeast of Xuzhou. This would set the stage for moving west to cut the Xu-Beng (<u>Xu</u>zhou-<u>Beng</u>bu) railroad and isolate Xuzhou from the east.[24]

After examining these two options with his staff, Su Yu decided that an offensive to the east of Xuzhou in the direction of Huaian and Huaiyin was the better choice. Logistics considerations and the desire to keep the ECFA's combat power relatively concentrated were the deciding factors. Moving southwest into central Henan would put the ECFA far from its Shandong base area and make it difficult to obtain food for the troops. This was not the case in northern Jiangsu. Not only was this area close to Shandong, it was also a rich grain-producing area that could help supply the army with food. Moving southwest also had the disadvantage of placing the ECFA between the Nationalist forces in Xuzhou and those along the Ping-Han railroad in central Henan. In such a situation it would be difficult to concentrate ECFA forces for an attack toward Xuzhou, while conversely it would be easier for Nationalist armies to concentrate against the ECFA.[25]

Scattered fighting was still continuing in Jinan when at 0700, 24 September, Su Yu sent a message to the CMC and the CCP's East China and Central Plains Bureaus presenting his views on the situation along with four possible future courses of action. The Nationalists had been organizing a force to move north from the area around Xuzhou to relieve their encircled army at Jinan, but as of that morning, Qiu Qingquan's Second Army was just leaving Shangqiu and Huang Baitao's Seventh Army had not yet completed assembling in Xuzhou. Su felt that once the Nationalist command in Xuzhou learned of Jinan's fall, it would probably halt its forces' northern advance and begin preparing to counter a southern ECFA advance. If, however, the forces continued to advance, he was prepared to block their movement in accordance with plans already made to isolate the Jinan battlefield. "However, if the enemy stops moving north," Su told the CMC, "then here are options for our next operations:"

> 1. In order to improve the war situation in the Central Plains, isolate the Jin-Pu railroad, force the enemy to withdraw to defend (at least strengthen) the areas along the Yangzi River and the Jin-Pu railroad, thereby reducing his maneuver strength, which will make it easier for us to renew our work along the

1. 为更好的改善中原战局，孤立津浦线，并迫使敌人退守（至少要加强）江边及津浦沿线，以减少其机动兵力，与便于我恢复江边工作，为将来渡江创造有利条件，以及便于尔后华野全军进入陇海路以南作战，能得到交通运输供应的方便，和争取华中人力，物力对战争的支持，建议即进行淮海战役，该战役可分为两阶段：

第一阶段以苏北兵团（须加强一个纵队）攻占两淮，并乘胜收复宝应，高邮，而以全军主力位于宿迁至运河车站沿线两岸，以歼灭可能来援之敌。如敌不援或被阻，而改经浦口，长江自扬州北援，则我于两淮作战结束前后，即进行战役第二步，以三个纵队攻占海州，连云港，结束淮海战役，尔后全军转入休整。

2. 只进行海州作战，仅以攻占海州，新浦，连云港等地为目的，并以主力控制于新安镇，运河车站南北及峄枣线，以备战姿态进行休整。此案对部人休整（只有攻城部队须稍事休整，至昨黄昏为止，攻城部队之六个纵队仅伤亡八千余人，昨晚及今晨伤亡尚不在内，依此伤亡并不算大）更便利，但亦增加今后攻占两淮的困难（敌可能增兵）。

3. 全力向南求援敌之一部而歼灭之，但在济南攻克敌人加强警惕，可能退缩，恐不易求战。

4. 全军即进入休整，如此对部人有好处，但易失去适宜作战—"秋凉气候和济南失守后加于敌人之精神压力"。

究应如何请电示，但不论采何方案，建议华东局立即令鲁南及滨海地武将临沂之王洪九部包围，以待济，徐作战结束后，加派一部主力（如仅以地武歼该敌很难奏效）攻歼该敌。

饶政委今明可抵职部，到后当将尔后行动再请示饶政委。

粟

敬晨七时

Su Yu's proposal to the Central Military Commission to undertake the Huai Hai Campaign. The first paragraph of this message appears on the front cover of this book.

Yangzi and establish favorable conditions for crossing the Yangzi in the future and will also make it easier for the entire ECFA to move south of the Long-Hai railroad to conduct operations, make our communication and transportation more convenient, and obtain the human and material resources for sustaining the war that are available in central eastern China, I propose that we promptly execute the Huai Hai Campaign.

This campaign can be divided into two stages: In the first stage the Subei Army (one additional column must be added to strengthen it) will seize Huaian and Huaiyin and then follow up on this victory by recovering Baoying and Gaoyou. Meanwhile the main body of the army will position itself on both sides of the Grand Canal between Suqian and Yunhechezhan in order to destroy any enemy relief forces. If the enemy does not dispatch a relief force [from the west], or this relief force is blocked and he sends a relief force by way of Pukou and the Yangzi River to advance northward from Yangzhou, then at about the time the fight for Huaian and Huaiyin is ending, we will execute the second stage of the campaign. This will be the use of three columns to take Haizhou and Lianyungang. With this the Huai Hai Campaign will be over and the entire army will enter a period of rest and reorganization.

2. We would only execute the Haizhou operation. The objectives would be to take Haizhou, Xinpu, Lianyungang, and other places in that area. Meanwhile, the main body of the army would occupy the area to the north and south of Xinanzhen and Yunhechezhan and along the Yixian-Zaozhuang railroad and then rest and reorganize while being in a posture of readiness to fight. This option, as far as rest and reorganization is concerned (Only the columns used to attack Jinan need some rest and reorganization. As of the evening of 23 September the reported total of dead and wounded for those six columns was only a little over 8,000. The casualties incurred from last night to this morning are not included. These losses aren't great.), would be convenient. However, it would increase the difficulty of attacking Huaian and Huaiyin in the future because the Nationalists would probably reinforce their forces there after an ECFA attack on Haizhou.

3. Advance southward from Jinan with the whole army and try to draw part of the Nationalist relief forces into a battle where they can be destroyed. However after the fall of Jinan these forces will be extra vigilant and will probably withdraw, making it hard to engage them.

4. The entire ECFA will enter a period of rest and reorganization. There are benefits to doing this, but we will be easily passing on a good opportunity for an operation. The onset of cold autumn weather coupled with the loss of Jinan have placed heavy psychological pressure on the enemy.[26]

Su Yu's clear preference was for option one. This option was accompanied by the most analysis and was the only one earning his recommendation to be "promptly executed." His reasoning established clear links between the objectives of that course of action and broader strategic objectives. Successfully completing the Huai Hai Campaign would facilitate mobilizing more resources for the war effort. It would improve transportation. It would set the stage for further operations of even greater significance such as crossing the Yangzi River and bringing the war into the heartland of Nationalist economic and political power. A few months earlier, Su had taken it upon himself to convince the CMC that the time was not right to send large regular forces south across the Yangzi River. Now he was telling them that after victory in the Huai Hai Campaign the time for such a move would be close at hand.

In Su Yu's view, an opportunity to deliver a major blow against the enemy lay before him, and he wanted to take advantage of it. His perspective, in this regard, was very Sunzian. His inference that attacking soon would be beneficial because the loss of Jianan and the arrival of cold weather would weigh heavily on Nationalist morale could have come straight from Sunzi's advocacy of attacking an army when its spirit is waning.[27] But an even more profound similarity to Sunzi's thought is Su Yu's simple desire to take advantage of the *shi* he saw before him. *Shi* is the title of chapter five in Sunzi's *The Art of War* where it has been translated as "energy," "strategic advantage," or "strategic military power," among other terms. In that chapter Sunzi describes *shi* as being like the force of rushing water that lifts stones from a stream bed, like a drawn crossbow, and like round rocks rolling down a steep mountain slope. These images clearly express the sense of potential energy in a situation and the existence of momentum and force. Sunzi states that the truly competent commander seeks victory from *shi* and does not demand it from his soldiers. Su Yu's advocacy of the Huai Hai Campaign expresses that very sentiment of seizing the moment and striking while the iron is hot.

Looked at in terms of US Army doctrine, Su Yu's proposal was an attempt to avoid, as much as possible, the sapping of operational momentum that the introduction to FM 3-0, written by General Eric K. Shinseki, Chief of Staff, US Army, states is a problem in every transition.[28] To paraphrase Shinseki, Su wanted to "master the transition" from the Jinan Campaign to the Huai Hai Campaign by moving forward quickly with this new offensive. Su's desire to maintain the physical and psychological momentum the successful Jinan Campaign had generated and use it to exploit existing opportunities and create new ones was also in keeping with PLA operational doctrine. Two of the PLA's 10 principles of operation at the time clearly stated the value of keeping transitions brief and pressure on the enemy high:

> 6. Give full play to our style of fighting—courage in battle, no fear of sacrifice, no fear of fatigue, and continuous fighting (that is, fighting successive battles in a short time without rest).
> 10. Make good use of the intervals between campaigns to rest, train and consolidate our troops. Periods of rest, training and consolidation should in general not be very long, and the enemy should so far as possible be permitted no breathing space.[29]

Su Yu's proposal for the Huai Hai Campaign won quick approval from his superiors. At 1200, 25 September, Liu Bocheng, Chen Yi, and Li Da sent a message to the CMC and Su Yu saying that the ECFA should exploit its victory at Jinan by acting with dispatch to carry out Su's proposed Huai Hai Campaign: "Su's message of 0700 24 September has been received. We agree that after taking Jinan he should exploit the victory by carrying out the Huai Hai Campaign. His first option, the one calling for attacks on Huaian and Huaiyin and any relief force is the best."[30]

CMC approval for the campaign came in a message sent out at 1900, 25 September, to Su

Yu; Rao Shushi, Political Commissar, East China Military Region (ECMR); Xu Shiyou, Commander, ECFA's Shandong army; Tan Zhenlin; Wang Jian'an, Deputy Commander, Shandong army; as well as Liu Bocheng, Chen Yi, and Li Da. "We think that carrying out the Huai Hai Campaign is absolutely essential," the message began.[31] The CMC also emphasized a rapid transition to the new campaign. Those units that had participated in the attack on Jinan were to be allowed a short rest of two weeks, but the rest of the army would have to wait until after the campaign to rest and reorganize. 10 October, China's National Day, a date little more than two weeks away, was set as the day to start the campaign.[32]

The Huai Hai Campaign Plan Evolves

Along with CMC approval of the general concept of Su Yu's campaign came an important change. Based on intelligence reports, the CMC believed that the Second Army would soon return to its defensive positions along the Long-Hai railroad in the Shangqiu-Dangshan area and considered it likely that the Seventh Army would be moving from Xuzhou back to its former area of operations east of the Grand Canal around Xinanzhen. Deployed in this area, the Seventh Army would be a major obstacle in the way of Su Yu's proposed operations, but it would also become the most exposed of the Nationalist armies around Xuzhou. For these reasons, the CMC message approving the campaign also stated that Su's first objective should be to annihilate the Seventh Army:

> Prepare to carry out several operations as follows:
>
> (1) Your first operation should have the destruction of Huang's army along the line between Xinanzhen and the Grand Canal as its objective.
> (2) The destruction of enemy forces in the Huaian-Huaiyin, Gaoyou, and Baoying areas will be the second operation.
> (3) The destruction of enemy forces in the Haizhou, Lianyunguang, and Guanyun areas will be the third operation.[33]

The CMC message of 25 September concluded with a paragraph describing the importance of the campaign and placing it within a larger strategic context. In the CMC's view, if well fought, these three operations could destroy more than 10 enemy divisions, link Shandong and northern Jiangsu together, and force the enemy to disperse its troop strength to protect the Yangzi River. This would be helpful, the CMC noted, to the ECFA's next operation, a westward thrust against the Xu-Pu (Xuzhou-Pukou) railroad.[34] With this last comment, the CMC endorsed Su Yu's concept of strategically encircling Xuzhou by attacking from the east.

The CMC had hardly approved the concept of the Huai Hai Campaign and set 10 October as the target date for the start of the offensive when it began to reconsider its timetable. On 28 September the CMC sent a message to Su Yu, Rao Shushi, Tan Zhenlin, Chen Yi, Liu Bocheng, and the CCP Central Committee's East China Bureau outlining the anticipated difficulties of the campaign and pushing the start of the campaign back 10 days to 20 October. As the following excerpt from this message indicates, the scale of fighting was expected to be larger than any the ECFA had previously experienced, and this meant that extensive preparations had to be made:

> The transfer of Huang's army back to the Xinanzhen area has been confirmed. The first, and also the most important, operation of your Huai Hai Campaign will be to block the two armies under Qiu [Qingquan] and Li [Mi] and destroy

Huang Baitao's army. The Xinanzhen area is very close to Xuzhou so Qiu and Li's army will come very quickly to provide support. The scale of fighting during this campaign will certainly be greater than that of the Jinan Campaign and will possibly certainly exceed that of the Sui-Qi [Eastern Henan] Campaign. Because of this you must have enough time to allow the armies that attacked Jinan to rest, reorganize, and replenish. Moreover, all operational requirements for the entire army, including all logistical work, must be completely prepared before you start to move.

The time required for the campaign, including attacking Huang's army, Haizhou, and Huaian and Huaiyin will be from one to one and a half months. After the fighting is over there will be a month for rest and reorganization. As a result, you must prepare two to two and a half months of rations and fodder. The Jinan Campaign only took 10 days, and it seems that rest and reorganization after it will require about 20 days. The Huai Hai Campaign is expected to take one and half months and adding rest and reorganization time makes approximately two and a half months. Originally, we were prepared for this period to be a most difficult time for us when we would be attacking Jinan and fighting a relief force. If you are now able during this period to achieve victories in two great campaigns, the Jinan Campaign (This you've already won.) and the Huai Hai Campaign, this will really be quite an achievement.

The meeting for all cadre at the level of division commander and above that is to be held at Qufu should be delayed for several days so that each column and division in the armies used to attack Jinan is able to carry out some adjustments prior to the meeting. The 9th and 13th Columns, which suffered the most casualties, should be given replacements as quickly as conditions allow. If it's possible to transfer some local units into these two columns, the 73d and 109th regiments are in special need. When carrying out the Huai Hai Campaign these two columns would be best suited for a reserve role during the first phase. Among the 60,000 prisoners, more than half can be used as replacements in those columns where the need for men is most acute. In consideration of the necessity for those armies that participated in the attack on Jinan to rest and have losses replaced, it seems that the time for launching the Huai Hai Campaign has to be pushed back to 20 October.[35]

After being told that destroying Huang Baitao's Seventh Army should be the Huai Hai Campaign's first objective, Su Yu's initial concept of operations was to use five columns to surround and destroy the Seventh Army while one column attacked Tancheng, one column to provide right flank security by keeping watch on Nationalist units in the Lincheng-Taierzhuang area, and seven columns to isolate the battlefield by blocking Qiu Qingquan and Li Mi's anticipated relief efforts.[36] On 11 October the CMC suggested a number of refinements to this deployment. Basically, the CMC's view was that isolating the battlefield would be accomplished more effectively by creating at least the illusion of multiple major threats rather than by simply placing a large blocking force in front of the Nationalist relief forces. The CMC proposed that the ECFA put more men into the areas north and south of the corridor east of Xuzhou through which any Nationalist force attempting to relieve the Seventh Army would have to move. From those areas the ECFA troops would not only threaten the flanks of Nationalist relief columns, but by seeming to pose a threat to Xuzhou itself, they would also make it more difficult for the Nationalists to send a relief force out of the city.

The CMC also proposed that the ECFA send a column into southwestern Shandong to tie down elements of Qiu Qingquan's Second Army by attacking the Xuzhou-Shangqiu section of the Long-Hai railroad.[37] As the campaign's complexity and scale increased, so, too, did the time required to prepare. On 12 October Su Yu sent a message to the CMC in which he mentioned some problems that were arising and moved the starting date for the campaign from 20 October to 25 October.[38] On 14 October the CMC replied that only after all such major issues as winter clothing and troops replacements were resolved could the campaign begin. They set the launch date as somewhere between 5-10 November.[39]

The CPFA's Increasing Role in the Campaign

With every delay in the campaign's launch date, the CPFA's place in the campaign became more important. Before 11 October the CPFA's contribution to the Huai Hai Campaign had been to carry out attacks in west and southwest Henan to draw Nationalist forces in that area farther west of the Ping-Han railroad. The purpose was to make it more difficult for the Nationalists to shift those forces that were under the command of Bai Chongxi's Central China Bandit Suppression Headquarters at Wuhan and not the Xuzhou Bandit Suppression Headquarters to the Xuzhou area after the Huai Hai Campaign began. This was a subtle shaping operation, a small ripple appearing at the far western edge of the central plains even before the rock of the ECFA's offensive struck in the east. Conceived out of consideration of space-time relationships, these attacks did not seek to destroy the Nationalist units that might be used to reinforce Xuzhou. The objective was to neutralize them by distance.

Beginning on 11 October, the CPFA's role in the Huai Hai Campaign started to grow as it was ordered to conduct a shaping operation aimed directly at fixing forces that were under Xuzhou Bandit Suppression Headquarters command and limiting their freedom of action. The impetus for this development was the Nationalist decision on 6 October to have Sun Yuanliang shift his Sixteenth Army east from Zhengzhou and assemble at Liuhe, a town some 40 kilometers (km) west of the Second Army headquarters at Shangqiu. This move was part of Nationalist preparations for the Sixteenth and Second armies' offensive into southwest Shandong that was to begin on 15 October. The CMC was concerned that the Sixteenth Army's eastward shift would create a potential threat to the Huai Hai Campaign's success and acted accordingly. In its 11 October message to Su Yu and others that was referred to earlier, the CMC stated: "As three enemy corps under Sun Yuanliang are about to move east, it is hoped that Liu Bocheng, Chen Yi, and Deng Xiaoping will dispose their troops at once to attack the Zheng-Xu [Zhengzhou-Xuzhou] railroad so as to tie down Sun Yuanliang's army."[40] In another message sent the same day directly to Liu, Chen, Deng, and Li Da, the CMC made it clear that this "hope" was really an expectation: "You should quickly deploy forces and tie down Sun's army by attacking the Zheng-Xu railroad and wiping out some enemy units. Otherwise, his army will be added to forces in the Xuzhou area, and will greatly obstruct the ECFA's new operation."[41]

The response of Liu Bocheng, Chen Yi, and Deng Xiaoping to the 11 October directive from the CMC was immediate and forceful. After realizing that only two understrength divisions remained in Zhengzhou to defend the city and the section of the Ping-Han railroad between

Zhengzhou and the Yellow River, they devised an ambitious plan. They would use local irregular forces to sabotage the Long-Hai railroad to the east and west of Kaifeng while the CPFA main body—the 1st, 3d, 4th, and 9th columns—attacked Zhengzhou. Liu Bocheng was to continue leading the CPFA's 2d and 6th columns in their shaping operation in west Henan.[42] This proposal was transmitted to the CMC on 12 October. Approval came back the following day.

On the night of 21 October the four ECFA columns moved into positions on all sides of Zengzhou, and early in the morning of 22 October they began their attack. Within hours the Nationalist forces abandoned the city and fled to the north where they were surrounded and captured. Taking Zhengzhou was an important military and psychological victory for the Communists, but it did not diminish the threat the Second and Sixteenth armies posed to the ECFA's Huai Hai Campaign. These armies were ready to begin advancing into Shandong on 15 October only to have Jiang Jieshi cancel their offensive abruptly because of the rapidly collapsing Nationalist position in Manchuria. Furthermore, Jiang had ordered Du Yuming, Deputy Commander, Xuzhou Bandit Suppression Headquarters, and the major proponent of this offensive, to accompany him to Shenyang and take command of the remaining Nationalist armies in northeast China. After this operation was canceled, these two armies remained in place in the Liuhe-Shangqiu area while the Xuzhou command considered what to do next. At the same time the CMC was busily considering ways to keep them from moving into the area around Xuzhou. At 0100, 22 October, before the battle for Zhengzhou had begun, the CMC sent a message to Chen Yi and Deng Xiaoping, with information copies to Rao Shushi, Su Yu, Tan Zhenlin, and the CCP Central Plains Bureau, stating for the first time the possibility that the CPFA might have to advance all the way to the Xu-Beng railroad:

> In order to guarantee the total victory of the ECFA in the Huai Hai Campaign, please prepare to move your entire army quickly to the east after you have captured Zhengzhou and rested for a few days. Look for an opportunity to take Kaifeng, or bypass Kaifeng and move directly toward the Xu-Beng railroad. This will not only tie down Sun Yuanliang and Liu Ruming [Fourth Pacification Area commander], but will also tie down part of Qiu Qingquan's army and Li Mi's army.[43]

Chen Yi and Deng Xiaoping also saw the importance of moving east as rapidly as possible. At 2200, 22 October, they informed the CMC that Zhengzhou had fallen and that the retreating Nationalist forces were under attack 17 km north of the city. Their intention was to give the four columns that had been involved in the fighting two days to rest and reorganize and then set out on 25 October to attack Kaifeng. "If the enemy forces in Kaifeng withdraw to the east," they told the CMC, "then, in accordance with your message of 0100 22 October, we will either move eastward toward Shangqiu or go directly toward the Xu-Beng railroad in order to clamp down on Sun Yuanliang and Liu Ruming and coordinate with the ECFA operation."[44]

On 24 October, the Nationalist force defending Kaifeng evacuated the city without a fight, and a Communist regional force occupied it. Within two days, objectives that had formerly been seen as requiring a significant CPFA effort to take had fallen into Communist hands. These tactical successes made it possible for the CPFA to increase its contribution to the ECFA's campaign. Deciding how the CPFA should contribute, however, was not an easy matter for the CMC. This was because those shaping operations that would potentially do the most to reduce the number of Nationalist forces that could be deployed to fight the ECFA were ones that the CPFA would have the greatest difficulty executing.

As the agency responsible for employing the military instrument of power effectively in pursuit of the overarching CCP goal of achieving political power, the CMC provided overall strategic direction to the ECFA and CPFA and coordinated their actions and movements. Ultimately, the CMC was responsible for ensuring that the campaigns and major operations these two field armies conducted contributed to achieving strategic objectives. But in meeting this responsibility, the CMC relied heavily upon its field commanders' judgment. The example of Su Yu changing the CMC's decision to dispatch three ECFA columns to an area south of Yangzi River was discussed earlier. As options for CPFA future operations were being discussed following the capture of Zhengzhou and Kaifeng, the opinions of Chen Yi and Deng Xiaoping would have an equally determinative influence.

The CMC message of 0100, 22 October, and the Chen-Deng message of 2200, 22 October, indicate that at this time two options for CPFA movement were being considered. One option was for the CPFA to go east along the Long-Hai railroad and force the Nationalist forces that were withdrawing along this line to stop and engage the pursuing Communist force. The other option was to move to the southeast and attack the Xu-Beng railroad, the logistics lifeline for the several hundred thousand Nationalist troops under the command of Liu Zhi's Xuzhou Bandit Suppression Headquarters. The following excerpt from a CMC message that was sent to Rao Shushi, Su Yu, Tan Zhenlin, Chen Yi, Deng Xiaoping, and the CCP Central Plains Bureau at 1300, 22 October, shows that the CMC felt the CPFA would be executing some version of option one but that option two would have the biggest effect:

> A very favorable situation now is that Bai Chongxi's [Third Army], Zhang Gan commanding, and [Twelfth Army], Huang Wei commanding, have been drawn into the Tongbai Mountains by the CPFA 2d and 6th columns and local forces. For quite some time they will be unable to turn around and advance to the Yellow River flood plain to threaten the operations of our troops in the northeastern part. This will enable Chen Yi and Deng Xiaoping, after their victory in Zhengzhou, to move eastward with all or part of their force and in coordination with your 3rd and Liangguang columns tie down all of Sun Yuanliang's and Liu Ruming's forces and also possibly some of Qiu Qingquan's army and Li Mi's army.
>
> Actual movements can be decided after Zhengzhou is taken. Our present calculation is to have part of their force stay along a line from Zhenghou to Huaiyang and have their main force carry out a Xu-Beng operation when Qiu and Li are deeply engaged in trying to relieve Huang Baitao's army. At that time they would look for an opportunity to seize Suxian and Bengbu and utterly and completely destroy the Jin-Pu railroad. This would cut the enemy's line of communication and isolate Liu Zhi's entire force.
>
> If the Zhengzhou operation can be successfully completed in a few days, then, after a few days of rest, Chen and Deng will be able to begin moving east. This will be at the end of this month or early next month. It will take about ten days to reach the vicinity of Suxian and Bengbu where they can rest for a day or so and then begin the Xu-Beng operation. This will be just at the time

when the ECFA's battle will be the fiercest. The circumstances created by this CPFA attack will absolutely draw a large portion of Qiu and Li's forces away as reinforcements for this fight [for the railroad]. This will have a great impact on guaranteeing that the Huai Hai Campaign will achieve a great victory.

However, we don't know if there is enough time to do this. We ask Chen and Deng to carefully consider all aspects of the situation after the battle for Zhengzhou is won and send their views to us.[45]

Chen and Deng's reply to the CMC, which also went to Rao Shushi; Su Yu; Tan Zhenlin; Liu Bocheng; Li Da; and Deng Zihiu, political commissar, CPMR, and deputy political commissar, CPFA, was sent at 1200, 24 October. The message touched on several factors that might affect future operations and presented three options for the CMC to consider. The main points of the message, by paragraph, follow:

(1) The 119th Division at Kaifeng is preparing to flee. There is a great possibility that we can occupy Kaifeng without a fight. Yesterday, 23 October, Bai Chongxi ordered Huang Wei's three corps to move north. . . . We estimate that . . . he will attempt to make us turn back or will move east as reinforcements. . . . We don't know if Zhang Gan's army will follow Huang Wei or not.

(2) We have decided to start moving east tomorrow. In case of rain we will probably delay one day. . . . As of now we plan for our main body to be in Kaifeng on 25 October and rest for one day. After five days of march we expect to reach an area south and southwest of Shangqiu on 2 November. After the fighting begins on the eastern front we can again look at the situation and decide what actions to take.

(3) There are three options for maneuver after we reach the area mentioned above:

    (a) After fighting begins on the eastern front, we can take advantage of Qiu Qingquan's movement to the east and Huang Wei's army still being far away to use the [CPFA] 1st, 3rd, 4th, and 9th columns and the ECFA 3rd and Liangguang columns to grab hold of Sun Yuanliang's army and attack it. The good point of this move is that we can be quite sure of destroying one or two of Sun's corps. We might also hold part of Qiu's army back.

    (b) If conditions aren't right for attacking Sun's army, then we can march for six days and on the 9th or 10th reach the Xu-Beng railroad and carry out the mission that the CMC formerly gave us.

    (c) If, by the time we have reached the area around Shangqiu, Huang Wei's three corps are advancing eastward alone (that is, Zhang Gan is not following behind), then there is a good opportunity to destroy one or two of those corps. The shortcomings of this course of action are that it would make it difficult to coordinate with the eastern front and the only forces left to draw Sun Yuanliang back would be the [ECFA] 3rd and Liangguang columns.

(4) No matter which course of action is selected, once we're positioned southwest of Shangqiu any of them could be done. If Qiu and Sun move their armies eastward earlier, we intend to follow them and carry out option (b).

(5) If we advance to the Xu-Beng railroad, we will surely grab hold of Sun

Yuanliang and part of Qiu and Li's armies. However, if the fighting on the eastern front is not over in ten days, by then Huang Wei's army would probably have rushed over and we would be in a difficult position. We would be in a constricted area crossed by many rivers. Maneuver would not be easy.

(6) If Huang Wei's army goes north, we propose that Liu Bocheng and Li Da order the 6th Column to follow them.

(7) We request that the CMC consider these points and provide directions.[46]

The CMC response to this message, which was sent at 0300, 25 October, was a shock to Chen Yi and Deng Xiaoping. They had just proposed a course of action that had them fighting not too far east from their current position between Zhengzhou and Kaifeng. The CMC replied with a plan to have them move approximately 450 km to the southeast, cross the Huai River, and prepare to attack the segment of the Jin-Pu railroad that lay between Bengbu and the Yangzi River town of Pukou. Clearly, the precedent for such an operation was there. Just a little over a year earlier the Liu-Deng army had made a similar deep thrust from southwest Shandong across Anhui to the Dabie Mountains. Now the CMC wanted this army to once again drop its line communication to the rear area and move deep into enemy territory. This was, in the CMC's estimation, the way to have the four columns exert the maximum pressure possible on the Nationalists to compel them to redeploy forces away from their effort to save Huang Baitao's Seventh Army. In *The Art of War*, Sunzi wrote of moving the enemy by attacking that which is important to him. This concept was at the heart of the CMC's newly conceived shaping operation. The CMC understood that executing this operation carried with it risks and difficulties but felt they were outweighed by the potential benefits to be gained:

> [Chen and Deng's] message of 1200, 24 October has been received. The enemy has already fled Kaifeng. Do not go to Kaifeng or to the area near Shangqiu. From your present position take the shortest route to Mengcheng and assemble there. After resting for a few days move directly to capture Bengbu. Also, prepare to cross the Huai River and move south to seize the Beng-Pu [Bengbu-Pukou] railroad.
>
> Use all four of your army's columns . . . to gain control over the broad area south of the Huai River, north of the Yangzi River, east of the Huai-Southern railroad, and west of the Grand Canal, and thereby draw the enemy to attack you. When this happens you can use the tactic of rapid concentration and rapid dispersal to maneuver against the enemy. Be prepared to maintain operations in this area for 2-3 months.
>
> This move will be beyond the expectations of the enemy. In order to defend against us crossing the Yangzi, the enemy will have to send forces south from around Xuzhou. It is also possible that units from Bai Chongxi's command will be shifted eastward.
>
> Within two months the ECFA may be able to destroy approximately one-third of the 55 divisions under Liu Zhi's command, that is, about 18 divisions, and achieve a great victory. If the enemy deploys a large number of troops against you, then you can temporarily adopt the dispersed fighting method and spread all twelve of your divisions out across the area between the Yangzi River, the

Huai River, Lake Chao, and the Grand Canal in order . . . to avoid his pressure while awaiting the southward movement of the ECFA.

Please consider whether this plan is feasible or not. We can wait until after you arrive in Mengcheng before making a final decision. If at that time you feel that this plan cannot be carried out, then you can attack the Xu-Beng railroad. Or, if Sun Yuanliang's army is vulnerable you can move north and attack him. If Huang Wei moves eastward behind you, you can turn back and attack him. The Mengcheng area is good for maneuvering. You can move east, west, south, or north. Before you reach Mengcheng the enemy won't know which way you are going.

We look forward to hearing whether or not you agree with the idea of going to Mengcheng and how long it will take to go from Zhengzhou to Mengcheng.[47]

Chen Yi and Deng Xiaoping did not believe that their force was capable of fulfilling this ambitious plan. Working quickly, they drafted a message that laid out their concerns and presented an alternative. At 1500 the same day they sent the following reply to the CMC:

We have received your message of 0300.

1. We propose changing our first assembly point to the area between Yongcheng, Bozhou, and Guoyang. From there it will be easier to either move against the Su-Beng railroad or attack Sun Yuanliang. Going from Zhengzhou to that area will take about ten days (including one day for rest). Tomorrow, the 26th, we will start out and on 4 November we can be there.
2. We think that seeking the destruction of Sun Yuanliang should be the first move. If Sun can't be attacked easily, then we can attack the Suxian-Bengbu Railroad. Bai Chongxi has already ordered Huang Wei to move east as reinforcements, but that force will arrive too late. If the opportunity presents itself, destroying most of Sun Yuanliang's army is the best course of action.
3. As for pressing forward to the area south of the Huai, this should be done only in the case of extreme necessity. That area is constricted with lakes and mountains and it lacks grain and water. A large force would have difficulty maneuvering there and conditions for sustaining a force are unfavorable. As of now we still haven't replaced all of the shoes, socks, cotton-padded trousers, caps, and belts that we need. We have made no financial preparations whatsoever and will be unable to take supplies with us.
4. If there is the utmost need to move south of the Huai, then the best approach would be to use one column to destroy the railroad running between Bengbu and Nanjing while the main force captures Hefei and other cities and then, with the Dabie Mountains behind it, links the area south of the Huai River together and guarantees that there is a supply line from the rear. To sum up, adopting this course of action will make it very difficult for us to fight and will probably increase our casualties.[48]

In the face of this strong opposition from Chen Yi and Deng Xiaoping, the CMC quickly rescinded its directive that the CPFA move to Mengcheng. A short message sent to Chen and Deng on 26 October expressed agreement with their proposal that the four columns under their direct command move to an area bounded by Yongcheng, Bozhou, and Guoyang and assemble there on 4 November.[49]

While the CPFA's main force was marching toward Yongcheng, the two CPFA columns in southern Henan and northern Hubei were trying to delay the shift of Huang Wei's Twelfth Army to the Xuzhou area. After learning that Huang Wei had received orders to assemble and move his army to the east, Liu Bocheng began trying to slow the movement of Nationalist units toward their assembly areas around Queshan. These operations only had limited success. Since early October, Liu had been trying to draw Huang Wei's forces west and south away from the forthcoming battle area in East China. To do this, his columns had been to the west and south of the Twelfth Army. Now, as Nationalist forces moved east and north toward Queshan, it was difficult to interfere with their movement.

This was especially true of the X, XIV, and XVIII Corps, which were located almost directly west of Queshan around the cities of Biyang and Tanghe. Only the LXXXV Corps, which was operating in the Anlu-Yingshan-Suixian area in northern Hubei had a great distance to travel. Since the LXXXV Corps would have to use the Ping-Han railroad to move to Queshan and because this railroad was the major route for transporting supplies north from Wuhan for the other corps, Liu made destroying this line south of Xinyang a top priority.[50] As part of this effort, the 2d Column pushed its attack as far south as Xiaogan, a town only 70 km north of Wuhan, and succeeded in tearing up 2 km of track on 31 October and 1 November. However, assembling and resupplying the Twelfth Army could not be stopped. On 8 November, the X, XIV, and XVIII Corps left Queshan and began their movement toward Xuzhou. Five days later the LXXXV Corps, which had taken more time to reach Queshan, completed its preparations and set out to catch up with the rest of the army.

Even while fighting to delay the Twelfth Army's assembly, Liu Bocheng was thinking of ways to slow the army's eastward movement after it left Queshan. It was apparent, and confirmed by intelligence reports, that Huang Wei's force would pass through Xincai and Fuyang on its way to the Huai River plain. On 2 November Liu informed Chen Yi, Deng Xiaoping, and the CMC that he was ordering the 2d and 6th Columns to move into positions north and south of this route. From there they would conduct flank attacks against Huang's columns and continue attacking Huang's rear as he moved east. The 2d Column received its orders that day. It was directed to move from its location in the vicinity of Xiaogan through the Dabie Mountains to Xixian, a small city on the north bank of the Huai River some 100 km east of Queshan, and prepare to conduct a flank attack against Huang Wei.[51] This sometimes mountainous 150-km route was to be covered by 6 November.[52] The 6th Column received its orders on 3 November. The column was told to break contact with Nationalist forces around Nanyang and go to Shangcai by way of Fangcheng, a distance of nearly 200 km. The deadline for reaching Shangcai was set at 8 November.[53] Once there the column was to begin preparing to carry out its attacks.

Conditions did not permit the execution of this plan. Advance elements of the 2d Column reached Xixian on 6 November and quickly captured the city from the local Nationalist defense force. However, as the rest of the column assembled, it became apparent that sickness among the soldiers had seriously reduced the column's combat effectiveness. The troops were not fitted with padded cotton jackets, and the colder weather north of the Dabie Mountains, coupled with the physical stress of their arduous march, had caused many to fall ill. Faced with this problem, Liu Bocheng abandoned his plan for attacking the Twelfth Army. On 6 November he issued orders for the 2d Column to continue marching north to the Huaidian-Lutaiji area where it would receive winter clothing and then go east as rapidly as possible to reach the Guoyang-Mengcheng area ahead of Huang Wei.[54] The 6th Column received similar orders. With Huang Wei's preparations for leaving Queshan nearing completion, it had been decided not to use the regular columns to slow Huang's movement through eastern Henan. Instead, they went east to help establish blocking positions somewhere in the Guoyang-Mencheng area while local guerrilla units were to delay Huang Wei's advance. They did this over the following 10 days by sabotaging roads and bridges and placing harassing fire on the Nationalists wherever they could.

While Liu Bocheng's operations to impede the Twelfth Army's assembly and its movement to the east were taking place, Chen Yi and Deng Xiaoping were leading the CPFA's 1st, 3d, and 4th Columns from Zhengzhou toward Xuzhou with the 9th Column following about two days behind. They also were establishing communications with the two ECFA columns (the 3d and Liangguang) that were moving southwest from Jinan into southwest Shandong. When Su Yu and the CMC had decided on 14 October to send two columns into the area northwest of Xuzhou, the purpose had been to help create the impression that the objective of the coming offensive was to capture Xuzhou, not to destroy Huang Baitao's army.[55] The CPFA's quick victory at Zhengzhou and the prospect that this army's main body would be moving east added new possibilities to this concept. To increase coordination between all forces west of Xuzhou, on 23 October, operational control of the two ECFA columns was transferred from the ECFA to Chen and Deng.[56]

During the march to the assembly area between Boxian and Yongcheng, various options for using the six columns were considered. On 31 October Chen Yi and Deng Xiaoping proposed using three of their columns and the two ECFA columns that were moving into positions about 48 km north of the Shangqiu-Tangshan segment of the Long-Hai railroad to launch a pincer attack on Sun Yuanliang's army.[57] On 2 November they proposed the possibility of cutting between Qiu Qingquan and Xuzhou.[58] On 3 November Liu Bocheng pointed out the importance of the Jin-Pu railroad to the Nationalists and proposed that the Chen-Deng force cut this line between Xuzhou and Suxian to force Second Army units to redeploy away from Xuzhou.[59] On 5 November the CMC proposed two courses of action that expanded on Liu's concept. In both cases the three CPFA columns would not tarry at Yongcheng but would keep marching to the southeast. In one case the objective was to encircle and possibly capture Suxian. The other objective was to destroy parts of the railroad between Xuzhou and Bengbu and capture Mengcheng.[60]

None of the proposed operations was carried out. By the time Chen and Deng were approaching Yongcheng on 5 November, Sun Yuanliang's army had been shifted from the area west of Xuzhou to the Suxian-Mengcheng area. Also, an attack on the railroads close to Xuzhou appeared to be counterproductive because it would draw Qiu Qingquan's army closer to the city. Advancing to Suxian or Mengcheng without rest would be asking much of soldiers who had just completed an 11-day road march. Such a maneuver would place the army farther from Xuzhou and disperse its strength. Instead of following any of the earlier proposals, on 5 November, Chen Yi and Deng Xiaoping proposed an operation that would attack Liu Ruming's Fourth Pacification Area force, which had been left exposed along the Long-Hai railroad when Sun Yuanliang's army changed location and the Second Army had shifted closer to Xuzhou. In

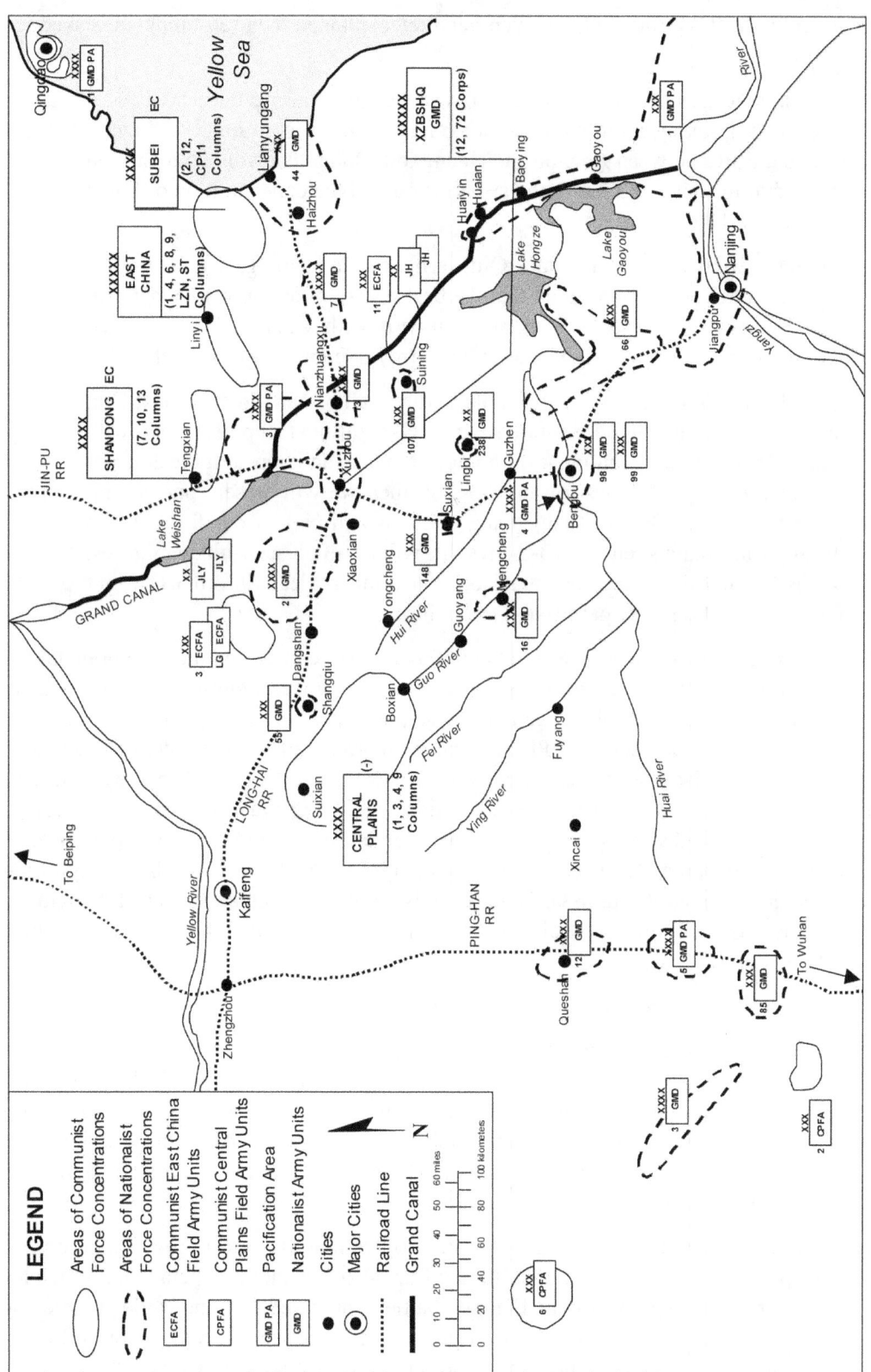

Map 1. Location of forces, 5 November 1948.

a message sent to the CMC at 1300, 5 November, they explained their reasoning and asked for permission to proceed:

> We estimate that the enemy situation won't change during the next two or three days. Looking at this situation, it's not good for us to go south of Xuzhou or into the area between Xuzhou and Huangkou. Doing that would only hasten the withdrawal of Qiu's Army toward Xuzhou and the concentration of Sun's army toward the north.
>
> Our only two options are to attack Qiu's army or Liu Ruming. After considering the matter, we have decided that the best course of action is to attack Liu Ruming first. Liu's force is weak and can be quickly destroyed or pressured into revolting. Also, we might cause Qiu's army to come to Liu's relief.
>
> Once Liu is eliminated we will be able to direct all of our forces against Qiu. We will also be in a good position to undertake our next step of dealing with Huang Wei and Sun Yuanliang. If Qiu does not take an interest in the destruction of Liu and withdraws toward the east, then we will closely pursue him using the ECFA's 3d and Liangguang columns and part of our force. If we destroy Liu's main strength in 3-5 days this will be all pluses with no minuses. We have decided to launch our attack on 7 November. Please inform us tonight whether or not we have permission to do this.[61]

CMC approval of this plan was sent out at 0600 on 6 November, and that afternoon CPFA elements began moving north toward their objectives.[62] The general mission was the same as that given the CPFA on 11 October—conduct a shaping operation in support of the coming ECFA offensive. On 11 October the CPFA had been far from Xuzhou in western Henan, now it was within striking distance of Xuzhou and the Xu-Beng railroad. It had become an integral part of the Huai Hai Campaign. In recognition of this developing situation, just a week earlier, on 31 October, Su Yu had already asked the CMC to give Chen Yi and Deng Xiaoping overall command of the campaign: "The scale of this campaign is very large. I ask that Army Commander Chen and Political Commissar Deng exercise unity of command."[63] On 1 November the CMC made this appointment official, and the Huai Hai Campaign clearly became a joint ECFA-CPFA endeavor.[64]

The ECFA Prepares for the Huai Hai Campaign

When Su Yu proposed the Huai Hai Campaign, he did not foresee a battle to destroy the Seventh Army as being part of the campaign. The lack of a major force blocking his path made it reasonable to push ahead quickly after taking Jinan. Even when, in its approval of the campaign given the next day, the CMC made annihilating the Seventh Army the first objective of the campaign, speed in launching the campaign was emphasized. After a short transition period, the campaign was set to begin on 10 October.

As discussed earlier, keeping the time between operations short to keep pressure on the enemy was a principle of PLA operations. But the PLA also had another operational principle, principle 5, that dealt with preparation: "Fight no battle unprepared, fight no battle you are not sure of winning; make every effort to be well prepared for each battle, make every effort to ensure victory in the given set of conditions as between the enemy and ourselves."[65]

Due to the complexity, scale and importance of the coming campaign, both Su Yu and the CMC soon began to tilt in favor of preparedness over speed in launching the campaign. The CMC message of 28 September pointed out numerous things that needed to be done before the campaign could begin. Then on 12 October Su reported problems in getting troop replacements for the 9th and 13th Columns and suggested the campaign begin on 25 October.[66] The CMC responded by saying that the start of the campaign should be delayed until 5-10 November. It reminded Su that he should wait until all units that had seen combat in Jinan had replaced their losses. The CMC also mentioned the need to wait until winter clothing had been completely distributed, food and ammunition were ready, and political work had been done.[67]

While all these preparations for sustaining the campaign were under way, plans for achieving the campaign's objectives were being developed and modified. As time went by, possible CPFA shaping operations became a larger part of the planning process, but the decisive operation remained the ECFA's maneuver to encircle and annihilate the Seventh Army. On 27 October the CMC advised Su Yu not to expect too much from CPFA shaping operations. The ECFA had to be prepared to achieve the campaign's objective by itself:

> The eleven divisions led by Chen and Deng will arrive in the Guoyang-Yongcheng-Bozhou area on 4 November. By striving to fight Sun Yuanliang and threatening both Xuzhou and Bengbu they will naturally play a major supporting role in your operation. They may possibly draw one of Qiu Qingquan's corps and possibly all of Sun Yuanliang's army toward them. However, your plans should be based on the ability of the ECFA itself to directly and effectively tie down Qiu Qingquan. This is the only reliable approach because the enemy is fighting on internal lines and can nimbly shift forces. Also, Chen and Deng cannot become a mortal threat to Liu Zhi.[68]

On 22 October when the CMC approved a revised deployment scheme that Su Yu had submitted on 21 October, the concept of operations for ECFA units was basically set. The next day, 23 October, ECFA headquarters issued a warning order for the campaign that fixed the time for starting the campaign as the evening of 5 November. This order laid out in detail the mission of each column, command and control relationships, the routes that columns would take from their current locations to forward assembly areas, and a time schedule for moving the columns. To avoid creating traffic congestion on the limited road network, column movement was staggered with the first starting out on the evening of 25 October and the last one beginning its move on the evening of 30 October. Strict security measures regarding this movement were imposed:

> 1. Before beginning to move, each headquarters must dispatch a liaison group to their designated assembly area and work with the local militia government to establish ways to block the flow of information.
> 2. In mountainous areas units can move forward by day if they are dispersed. In all other areas they must march forward by night and pay great attention to countering detection from the air.
> 3. In order to prevent a premature revelation of what we're doing, all columns on the march should make every effort to communicate by long distance land line telephone or motor vehicles. After reaching assembly areas, the use of radios for communication will start again.[69]

The warning order also assigned reconnaissance responsibilities and presented communications information. Those columns that were going to have additional artillery from the Special Type (ST) Column (artillery-armor-engineer column) attached to them were directed to send representatives to the ST Column assembly area to link up with the artillery unit assigned to them and bring it back. This was to be done by 31 October. Those columns having an engineer company from the ST Column attached for the purpose of enhancing their river-crossing ability were told to do the same thing by 1 November. Separate messages dealt with such other matters as sustainment operations, medical treatment and casualty evacuation, and laying telephone lines. The overall objective was clearly stated as annihilating Huang Baitao's army, including every unit of the XXV, LXIV, LXIII, and C Corps.[70]

On 31 October the date for starting the campaign was set back to 8 November, but that was the last delay. On 4 November ECFA headquarters issued the order to execute the Huai Hai Campaign. Units were directed to begin moving from their forward assembly areas to their attack positions on the evening of 6 November and to be ready to launch the general attack on the evening of 8 November.

PLA Doctrine, Sunzi's *The Art of War*, and Su Yu's Campaign Design

When Su Yu proposed the Huai Hai Campaign as a quick sequel to the Jinan Campaign, he was expressing the sentiment of PLA operational principles 6 and 10. His desire to take advantage of the situation to maintain and build momentum was also in keeping with Sunzi's advocacy of using *shi* (the potential energy present) to maximum effect. It should, therefore, not be surprising that the operational design presented as part of his proposal also manifested concepts contained in the PLA's 10 operational principles and Sunzi's *The Art of War*.

The PLA's 10 operational principles, which were codified in 1947, were an expression of Communist strategy and a guide to military planning. They were, as Mao Zedong described them, "the main methods the People's Liberation Army has employed in defeating Chiang Kai-shek . . . , the result of the tempering of the People's Liberation Army in long years of fighting against domestic and foreign enemies and completely suited to our present situation."[71] Operational principles 6 and 10 (advocacy of short transitions) and 5 (advocacy of preparedness) were discussed earlier in the context of Su Yu envisioning the Huai Hai Campaign and preparing for it. The other seven principles are:

> 1. Attack dispersed, isolated enemy forces first; attack concentrated, strong enemy forces later.
> 2. Take small and medium cities and extensive rural areas first; take big cities later.
> 3. Make wiping out the enemy's effective strength our main objective; do not make holding or seizing a city or place our main objective. Holding or seizing a city or place is the outcome of wiping out the enemy's effective strength, and often a city or place can be held or seized for good only after it has changed hands a number of times.
> 4. In every battle, concentrate an absolutely superior force (two, three, four and sometimes even five or six times the enemy's strength), encircle the enemy forces completely, strive to wipe them out thoroughly and do not let any escape from the net. In special circumstances, use the method of dealing crush-

ing blows to the enemy, that is, concentrate all our strength to make a frontal attack and also to attack one or both of his flanks, with the aim of wiping out one part and routing another so that our army can swiftly move its troops to smash other enemy forces. Strive to avoid battles of attrition in which we lose more than we gain or only break even. In this way, although we are inferior as a whole (in terms of numbers), we are absolutely superior in every part and every specific campaign, and this ensures victory in the campaign. As time goes on, we shall become superior as a whole and eventually wipe out all the enemy.

7. Strive to wipe out the enemy through mobile warfare. At the same time, pay attention to the tactics of positional attack and capture enemy fortified points and cities.

8. With regard to attacking cities, resolutely seize all enemy fortified points and cities which are weakly defended. Seize at opportune moments all enemy fortified points and cities defended with moderate strength, provided circumstances permit. As for strongly defended enemy fortified points and cities, wait till conditions are ripe and then take them.

9. Replenish our strength with all the arms and most of the personnel captured from the enemy. Our army's main sources of manpower and materiel are at the front.[72]

Most of these principles found expression, to some extent, in Su Yu's original proposal for the Huai Hai Campaign. After he laid out the military, political, and economic conditions with strategic significance that winning the campaign would create, he presented a sequence of actions that, if followed, would produce that victory. Those actions were basically the ones contained in operational principles 1, 2, 4, 7, and 8.

Su Yu did not propose conducting the decisive battle for the central plains in his message of 24 September. He did not envision a major battle against a large Nationalist army. His proposed sequence of actions, therefore, involved attacks at the lower end of the scale of violence expressed in principles 1, 2, 4, 7, and 8. Dispersed, relatively isolated enemy forces were to be attacked. Small cities and extensive rural areas were to be occupied. An absolute superiority in forces was to be attained, but given the low density of Nationalist forces then in the area, that would be easily attainable. Mobile warfare, not positional attack, was to be emphasized. Weakly or moderately defended strong points and cities would be seized. Success in these endeavors would lay the groundwork for the larger battles to come.

Su Yu's concept of operational-level maneuver through the weakly defended area between the Grand Canal and Haizhou instead of directly attacking the main Nationalist strong point of Xuzhou not only followed PLA operational doctrine but it also was in accordance with Sunzi's concept of avoiding strength and attacking weakness. Because the Communists held the initiative, were able to ascertain Nationalist dispositions, and were able to conceal their own dispositions and intentions, the Nationalists were forced to disperse forces in ways that created vulnerabilities. Su Yu sought to exploit those vulnerabilities through maneuvers that were close to Sunzi's theoretical ideal presented in chapter six of *The Art of War*. In that chapter Sunzi deals extensively with the way in which information superiority leads to a numerical superiority that, in turn, creates the potential for victory through maneuver:

> If I am able to determine the enemy's dispositions while at the same time I conceal my own then I can concentrate and he must divide. And if I concentrate while he divides, I can use my entire strength to attack a fraction of his. There, I will be numerically superior. Then, if I am able to use many to strike few at the selected point, those I deal with will be in dire straits.
>
> The enemy must not know where I intend to give battle. For if he does not know where I intend to give battle he must prepare in a great many places. And when he prepares in a great many places, those I have to fight in any one place will be few.
>
> When he prepares everywhere he will be weak everywhere.[73]
>
> Now an army may be likened to water, for just as flowing water avoids the heights and hastens to the lowlands, so an army avoids strength and strikes weakness.
>
> And as water shapes its flow in accordance with the ground, so an army manages its victory in accordance with the situation of the enemy.[74]

In addition to reflecting Sunzi's idea of avoiding strength and attacking weakness, Su Yu's scheme of maneuver also used another Sunzian concept, the simultaneous, complementary, or interchangeable use of what Sunzi called the *zheng* (cheng/fixing/orthodox/normal/straightforward) force and the *qi* (ch'i/maneuver/unorthodox/extraordinary/surprise) force. Sunzi devotes much of chapter five in *The Art of War* to discussing *zheng* and *qi* forces. "Battle, in general," he states, "is using the *zheng* force to engage the enemy and the *qi* force to obtain victory."[75] Sunzi also saw the *zheng* and *qi* forces as not really being mutually exclusive but as being related parts of a cyclical continuum. He saw them interacting and even transforming their nature so that in the course of a battle one might become the other: "Battle situations do not go beyond *qi* and *zheng*. The possible changes of *qi* and *zheng* are inexhaustible. *Qi* and *zheng* mutually transform themselves into each other as if moving around a seamless ring. How can anyone exhaust the possible combinations."[76]

Su Yu's initial campaign proposal contained a straightforward use of *zheng* and *qi* forces. The Subei army (*qi* force) was to move south toward Huaian and Huaiyin to take the campaign's geographical objectives. Meanwhile the ECFA's main body (*zheng* force) was to establish blocking positions along the Grand Canal to engage any Nationalist forces that might try to move east to interfere with Subei army operations.

The decision to destroy the Seventh Army during the first phase of the campaign did not fundamentally alter this campaign design. Maneuver that avoided strength while flowing into areas of weakness was still to be the central part of the campaign. This *qi* force action was intended to achieve the all-important encirclement and separation of Seventh Army's units. It was also to be the basis for establishing the *zheng* force along the Grand Canal that would isolate the battlefields upon which the Seventh Army was to be annihilated.

However, from the perspective of PLA operational principles, making the Seventh Army's destruction the campaign's primary objective was a significant shift. Whereas Su Yu's proposal was in accordance with principles 1 and 2, attacking dispersed isolated enemy forces and seizing small cities and rural areas, the CMC was obviously looking at principle 3, wiping out a

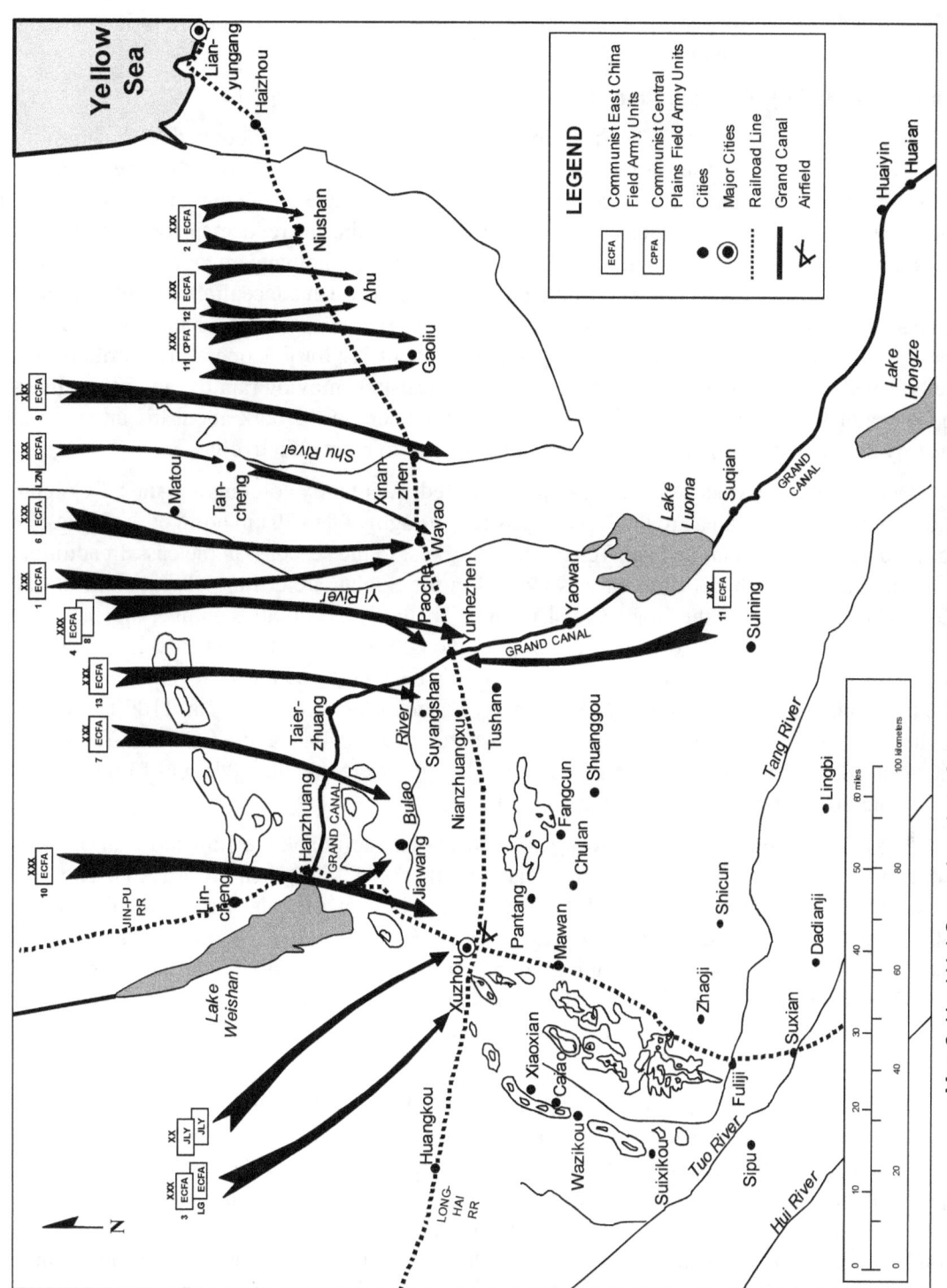

Map 2. Huai Hai Campaign plan of attack according to ECFA order issued 4 November 1948.

large portion of the enemy's effective strength. After the CMC focused on this principle, it was assumed that the campaign would involve heavy fighting. As noted earlier, it was this anticipation that led to a longer period of preparation for the campaign and the desire to increase the impact of CPFA shaping operations.

The Final ECFA Campaign Plan

The attack order that ECFA headquarters issued on 4 November elaborated on the missions assigned each column in the warning order and emphasized the need for speed in execution. Su Yu sought to achieve a high tempo during the operation by emphasizing that infiltration movements and encirclements should be completed before turning to reduce surrounded pockets of Nationalist soldiers. He also granted authority to column commanders to act on the spot to respond to emerging opportunities. Sending his columns between concentrations of Nationalist forces and fighting to keep them apart was an audacious concept, but Su had concentrated a large force that outnumbered the Seventh Army by about 3:1 for this operation. Furthermore, he believed that by employing operations security measures, moving rapidly, and using diversionary attacks he could keep the Nationalist commanders in the dark about his intention to destroy the Seventh Army until it was too late for them to react effectively.

During the two weeks before the campaign started, 12 infantry columns and the ST Column moved south from the area around Jinan to positions roughly 48 to 80 km north of the Long-Hai railroad along a line running from Tengxian in the west to the seacoast in the east. In addition, the Subei army's 11th (E) Column was located in the Suqian area, some 48 km south of the Long-Hai railroad along the Grand Canal. (The "E" behind this column's number indicates that this was the ECFA's 11th Column as opposed to the CPFA's 11th column that was attached to the ECFA. In this work the CPFA's 11th column is designated as the 11th [C] Column.) On the left flank, under the command of Subei army headquarters, were the 12th, 11th (C), and 2d Columns. In the center were the 1st, 4th, 6th, 8th 9th, Luzhongnan, and ST Columns under the ECFA headquarters' direct command. On the right flank were the 7th, 10th, and 13th Columns under the Shandong army headquarters' command.

These 13 columns had the following missions. On the left flank the 12th and 11th (C) Columns were to advance abreast through the area northeast of Xinanzhen toward Ahu. The 12th Column's objective was to surround the XXV Corps base at Ahu and cut all possible routes of withdrawal out of Ahu either to the west or to the east. The 11th (C) Column was to pass to the northwest of Ahu, capture the high ground east of Xinanzhen, and move south to surround the LXIV Corps at Gaoliu. The 2d Column was to be held in reserve the first day; the second day it was to be committed to support the other two columns' major attacks against surrounded Nationalist units.[77]

While the three columns on the left were dealing with the XXV and LXIV Corps, the four center columns were to attack, encircle, and destroy the other two Seventh Army corps—the LXIII at Wayao and the C at Xinanzhen—plus the units attached to the Seventh Army headquarters at Xinanzhen. The 9th Column was to move south toward Xinanzhen on the east side of the Shu River and slide past the city on the east, cutting all lines of communication as far south as the Xinanzhen-Gaoliu road. To the right of the 9th Column the Luzhongnan Column was to attack Tancheng on the evening of 7 November and then move down the west side of the Shu River to cut both the road between Xinanzhen and Wayao and the Long-Hai railroad. On the right of the Luzhongnan Column the 6th Column was to move south to attack Wayao. If it appeared that Wayao could be taken quickly, the 6th Column was to press the attack with part of its force while sending the rest south across the Long-Hai railroad into the area southwest of Xinanzhen to encircle the city. The 1st Column was to follow behind the Luzhongnan and 6th Columns and wait in an area approximately 6 kms north of Wayao while the 6th Column attacked. If this attack faltered, the 1st Column was to add its weight to the attack. If the 6th Column attack succeeded quickly, the 1st Column was to coordinate with the 6th, Luzhongnan, and 9th Columns to launch an attack on Xinanzhen. While these attacks were taking place, the ST Column's main body was to move into an area 40 km north of Tancheng and await further orders.[78]

To the right of the 6th Column, the 9th and 4th Columns were to occupy the area between the Yi River and the Grand Canal and construct strong defensive positions along the Grand Canal. The purpose was to block the expected Nationalist relief force moving east from Xuzhou. As part of their mission, these columns were also directed to send reconnaissance teams 20 to 25 kms west of the Grand Canal to establish contact with local guerrilla units, the 11th (E) Column that was to advance northwest along the Grand Canal from Suqian, and the 13th Column that was to move south from the Taierzhuang area. Establishing contact between all of these units was an essential prerequisite for mounting an effective defense.

The three columns on Su Yu's right flank were assigned the task of creating a realistic threat to Xuzhou. The 10th Column was to move south along the Jin-Pu railroad, bypass Lincheng, capture the long bridge across the Grand Canal, and advance as near to Xuzhou as possible. Once across the Grand Canal, the 10th Column was also supposed to dispatch a force toward Jiawang, the location of Feng Zhian's Third Pacification Area headquarters. This force would support the 7th Column that was to start out from the Zaozhuang area and move directly south across the Grand Canal toward Jiawang. The ECFA high command hoped that the military pressure of a two-pronged attack, when added to an ongoing psychological warfare effort, would be enough to convince Feng Zhian to change loyalties and surrender his forces. To ensure coordination between the 7th and 10th Columns, the 7th Column was placed under the command of the 10th Column commander during this operation.

To the east of the 7th Column, the Shandong army's easternmost column, the 13th, was directed to move directly south toward Taierzhuang. If the city could not be taken easily, the column was to cross the Grand Canal west of the city and push on to Suyangshan on the southern bank of the Bulao River. After destroying Nationalist units holding defensive positions along the Grand Canal from the area south of Taierzhuang to the Bulao River, the column was to dig in along the Bulao River and send units south to Bayiji and Nianzhuangxu. These units would try to make contact with the 4th and 8th Columns and start joint preparations for the anticipated defensive battle.[79]

As noted earlier, the order to execute the final plan was issued 4 November. Movement to attack positions was to begin on the evening of 6 November, and the general attack was to be launched 8 November. Events did not develop this way. Before the ECFA began moving to its attack positions, the Nationalists ordered a redeployment of forces that quickly began to make large portions of the campaign plan irrelevant. Faced with a new and rapidly changing situation, the ECFA quickly altered the missions of some columns and directed others to execute their original orders earlier than planned. However, despite all of the changes, the general concept of the campaign remained the same. The objective was still to destroy the Seventh Army. The problem was that because the Seventh Amy was not where Su Yu had planned for it to be, surrounding and destroying that army became a much greater challenge.

Notes

1. Su Yu, "*Huaye san ge zongdui zan bu dujiang nanjin de jianyi*" [A Proposal That for the Time Being the Three Columns of the ECFA Not Cross the Yangzi River and Advance to the South], in *Su Yu junshi wenji* [A Collection of Su Yu's Military Documents], hereafter cited as *SYJW*, Su Yu Junshi wenji bianjizu [Editorial Committee for *A Collection of Su Yu's Military Documents*], ed. (Beijing: Jiefangjun chubanshe, 1989), 350.

2. Ibid.

3. Ibid., 357.

4. Su Yu, "*Dui jin hou zuozhan jianjun zhi yijian*" [Thoughts on Future Military Operations and Army Building], *SYJW*, 344-45.

5. Su Yu, "*Huaye san ge zongdui zan bu dujiang nanjin de jianyi*" [A Proposal That for the Time Being the Three Columns of the ECFA Not Cross the Yangzi River and Advance to the South], *SYJW,* 350.

6. Zhang Zhuen, "*Su Yu zai zujian dongnan yezhanjun yihou*" [Su Yu After the Organization and Establishment of the Southeast Field Army], *Junshi Lishi* (Military History), 1994, No. 2, 4.

7. Ibid.

8. Ibid., 5.

9. Ibid.

10. Ibid.

11. Su Yu, "*Huaye san ge zongdui zan bu dujiang nanjin de jianyi*" [A Proposal That for the Time Being the Three Columns of the ECFA Not Cross the Yangzi River and Advance to the South], *SYJW*, 356-57.

12. Ibid., 357.

13. Ibid.

14. Zhu Ying, "*Su Yu zui gan jinzhang de san ci zhanyi zhihui*" [Su Yu's Three Most Anxious Moments as a Campaign Commander], *Junshi Lishi* [Military History], 1998, No. 2, 48.

15. Mao Zedong, "On the September Meeting—Circular of the Central Committee of the Communist Party of China," *Selected Works of Mao Tse-tung* (hereafter cited as *SWM*), (Peking: Foreign Languages Press, 1967), vol. 1, 272.

16. Mao Zedong, "The Concept of Operations for the Liaohsi-Shenyang Campaigns," *SWM*, vol. 1, 261.

17. Mao Zedong, "On the September Meeting—Circular of the Central Committee of the Communist Party of China," *SWM*, vol. 1, 273.

18. Ibid., 270.

19. Zhu De, "Four Talks at the War Briefing Meetings Held by the Operations Bureau of the Chinese People's Liberation Army Headquarters, August-November 1948," *Selected Works of Zhu De* (Beijing: Foreign Languages Press, 1986), 250, hereafter cited as *SWZD*.

20. Ibid., 249-50.

21. *Zhongguo renmin jiefangjun quan guo jiefang zhanzheng shi* [A History of the People's Liberation Army's War to Liberate the Entire Country], Wang Miaosheng and Jiang Tiejun, eds. (Beijing: Junshi kexue chubanshe, 1997), 50.

22. Ibid., 53.

23. *Mingjiang SuYu* [The Famous General Su Yu], Lao zhanshi shiwenji bianweihui zhongguo geming bowuguan [The Committee for Editing the Poetry and Writings of Old Warriors and the Museum of the Chinese Revolution] ed. (Beijing: Xinhua chubanshe, 1986), 377.

24. Ibid.

25. Ibid.

26. Su Yu, "*Guanyu juxing huaihai zhanyi zhi zhongyang junwei de dianbao*" [Telegram to the Central Military Committee Concerning Carrying Out the Huai Hai Campaign] in *Huai hai zhanyi* [The Huai Hai Campaign], vol. 1, Zhonggong zhongyang dangshi ziliao zhengji weiyuanhui [Chinese Communist Party Central Committee's Committee for the Collection of Party Historical Material], ed. (Beijing: Zhonggong dangshi ziliao chubanshe, 1988), 48, hereafter cited as *HHZY*. The Huai Hai Campaign's name comes from the names of the geographical objectives in the proposed campaign. They are the two "Huai cities," Huaian and Huaiyin, and Haizhou. In this study the transmission times for PLA messages are given as being on the hour. This is because the transmission time on a message is either given as being on the hour or as occurring during one of the 12-hour periods that a day includes. In the latter case, a message said to have been sent during 1300-1500 will arbitrarily be given a 1300 transmission time.

27. Sunzi, *The Art of War*, Samuel B. Griffith, trans. (New York: Oxford University Press, 1963), 108.

28. Field Manual 3-0, Operations, (Washington, DC: US Government Printing Office, June 2001), foreword.

29. Mao Zedong, "The Present Situation and Our Tasks," *SWM*, vol. 4, 161-62.

30. "*Liu Bocheng, Chen Yi, Deng Xiaoping tongyi chengsheng jinxing Huaihai zhanyi zhi zhongyang junwei, Su Yu de dianbao*" [Telegram From Liu Bocheng, Chen Yi, and Deng Xiaoping to the CMC and Su Yu Agreeing That the Huai Hai Campaign Should be Carried Out as the Way to Exploit the Victory at Jinan], *HHZY*, vol. 1, 50.

31. "*Zhongyang junwei guanyu pizhun juxing Huaihai zhanyji ji zhanyi di yi ge zuozhan ying jianmie Huang Baitao bingtuan zhi Rao Shushi, Su Yu de dianbao*" [Telegram From the CMC to Rao Shushi and Su Yu Concerning Approval for Carrying Out the Huai Hai Campaign and the Need to Make Destroying Huang Baitao's Army the First Operation], *HHZY*, vol. 1, 52.

32. Ibid.

33. Ibid., 52-53.

34. Ibid., 53.

35. "*Zhongyang junwei guanyu ying zuohao Huaihai zhanyi de chongfen zhunbei zhi Rao Shushi, Su Yu, Tan Zhenlin de dianbao*" [Telegram From the CMC to Rao Shushi, Su Yu, and Tan Zhenlin Concerning the Need to Be Fully Prepared for the Huai Hai Campaign], *HHZY*, vol. 1, 54-55.

36. Zhang Zhen, "*Huadong yezhanjun zai Huaihai zhanyi zhong de zuozhan xingdong*" [The Combat Operations of the ECFA During the Huai Hai Campaign], *HHZY*, vol. 2, 29.

37. "*Zhongyang junwei guanyu Huaihai zhanyi bushu de jidian yijian zhi Rao Shushi, Su Yu, Tan Zhenlin te dianbao*" [Telegram From the CMC to Rao Shushi, Su Yu, and Tan Zhenlin Concerning Some Ideas for Deploying Forces During the Huai Hai Campaign], *HHZY*, vol. 1, 63.

38. "*Rao Shushi, Su Yu, Tan Zhenlin guanyu jianmie Huang Baitao bingtuan de bushu zhi zhongyang junwei de dianbao*" [Telegram From Rao Shushi, Su Yu, and Tan Zhenlin to the CMC Concerning the Deployment of Forces for the Destruction of Huang Baitao's Army], *HHZY*, vol. 1, 68.

39. "*Zhongyang junwei guanyu qianzhi Xuzhou ge bu yuandi de bushu zhi Rao Shushi, Su Yu, Tan Zhenlin de dianbao*" [Telegram From the CMC to Rao Shushi, Su Yu and Tan Zhenlin Concerning the Deployment for Tying Down All Xuzhou Units That Could Provide Aid (to Huang Baitao)], *HHZY*, vol. 1, 72.

40. "*Zhongyang junwei guanyu Huaihai zhanyi bushu de ji dian yijian zhi Rao Shushi, Su Yu, Tan Zhenlin te dianbao*" [Telegram From the CMC to Rao Shushi, Su Yu, and Tan Zhenlin Concerning Some Ideas for Deploying Forces During the Huai Hai Campaign], *HHZY*, vol. 1, 63-64.

41. Li Da, "*Huigu Huaihai zhanyi zhong de zhongyuan yezhanjun*" [The CPFA in the Huai Hai Campaign], *HHZY*, vol. 2, 3.

42. Wei Minshi, "*Jiefang Zhengzhou zhi yi*" [The Campaign to Liberate Zhengzhou] in *Liu Deng dajun nanzhengji* [Record of the Southern Campaign of the Liu-Deng Army], Tian Xiaoguang and Wei Minshi, eds. (Xinxiang, Henan: Henan renmin chubanshe), 1985, 383-84.

43. "*Zhongyang junwei guanyu zhongye gongke Zhengzhou hou quanjuin dongjin zhi Chen Yi Deng Xiaoping de dianbao*" [Telegram From the CMC to Chen Yi and Deng Xiaoping Concerning a Move to the East by the Entire CPFA After it Takes Zhengzhou], *HHZY*, vol. 1, 75.

44. "*Chen Yi, Deng Xiaoping guanyu zhanling Zhengzhou ji zhuli dongjin jihua zhi zhongyang junwei deng de dianbao*" [Telegram From Chen Yi and Deng Xiaoping to the CMC and Others Concerning the Plans for Occupying Xuzhou and the Eastward Movement of the Main Body], *HHZY*, vol. 1, 78.

45. "*Zhongyang junwei guanyu xiugai Huaihai zhanyi bushu deng wenti zhi Rao Shushi, Su Yu, Tan Zhenlin de dianbao*" [Telegram From the CMC to Rao Shushi, Su Yu and Tan Zhenlin Concerning Changes in the Dispositions for the Huai Hai Campaign and Other Questions], *HHZY*, vol. 1, 76-77.

46. "*Chen Yi, Deng Xiaoping guanyu zhongye zhuli dongjin hou, san ge zuozhan fangan zhi zhongyang junwei deng de dianbao*" [Telegram From Chen Yi and Deng Xiaoping to the CMC and Others Concerning Three Operational Options for the CPFA Main Force After it Advances to the East], *HHZY*, vol. 1, 88-89.

47. "*Zhongyang junwei guanyu zhongye zhuli chu Huainan de fangan zhi Chen Yi, Deng Xiaoping de dianbao*" [Telegram From the CMC to Chen Yi and Deng Xiaoping Concerning a Plan for Going Into the Area South of the Huai River], *HHZY*, vol. 1, 90-91.

48. "*Chen Yi, Deng Xiaoping jianyi bu chu Huainan wei hao zhi zhongyang junwei deng de dianbao*" [Telegram From Chen Yi and Deng Xiaoping to the CMC Suggesting That It's Best Not to Go South of the Huai River], *HHZY*, vol. 1, 92.

49. "*Zhongyang junwei tongyi zhongye bu chu Huainan zhi Chen Yi, Deng Xiaoping de dianbao*" [Telegram From the CMC to Chen Yi and Deng Xiaoping Agreeing That the CPFA Should Not Go South of the Huai River], *HHZY*, vol. 1, 93.

50. "*Liu Bocheng, Deng Zihui, Li Da guanyu poji Ping Han lu shi zhi zhongyang junwei deng de dianbao*" [Telegram From Liu Bocheng, Deng Zihui, and Li Da to the CMC and Others Concerning the Wrecking of the Ping-Han Railroad], *HHZY*, vol. 1, 106.

51. Chen Zaidao and Fan Zhaoli, "*Wei liao Huaihai zhanyui de shengli*" [For Victory in the Huaihai Campaign], *HHZY*, vol. 2, 97.

52. Ibid.

53. Du Yide, "*Huiyi zhongye liu zong canjia weijian Huang Wei bingtuan zhi zhan*" [Recollection of the CPFA 6th Column's Participation in the Battles to Encircle and Destroy Huang Wei's Army], *HHZY*, vol. 2, 145. This is also mentioned in the telegram noted in note 50.

54. Chen and Fan, 97-98.

55. "*Zhongyang junwei guanyu qianzhi Xuzhou ge bu yuandi de bushu zhi Rao Shushi, Su Yu, Tan Zhenlin de dianbao*" [Telegram From the CMC to Rao Shushi, Su Yu and Tan Zhenlin Concerning the Deployment for Tying Down All Xuzhou Units That Could Provide Aid (to Huang Baitao)], *HHZY*, vol. 1, 71.

56. "*Zhongyang junwei guanyu zhongye dongjin hou de zuozhan xingdong zhi Chen Yi, Deng Xiaoping deng de dianbao*" [Telegram From the CMC to Chen Yi, Deng Xiaoping, and Others Concerning Combat Operations of the CPFA After it Advances to the East], *HHZY*, vol. 1, 79.

57. "*Chen Yi, Deng Xiaoping guanyu qianzhi Qiu Qingquan Sun Yuanliang bingtuan de zuozhan fangan zhi zhongyang junwei deng de dianbao*" [Telegram From Chen Yi and Deng Xiaoping to the CMC and Others Concerning Operational Plans for Tying Down the Armies of Qiu Qingquan and Sun Yuanliang], *HHZY*, vol. 1, 104-105.

58. "*Chen Yi, Deng Xiaoping guanyu qianzhi Qiu Qingquan, Sun Yuanliang bingtuan de xin fangan zhi zhongyang junwei deng de dianbao*" [Telegram From Chen Yi and Deng Xiaoping to the CMC and Others Concerning a New Plan for Tying Down the Armies of Qiu Qingquan and Sun Yuanliang], *HHZY*, vol. 1, 110-11.

59. "*Liu Bocheng, Deng Zihui, Li Da jianyi zhongye zhuli jieduan Xu-Su jian tielu zhi zhongyang junwei, Chen Yi, Deng Xiaoping de dianbao*" [Telegram From Liu Bocheng, Deng Zihui, and Li Da to the CMC, Chen Yi, and Deng Xiaoping Proposing That the CPFA Main Force Cut the Xuzhou-Suxian Railroad], *HHZY*, vol. 1, 114.

60. "*Zhongyang junwei guanyu Su-Beng diqu zuozhan fangan zhi Chen Yi, Deng Xiaoping de dianbao*" [Telegram From the CMC to Chen Yi and Deng Xiaoping Concerning Plans for Operations in the Area of Suxian and Bengbu], *HHZY*, vol. 1, 122-23.

61. "*Chen Yi, Deng Xiaoping guanyu xian da Liu Ruming bu zhi zhongyang junwei de dianbao*" [Telegram From Chen Yi and Deng Xiaoping to the CMC Concerning First Striking at Liu Ruming's Force], *HHZY*, vol. 1, 124-25.

62. "*Zhongyang junwei tongyi zhongye da Liu Ruming bu zhi Chen Yi, Deng Xiaoping de dianbao*" [Telegram From the CMC to Chen Yi and Deng Xiaoping Agreeing That the CPFA Should Strike Liu Ruming's Force First], *HHZY*, vol. 1, 126.

63. "*Su Yu guanyu qing Chen Yi, Deng Xiaoping tongyi zhihui zhi zhongyang junwei de dianbao*" [Telegram from Su Yu to the CMC Asking That Chen Yi and Deng Xiaoping Have Overall Command], *HHZY*, vol. 1, 103.

64. "*Zhongyang junwei guanyu Huaihai zhanyi tongyi zhihui wenti zhi Chen Yi, Deng Xiaoping, Su Yu de dianbao*" [Telegram From the CMC to Chen Yi, Deng Xiaoping, and Su Yu Concerning the Question of Unity of Command for the Huai Hai Campaign], *HHZY*, vol. 1, 107.

65. Mao Zedong, "The Present Situation and Our Tasks," *SWM*, vol. 4, 163.

66. "*Rao Shushi, Su Yu, Tan Zhenlin guanyu jianmie Huang Baitao bingtuan de bushu zhi zhongyang junwei de dianbao*" [Telegram From Rao Shushi, Su Yu, Tan Zhenlin to the CMC Concerning the Deployment of Forces for Destroying Huang Baitao's Army], *HHZY*, vol. 1, 68.

67. "*Zhongyang junwei guanyu qianzhi Xuzhou ge bu yuandi de bushu zhi Rao Shushi, Su Yu, Tan Zhenlin de dianbao*" [Telegram From the CMC to Rao Shushi, Su Yu and Tan Zhenlin Concerning the Deployment for Tying Down All Xuzhou Units That Could Provide Aid (to Huang Baitao)], *HHZY*, vol. 1, 72.

68. "*Zhongyang junwei guanyu yao shexiang di keneng bianhua de ji zhong qingkuang yu wo duifu*

de banfa zhi Rao Shushi, Su, Yu Tan Zhenlin de dianbao" [Telegram From the CMC to Rao Shushi, Su Yu, Tan Zhenlin Concerning Several Possible Enemy Situations That We Can Imagine and Our Ways to Respond], *HHZY*, vol. 1, 95.

69. "*Huadong yezhanjun Huaihai zhanyi yubei mingling*" [ECFA Warning Order for the Huai Hai Campaign], *HHZY*, vol. 1, 80-87.

70. Ibid.

71. Mao Zedong, "The Present Situation and Our Tasks," *SWM*, vol. 4, 162.

72. Ibid., 161-62.

73. Sunzi, *The Art of War*, Samuel B. Griffith, trans. (New York: Oxford University Press, 1963), 98.

74. Ibid., 101.

75. Author's translation. Griffith's translation of this passage is "Generally, in battle, use the normal force to engage; use the extraordinary to win." See Sunzi, 91, passage 5.

76. Author's translation. Griffith's translation of this passage is "In battle there are only the normal and extraordinary forces, but their combinations are limitless; none can comprehend them all. For these two forces are mutually reproductive; their interaction as endless as that of interlocking rings. Who can determine where one ends and the other begins." See Sunzi, 92, passages 11 and 12.

77. "*Huadong yezhanjun Huaihai zhanyi gongji mingling*" [ECFA Attack Order for the Huai Hai Campaign], *HHZY*, vol. 1, 118.

78. Ibid., 119-20.

79. Ibid., 118.

Chapter Three

Nationalist Strategy During Summer and Early Fall 1948

The wise general is always considering both favorable and unfavorable factors. Thinking about what is not favorable in advantageous situations enables him to complete his mission. Thinking about the advantages he has in the midst of a difficult situation enables him to find a way out.

—Sunzi, *The Art of War*

To visualize the desired outcome, commanders must clearly understand the situation in the battlespace.

—FM 3-0, *Operations*

The August Strategy Session in Nanjing

Just as the CCP Central Committee met at Xibaipo, a small village in the hills of western Hebei, from 8 to 13 September to review the previous two years of civil war and set policy and strategy for the future, President Jiang Jieshi held a meeting of his military commanders in Nanjing on 3-7 August to assess the situation facing the Nationalists. The Nationalist leaders saw that their military position had seriously deteriorated during the past six months and urgently discussed ways to reverse this trend. The conference concluded with agreement on a comprehensive program to raise the level of national mobilization; increase munitions production; eliminate shortcomings in operational command and control, operations security, intelligence gathering, logistics, and soldier recruitment and training; and improve troop morale. The goal was to halt the rising tide of Communist victories and regain the initiative on the battlefield.

At the strategic level, the effort to stop the Communists' southward expansion toward the Yangzi River valley received top priority. The area between the Yellow River and the Yangzi, the central plains, was designated as the decisive area of combat for the coming year. Nationalist armies in northeastern, northern, and northwestern China received local objectives to accomplish, but behind those objectives lay the strategic mission of containing Communist forces so they could not be sent to central and east central China. In addition, a plan was adopted to increase the army's size by 1,500,000 men. The purpose was to create a strategic reserve that would provide strategic and operational-level flexibility.[1]

At the operational and tactical levels, attention was focused on how to effectively counter the Communist strategy of achieving local superiority and destroying varying sizes of Nationalist units one by one. The Nationalists faced a dilemma. They were almost compelled by their position as the government of China to disperse forces to try to defend everywhere, but dispersed small units were vulnerable to attack and so, too, were reinforcements sent to assist them. Through two years of civil war the Communists had taken advantage of this situation to successfully encircle and destroy innumerable Nationalist units. Now the Nationalists sought to combat this strategy and possibly turn it to their advantage by more effectively applying the principles of mass and maneuver. Some commands were to be consolidated, maneuver forces were to be made more powerful, and defensive positions around important cities and strategic locations were to be strengthened.

The idea was to take an old concept, trapping Communist units between the hammers of maneuver forces and the anvils of forces defending in place, and really make it work. By making it easier to designate forces to meet a threat, giving maneuver forces the combat power to push quickly through opposing forces, and ensuring that the garrisons manning fixed defenses had the staying power to resist for a long time, the Nationalists hoped to change the time equation that up to then had so often meant that isolated units were destroyed before they could be relieved. Theoretically, if encircled units could hold out longer and relief forces could maneuver into place more rapidly, Communist units would indeed be crushed between these anvils and hammers.

The first major test of this reinvigorated "hammer and anvil" strategy came when the ECFA attacked Jinan on 16 September. The result was a complete failure. The defense of the approaches to the city and the city itself was ineffective, lasting only eight days. Perhaps even more disappointing was the slowness with which the Xuzhou Bandit Suppression Headquarters organized relief forces. At the time the last Nationalist holdouts in Jinan were surrendering, relief columns were just beginning to move north toward them. Instead of forming an anvil and hammer, the Nationalist army had formed nothing.

The fall of Jinan and the loss of its 90,000 defenders posed a direct threat to the Nationalist strategic aim of keeping the Communists from expanding south out of Shandong. ECFA forces that had been defending against Nationalist offensive operations out of Jinan were now available for use elsewhere. Several Nationalist armies under the command of the Xuzhou Bandit Suppression Headquarters still stood between the ECFA and the Yangzi River valley. However, in both Xuzhou and the central headquarters in Nanjing there was uncertainty about what these forces should do to thwart the ECFA's next move.

Du Yuming Seeks the Initiative

Du Yuming, deputy commander, Xuzhou Bandit Suppression Headquarters, quickly took the position that the best approach was to launch an offensive into Shandong before the ECFA recovered from the Jinan Campaign. He presented several reasons to support his argument. First, Nationalist maneuver forces had been reorganizing and replenishing since the end of large-scale fighting with the ECFA early in July and were ready to fight. Second, during this period, the defenses around Xuzhou had been strengthened so that the Communists' small-unit attacks would not be a threat to the city after the Nationalist armies moved north. Third, the disposition of the ECFA seemed to offer the possibility that a Nationalist attack could be successful. Intelligence reports indicated that the ECFA was currently divided, with part resting and reorganizing in central Shandong while the remainder did the same in the Yanzhou-Jining area of southwest Shandong. In addition, there was no evidence that the columns in the Yanzhou-Jining area had constructed defense works that could greatly delay a Nationalist advance. Fourth, at this time the CPFA was far to the west in central Henan and therefore could not threaten the Nationalist forces' left flank or rear.[2] Fifth, Du noted that waiting passively while the ECFA recovered from its Jinan Campaign left the initiative with the enemy. In his opinion, allowing the ECFA to prepare for an offensive at the time and place of its own choosing virtually guaranteed that the Nationalists would find themselves at a serious disadvantage. Finally, Du felt the need, especially after the bitterly disappointing failure to save Jinan, to somehow reestablish confidence and an offensive spirit in the army. He understood the need to raise the morale of his officers and men and believed a victory would do more than anything else to achieve this goal. In July Du had been assigned as deputy commander, Xuzhou Bandit

Suppression Headquarters, in an attempt to put more vigor into Liu Zhi's command.³ Now, shortly after the fall of Jinan, he put together a plan for a Nationalist offensive into Shandong and submitted it to Liu Zhi, hoping that Liu would be moved to act.

Du Yuming's concept of operations for this offensive was to have all four armies under the command of the Xuzhou Bandit Suppression Headquarters—the Seventh, Thirteenth, Second, and Sixteenth—advance on a broad front toward Yanzhou. The objective was to trap part of the ECFA in the Yanzhou-Jining area and destroy it quickly, thereby gaining that much-needed Nationalist victory and establishing more favorable conditions for subsequent fighting with the ECFA. If the ECFA avoided battle, the Nationalist forces would advance as far as Dongping, Dawenkou, and Sishui but would not enter the mountainous areas farther to the east or north. Instead, Du envisioned using what he called a "fishing" tactic. In this tactic a powerful corps would be placed in an easily defensible position and given an abundant supply of food and ammunition. Then the other units would withdraw and wait for the Communists to launch an attack against this lone corps. If the Communists took the bait and attacked, the Nationalist units that had withdrawn earlier would quickly return along external lines, surround the Communist forces, and destroy them.

As for the CPFA, Du assumed that it could not become involved in the fighting because it was so far away. However, to make it even more unlikely that the CPFA would move east, he wanted the Nationalist forces in west Henan, such as Huang Wei's Twelfth Army, to launch operations that would keep the CPFA tied down there. If somehow, despite these efforts, the CPFA still moved east, Du wanted Nationalist forces from central China to follow the CPFA as it advanced. In that scenario, Du planned that at a certain point part of the Nationalist forces in Shandong would go on the defensive to contain the ECFA while his main force moved west to crush the CPFA between them and the Nationalist forces moving east behind the CPFA.⁴

Liu Zhi, Du's ever-cautious superior, agreed with Du's "Plan for Attacking the Communist Army in Shandong" in principle, but he felt that Du was committing too large a force to the operation. Also, he opposed entrusting Xuzhou's defense to Feng Zhian's Third Pacification Area force because he had doubts about its political reliability. Only after a heated argument, during which Du agreed to assign Xuzhou's defense to the Thirteenth Army and place Third Pacification Area units in the attacking force, did Liu give his final consent.⁵

With Liu Zhi's approval in hand, on 30 September Du Yuming flew to Nanjing to present his plan to the Army chief of staff, Gu Zhutong. Since Gu lacked the authority to approve such an operation on his own, on 2 October Du flew to Beiping (Beijing's name since 1928 after the Nationalists changed it before establishing the national capital in Nanjing) where he met with Jiang that afternoon. Following further discussions the next morning, Jiang wrote out his approval, and Du quickly went back to Nanjing. On 4 October he and Gu discussed how to implement the plan. Since the supporting diversionary operations the Nationalist forces would carry out against the CPFA in central China were a key part of the plan, before returning to Xuzhou, Du wanted to be sure that Bai Chongxi, commander, Central China Bandit Suppression Headquarters in Wuhan, was willing to carry out these operations. Also, he wanted Bai's assurance that if the CPFA moved east Bai would send the Twelfth Army in pursuit.⁶ On 5 October Gu obtained Bai's agreement to do these things, and Du returned to Xuzhou to report to Liu. That same day Du also decided that in preparation for the offensive Sun Yuanliang's Sixteenth Army should move from Zhengzhou to Liuhe to be close to Second Army headquarters at Shangqiu.

On 7 October Du convened a meeting with Qiu Qingquan, Li Mi, Huang Baitao, and others to go over the planned operation in detail. At this time it was decided that the offensive would begin on 15 October.[7]

Du Yuming's offensive never took place. Early on the morning of 15 October, as Du stepped into his car to go to his forward command post, an aide rushed up and handed him an urgent message from Jiang Jieshi canceling the operation. Jiang was deeply concerned about the increasingly desperate situation his army faced in Manchuria and did not want another major campaign to begin at this time. Furthermore, he was about to fly from Nanjing to Shenyang (Mukden) to look at conditions firsthand, and he wanted Du to go with him and assume command of all remaining Nationalist forces in Manchuria. With hardly time for farewells, Du proceeded to the Xuzhou airfield to await the arrival of Jiang's airplane from Nanjing. Then he was gone.[8]

He Yingqin and Gu Zhutong Develop an Active Defense Concept

The cancellation of the 15 October offensive left the Nationalist forces under the Xuzhou Bandit Suppression Headquarters with no operational plans and a great deal of uncertainty. Intelligence reports indicated that the ECFA was preparing to move south and the CPFA was moving toward Zhengzhou. It was assumed that the Communists intended to bring the CPFA onto the Yellow River-Huai River plain and employ it in conjunction with the ECFA to carry out a large offensive. At all command levels there was considerable discussion about how to respond to this developing threat.

After a week of deliberating, on 22 October, Defense Minister He Yingqin and Gu Zhutong finally agreed that the forces in and around Xuzhou should adopt a defensive posture that conformed closely to the Nationalist forces' existing deployment. They envisioned a significant consolidation west of Xuzhou where they called for all cities west of Shangqiu on the Long-Hai railroad to be abandoned, including the Henan provincial capital of Kaifeng and the railroad center of Zhengzhou. However, they advocated maintaining an area defense to the east of Xuzhou along the Long-Hai railroad between Xuzhou and Haizhou to block an ECFA penetration into north Jiangsu. They also proposed that the Twelfth Army go to Zhoujiakou to prepare to move east behind the CPFA. He and Gu hoped that at some point conditions would be right for the Twelfth Army and Second Army to catch the CPFA between them and destroy it. Recognizing the need to more effectively cope with what seemed to be increasing coordination between the ECFA and the CPFA, He and Gu proposed the subordination of the Xuzhou and Wuhan Bandit Suppression Headquarters to a new headquarters to be established in Bengbu with Bai Chongxi as commander. Establishing this new headquarters was a way to facilitate transferring forces from central to eastern China. It also would provide a graceful way to reduce Liu Zhi's the responsibilities.[9]

Early on the morning of 23 October, Guo Rugui, chief of operations, Defense Ministry, flew to Beiping where he presented He Yingqin and Gu Zhutong's proposal to Jiang Jieshi. After obtaining Jiang's approval, Guo flew back to Nanjing that same evening. The next day orders for the various troop movements were issued. However, the new headquarters at Bengbu could not be established until Bai Chongxi's agreement to serve as commander was obtained.

The orders the High Command issued on 24 October assigned the following broad missions. East of Xuzhou the Thirteenth Army, centered around Bayiji, and the Seventh Army, centered around Xinanzhen, were to block any attempt by the ECFA to advance south across the Long-Hai railroad. These two armies were also directed to provide assistance if there was an attack against Haizhou. West of Xuzhou the Second Army was to maintain control of the area around Dangshan and prepare to make a joint attack on the CPFA in conjunction with the Twelfth Army after the CPFA entered the Yellow River plain. The Sixteenth Army was to remain in the Liuhe area until after the CPFA entered the Yellow River plain. Then it was to move to the Suxian-Mengcheng area to provide protection for Bengbu. The Third Pacification Area was to defend the area along the Grand Canal from Weishan Lake east to Taierzhuang. The Fourth Pacification Area was to provide a garrison force for Shangqiu and troops to patrol the railroad between Shangqiu and Xuzhou. Xuzhou Bandit Suppression Headquarters was to strengthen defensive works around Xuzhou, Bengbu, and Huaiyin to provide a central core around which the Nationalist armies could maneuver. The Twelfth Army would prepare to follow the CPFA to the east and be ready to join the Second Army in attacking it.[10]

Reconsidering He Yingqin and Gu Zhutong's Plan

Issuing orders on 24 October to carry out the plan He Yingqin and Gu Zhutong developed did not end the debate about how Nationalist forces in east and east central China should deploy to counter the expected Communist offensive. A number of officers thought the forces positioned along the Long-Hai railroad were dangerously exposed. The railroad provided east-west mobility, but there was no north-south depth to the defense. Furthermore, the officers were concerned that virtually the entire Xuzhou command depended on the Xu-Beng railroad for logistics support. They pointed out that if that line was cut and the CPFA's eastward movement was making a Communist attack against it look more likely, all of the armies around Xuzhou would be isolated. To remove these vulnerabilities from the Nationalist deployment, the officers proposed that Xuzhou be abandoned and that all Nationalist forces withdraw south of the Huai River. They argued that because the river was a major natural obstacle, a defense line constructed along the south bank would be able to withstand any Communist attack. To show that they still possessed offensive spirit, the plan's advocates also stated that once the Communists had exhausted themselves trying to break through the Huai River line the Nationalist army would be in a good position to counterattack to the north.[11]

Recognizing that the deployment ordered on 24 October did have serious defects, on 29 October, Gu Zhung invited He Yingqin and others to army headquarters to reassess Nationalist strategy. The option of withdrawing south of the Huai River was thoroughly discussed but then rejected because of the reluctance to give up Xuzhou and its position astride the Long-Hai railroad. As long as the Nationalists held Xuzhou they could keep the Communists from using this railroad to transport men and materiel from west to east and east to west. If the railroad fell into Communist hands, the Communists would immediately gain a significant advantage in strategic mobility in the key region between the Yellow and Yangzi Rivers. Moving south of the Huai River was also opposed because it would limit the Nationalist armies' ability to maneuver. The argument was made that once Nationalist armies had withdrawn south of the river it would be very difficult for them to again project combat power into northern Jiangsu or west toward the Ping-Han railroad.[12] One more reason given for not withdrawing south of the Huai River was the adverse psychological impact such a move would have on the army and the civilian population. It was feared that abandoning Xuzhou and all the remaining area north of the Huai River at a time when the Nationalist position in Manchuria was crumbling would be another blow to army morale and would further reduce public confidence in the Nationalist government.

Not surprisingly, the plan that finally emerged from Gu Zhutong's strategy session of 29 October was a compromise. The obvious vulnerabilities to attack that were inherent in the existing Nationalist deployment were to be eliminated without withdrawing south of the Huai River. All Nationalist positions along the Long-Hai railroad east and west of Xuzhou were to be abandoned. Xuzhou was to be defended, but only be one or two reinforced corps. The rest of the forces under the Xuzhou Bandit Suppression Headquarters were to be deployed along both sides of the Xu-Beng railroad between Xuzhou and Bengbu.[13] There the forces would establish strong area defenses to protect the railroad and prepare to maneuver either to the east or west to encircle and destroy parts of the ECFA or CPFA.[14] The coming battle was potentially the decisive battle of the civil war, and all possible combat power was to be concentrated to fight it. Therefore, the plan continued to call for shifting the Twelfth Army to the East China theater. This army's presence was considered crucial in coping with the CPFA.

Nationalist Indecision

Had this proposed redeployment been implemented quickly, it might have become impossible for the ECFA to isolate and destroy the Seventh Army. On 30 October some of the ECFA columns that had important roles in cutting the Seventh Army's route of withdrawal toward Xuzhou, such as the 13th and the 8th, were still three days' march from their forward assembly areas, and the scheduled start of the offensive was 10 days away. However, for several critical days Jiang Jieshi failed to approve this or any other general redeployment plan. Late on the evening of 29 October Gu Zhutong sent a message to the Xuzhou command giving permission for Liu Ruming's Fourth Pacification Area force to evacuate Shangqiu if necessary.[15] However, the major redeployment and concentration of forces He Yingqin and Gu Zhotong proposed was not authorized. While time passed, the armies around Xuzhou remained in place.

Jiang Jieshi's delay in making a decision was due to many factors. On 30 October he deactivated his temporary headquarters in Beiping and returned to Nanjing. He had gone to Beiping mid-month to better direct his armies in Manchuria, only to see those armies destroyed in a series of crushing defeats. As he returned to Nanjing he was concerned about the need to preserve the armies that were now spread out around Xuzhou. Impressed by the Communist forces' ability to carry out deep attacks and encircle Nationalist forces in Manchuria, Jiang saw the military benefit of withdrawing south of the Huai River and creating a strong linear defense line to protect Nanjing. At the same time, he believed that such a withdrawal would reflect poorly on his leadership. Torn between unpleasant alternatives he hesitated. Instead of deciding to redeploy his forces around Xuzhou, Jiang focused first on establishing a new command structure and filling the leadership void left at the Xuzhou Bandit Suppression Headquarters by Du Yuming's departure. Overestimating the time the ECFA would spend preparing for another offensive after the end of its campaign to take Jinan, he assumed that after his new commanders were in place there would be ample time to work with them on a plan to meet the expected Communist attack.

After He Yingqin and Gu Zhutong had proposed that a new headquarters be established at Bengbu to command the Nationalist forces in both east and central China and that Bai Chongxi be appointed as the overall commander, Jiang Jieshi had quickly given his approval. However, nothing had happened since then because Bai had not agreed to accept the post. Bai considered the position to be filled with problems. He knew that creating a new headquarters staff would require considerable time and that time was limited. He could not simply move his staff from Wuhan because that would disrupt, and possibly fatally weaken, the Nationalist military effort in central China. Also, anyone coming to east China from elsewhere, including Bai, would face an unfamiliar situation. Bai was especially concerned because he knew so few of the corps or division commanders serving under the Xuzhou Bandit Suppression Headquarters. How, he wondered, could he be an effective commander if he did not know the qualities of the men responsible for executing his orders? He did not want to take the position and then become the scapegoat if the Nationalists suffered a major defeat.[16]

As Jiang Jieshi prepared to leave Beiping for Nanjing, creating the new headquarters with Bai Chongxi as commander had become a high priority. In an attempt to accelerate the decision-making process, Jiang ordered Bai to fly to Nanjing on the same day that Jiang was returning to the capital. Bai did so, and late that afternoon, he attended a long meeting with He Yingqin at the Defense Ministry. He Yingqin reviewed the situation in east China, described the function of the proposed new headquarters, and told Bai that he would be making a very important contribution to the war effort by assuming the position of commander. Despite the pressure, the next day Bai announced that he could not accept the post. His action, in effect, killed the idea of creating a new headquarters because Bai was the only officer with the necessary rank, prestige, and position to make the proposal work on such short notice. Bai did agree, however, that the Twelfth Army could be shifted eastward to the central plains. Orders were issued late on the night of 31 October for the Twelfth Army to assemble at Queshan as rapidly as possible and be fully assembled by 10 November.[17]

By 31 October Jiang Jieshi also had to admit failure on another personnel matter. He had attempted to convince Song Xilian, who was concurrently serving as Bai Chongxi's deputy in Wuhan and commander, Fourteenth Army, to go to Xuzhou to be Liu Zhi's deputy. Jiang and others doubted that Liu Zhi, who had already been relieved from command once for poor performance during fighting in northeastern Henan in September 1946, could command a great battle by himself. Therefore, after Du Yuming left Xuzhou for Manchuria, every effort was made to replace him. On 24 October Jiang sent a message to Song asking him to go to Xuzhou. Song, however, used a series of excuses to delay the move. Finally, on 31 October an exasperated Jiang Jieshi decided not to press the matter further. The next morning he dispatched Xu Langxuan, deputy chief of operations, Defense Ministry, to go to the Manchurian port city of Huludao to ask Du Yuming to return to Xuzhou to resume his former duties. Du consented, but he asked permission to stay in Huludao until the Nationalist forces squeezed into a defense perimeter around the port were safely evacuated by sea. Jiang granted Du's request, which at the time did not appear to hold any risks. This decision, however, soon had serious consequences. Just a week later, during the critical early phase of the fighting around Xuzhou, Du would not be there when he was needed.

On 3 November Xu Langxuan returned to Nanjing from Huludao. The same day Jiang Jieshi agreed to two relatively minor shifts of Xuzhou command forces to strengthen the defenses of Bengbu and the area west of the Xu-Beng railroad. One shift, moving the Sixteenth Army from Suxian to the Mencheng-Guoyang area had been included in the redeployment plan approved on 23 October. The other, moving the Fourth Pacification Area from Shangqiu to the

Guzhen-Bengbu area, had been under consideration for several days. There was, however, still no decision on a major redeployment of the forces around Xuzhou.

When Jiang Jieshi came back to Nanjing from Beiping on 30 October he was leaning heavily toward ordering his forces to withdraw south of the Huai River.[18] Thinking that he might lose his armies in a battle to defend Xuzhou, he was prepared to err on the side of caution and not fight for the city. This led him to hesitate to give final approval to He Yingqin and Gu Zhutong's proposal of 29 October. As the days passed, however, a touch of optimism began to replace his earlier pessimism. The ECFA's move south to its forward assembly area had not been detected, so this developing threat was not known. The CPFA's move toward the east seemed to have slowed, and there was hope that the eastward advance of the Twelfth Army would further slow or even stop this move. Nationalist assessments of enemy intentions were now concluding that in the near term the CPFA and the ECFA were not likely to combine forces and carry out a great offensive together. Since the benefits of holding Xuzhou were so great, this changed perception of the threat led Jiang to decide to defend the city.[19] To see the situation for himself and decide how to redeploy his forces to achieve this objective, he made plans to visit Xuzhou on 4 November.[20]

Last-minute pressure to attend to other matters kept Jiang Jieshi from making this trip. In his place he sent Gu Zhutong and Guo Rugui. Gu and Guo flew to Xuzhou on 4 November, and the next morning they held a meeting with Liu Zhi, Liu's army commanders, and the corps commanders who were able to attend to discuss the overall military situation in the civil war and possible courses of action for the forces around Xuzhou. Gu wanted to know about the logistics situation and the level of combat readiness in all units. He also wanted to learn, firsthand, what the army commanders thought about the options of either defending Xuzhou or withdrawing south of the Huai.[21]

The Nationalists Decide to Defend Xuzhou

At the senior commanders' meeting on the morning of 5 November, Sun Yuanliang, commander, Sixteenth Army, believed the best option was to withdraw south of the Huai River. He pointed out that the surrounding terrain made Xuzhou hard to defend and easy to attack. He noted the exposed position of Xuzhou at the end of a long supply line. Withdrawing to the Huai River, he stated, would greatly shorten that supply line and would add a major natural obstacle to the defense's strength. Furthermore, with the Huai River before them and the region of lakes and marshes on the right, the Nationalists would be able to conduct economy-of-force operations and mass forces in places of their choosing for attacks back north.[22] Sun's advocacy of withdrawing south of the Huai may also have been related to the situation his army faced. Just a few days earlier he had been ordered to send his XCIX Corps south to Bengbu on the Huai River to add to the forces defending that city and to defend the broad area between Mencheng and Guoyang with only two corps.[23]

Li Mi, commander, Thirteenth Army, agreed with Sun's suggestion that the Nationalist armies withdraw south of the Huai.[24] However, Qiu Qingquan, commander, Second Army, and Huang Baitao, commander, Seventh Army, both argued strongly for defending Xuzhou. Qiu did not think the logistics situation was a problem. He pointed out that Xuzhou could receive supplies by rail, road, and air and that large stockpiles of food and ammunition were already there. He also thought the extensive network of fortifications that had been constructed in and around the city made it possible to mount an effective defense.[25] Because Qiu and Huang commanded the two most powerful armies under the Xuzhou Bandit Suppression Headquarters, their views carried more weight than Sun's and Li's. Most important, after the four army commanders had spoken, Gu Zhutong informed them that Jiang Jieshi wanted to defend Xuzhou. This settled the matter and from that point on the meeting focused on how to redeploy forces to achieve that objective.[26]

The plan for defending Xuzhou and the area between Xuzhou and Bengbu that they developed was similar to the deployment plan He Yingqin and Gu Zhutong proposed on 29 October. However, the center of mass of the Nationalist forces was to be farther north. Instead of leaving only one or two reinforced corps inside Xuzhou and deploying the rest of the forces to the south along the Xu-Beng railroad, the new plan envisaged holding a line blocking possible avenues of approach to the city from the north, west, and east. To the northeast the Third Pacification Area force was to remain in place and defend the area along the Grand Canal from Weishan Lake east to Taierzhuang. Southeast of Taierzhuang the Seventh Army was to establish a defensive line along the west bank of the Grand Canal as far south as Suqian where it would link up with First Pacification Area forces operating out of Huaiyin.

This meant that all cities along the Long-Hai railroad east of the Grand Canal, including Haizhou and the port of Lianyungang were to be abandoned. The Thirteenth Army was to move south to the Lingbi-Sixian area to provide depth to the Grand Canal defensive line and security for lines of communication. West of Xuzhou the Second Army was to abandon all cities west of Dangshan and control the area running north from Weishan Lake, through Dangshan, and south to Yongcheng. South of the Second Army, the Sixteenth Army was to operate out of Mengcheng to control the area from Yongcheng to the Huai River. The Fourth Pacification Area force that had by now reached Bengbu was to move east of the city and provide security in the Huaiguan area. The Eighth Pacification Area, which up to this time had been responsible for security around Huaiguan, was to be deactivated and its units attached to the Fourth Pacification Area. The Ninth Pacification Area force at Haizhou was to be evacuated by sea from Lianyungang.[27]

After this plan was agreed to, Gu Zhutong told Liu Zhi and the army commanders that they did not need to wait for an official order but could start to execute the plan immediately. Liu Zhi, however, said that he wanted an order in hand before he directed the armies to act. Gu assured Liu that such an order would be issued from Nanjing later in the day. Gu departed Xuzhou around 1400, 5 November, and as he had promised, the orders were issued that evening. There was, however, one very important change. After returning to Nanjing, Gu learned from the Army Logistics Command that no ships were currently available to evacuate the Ninth Pacification Area's XLIV Corps from the port of Lianyungang. As a result, the orders that were issued directed this corps to move west by land to Xuzhou.[28]

On 6 November Nationalist units began to redeploy. East of Xuzhou the XLIV Corps hurriedly marched out of Haizhou on its way to Xinanzhen. West of Xuzhou the Second Army abandoned Shangqiu. However, the redeployment would not be completed as planned. Just as the Nationalist forces were beginning to move toward new locations the Communists were starting to advance into positions to launch their offensive. Upon learning that Nationalist forces were abandoning many outposts and bases and were starting to shift forces toward Xuzhou and areas to the south, the Communist command ordered all units to begin their attacks as quickly as possible. Soon the two armies were locked in combat, and a very fluid battlefield situation developed. This rapidly changing situation quickly brought many new challenges to the commanders on both sides. It also provided additional opportunities for them to practice operational art.

Notes

1. *Zhongguo renmin jiefangjun zhanshi* [A History of the Chinese People's Liberation Army's Wars], Mo Yang and Yao Jie, eds. (Beijing: Junshi kexue chubanshe, 1987), vol. 3, 234.

2. Du Yuming, "*Huaihai zhanyi shimo*" [The Huai Hai Campaign From Beginning to End] in *Huaihai zhanyi qinli ji* [A Record of Personal Experiences During the Huai Hai Campaign], Zhongguo renmin zhengzhi xieshang huiyi quanguo weiyuanhui wenshi ziliao yanjiu weiyuanhui [The Historical Materials Research Committee of the National Committee of the Chinese People's Political Consultative Conference], eds. (Beijing: Wenshi ziliao chubanshe, 1983), 3, hereafter cited as *QLJ*.

3. Sanjun daxue zhanshi bianzuan weiyuan hui [Armed Forces University's Committee for Compiling War Histories], *Guojun kanluan zhanshi Xu-Beng huizhan zhi bu* [The Xu-Beng Campaign Portion of the History of the National Army's War to Suppress Rebellion], (Taibei: Sanjun daxue, n.d.), 12.

4. Du Yuming, 7.

5. Ibid.

6. Ibid.

7. Ibid., 8.

8. Ibid.

9. Guo Rugui, "*Huaihai zhanyi zhong wo suo zhidao de Jiangjun guanjianxing juece*" [What I Know About Key Strategic Decisions Made by Jiang's Military During the Huai Hai Campaign], *Junshi lishi* [Military History], 1988, No. 6, 32.

10. Ibid.

11. Ibid. This plan is also discussed in Du Yuming, 10.

12. Ibid., 33.

13. Ibid., 32-33.

14. Ibid.

15. Ibid., 33.

16. Tan Geming, "*Guixi zai Huaihai zhanyi zhong de taidu ji Bai Chongxi "bei zhan qiu he" yinmou de huanmie*" [The Attitude of the Guangxi Clique During the Huai Hai Campaign and the End of Bai Chongxi's Scheme of 'Preparing for War While Asking for Peace'], *QLJ*, 126-27.

17. Guo Rugui, 33.

18. Du Yuming, 8.

19. Li Yikuang, "*Huaihai zhanyi guomindangjun bei jian gaishu*" [A General Account of the Destruction of the Nationalist Army During the Huai Hai Campaign], *QLJ*, 63.

20. Guo Rugui, "*Huaihai zhanyi qijian guomindangjun tongshuaibu de zhengchao he juece*" [Wrangling and Decision Making Within the Nationalist High Command During the Time of the Huai Hai Campaign], *QLJ*, 55.

21. Zhou Kaicheng, "*Huaihai zhanyi zhong de di bajun*" [The VIII Corps in the Huai Hai Campaign], *QLJ*, 243.

22. Ibid.

23. Hu Lincong, "*Di sishiyijun gongji shoucuo yu tuwei wajie*" [The Failure of the XLI Corps' Attack and the Collapse of the Breakout Attempt], *QLJ*, 431-32.

24. Zhou Kaicheng.
25. Ibid.
26. Ibid.
27. Guo Rugui, "*Huaihai zhanyi zhong wo suo zhidao de Jiangjun guanjianxing juece,*" 33.
28. Ibid., 33-34.

Chapter Four

The Physical Setting of the Huai Hai Campaign and a Comparison of the Opposing Forces

To gauge the outcome of a war, consider it in terms of the following five factors and compare the strengths of the two sides. The first of the five factors is the moral stature of the ruler, the second is weather, the third is the terrain, the fourth is command, and the fifth is regulations.
—Sunzi, The Art of War

Unquestionably, victory or defeat in war is determined mainly by the military, political, economic and natural conditions on both sides. But not by these alone. It is also determined by each side's subjective ability in directing the war. In his endeavour to win a war, a military man cannot overstep the limitations imposed by the material conditions; within these limitations, however, he can and must strive for victory. The stage of action for a military man is built upon objective material conditions, but on that stage he can direct the performance of many a drama, full of sound and colour, power and grandeur.
—Mao Zedong, Problems of Strategy in China's Revolutionary War

Operational art, if practiced well, can indeed be, to repeat a portion of the quote above from Mao Zedong, "full of sound and colour, power, and grandeur."[1] A successful operational commander may be likened to a performing virtuoso. But as Mao notes, the operational commander performs on a stage formed by objective material conditions. Those conditions may restrain an operational commander, but they can also create opportunities. This is where the commander's subjective ability—his knowledge, understanding, instincts, intuition, will, and determination—come into play. Using the instruments at hand, he must work within the framework set by objective reality to fashion a path to victory.

The Physical Environment of the Huai Hai Campaign Area

A significant part of the objective reality operational commanders faced is what the 1993 edition of FM 100-5 describes as "the four major physical elements of the environment of operations . . . [namely,] geography, terrain, weather, and infrastructure."[2] These elements play an important role in military operations by affecting the time needed to carry out virtually every type of activity. They can shape movement and maneuver, strengthen defenses, or facilitate offensive action. In the words of FM 100-5, "they form an important component of the planning tool METT-T . . . and must be considered in operations planning."[3]

In broad geographic terms, the Huai Hai Campaign was fought on the southeastern part of the great alluvial plain formed by the Yellow River. The area of operations was large, stretching from Haizhou in the east to Shangqiu in the west and from Zaozhuang in the north to Bengbu in the south. This region was densely populated with most of the people living in small rural villages and working the land. The area was intensely cultivated; the major crops were wheat, corn, gaoliang (Chinese sorghum), and soybeans. At the time of the campaign, the houses were generally constructed of dried adobe bricks and had roofs made from gaoliang stalks and leaves. The villages were surrounded by earthen walls 6 to 9 feet high that were constructed to provide protection from periodic flooding. The dirt used in these walls was dug from the ground beyond them. Due to the high water table, this excavated area would fill with water, creating a moat effect. In larger towns, some buildings and the surrounding walls were constructed of more substantial material, including fired brick and stone. During the campaign, villages and towns were important militarily because their walls and moats provided ready-made defensive positions and their houses provided valuable shelter against the elements.

The climate of the Huai Hai Campaign area is a combination of continental and maritime. A summer monsoon prevails from May through July and brings with it moist, warm air masses. During the winter the Siberian High brings in cold, continental weather. The mean July temperature is 80 degrees Fahrenheit (F), and the mean January temperature is 30 degrees (F). The mean annual precipitation across the campaign area varies from 31 inches in the north to 37 inches in the south. On the average, more than 50 percent of the precipitation falls during June, July, and August.

As noted, the Huai Hai Campaign was fought predominantly on an alluvial plain. However, in the north central portion of the campaign area there is an area of hills that extends south from the higher mountains in Shandong province to an east-west line running roughly from Suining to Fuliji. These hills generally have steep slopes and often rise dramatically from the surrounding plain to heights of several hundred feet. They do not, however, form a unified mass of elevated terrain. Instead, they rise here and there from the flat surface of the plain, looking almost as if they were still the islands they once were in an ancient sea long since filled in with Yellow River alluvium. One significant gap in the hills was once the old course of the Yellow River when the river flowed through Xuzhou, Shuanggou, and Gupi on its way to the Yellow Sea. The other major gap is the Hanzhuang-Taierzhuang corridor of the Grand Canal east of Weishan Lake. Within this area of hills, the largest contiguous area of elevated terrain lies southwest of Xuzhou. Between Xuzhou and Fuliji several hills reach more than 1,000 feet in height, and the high ground between them forms a significant terrain feature.

The most prominent terrain of the area, however, is the east China plain. The plain is nearly level with an almost imperceptible gradient of increasing elevation going from east to west. Hongze Lake, the large lake southeast of the campaign area, is only 5 meters above sea level, and at Guzhen and Bengbu, 280 km from the seacoast, the elevation is only 20 meters. A report on Chinese geography the US Far East Command prepared in December 1947 noted that basically the entire plain south of a line from Haizhou through Suxian to Fuyang was poorly drained with ditches, canals, and small rivers creating serious barriers to movement.[4]

The transportation infrastructure, or lack of it, was another important feature of the Huai Hai Campaign's physical environment. Large towns were connected by improved roads, but the improvements consisted of nothing more than grading and rolling the natural earth. If pebbles were available, they were added and pounded into the road surface. In some cases, clay was then poured on top of the stones to bind and level the surface. Due to poor drainage, roads were often weakened by water seeping under them from neighboring fields. Heavy rains also took a toll. Four days of clear weather might be required after a heavy rain before normal vehicular traffic could resume. Road maintenance in poorly drained areas was especially difficult because gravel, timber, and crushed rock were not available locally.[5]

The poor quality of the roads made the two rail lines in the area very important. The Long-Hai railroad ran from the seaport of Lianyungang on the east through Xuzhou to Gansu province on the west. The Jin-Pu railroad ran from Tianjin in the north to Pukou, a town on the north bank of the Yangzi River opposite Nanjing, in the south. The two lines crossed at Xuzhou, and consequently this city was a major railroad center. When the Huai Hai Campaign began, the Long-Hai railroad west of Shangqiu and the Jin-Pu railroad north of Xuecheng were under Communist control, with the rest of the two lines under Nationalist control. The railroads were at the heart of the Nationalists' strategy. They had relied on railroads to establish a mobility advantage over the Communists in 1946 and 1947. Rail transportation was the backbone of their logistics system and a key element in their plans to respond effectively to Communist moves and regain the initiative.

The only modern airfield within the campaign area was in Xuzhou. It was an important air base and transportation link for the Nationalists during the first three weeks of the campaign, but it was abandoned on 30 November. After that, Nationalist aircraft had to operate out of the airfield at Nanjing. The primary port for the campaign area was Nanjing. Lianyungang, the seaport at the east terminus of the Long-Hai railroad, might have played a role in the campaign if the Nationalists had had more shipping and more reserves to deploy to that area, but the Nationalists abandoned it on the eve of the Communist offensive.

Weaknesses in the transportation infrastructure caused more problems for the Nationalists than for the Communists. One reason for this was that the Communists relied more heavily on human and animal muscle power than on mechanical power for movement. This was true for moving both soldiers and supplies. Communist commanders took pride in their troops' ability to move across country. Human porters did not need prepared roads, railroads, or airfields to transport food and ammunition. The fixed transportation infrastructure the Nationalists relied on was vulnerable to attack and destruction. Communist attacks damaged roads and railroads, and with few alternative routes to use, the Nationalist forces' ability to generate combat power was soon affected. On the other hand, the long lines of peasants carrying rice on their backs or pushing wheelbarrows filled with artillery shells that the Communists organized could not be interdicted with the means that were available to the Nationalists. Their routes and destinations could also be changed with ease.

Comparing Nationalist and Communist Political and Economic Strengths

A comprehensive comparison of the Nationalists' and Communists' political and economic strength is far beyond the scope of this work. Those interested in this aspect of the war can refer to such books as *Civil War in China: The Political Struggle 1945-1949* by Suzanne Pepper. Suffice it to say here that at the time of the Huai Hai Campaign the Nationalists were suffering because they had failed to fully mobilize the resources that were potentially available to them, and they were not effectively using the resources they had already mobilized in their fight against the Communists. The Communists, however, were reaping the benefits of their efforts to tightly organize areas under their control and mobilize all possible human and materiel resources to support the armed struggle.

Those attending the Nationalist strategy conference in Nanjing in August 1948 recognized the problem. Looking at the Communists they saw an organizational structure that ensured that the party, government, and army were a unified whole working for a common purpose. They themselves, in contrast, had been approaching "eradicating the bandits" as simply a matter of building military strength and conducting military operations. This approach was clearly failing. The conference concluded with a call to coordinate work across the full spectrum of military, governmental, economic, political, educational, and cultural activities. Nationalist government leaders resolved to completely mobilize all human and materiel resources and unleash what they called the power of total war.[6]

Specific areas of Nationalist weakness were revealed by the changes recommended by the "Resolution on Strategic Policy" the conference adopted. There was to be full national mobilization for war. Political and military activities were to be integrated. Government organizations were to be strengthened. Government finances were to be improved by tax changes and changes in the tax collection system. Measures were to be taken to control inflation, including implementing rationing in large cities. It was particularly relevant to the politico-military situation in the Huai Hai Campaign area that north of the Yangzi River every province was to become a pacification area so there could be the closest possible coordination between political and military organizations. At the county level and below, every government organization was to be strengthened and given more authority so that it could defend and save itself.[7]

The new policies to improve economic and political conditions, mobilize popular support, and strengthen the connection between military operations and government programs might have made a difference for the Nationalists if there had been time to implement them and they had been carried out effectively. It was not possible, however, to put the measures into practice in time to reduce in any way the advantage in organization the Communists had in east central China before the start of the Huai Hai Campaign. The Communists did not have as many economic resources as the Nationalists. Despite expanding their base areas and linking many of them together, they had relatively little industrial production. They also did not have the hundreds of millions of dollars in foreign aid that the United States was giving the Nationalists. However, they compensated for these weaknesses by means of organization. During years of struggle they had forged and refined an organizational structure that enabled them to deeply tap rural China's resources. Chapter One contains a description of the thoroughness of the Chinese Communist Party's (CCP's) organizational effort. Organizations were established to connect as many people as possible to the party's voice and reach. Organizations were also set up to ensure that the military served party goals and there was unity of effort between the military and political cadres. While the Nationalists were deciding in August 1948 to organize to fight a "total war," the Communists had already long been doing that.

Figure 1 shows the Communist military and political organization from the national level down to the regional level. Regional party bureaus implemented the CCP's political, economic, and social programs in the various areas under CCP control. Within these areas there was also a military region organization responsible for defending and expanding Communist-controlled territory. Coordination between political and military activities was achieved by appointing people to serve concurrently in CCP regional bureau positions, military region positions, and field army command positions.

No better example of this phenomenon exists than Chen Yi. At the time of the Huai Hai Campaign, Chen was commander and political commissar, East China Military Region (ECMR); commander and political commissar, East China Field Army (ECFA); and assistant secretary, CCP East China Bureau. In addition, since May 1948, when the CCP Central Committee had decided to strengthen the CCP's military and political work in the Henan province area, he had served as deputy commander, Central Plains Military Region (CPMR); deputy commander, Central Plains Field Army (CPFA); and second secretary, CCP Central Plains Bureau. The multiple positions other Central Plains Bureau members held at this time, as shown in

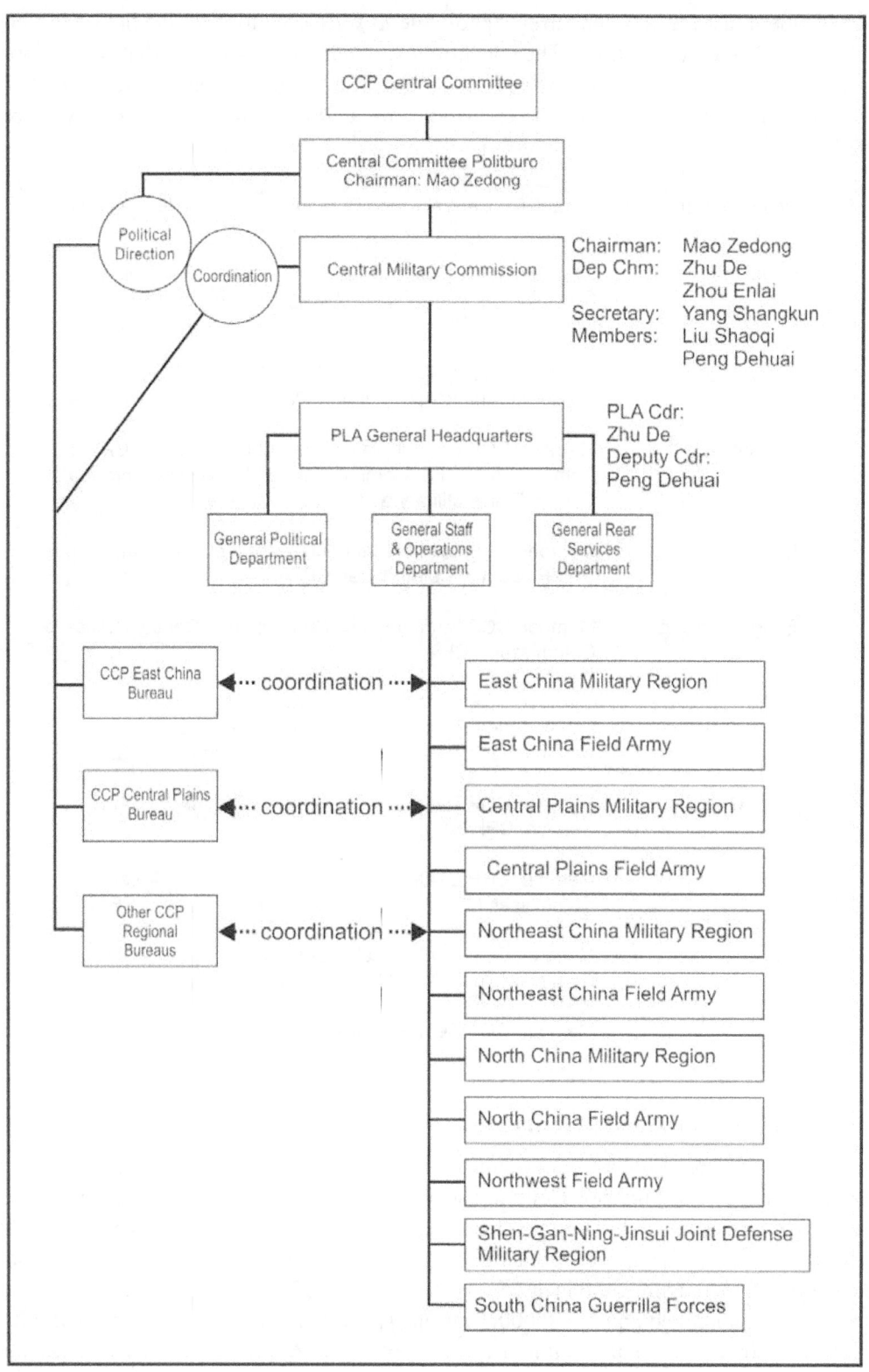

Figure 1. Communist military and political organization down to the regional level, summer-fall 1948.

table 1, further illustrate how concurrent appointments were used to forge the links between the CCP's political and military tasks. The concurrent appointments also show that well before the Huai Hai Campaign was even conceived the outline of an organizational structure that could bring east and central China's resources together to support such a large campaign already existed.

Table 1. Concurrent Appointments That CCP Central China Bureau Members Held, Summer-Fall 1948

Deng Xiaoping	First Secretary, CCP Central Plains Bureau; Political Commissar, Central Plains Military Region; Political Commissar, CPFA
Deng Zihui	Third Secretary, CP Central Plains Bureau; Deputy Political Commissar, CPMR; Deputy Political Commissar, CPFA
Liu Bocheng	Member, CCP Central Plains Bureau; Commander, CPMR; Commander, CPFA; Commandant and Political Commissar, Central Plains Military and Political College
Li Xiannian	Member, CCP Central Plains Bureau; Deputy Commander, CPMR; Deputy Commander, CPFA
Song Renqiong	Member, CCP Central Plains Bureau; Third Deputy Political Commissar, ECFA
Su Yu	Member, CCP Central Plains Bureau; Acting Commander, ECFA; Acting Political Commissar, ECFA; Deputy Commander, ECFA; Second Political Commissar, ECFA
Chen Geng	Member, CCP Central Plains Bureau; Commander, 4th Column, CPFA
Zhang Jichun	Member, CCP Central China Bureau; Deputy Political Commissar, CPMR; Deputy Political Commissar, CPFA
Tan Zhenlin	Member, CCP Central Plains Bureau; First Deputy Political Commissar, ECFA; Political Commissar, Shandong Army
Li Da	Member, CCP Central Plains Bureau; Chief of Staff, CPFA

Quantitative Comparison of Military Forces

A common theme in Chinese Communist histories of the Huai Hai Campaign is that in this campaign a numerically inferior Communist force defeated Nationalist forces that not only had a numerical advantage but enjoyed technological superiority. As far as the regular forces involved in the campaign are concerned, this is true. The ECFA's 15 infantry columns and the Special Type (ST) Column contained approximately 360,000 soldiers.[8] The CPFA's seven infantry columns contained about 150,000.[9] Various regional forces that were attached to these field armies brought the total Communist troops to around 600,000.[10] Opposing these forces the Nationalists committed approximately 800,000 troops.[11] In addition, the Nationalists had a

2-to-1 advantage in artillery, had more than 200 American M3A Stuart light tanks for at least a 10-to-1 advantage in armor, and possessed a small, modern air force that had no opposition in the air.[12] However, as explained in chapter one, the Communists had long used a three-tier structure in building military forces. All three tiers—the regular conventional forces, regional forces, and local militia —participated in the campaign. The Communist regular forces, the ECFA and CPFA, were certainly the key to winning, but the approximately 500,000 members of regional forces and local militias also made a significant contribution.[13] In addition, more than 5 million civilians were eventually mobilized to form a logistics system that sustained the regular forces in the field. Militia members and transport laborers do not show up in a simple quantitative comparison of opposing regular military forces. Their efforts, though, made a huge difference in the campaign.

The map shows the military districts and subdistricts the Communists organized in the area where the Huai Hai Campaign was fought. Their names reflect their location. The Yu (Henan)-Xi (West) district is in western Henan province. The Yu-Wan-Su district covers parts of Yu (Henan), Wan (Anhui), and Su (Jiangsu) provinces. The Ji-Lu-Yu district includes part of Ji (Hebei), Lu (Shandong), and Yu (Henan) provinces. The Lu-Zhong-Nan district is in the Zhong-Nan (central-southern) part of Lu (Shandong) province. The Jiang-Huai district is north of the Chang Jiang River (Yangzi River) and is centered on the Huai River. The Su (Jiangsu)-Bei (North) district is in the northern part of Su (Jiangsu) province. Except for the case of the Su-Bei district, the regional forces of these districts appear on the PLA organization table (see figure 2).

Figure 2 shows the ECFA and CPFA organization down to the column level. It also lists the independent divisions in each army. In the CPFA the field army headquarters exercised direct control over the columns, but in the ECFA one-half of the columns were grouped under two intermediate army commands, the Shandong army and the Subei (Northern Jiangsu) army. These titles reflected the general geographical areas where the armies had been formed and where they had operated during the previous 2 years. Su Yu's ECFA headquarters directly controlled the remaining ECFA columns.

Within the People's Liberation Army (PLA) of 1948 a column was equivalent to a US corps in terms of size and function. Columns were the largest tactical units used to conduct maneuver at the operational level. They usually contained two to three divisions and ranged in size from 20,000 to 30,000 men. A notable exception was the CPFA's 4th Column, the largest column in the Huai Hai Campaign. After the Southern Shaanxi Division was attached to this column on the eve of the campaign it contained five divisions and numbered approximately 45,000 soldiers.[14]

Generally speaking, ECFA columns were larger than the CPFA's because ECFA divisions had more men than did CPFA divisions. At this time there was no fixed size for a division in the PLA, but the PLA was moving toward establishing a standard of approximately 10,000 men each. Reflecting the fact that the ECFA had advanced farther along the path of "regularization" in organization, weaponry, and style of fighting than the CPFA, ECFA divisions were closer in strength to the 10,000-man figure than the CPFA was. On average, ECFA divisions had more than 9,000 men while CPFA divisions numbered between 7,000 and 8,000 men.

PLA divisions, as shown in figure 3, were organized on a triangular basis. Divisions had

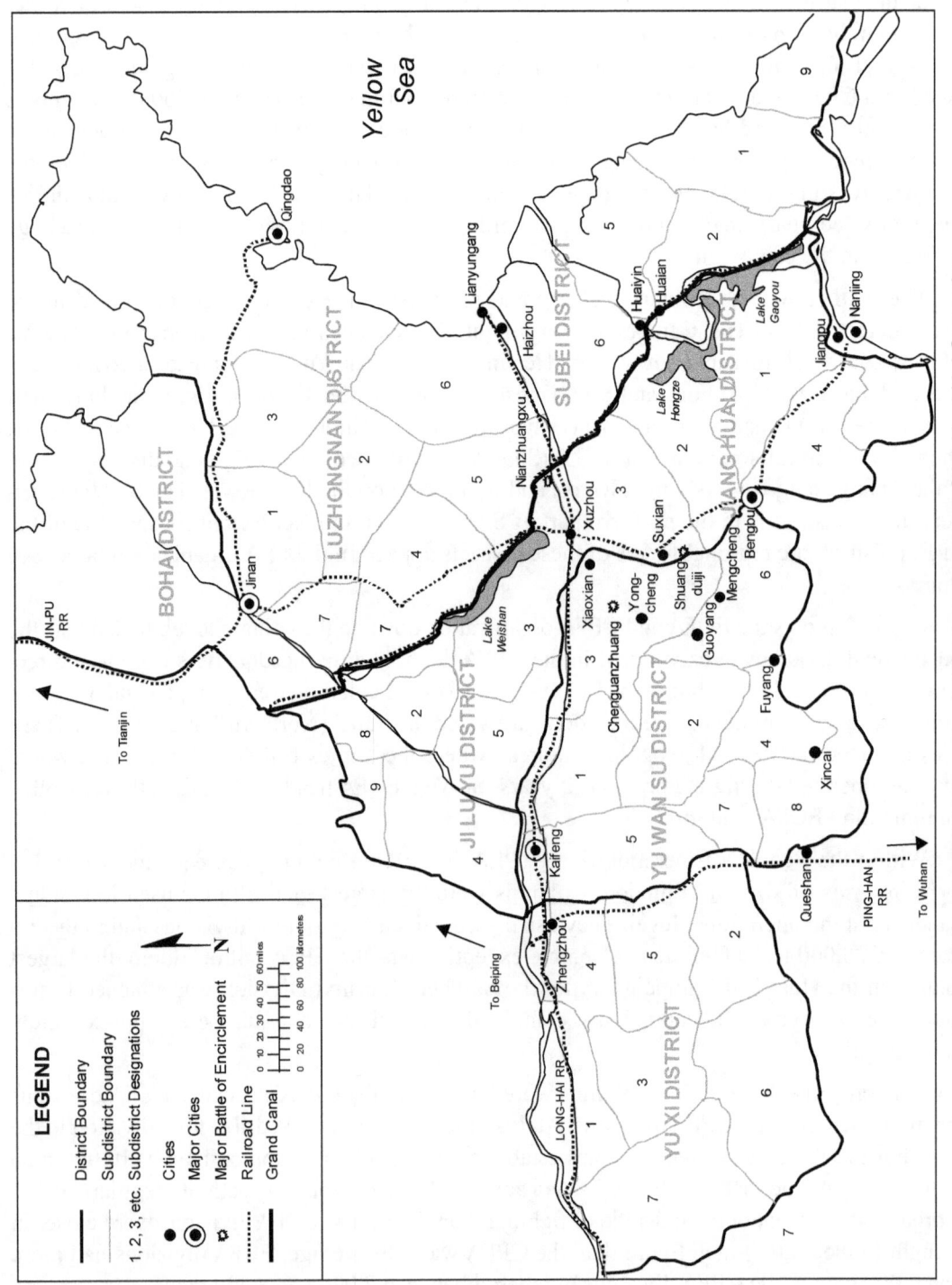

Communist military districts and subdistricts in the area of the Huai Hai Campaign.

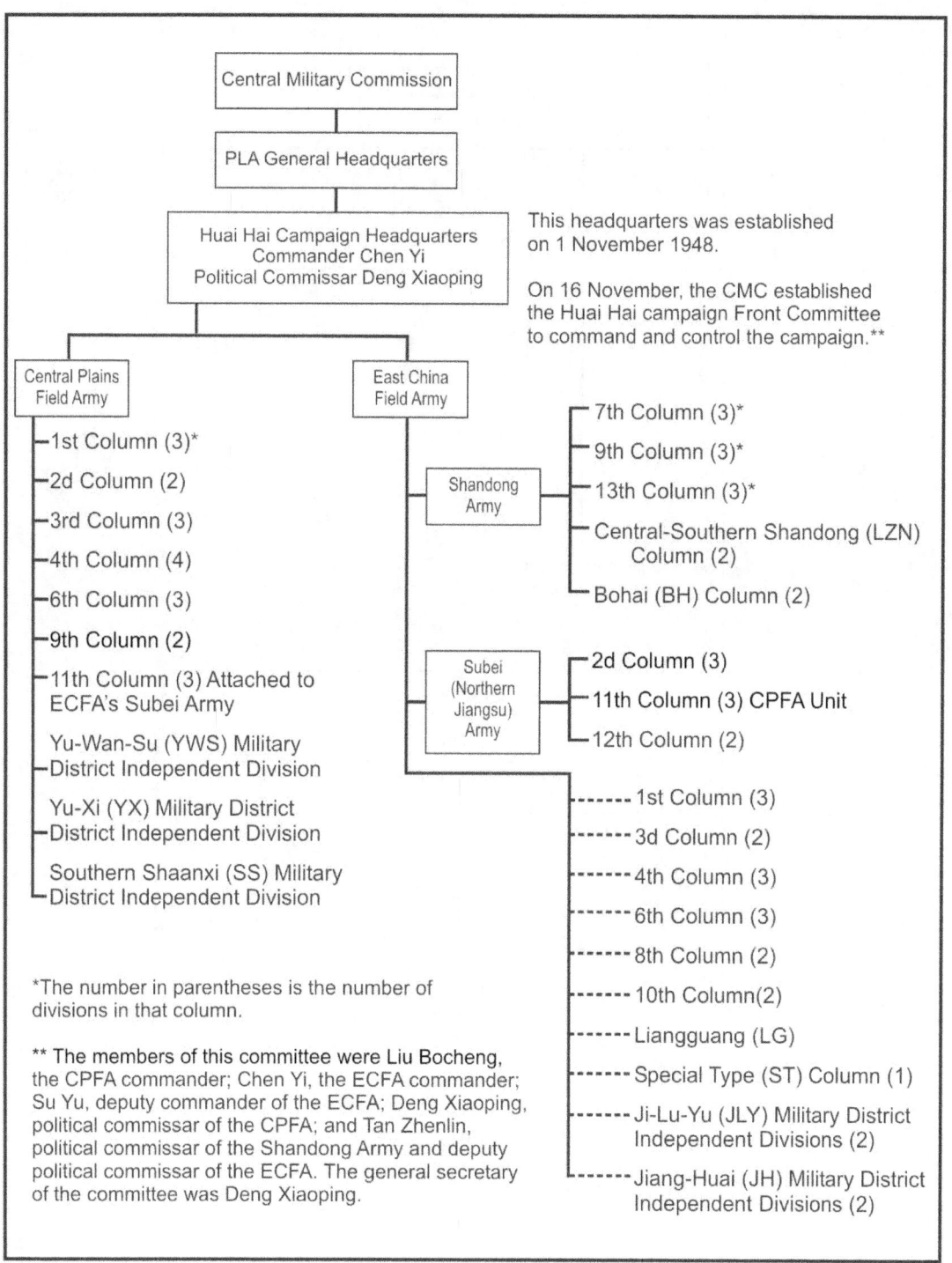

Figure 2. PLA organization for the Huai Hai Campaign.

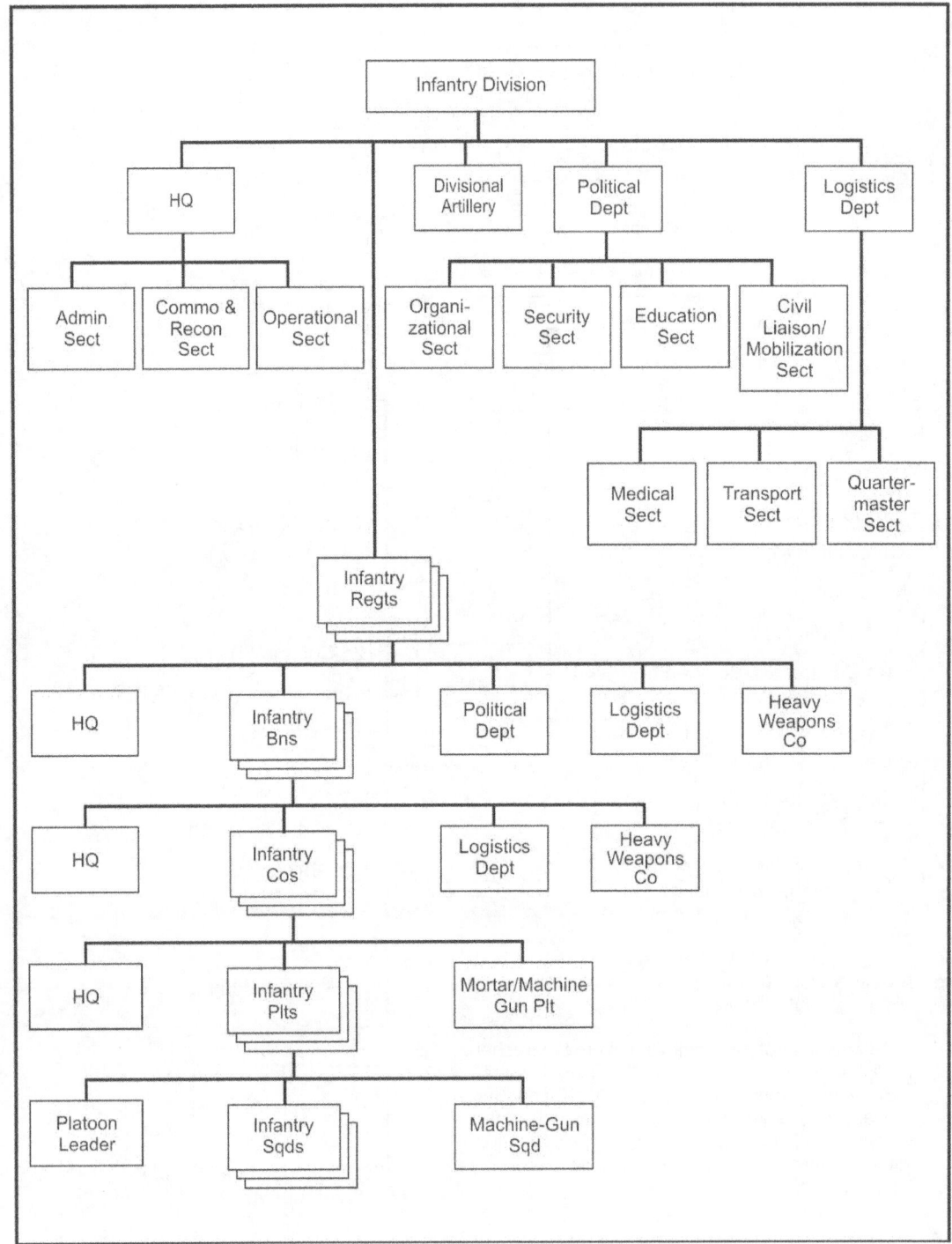

Figure 3. PLA infantry division organization, autumn 1948.

three regiments, regiments had three battalions, battalions had three companies, companies had three platoons, and platoons had three squads. At each level a separate unit provided additional firepower. Just as ECFA divisions had more soldiers than CPFA divisions, they also had greater

Table 2. ECFA Divisional Weapons

75mm Pack Howitzers	4-8
82mm Mortars	20
60mm Mortars	36
Heavy Machine Guns	36
Light Machine Guns	180
Automatic Rifles	250
Rifles	2800
Carbines	350
Pistols	130

had firepower. ECFA divisions generally had a separate artillery battalion, and CPFA divisions usually only had a separate artillery company.

Tables 2 and 3 show the weapons in hypothetical "average" CPFA and ECFA divisions at this time. Since there was no standard table of organization and equipment (TOE) for PLA divisions and even within the same field army, divisions varied in size and weaponry, the chance any one division actually possessing weapons in these exact numbers is small. However, the numbers are reasonable general estimates and illustrate two important points: they show the "lightness" of PLA divisions, and they show that the CPFA divisions' firepower was much weaker than the ECFA divisions'. On average, CPFA divisions only had two 75-millimeter (mm) pack howitzers as opposed to an average of four in an ECFA division. Also, CPFA divisions had fewer mortars and machine guns than ECFA divisions. CPFA columns did not have many artillery assets to attach to their divisions. A CPFA column was fortunate if it had a full artillery battalion with three companies and 12 guns to supplement the artillery in its divisions. There was not a single 105mm howitzer in the entire CPFA. The difference in weaponry was due, in part, to the ECFA's success in capturing the weapons of some of the Nationalist army's

Table 3. CPFA Divisional Weapons

75mm Pack Howitzers	2-4
82mm Mortars	9
60mm Mortars	12
Heavy Machine Guns	30
Light Machine Guns	150
Automatic Rifles	150
Rifles	2000
Carbines	300
Pistols	100
Explosive Launching Tube*	10 (?)

*The so-called explosive launching tube was an improvised weapon fabricated from local material. It was basically a metal cylinder approximately 70 centimeters in diameter and 70 centimeters high. It was used to shoot a 20-kilogram bundle of explosives a few hundred yards at low velocity. The weapon was highly inaccurate, but against fixed encircled forces it created important psychological as well as physical effects.

best divisions. It also reflects the residual effects of the heavy artillery losses the Liu-Deng army suffered during its August 1947 march to the Dabie Mountains.

The small amount of artillery in the CPFA meant that this field army was not well equipped to fight positional warfare. The ECFA, on the other hand, did have the firepower for positional warfare and to support frontal assaults where necessary. During 1948, divisional firepower had been increased across the board as large quantities of weapons were captured from the Nationalists. Furthermore, four ECFA columns—the 3d, 9th, 10th, and 13th—were designated as special attack columns and given additional artillery, mortars, and heavy machine guns so they could destroy fixed fortifications and successfully attack heavily defended large cities. For the 3d Column this meant each of its divisions was given two 75mm pack howitzer batteries instead of the usual one, and the column received a battery of 105mm howitzers. As part of this transformational program, these special attack columns also underwent special training in assault tactics and artillery-infantry coordination. Perhaps even more important in concentrating firepower at decisive points on the battlefield, during 1948 the ECFA was able to field several batteries of 105mm howitzers. Some of the batteries were placed under the control of Shandong army headquarters, but most were placed in the ST Column under direct ECFA command.

By the time of the Huai Hai Campaign, the ST Column, which was also known as ECFA "Artillery Headquarters," was the size of an expanded division with approximately 11,000 soldiers. It had three artillery regiments and contained the ECFA's small light tank force and a number of engineer battalions. Each of the three artillery regiments had three battalions, and every battalion had three companies with a battery of four guns in each company. Two of the regiments had 105mm howitzers, and the third had 36 Japanese 75mm guns.

Quantitatively, the Nationalists committed more regular military assets to countering the Huai Hai Campaign than the Communists began with. Because they had not matched the Communist effort to organize and mobilize the rural peasants in the region, the Nationalists did not have military or paramilitary units that were comparable to the regional forces or local militias the Communists had established. In some places, landlords and others seeking to keep their dominant positions in society and maintain order had raised anti-Communist units, but such units' ability to contribute to regular military operations was minimal. For the Nationalists, the instruments to defend the Xuzhou-Bengbu area had to be their regular professional army and their air force. On paper, this was a large, formidable looking force.

Figure 4 shows the command structure for Nationalist forces in east central China as it existed on the eve of the Huai Hai Campaign. Chief of the Supreme General Staff General Gu Zhutong provided overall unity of command acting under Commander in Chief of the Armed Forces President Jiang Jieshi authority. In the broad area around Xuzhou all Nationalist ground forces were under the command of the Xuzhou Bandit Suppression Headquarters. This headquarters had operational control over the Second, Seventh, Thirteenth, and Sixteenth Armies, the First, Third, Fourth, and Ninth Pacification Areas, two independent corps, railroad protection troops headquartered in Suxian, and several independent regiments located in Xuzhou. However, this headquarters did not control the Twelfth Army that was about to begin moving from Queshan toward Xuzhou. That army was under the direct command of the Army Supreme Command in Nanjing and would remain under its control during the campaign. Also, The Xuzhou Bandit Suppression Headquarters did not control the Chinese air force units stationed in Xuzhou. They were under the command of Air Force Headquarters in Nanjing.

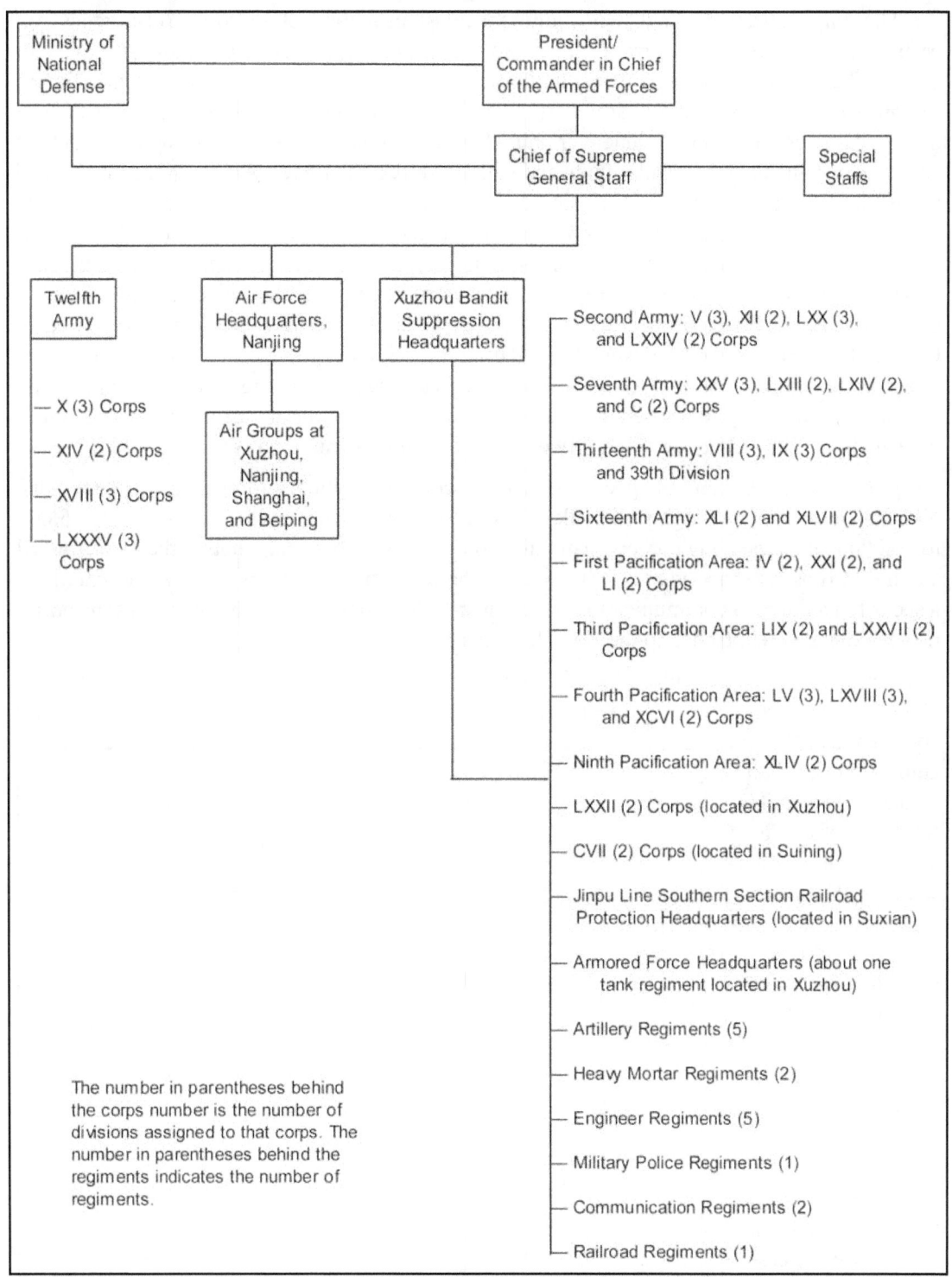

Figure 4. Nationalist military organization during the Huai Hai Campaign.

The Nationalist army had two traditional missions—conducting counterinsurgency operations against irregular guerrilla forces and destroying large mobile Communist maneuver forces. These missions were reflected in the two types of large units under the Xuzhou Bandit Suppression Headquarters. The armies were designed to conduct offensive operations against the regular large Communist maneuver units. Pacification area forces were designed to defend areas against attacks by irregular units and small-size regular forces. Although the armies and the pacification areas were roughly similar in size and organization, they were significantly different. The armies were made up of units the central government raised and trained. Their weapons and training were the best in the Nationalist army. Pacification area forces, on the other hand, had generally not been formed by the central government but were created originally by one of China's regional warlords. The Third Pacification Area, for example, had its roots in General Feng Yuxiang's Northwest Army. Differences in background and fighting ability between army and pacification area units sometimes led to tension among their commanders and hampered their ability to cooperate. The officers in the armies felt the pacification area forces were definitely less effective than army units at generating combat power.

In both the armies and the pacification areas, corps were the next lower subordinate units. Nationalist corps were roughly equivalent in size to Communist columns, ranging from 25,000 to 40,000 men, depending on how many divisions were attached and whether they were at full strength. Corps also had their own assets. In the better Nationalist corps, an engineer battalion, a security battalion, a communication battalion, a 105mm howitzer battalion, and a transportation regiment were attached to the corps headquarters.

Nationalist divisions, like PLA divisions, were organized on a triangular basis. In early 1948 the size of a Nationalist division was set at 14,488.[15] However, in August the military conference in Nanjing authorized a change in the divisional TOE for Nationalist infantry divisions (all divisions were infantry divisions) that reduced the standard size of divisions to 10,445. How far this reorganization had proceeded, division by division, by the time of the Huai Hai Campaign is unclear. However, given the problems that the Nationalist army was having finding replacements for battle casualties, this change in the TOE certainly brought the TOE closer to the

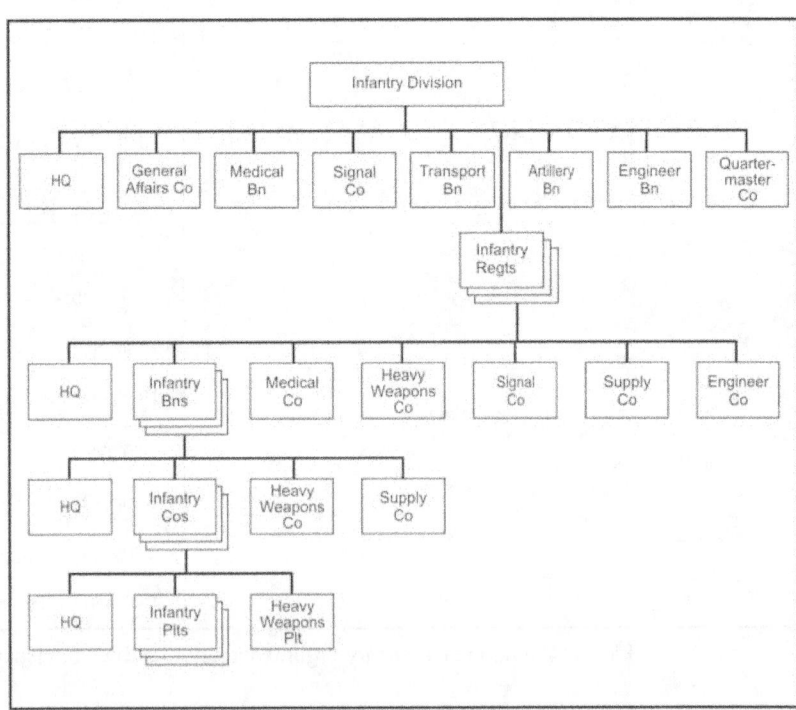

Figure 5. Nationalist infantry division organization, autumn 1948.

manpower situation as it existed in the field. Figure 5 shows the organizational structure for the smaller division that was adopted in August 1948.

Nationalist divisions, on average, had greater firepower than PLA divisions. Weapons in a division with 10,000 soldiers would probably have been close to the numbers shown in table 4. The divisional TOE in early 1948 called for a four-gun 75mm pack howitzer company in each of the three infantry regiments. Each regiment was to have a 4.2-inch mortar company with eight mortars. The TOE adopted in August consolidated the three regimental artillery companies into a regimental artillery battalion and dropped the 4.2-inch mortar company. Given the other TOE changes for divisions decided on at this time and the general reduction of division size that was occurring, the actual type and number of weapons in any given division in early November are uncertain. In some cases, at least, divisions still had three artillery companies and a 4.2-inch mortar company.

At corps level the Nationalists had additional firepower assets. Usually this consisted of an artillery battalion containing three artillery companies equipped with four 75mm pack howitzers each and a 4.2-inch mortar company with eight mortars. In the best corps—V and XII Corps, Second Army; XVIII Corps, Twelfth Army; and VIII Corps, Thirteenth Army—the artillery battalion was equipped with 105mm howitzers.

Nationalist army-level headquarters usually did not directly control their artillery units. They generally only had a security battalion and a communication battalion attached to them. However, it is worth noting that at the beginning of the Huai Hai Campaign Seventh Army headquarters had two artillery battalions and an engineer battalion attached.[16]

In early November, as shown on figure 4, the Xuzhou Bandit Suppression Headquarters (Army Group Headquarters) theoretically had direct control over a large number of units. These units included the LXXII Corps plus armor, artillery, 4.2-inch mortar, military police, engineer, communications, and railroad regiments. However, except for the troops needed to maintain communication with the various army headquarters and provide security, almost all of these regiments had already been parceled out to the armies around Xuzhou. Only the LXXII Corps and the armored regiment were readily available to provide additional firepower where they might be needed.

In addition to the firepower available from artillery in every division, several American-trained and -equipped divisions also had an organic tank battalion with 18 light Stuart tanks.

Table 4. Nationalist Army Divisional Weapons

Weapon	Count
75mm Pack Howitzers	8
4.2inch Mortars	4
82mm Mortars	27
60mm Mortars	54
Heavy Machine Guns	54
Light Machine Guns	285
Automatic Rifles	250
Rifles	3100
Carbines	600
Pistols	450

These tanks mounted a 37mm main gun and three 30-caliber machine guns. The Nationalists employed these tanks in an infantry support role where their protected firepower proved effective against the lightly armed PLA infantry. The tank regiment in Xuzhou had 60 to 80 operational tanks, and later in the campaign the Nationalists committed as many as 80 more tanks to the fighting on the southern front north of the Huai River.

The Nationalist air force could also bring firepower to the battlefield. It was the most modern of China's three military services, having received a large amount of American assistance during World War II. Table 5 shows that at the start of the campaign the Nationalists could put 80 fighters, 40 bombers, and 40 transports into the air around Xuzhou.[17]

Qualitative Comparison of Military Forces

The quantitative comparison of Communist and Nationalist forces already presented shows that both sides possessed the potential for generating significant combat power, or what FM 3-0 defines as "the ability to fight."[18] However, having potential means little unless that potential is realized when called for on the battlefield. Only when the potential capabilities of the military assets available actually become destructive or disruptive force do those assets have value. Then those assets become the means for reducing enemy combat power, eventually to the point at which the enemy is either destroyed or forced to surrender.

FM 3-0 describes the process by which military assets become combat power as a matter of combining and applying what it calls the elements of combat power. These elements are maneuver, firepower, leadership, protection, and information.[19] They are the building blocks that commanders use to produce desired effects—developing a destructive force and reducing the enemy's ability to fight. The quantitative comparison of Communist and Nationalist forces shows that the Nationalist army possessed substantial potential for generating combat power and that the Communists had some significant weaknesses. This qualitative comparison looks at the two sides in terms of where they stood regarding the five elements of combat power and provides a basis for understanding why, as the Huai Hai Campaign developed, the Nationalists failed to do better and the Communists were so successful.

Firepower is one element of combat power in which the Nationalists had an advantage in both capability and in application during much of the campaign. The quantitative comparison of available weapons to both sides on the eve of the campaign showed the Nationalists' superior potential to generate destructive force. They had more artillery, more armor, more and heavier mortars, and an air force. However, the amount of armor available was not sufficient to have a significant effect across such a broad campaign area. Dispersing tanks to support infantry operations further lessened their impact. The lack of an overall joint command within the theater of operations hindered the air force's ability to contribute firepower. As shown in table 5, Nationalist air assets in Xuzhou were not under the command of the Xuzhou Bandit Suppression Headquarters, making it difficult to coordinate ground and air operations. Furthermore, poor communication links between aircraft and ground units and a lack of training in close air support made it difficult for the air force to contribute effectively to ground combat. Despite such problems, at certain times and in certain places the Nationalists were able to use their advantage in weaponry to dominate the Communist forces. However, due to weaknesses in the other elements of combat power, that dominance was localized and transitory. As the campaign developed, because the Communists were able to maneuver and concentrate their fewer artil-

Table 5. Nationalist Aircraft Available for Use During the Huai Hai Campaign

Type of Aircraft	Air Base	Model	Number
Fighters	Xuzhou	P-51	41
Fighters	Nanjing	P-51	16
Fighters	Nanjing	P-47	16
Fighters	Unspecified	P-51 and P-47	20
Bombers	Xuzhou	B-25	5
Bombers	Xuzhou/Nanjing	B-26	27
Bombers	Nanjing/Shanghai/Beiping	B-24	18
Reconnaissance	Nanjing	F-5	3
Reconnaissance	Nanjing	F-10	1
Transport	Nanjing	C-46	30
Transport	Nanjing	C-47	10

Source: *Xubeng huizhan zhi bu* [The Xu-Beng Battle Section], Sanjun daxue zhanshi bianzuan weiyuanhui [The Armed Forces University War History Compilation Committee], ed. (Taibei: Sanjun daxue, n.d.), 5-6.

lery assets, in the final phase of every major battle they had the advantage in firepower.

Firepower and maneuver complement each other. According to FM 3-0, "Firepower magnifies the effects of maneuver by destroying enemy forces and restricting his ability to counter friendly actions; maneuver creates the conditions for the effective use of firepower."[20] During the Huai Hai Campaign the Communists used maneuver to bring their firepower to bear on the Nationalists. They also used maneuver to create conditions that diminished the Nationalist artillery's effectiveness.

Looking at the maneuver element of combat power, here, too, the Nationalists had certain assets that gave them significant maneuver potential. The Nationalists could use the Jin-Pu railroad and the Long-Hai railroad to quickly move troops, equipment, and supplies from place to place along the railroad. The Nationalist army was also more motorized and more mechanized than the PLA. Furthermore, the Nationalist air force had the potential to airlift limited numbers of troops and supplies over great distances quickly and to add firepower rapidly to any battlefield.

In actuality, however, these potential areas of advantage in maneuver meant little. Relying on railroads for logistics support created areas of obvious vulnerability that had to be defended and restricted options for maneuver. Moving mechanized and motorized units was difficult in an area with a poor road network. Lack of airfields limited air support, both for attacking Communist forces and for transporting men and materiel. In addition, the Nationalist army had a weak intelligence-gathering capability, did not fight well at night, had developed a defensive mind-set, and suffered from an overcentralized command structure. Too many matters had to be referred to the Supreme General Staff in Nanjing for decision, and often action had to wait until Jiang Jieshi had examined the issue and passed judgment. By then the benefits of a possible maneuver would have long since disappeared.

As far as the Communists were concerned, maneuver had been a centerpiece of their operational doctrine from the time the PLA was established in 1927. Inferior in size and firepower to the Nationalists since then and to the Japanese army from 1937 to 1945, the PLA relied on maneuver to protect its units and set favorable terms for its battles. In early 1928 the Red army (PLA) adopted the following maneuver-centered principles of guerrilla warfare: "The enemy advances, we retreat; the enemy camps, we harass; the enemy tires, we attack; the enemy retreats, we pursue."[21] In December 1936 Mao Zedong reminded students at the Red Army College in northern Shaanxi of the Red army's need to "oppose fixed battle lines and positional warfare and favor fluid battle lines and mobile warfare."[22] The PLA's principles of operations set forth in December 1947 continued to stress the importance of maneuver.

Su Yu's concept of operations for the Huai Hai Campaign relied heavily on maneuver. By inserting forces between Nationalist units, he sought to achieve a situation in which many of his columns were fighting on the tactical defense even as they contributed to the operational-level offense. Through maneuver, Su sought to achieve surprise, create psychological shock, build and maintain momentum, occupy advantageous positions, and gain moral dominance. Su believed that rapid, deep maneuver would soon create a situation on the ground that would ensure the Seventh Army was destroyed. Firepower was not the critical piece in achieving that situation. In keeping with Sunzi's admonition to avoid places where the enemy is strong and attack into voids, Su Yu ordered his commanders not to become involved in fighting that would slow their advance but to keep their forces flowing forward until all Seventh Army units were encircled.

To implement Su Yu's vision, campaign planning and preparation paid close attention to setting the pieces of the maneuver puzzle in place. An effective intelligence-gathering network provided detailed information on Nationalist troop dispositions and probable future action. Based on this intelligence, Su Yu stealthily concentrated his columns and moved them forward to locations that gave the PLA a positional advantage before the campaign began. High-ranking commanders met to discuss the problems of command, control, and communications that might arise in an operation of this scale. Chains of command were laid out clearly to facilitate coordination. The need for boldness, flexibility, and speed was emphasized. Perhaps most important, a large integrated logistics system capable of supporting operational-level maneuver was created.

To the 500,000 civilians mobilized to move supplies for the Jinan Campaign, 600,000 more were added. 142,000 of these laborers were assigned to move with the troops.[23] After the campaign began and the decision was made to expand the scale of operations, the system became even larger. Eventually, as shown in table 6, more than five million men served as laborers to transport materiel toward the front. Because the system ran primarily on human and animal muscle power it was slow, but it was also flexible. Wherever the fighting forces went, supply porters soon followed using canals, roads, rivers, cart trails, and even footpaths to bring supplies forward. The supply system's foot mobility complemented the PLA's foot mobility and enhanced its ability to maneuver across country. In the end, the Communist logistics system's ability to sustain very large forces spread across a broad area for an extended period of time played a key role in the Communists' victory.

Protection, according to FM 3-0, is "the preservation of the fighting potential of a force so the commander can apply maximum force at the decisive time and place."[24] In this element of combat power the advantage clearly lay with the Communists. Preserving military capability for future use had long been part of the PLA's doctrine. In 1936 Mao Zedong had stated

Table 6. Selected PLA Logistics Statistics for the Entire Huai Hai Campaign

Total Civilian Laborers	5,430,000
Long-Term Laborers (accompanied the army and worked for the entire campaign)	220,000
Rear Area Laborers (left their home areas to work for more than thirty days)	1,300,000
Base Area Workers (temporary laborers who worked in or near their home areas for about 10 days)	3,910,000
Draft Animals	767,000
Boats	8,539
Trucks	257
Handcarts, Pushcarts, Wheelbarrows, and Two-Wheeled Carts Pulled by Draft Animals	881,000
Shoulder Poles	305,000
Stretchers	206,000
Total Tonnage of Grain Transported	217,380
Mortar Rounds and Artillery Shells Transported	679,943
Rifle and Machine Gun Rounds Transported	20,149,633

Source: *Huaihai zhanyi* [The Huai Hai Campaign], Zhonggong zhongyang dangshi ziliao zhengji weiyuanhui [Chinese Communist Party Central Committee's Committee for the Collection of Party Historical Material], ed., vol. 3 (Beijing: Zhonggong dangshi ziliao chubanshe, 1988), 359.

a simple formula for force protection: "Fight when you can win, move away when you can't win."[25] In 1948 the PLA's operational principles still followed this strategy by directing commanders not to fight battles if victory was not assured or if casualties were likely to be high.[26] During the planning, preparation, and execution of the Huai Hai Campaign, protecting forces was a constant consideration.

The concept of operations for the Huai Hai Campaign reflected Su Yu's concern for force protection. Maneuver was to be used to weaken the Seventh Army's ability to mount a coherent defense. The blocking force assigned the mission of keeping the battlefield isolated was to use the Grand Canal to strengthen its defenses. Columns to the northeast and northwest of Xuzhou were to maneuver to create the impression that the city was the main objective and thereby make Nationalist commanders hesitate to send a large force to relieve the Seventh Army. Strict security measures were put in place to hide ECFA movements toward the south from Nationalist agents on the ground. The effective use of concealment, cover, dispersed movement, and darkness hid the moving units and their supplies from Nationalist reconnaissance aircraft.

During the campaign the Communists continued to protect their forces by using maneuver to counter Nationalist firepower. They worked to improve infantry assault tactics and infantry-artillery coordination. They improved field fortifications. They also carried out a comprehensive program to maintain individual soldiers' morale.

The Communists worked to keep morale high by addressing soldiers' material and psychological needs. First, adequate food, clothing, and shelter and at least rudimentary medical care were provided. Second, party commissars at various levels within the CPFA and ECFA convened regular meetings to explain the importance of the war against the Nationalists and the importance of each individual's contribution to the war. Bravery in battle was recognized, and exemplary soldiers were initiated into the CCP. Hardships were shared fairly equally, and soldiers' opinions were welcomed within the framework of what was called "military democracy."[27] By building good morale, this program helped promote and maintain an offensive spirit in the army. In addition, by creating conditions that were superior to those in the Nationalist army, this program made it easier for the PLA to recruit captured Nationalist prisoners into its ranks.

The deployment of the Nationalist armies in the Xuzhou-Bengbu area on the eve of the Huai Hai Campaign was not good in terms of "protection." They were spread out along the single rail line that they relied on for supplies, which made them vulnerable to ECFA-CPFA operational-level maneuver and firepower. This disposition also placed them at a maneuver disadvantage that they did not rectify soon enough. At the tactical level, the Communists respected Nationalist combat engineers for their ability to quickly construct strong field defenses. This ability greatly complicated Communist efforts to destroy encircled Nationalist units during the campaign. However, counterbalancing this ability were Nationalist shortcomings in cross-country mobility, night fighting, and maintaining effective command and control while moving. These weaknesses enabled the Communists to isolate and encircle Nationalist forces at all levels, from companies to army groups. Once units were encircled and relief was clearly impossible, field fortifications, no matter how good, could do nothing but delay their inevitable fate.

Keeping soldiers healthy and maintaining their fighting morale was another protection area in which Nationalists were not doing well. Their primary approach to raising morale was mass oath-taking ceremonies in which officers and men swore to fight hard to defend the nation against the Communists.[28] However, the reality of repeated defeats, inadequate food, poor medical treatment, and other hardships was such that despite the oaths, morale continued to decline. Some commanders still felt confident that their superior firepower would defeat the PLA in a positional battle, and they welcomed a Communist offensive that would bring large numbers of PLA infantry within range of their guns. But, on the whole, the army's fighting spirit was low. An intelligence summary the G2 section of the US Army Advisory Group (AAG) prepared on 5 October 1948 for Major General David Barr, Chief, AAG, captured the essence of the situation:

> The morale of the Nationalist Armed Forces appears to be steadily on the descent. A major factor in the poor morale is the total absence of a decisive Nationalist victory against the Communists. The second factor in the apparent lack of "will to fight" lies in the fact that it is extremely difficult to imbue the Nationalist soldier with a determination to fight for a cause which he feels is only of remote interest to him. For example, a Cantonese soldier has little interest in forcibly removing Communist forces from North China or Manchuria. A third factor of morale is the inability of the Government to properly house, clothe, and provide medical care for the soldier. The lack of medical care for the Nationalist soldier does not appear to be deliberate but rather caused by the lack of sufficient personnel and adequate facilities. The low pay scale of the Chinese Army contributes to the low morale of the Armed Forces.[29]

The information element of combat power was also an area of Communist superiority. Sunzi states that knowing one's enemy and oneself establishes the foundation of victory. FM 3-0 notes that information "enhances leadership and magnifies the effects of maneuver, firepower, and protection."[30] The tight organizational structure the Communists established in areas under their control made it difficult for the Nationalists to obtain information about the location and movements of Communist forces. Meanwhile, the Communists were not only able to acquire that kind of information about the Nationalists from reconnaissance teams or agents on the ground, underground Communists serving in the Nationalist army provided intelligence reports on Nationalist intentions. The latter type of information was of great value as the Communists planned the campaign, but it became less important once the campaign began. As the tempo of decision making increased, the time required to transmit this type of information reduced its usefulness.

The two most damaging cases of Nationalist officers supplying intelligence about Nationalist plans and troop deployments in eastern China to the Communists involved He Jifeng and Zhang Kexia, deputy commanders, Third Pacification Area, and Guo Rugui, Chief of Operations, Defense Ministry. He Jifeng's contacts with the Communists dated back at least to spring 1938 when he had secretly visited Yenan while convalescing from a wound suffered during fighting between Feng Yuxiang's Northwest army and the Japanese.[31] Zhang's contacts were also longstanding. Both He and Zhang had been members of the CCP for several years, and before the start of the Huai Hai Campaign they used their important positions in the Third Pacification Area to supply information on Nationalist plans and troop deployments around Xuzhou to the PLA. ECFA agents regularly visited He and Zhang in their headquarters in Jiawang to pick up the latest reports on Nationalist planning and to keep them informed about ECFA intentions.[32]

Guo Rugui had also been a longtime member of the CCP, having joined in the late 1920s while serving as a company commander.[33] His position within the Defense Ministry gave him access to Nationalist planning and troop movements at the highest strategic and operational levels. Because of the time required to pass information through Communist agents in Nanjing and Shanghai, it may have taken as many as three days for Guo's reports to reach PLA headquarters.[34] This meant that his reports had little value at the tactical level, but they did give the PLA High Command valuable insights into Nationalist staff thinking and helped the PLA anticipate large-scale Nationalist movements. Even worse for the Nationalists, Guo was the chief of operations, so he could propose and advocate courses of action that, while sounding reasonable, when implemented actually placed Nationalist forces in greater danger.

The Communists held an edge over the Nationalists in two other aspects of information—military deception (offensive information operations) and psychological operations. The Communists placed great emphasis on both. Deception was a key element in the original Huai Hai Campaign plan and played an important role in encircling the Twelfth Army. Psychological operations, or what the Communists called "political work," was an integral part of Communist efforts to weaken surrounded Nationalist units and cause them to disintegrate. Hot food was set out at night as a way to tempt hungry Nationalist soldiers to surrender. Using megaphones, Communist psychological operations teams would yell for hours about the good treatment awaiting those who would give up.

The last of the five elements of combat power to be addressed is leadership. It is the most important element because it provides the purpose and the direction for using the other elements.

According to FM 3-0, "Confident, audacious, and competent leadership focuses the other elements of combat power and serves as the catalyst that creates conditions for success."[35]

As shown in Chapter One on the historical background of the Huai Hai Campaign, the PLA leaders for this campaign were indeed confident, audacious, and competent. Through years of practical experience as commanders in combat and/or years of study in military schools, they had become skilled practitioners of military science and art. They believed in themselves, in each other, and in the forces they commanded. They were ready to act boldly to create opportunities and then take advantage of them.

Nationalist army leaders on the eve of the Huai Hai Campaign were equal, if not superior, to PLA leaders in terms of professional military education. The Huangpu Military Academy and other military schools the Nationalist government established later had taught military science and theories on the art of war to a large number of Nationalist officers. Between 1928 and 1937 German military advisers had worked with the Chinese army, and many Chinese officers had gone to Germany to study. Qiu Qingquan, commander, Second Army, for example, had studied at the German Army Engineer School in 1934 and the Berlin Army Academy from 1935 to 1937.[36] After China and the United States became allies during World War II, many more officers received professional training in the extensive education and training program established with US support. As a result, there was at this time a solid base of professional knowledge in the Nationalist army.

Nationalist warfighting experience was also equivalent to that of the Communists. During the preceding two and one-half decades the army had been involved in operations almost constantly, either fighting against regional warlord armies, the Communists, or the Imperial Japanese Army. This experience included large-scale conventional campaigns and small-scale counterinsurgency operations. The army had fought in all of the many types of terrain and climatic conditions existing in China.

Despite this body of professional knowledge and experience, at the time of the Huai Hai Campaign, Nationalist army leaders left much to be desired. At the heart of the Nationalist army's leadership problems was the army's long history of factionalism. Cliques had formed around several high-ranking leaders based on common regional backgrounds, relationships established during assignments at the Huangpu Military Academy, and/or shared experiences in the field. Objectivity often fell victim to the influence of cliques and personal interests when situations were analyzed and plans were developed. Conflicting loyalties and mutual suspicions hampered efforts to achieve unity of effort. In part, the overcentralized command structure Jiang Jieshi established was an attempt to overcome the effects of factionalism, but this created other problems. It stifled local commanders' flexibility and agility, wasted time, and often resulted in useless or even harmful orders being issued. An increased fear of failure caused by Jiang's tight control made Nationalist commanders even more defensive minded and further decreased their ability to respond rapidly to changing circumstances.

Writing years after the Huai Hai Campaign, Du Yuming placed much of the blame for the Nationalist army's defeat on factionalism and an overcentralized command structure. He had especially harsh words for Jiang Jieshi's leadership style:

> Jiang Jieshi's command style was personal and autocratic. The analyses of all military situations, large and small, and the shifting of all units, large and

small, had to pass through him for decision and direction. But Jiang was personally unable to concentrate his energy and grasp the big picture. Each day he relied on just one so-called 'official briefing' to make command decisions and shift forces. Or, relying on his own 'inspiration' he would wildly issue instructions. As a result, orders reaching the front were either outdated and inappropriate or were based on his own opinions and were therefore unreasonable. If a commander at the front did not follow them he would be guilty of disobeying orders; if he did follow them he would find himself in a trap.

Within the Jiang Jieshi clique feudal factional relationships held everything back. Whenever something happened, commanders only considered their small faction and did not think about the whole. They only thought about saving themselves and were not concerned about the overall situation. As a result, in every campaign large losses occurred because small gains were pursued and strategy was always changing.[37]

In addition to being harmed by factionalism and an overcentralized command structure, Nationalist army leaders were also being hurt by the actions of disloyal officers. The damage in the area of intelligence and planning that He Jifeng, Zhang Kexia, and Guo Rogui caused was mentioned previously. The possibility of officer-led unit defections during battle also existed. Such a development would be the complete antithesis of good leadership and represented a tremendous negative burden for the Nationalist army. A series of leadership failures had already placed Nationalist forces in east central China in a precarious position. To win, or even to just survive the coming battles, those forces would have to generate all of the combat power they were capable of producing. Weaknesses in leadership, coupled with the other relative weaknesses in information, protection, and maneuver, would make that hard to do.

Notes

1. Mao Zedong, "Problems of Strategy in China's Revolutionary War," *Selected Works of Mao Tse-tung* (hereafter cited as *SWM*), vol. 1 (Peking: Foreign Languages Press, 1967), 191.

2. US Army Field Manual (FM) 100-5, *Operations* (Washington, DC: US Government Printing Office [GPO], June 1993), 14-1.

3. Ibid., 14-3.

4. General Headquarters, Far East Command, Military Intelligence Section, *Military Geography of China* (Tokyo: Far East Command, December 1947), 2.

5. Ibid., 13.

6. *Zhongguo renmin jiefangjun quanguo jiefang zhanjeng shi* [The History of the Chinese PLA's War to Liberate the Entire Country], Wang Miaosheng, ed. (Beijing: Junshi kexue chubanshe, 1997), vol. 4, 23-24, hereafter cited as *QJZS*.

7. Ibid., 24.

8. *Zhongguo renmin jiefangjun zhanshi* [A History of the Wars of the Chinese People's Liberation Army], vol. 3, Junshi kexueyuan lishi yanjibu [Historical Research Department of the Academy of Military Science], ed., (Beijing: Junshi kexue chubanshe, 1987), 267.

9. Ibid.

10. Ibid.

11. Ibid., 271. Also see *Huaihai zhanyi* [The Huai Hai Campaign] Zhonggong zhongyang dangshi ziliao zhengji weiyuanhui [Chinese Communist Party Central Committee's Committee for the Collection of Party Historical Material], ed., vol. 1 (Beijing: Zhonggong dangshi ziliao chubanshe, 1988), 3, hereafter cited as *HHZY*.

12. *Xubeng huizhan* [The Xu-Beng Campaign], Guofangbu shizhengju [History and Political Department of the Ministry of Defense], ed. (Taibei: *Guofangbu shizhengju*, [n.d.], 4. This publication by the Nationalist Ministry of Defense puts the number of Nationalist tanks at 70 and the number of Communist tanks at 42. This figure seems low on the Nationalist side and high on the Communist side. Communist sources state that they only had 22 tanks. They also claim to have captured 215 Nationalist tanks. See *HHZY*, vol. 1, 337.

13. *QJZS*, vol. 4. On page 47, regional and local militia strength for the East China Military Region is given as 312,000. On page 249, regional and local militia strength for the Central Plains Military Region is given as 210,000.

14. Liu Youguang, "*Huaihai zhanyi zhong de zhongye sizong*" [The CPFA's Fourth Column in the Huai Hai Campaign], *HHZY*, vol. 2, 127.

15. *Organizational Changes in the Chinese Army 1895-1950*, Harry H. Collier and Paul Chin-chih Lai, eds. (Taipei, Taiwan: Office of the Military Historian, 1969), 257.

16. Li Shijie, "*Huang Baitao zai nianzhuangxu zhihui mudu ji*" [A Record of What I Saw of Huang Baitao Commanding at Nianzhuangxu], in Huaihai zhanyi qinli ji [A Record of Personal Experience During the Hau Hai Campaign], Zhongguo renmin zhengzhi xieshang huiyi quanguo weiyuanhui wenshi ziliao yanjiu weiyuanhui [The Historical Materials Research Committee of the National Committee of the Chinese People's Political Consultative Conference], eds. (Beijing: Wenshi ziliao chubanshe, 1983), 186, hereafter cited as *QLJ*.

17. See note 12 for a discussion of the number of Nationalist tanks in the campaign.

18. FM 3-0, *Operations* (Washington, DC: GPO, June 2001), 4-3.

19. Ibid.

20. Ibid., 4-6.

21. Mao Zedong, "Problems of Strategy in China's Revolutionary War," *SWM*, vol. 1, 213.

22. Ibid., 199.

23. *QJZS*, vol. 4, 271.

24. FM 3-0, 4-8.

25. Mao Zedong, "Problems of Strategy in China's Revolutionary War," *SWM*, vol. 1, 241.

26. Mao Zedong, "The Present Situation and Our Tasks," *SWM*, vol. 4, 161.

27. Mao Zedong, "On the Great Victory in the Northwest and on the New Type of Ideological Education Movement in the Liberation Army," *SWM*, vol. 4, 215.

28. *Nianzhuang zhandou* [The Battle of Nianzhuang], Guofangbu shizhengju [History and Political Department of the Ministry of Defense], ed. (Taibei: Guofangbu shizhengju, 1959), 12-13.

29. G2, US Army Advisory Group. "Summary of the China (Nationalist) Situation, 5 October 1948 to Chief AAG," (Nanjing: US Army Advisory Group, October 1948), 3.

30. FM 3-0, 4-10.

31. He Jifeng, "*Yunhe qianxian qiyi*" [Revolt on the Grand Canal Frontline], *QLJ*, 134.

32. Ibid.,138.

33. *Xubeng huizhan zhi bu* [The Xu-Beng Battle Section], Sanjun daxue zhanshi bianzuan weiyuanhui [The Armed Forces University's War History Compilation Committee], eds. (Taibei: Sanjun daxue, n.d.), 99.

34. Ibid., 100.

35. FM 3-0, 4-7.

36. *Zhongguo junshi renwu cidian* [Dictionary of Chinese Military Figures], Shu Shanyu, Bao Tong, and Zhang Yuji, eds. (Beijing: Kexue jishu wenxian chubanshe, 1988), 334.

37. Du Yuming, "*Huaihai zhanyi shimo*" [The Huai Hai Campaign From Beginning to End], *QLJ*, 12.

Chapter Five

The Huai Hai Campaign Begins

Warfare, in essence, is deception.
—Sunzi, *The Art of War*

Any operational plan must seek to achieve surprise.
—FM 100-5, *Operations*, May 1986

Deliberately creating misconceptions for the enemy and the springing surprise attacks upon him are two ways—indeed two important means— of achieving superiority and seizing the initiative.
—Mao Zedong, *On Protracted War*

In chapter four of *The Art of War*, the title of which has been translated as dispositions or positions, Sunzi discusses the relative strength and the functions of the defense and offense:

> Anciently the skilful warriors first made themselves invincible and awaited the enemy's moment of vulnerability. Invincibility depends on one's self; the enemy's vulnerability on him. It follows that those skilled in war can make themselves invincible but cannot cause an enemy to be certainly vulnerable. Therefore it is said that one may know how to win, but cannot necessarily do so. Invincibility lies in the defence; the possibility of victory in the attack.
>
> Therefore the skilful commander takes up a position in which he cannot be defeated and misses no opportunity to master his enemy.[1]

On the eve of the Huai Hai Campaign both sides were acting according to these Sunzian concepts. The Communists had established positions of invincibility—their secure rear bases in Shandong, Hebei, and Henan—and were now seeking to take advantage of any Nationalist vulnerability. They were seizing an opportunity to deliver a heavy blow. Victory was to come through offensive action. The Nationalists' plan to defend the Xuzhou-Bengbu area was an attempt to create invincibility. By concentrating their forces they hoped to create a situation in which Communist vulnerabilities would appear. When that happened, they intended to launch attacks and eventually once again establish mastery over the central plains.

The Nationalists Start to Redeploy

On 6 November Nationalist units began moving to the new locations designated in the plan agreed to the preceding day. West of Xuzhou the shifting of forces proceeded smoothly except for a breakdown in communications that left the 181st Division in an exposed position at Zhanggongdian. This division, which had been one of the better divisions in Liu Ruming's Fourth Pacification Area, had been detached from his command and attached to the Second Army's LXXIV Corps when the Fourth Pacification Area was ordered on 3 November to move by rail to Bengbu.[2] The LXXIV Corps had assigned the 181st Division a rear guard mission on 5 November as it moved east to Zhanggongdian, a small town 120 km west of Xuzhou. The division remained there on 6 November as other Second Army units continued to move farther east. Late in the afternoon the CPFA 1st Column, which was approaching this area from the south as part of Chen Yi and Deng Xiaoping's plan of 5 November to attack the Fourth Pacification Area, discovered its presence. Seeing that the 181st Division was vulnerable to encirclement, on his own initiative, the 1st Column commander ordered a predawn 7 November attack on the division's outer defense perimeter to keep the division in place. During the day the ECFA 3d Column's 8th Division and the Ji-Lu-Yu Military Region divisions arrived on the scene and completely encircled the division. A coordinated attack that evening failed to penetrate into Zhanggongdian, but an attack at 1100, 8 November broke through the Nationalist defenses. After a day of house-to-house fighting, the 181st Division's last elements surrendered that evening.[3]

Other than losing the 181st Division, the Second Army was able to move toward Xuzhou without interference. CPFA and ECFA columns under Chen Yi and Deng Xiaoping's command pursued the withdrawing Nationalist forces in an effort to hold them back, but the Nationalists stayed a step ahead. The pursuit, however, did bring the Communist forces much closer to Xuzhou in a short period of time. Late on 7 November the last Second Army units pulled out of Dangshan, and during the night, elements of the ECFA 3d Column's 9th Division entered the city.[4] On 8 November the ECFA Liangguang Column, the ECFA 3d Column's 9th Division, and the CPFA 4th Column were advancing east in a line abreast toward Huangkou, a town only 50 km from Xuzhou.

East of Xuzhou, Seventh Army's situation was very different from Second Army's. Huang Biatao, commander, Seventh Army, was pleased that this redeployment had been ordered. He had been advocating a pullback to the west bank of the Grand Canal since late October. However, he knew that both space and time were working against him. As he said to his XXV Corps commander on the night of 5 November while riding his special train from Xuzhou back to Seventh Army headquarters in Xinanzhen, "It's a shame that my plan was agreed to too late. I'm afraid that we might not be able to complete our withdrawal."[5]

Huang faced a huge problem. He had to move some 100,000 soldiers and their equipment and supplies quickly over distances as great as 80 km, and the only bridge he had to cross the Grand Canal was the 175-meter-long steel bridge on the Long-Hai railroad at Yunhezhen. Before leaving Xuzhou on the evening of 5 November, he tried to improve the situation by requesting that an engineer regiment be dispatched from Xuzhou to Yunhezhen to construct a temporary second bridge. However, during the night his problems got worse. The orders calling for the Ninth Pacification Area headquarters and its XLIV Corps to evacuate from Haizhou by sea were canceled, and the force was ordered to move west by land to Xinanzhen where the XLIV Corps would be attached to the Seventh Army. This meant the Seventh Army would have to wait for the XLIV Corps and that some 20,000 more soldiers and their equipment would have to cross the Grand Canal at Yunhezhen.

After reaching Xinanzhen, Huang directed his staff and corps commanders to meet with him early on the morning of 6 November to formulate a withdrawal plan. An area around Nianzhuangxu, a small village on the Long-Hai railroad approximately 15 km west of the Grand Canal and 50 km east of Xuzhou, was designated the army assembly area, and each corps was assigned an area around this town to occupy and defend. Corps missions while en route and the sequence in which they would cross the Grand Canal were laid out. To begin moving as quickly as possible, it was agreed that only one day would be given to preparation; the first units were to be on the road no later than 0500, 7 November.[6]

According to the plan, the LXIV Corps was to move directly from the Gaoliu area to

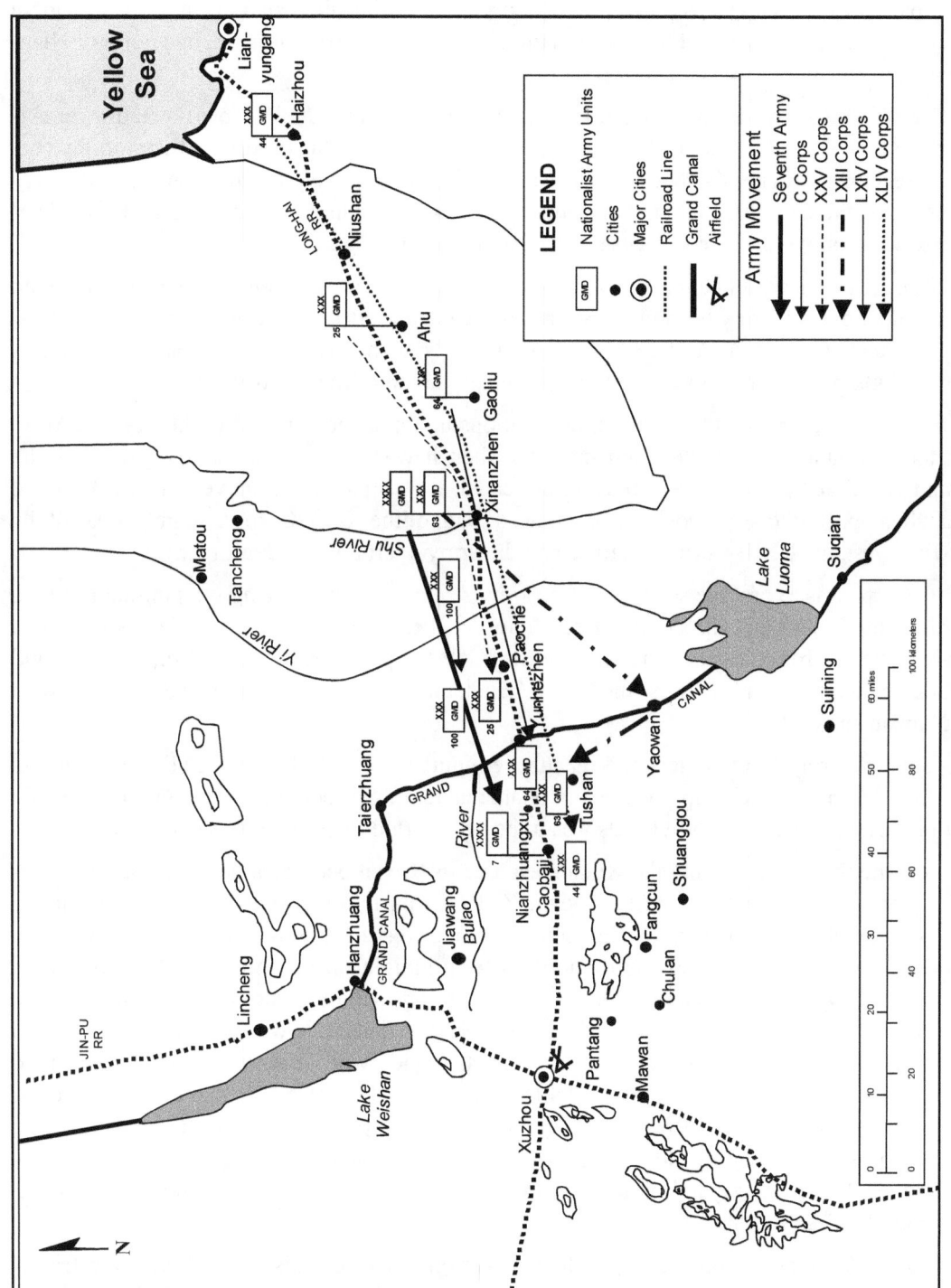

Map 1. Planned Seventh Army redeployment, 6-9 November 1948.

Yunhezhen and cross the Grand Canal. After crossing the canal it was to establish defensive positions along the west side of the canal near Yunhezhen and send a force south along the west bank of the canal to assist the LXIII Corps in crossing the canal at Yaowan. The main body of the corps was to establish itself in the villages to the east, northeast, and north of Nianzhuangxu.[7]

The XXV Corps was to send a unit to Niushan to screen the XLIV Corps' withdrawal. After the XLIV Corps had passed through Ahu, the XXV Corps was to follow it west to Paoche. Upon reaching Paoche, the XXV Corps was to take up defensive positions and coordinate a crossing of the Grand Canal at Yunhezhen with C Corps. Once across the Canal, the XXV Corps was to move into the villages northwest of Nianzhuangxu.[8]

The XLIV Corps was to move as quickly as possible from Haizhou to Xinanzhen and then follow the Seventh Army headquarters with its attached units to the Grand Canal. After crossing the canal, it was to move into the area around the Nianzhuangxu railroad station, which was 1 mile south of Nianzhuangxu, and into the villages south of the railroad.[9]

The LXIII Corps was to maintain its positions in Xinanzhen until after the Seventh Army headquarters and its units departed the city. Then it was to move southwest and cross the Grand Canal at Yaowan. After crossing the canal, the corps was to move northwest toward Nianzhuangxu and take up positions in villages south of the XLIV Corps assembly area. While moving west, the LXIII Corps was to screen the army's left flank and left rear.[10]

C Corps was to provide security on the army's right flank by moving west through an area north of the Long-Hai railroad. After reaching Paoche, it would establish a defensive screen against attacks from the north and wait for the XXV Corps. Once the XXV Corps arrived and arrangements were made to cross the Grand Canal, the C Corps was to move into villages west of Nianzhuangxu.[11]

Seventh Army headquarters and its attached units were to follow the LXIV Corps across the Grand Canal and take up positions in Nianzhuangxu. All food and ammunition that could not be carried by truck or individuals was to be transported directly to Xuzhou by train.[12]

For the four corps around the Xinanzhen area, 6 November was a day of frantic preparations. For the Ninth Pacification Area and the XLIV Corps, the conditions bordered on complete chaos. Official orders to abandon Haizhou and move west to Xuzhou did not reach the Ninth Pacification Area headquarters until shortly after midnight on the morning of 6 November, but by daybreak, the evacuation was already under way. Thousands of civilian refugees who had crowded into Haizhou from Shandong and northern Jiangsu now sought to flee to Xuzhou with the XLIV Corps. Masses of people and carts loaded with personal possessions clogged the roads and made movement slow and difficult. Still, by 1100, 6 November the XLIV Corps' last units were leaving Haizhou, and that night the corps stopped to rest just short of Ahu.[13] The XLIV Corps' main body passed through Xinanzhen late in the morning on 7 November and by nightfall had reached Wayao.[14] In two days it had covered more than 90 km, but it was still 25 km from the Grand Canal.

For Li Yannian, commander, Ninth Pacification Area, and his staff officers the trip to Xinanzhen went much faster. Traveling by jeep, they arrived at Seventh Army headquarters around 1800, 6 November. Huang Baitao had just received an urgent briefing on the military situation, and he brought Li over to the map to show him what was happening.[15] Huang was certain that the ECFA was preparing to strike at his army at any moment, and he was distressed by the options he faced. He knew he could not stand and fight at Xinanzhen because he would surely be cut off with no hope of relief. Yet, he also saw that moving west with a powerful enemy pressing against his right flank was an extremely unfavorable situation. Huang doubted that he could reach Xuzhou before encountering the enemy, and he felt the delay caused by waiting for the XLIV Corps was increasing the danger to his army. In addition, Huang was upset because the regiment of engineers that was supposed to come from Xuzhou to construct a second bridge at Yunhezhen had not yet arrived.[16] He knew that once his large force began to move the single railroad bridge would soon become a major bottleneck.

On 7 November, the Seventh Army's withdrawal went forward reasonably well. At 0330 the LXIV Corps began pulling out of Gaoliu, and by 1600 the corps' advance elements were crossing the Grand Canal at Yunhezhen.[17] That night while the rest of the corps completed its crossing, the units on the west side began to establish defensive positions. Also, a battalion was sent south to secure the LXIII Corps crossing point at Yaowan.[18] The XLIV Corps made steady progress during the day, and although the main body only moved as far as Wayao, some units moved as far west as Paoche and the corps headquarters crossed the Grand Canal and bivouacked at Zhaodun.[19] On the army's right flank and right rear, C Corps and XXV Corps carried out their screening missions without significant contact with the ECFA. The only corps encountering serious problems was the LXIII.

The LXIII Corps' troubles had begun on 6 November. After Huang Baitao and his corps commanders had agreed at their morning meeting that the LXIII Corps would provide left flank security for the Seventh Army and cross the Grand Canal at Yaowan, the corps commander, Chen Zhang, had ordered his 152d Division to send an infantry regiment and two engineer companies to Yaowan to construct a floating bridge for the corps to use.[20] However, when these troops arrived in Yaowan that evening and began collecting material for building the bridge they could only find four boats to use for the bridge's floating base. That night the regiment tried to use these boats to move a battalion across the canal, but the effort failed when local Communist irregulars began firing from the west bank.

When Chen Zhang learned of the failed attempt to establish a crossing point, he angrily ordered the 152d Division commander to move his division to Yaowan by noon, 7 November; find the material to make the floating bridge; force his way across the canal; and establish a firm bridgehead on the west bank.[21] By the time the additional forces arrived, 11th (E) Column elements had moved north from Suqian and established numerous interlocking firing positions covering the canal. Given the small number of boats available, there was nothing the 152d Division could do. By the evening of 7 November the only real chance the LXIII Corps had of crossing the canal was if the LXIV Corps unit starting to move down the west bank of the canal would reach it and provide help.

8 November was not a good day for the Seventh Army. On the positive side, Seventh Army headquarters and its attached units crossed the Grand Canal and reached the Nianzhuangxu area.[22] XLIV Corps units also crossed the canal, continued west, and began to set up defensive positions south of Nianzhuangxu.[23] However, during the day, PLA movements to counter the Nationalist redeployment began to take effect. With the XXV and C Corps still on the canal's east bank, serious threats to the Seventh Army were developing to its south, east, and north.

In the south the threat to the LXIII Corps increased markedly on 8 November. Its route to the west was blocked more firmly than ever. During the night of 7 November the battalion the LXIV Corps sent south along the Grand Canal's west bank was struck hard by 11th (E) Column elements. After losing two companies it withdrew back toward the Yunhezhen crossing.[24] By morning 11th (E) Column elements had advanced close enough to the Long-Hai railroad to begin harassing fire on the railroad from villages south of Zhaodun. Using two regiments, the LXIV Corps succeeded in pushing these lightly armed PLA units 5 km south of the railroad, but there was no second attempt to send a force south to Yaowan to help the LXIII Corps cross the canal.[25] During the night of 8 November at Yantou ECFA 9th Column elements attacked and overtook the part of the LXIII Corps that had stayed in Xinanzhen until that afternoon. Motivated by a desire to salvage as many supplies as possible for his corps to use before pulling out of Xinanzhen, the LXIII Corps commander had stayed in Xinanzhen with an infantry regiment, the corps reconnaissance battalion, and other units attached to his headquarters well beyond the completion of his assigned security mission.[26] When his force was attacked at Yantou, he and most of his soldiers escaped and made their way to Yaowan. Unfortunately for the LXIII Corps, the rice, blankets, ammunition, and other supplies this trailing force had been transporting were destroyed. Even worse, the arrival of a strong ECFA force into the area east of Yaowan meant the corps was in imminent danger of being encircled.

East of Yunhezhen on 8 November the ECFA pursuit was also drawing closer to the Seventh Army's main body. By nightfall, the XXV and C Corps were still on the east side of the canal because just as Huang Baitao had feared, the Yunhezhen bridge had become a bottleneck. A second bridge had not been constructed, and the single-track railroad bridge was jammed by a churning mass of soldiers, trucks, jeeps, and horse-drawn carts carrying artillery trying to cross as rapidly as possible. Thousands of civilian refugees crowding toward this only escape route to the west added to the confusion. On both sides of the bridge a few small boats were ferrying soldiers across the 50-meter-wide ribbon of water, but their capacity was limited. At about 2100 the sound of gunfire coming from the northeast added to everyone's sense of urgency. Lead elements of the ECFA 4th Column were attacking the defensive line that C and XXV Corps units had set up. This PLA force lacked the strength to penetrate the Nationalist defenses, but its arrival was a clear warning that the two corps had limited time to cross the canal.

The developing threats to the south and east of the Seventh Army were very serious, but on 8 November a still greater threat emerged to the northwest created by a large-scale defection within the Third Pacification Area. The defection began in the early hours of 8 November, and by day's end approximately 80 percent of the officers and men in the Third Pacification Area had surrendered. This defection opened a huge gap in the Nationalist defense line and created a tremendous opportunity for the PLA. At this time only 30 km separated the PLA positions along the Grand Canal between Hanzhuang and Taierzhuang and the Long-Hai railroad. Even though much of the Seventh Army had already crossed the Grand Canal, if the ECFA's 10th, 7th, and 13th Columns could advance quickly enough, they could still possibly cut in front of it and isolate it.

The Third Pacification Area units' defection also made it much easier for the Shandong army to pose a threat to Xuzhou. The possibility of an advance against the city was Liu Zhi's primary concern on the morning of 8 November, and he responded by ordering the Thirteenth Army to abandon its positions east of Xuzhou and move into the city.[27] At the same time he ordered the Second and Seventh Armies to move close to Xuzhou on the west and on the east. On 9 November Liu followed up on these orders by directing the Sixteenth Army to move with all possible speed from Mengcheng to Suxian to provide security for his line of communication between Xuzhou and the south.[28]

The movements Liu Zhi ordered on 8-9 November meant the end of the Nationalists' attempt to implement their redeployment plan of 5 November. A new fluid situation had developed, and new operational concepts and plans were required. Liu Zhi's hasty actions secured Xuzhou; however, at the same time, they opened up the area east of Xuzhou to PLA penetration and led to other problems.

The Third Pacification Area Defects

Surprise is a powerful aid to offensive action because it produces both psychological and physical effects. According to Field Manual 3-0, "Surprise delays enemy reactions, overloads and confuses his command and control (C2) systems, induces psychological shock in enemy soldiers and leaders, and reduces the coherence of the defense."[29] Surprise can cause enemy commanders to hesitate or misjudge a situation. It reduces the enemy forces' ability to generate combat power and magnifies the effects of one's own actions.

Surprise was very much a part of Su Yu's planning for the Huai Hai Campaign. His desire to move quickly after taking Jinan was based, in part, on his belief that by doing so he could achieve strategic surprise. Deception operations and operations security measures were implemented to gain surprise. Another major component of the search for surprise was the political work that was being done within Feng Zhian's Third Pacification Area to encourage his force to defect after the campaign began. Su's plans did not depend on such a defection happening. The 10th, 7th, and 13th Columns were assigned to attack the Third Pacification Area. They were given specific objectives as if they would have to fight their way south to the Long-Hai railroad. But the warning order for the campaign stated that the attack on Jiawang should be "coordinated with the political offensive to pressure Feng to revolt."[30] A revolt, Su knew, would greatly shock the Nationalist command structure and significantly aid the deep maneuver planned for the columns on his right flank.

Su Yu and the Central Military Commission (CMC) felt the political work within the Third Pacification Area held great promise because the primary Chinese Communist Party (CCP) contacts in this force were not only major generals who were serving as deputy commanders within the Third Pacification Area but they were also underground CCP members. Zhang Kexia and He Jifeng had been working quietly for several years providing intelligence to the Communists and subtly trying to promote sympathy for Communist ideas. Now the Third Pacification Area's location had placed them in position to make an important contribution to the Huai Hai Campaign by creating an opening at a critical place in the Nationalists' defenses.

Since mid-October Zhang and He had been meeting with agents the ECFA headquarters sent to the Third Pacification Area's forward command post in Jiawang. Working with such other high-ranking officers as Meng Shaolian, deputy commander, LIX Corps, and Guo Jianfang, commander, 132d Division, LXXVII Corps, they established the basic organization for implementing a defection and assured ECFA agents that they would act when the time came. Fear of discovery, however, limited these conspirators' activities and they were not sure how large a defection they could organize. Officer dissatisfaction with government mismanagement and corruption did not lead directly to a pro-Communist viewpoint. Even where feelings of disillusionment were strong, concerns about personal safety, fear for the well being of one's family, and a sense of loyalty to one's superiors kept many officers from abandoning the Nationalist cause. On 6 November He Jifeng could only tell the ECFA representative who had come to Jiawang for a final check on the prospects for a defection, "If we have a regiment, we'll have a regiment. If we have a division, we'll have a division. In any case, when the PLA moves south we will act. We will definitely not let this good opportunity slip by."[31]

When Shandong army units began to move south on the night of 6 November, He Jifeng, who was at the Third Pacification Area forward command post in Jiawang, facilitated their advance toward the Grand Canal by ordering Third Pacification Area units north of the canal to withdraw to the south.[32] However, on the evening of 7 November serious fighting broke out when a special force from the 7th Column moved to seize the important bridge across the Grand Canal at Wannianzha to use the next day when the general offensive was to begin. The 180th and 38th Division (LIX Corps divisions) commanders were still directing their troops to resist. They refused to defect due to fears for their families' safety in south China.[33]

That night, as both divisions were slowly pushed back from their positions along the canal, He Jifeng used his position to increase the psychological pressure on both division commanders. First, he ordered them to retake all lost ground south of the canal at all costs. Next, he called Feng Zhian at Third Pacification Area headquarters in Xuzhou, told him what he had done, and encouraged Feng to issue strict orders saying that unless the lost positions were regained by the next morning all division and regimental commanders responsible would be court-martialed.[34] Since their divisions were clearly incapable of complying with these orders, both division commanders felt compelled to reconsider their positions. After receiving assurances from the Communists that their families would be protected, around 0200, 8 November they agreed to defect and signed orders directing their divisions to move to assembly points to surrender to the PLA.[35] At this time He Jifeng ordered that all communications personnel be taken into custody and that all radio and telephone links with Third Pacification Area headquarters in Xuzhou be shut down. The communications personnel were considered to be the most loyal to the Nationalist government, and He wanted to keep word of what was happening from reaching Xuzhou until the last possible moment.

As the movement to defect gained momentum in the early hours of 8 November, so did the confusion. After daybreak He Jifeng and other officers who were in favor of defecting went around to units and talked to the officers and men about what was happening and asked that they join the defection. Most did join, but others refused and fled south. By evening all resistance from the Third Pacification Area had ended and the 23,000 officers and men who had voluntarily surrendered were starting to march north into Shandong to begin their reeducation process. Meanwhile, the rest of the Third Pacification Area, some 5,000 officers and men who were primarily from the 37th Division, LXXVII Corps, were moving in disarray toward Xuzhou.[36]

It was this sudden turn of events on the night of 7-8 November that led Liu Zhi to order the Thirteenth Army to move into Xuzhou. Caught by surprise and uncertain of Communist intentions, he misjudged the situation. Thinking that Xuzhou was under immediate threat from the northeast, he acted to protect the city, leaving the Seventh Army in an exposed position similar to the one that the Nationalist redeployment ordered on 5 November was supposed to eliminate. On 8 November the Seventh Army was closer to Xuzhou than it had been on 5 November. Most of the army was already on the west side of the Grand Canal, but the defections in the Third Pacification Area had opened up a large gap in the Nationalist defenses. Liu Zhi's order to the Thirteenth Army broadened and deepened that gap, providing Su Yu the chance to accomplish the primary objective of the Huai Hai Campaign, to encircle and destroy the Seventh Army.

Encircling the Seventh Army

As has been discussed, the Communists had a good intelligence network. Their operatives within the Nationalist army, agents on the ground, and reconnaissance teams gave leaders at the strategic, operational, and tactical levels vital information about Nationalist deployments, movements, and intended actions. However, there were limits on how quickly their intelligence system could collect, process, integrate, analyze, evaluate, and interpret information. In the case of the Seventh Army shift to the west bank of the Grand Canal ordered on the night of 5-6 November, it was not until the morning of 8 November that Su Yu learned that this movement was under way.[37]

Upon receiving this intelligence, Su Yu immediately ordered the 11th (E) Column to advance rapidly up the west side of the Grand Canal to keep the Seventh Army from crossing. He also ordered the Shandong army's 10th, 7th, and 13th Columns to push south with all possible speed and strength to reach positions where they could block Huang Baitao's movement west.[38] Originally, the Shandong army had the mission of creating the impression of an attack on Xuzhou and digging in along the north bank of the Bulao River to threaten the northern flank of any force sent out from Xuzhou to relieve the Seventh Army. The 11th (E) Column's original mission was to move north from the Suqian area and threaten the southern flank of such a relief force. It was not expected that these columns would be the main blocking force fighting to keep a Nationalist relief force from reaching the Seventh Army or to keep the Seventh Army from moving west. However, on 8 November the 10th, 7th, 13th, and 11th (E) Columns were the only columns in position to try to cut off the Seventh Army. All of the columns that had received this mission in the original plan were far east of the Seventh Army and had no chance of blocking its movement west.

Missions for the other ECFA columns were also changed to reflect the new situation. The 4th, 8th, 1st, 6th, 9th, and Luzhongnan Columns were ordered to exert every effort to overtake the Seventh Army and attack it as soon as possible. The Subei army—2d, 12th, and 11th (C) Columns—was directed to swing southwest, cross the Grand Canal in the Suqian area, and move up through Dawangji and Shuanggou toward Xuzhou.[39] Its mission was to threaten Xuzhou from the southeast and block any attempt by the Seventh Army to go south through Danji and reach Xuzhou by way of the Suqian-Xuzhou road.

On 8 November the Shandong army columns advanced rapidly through the area Third Pacification Area had formerly controlled. To create flexibility for maneuver when encountering Nationalist forces trying to harass or block them, column objectives were spread across 40 km east to west along the Long-Hai railroad. On the left flank, the 13th Column moved toward Caobaji; in the center, the 7th Column moved toward Daxujia. On the right flank, part of the 10th Column conducted a feint toward Xuzhou, but the main body moved toward the Damiaoshan-Houji area. To speed the advance, orders were issued to bypass Nationalist troops that offered no resistance. Only those found attempting to flee were to be attacked. Late that night the 7th and 13th Columns' lead elements reached the northern bank of the Bulao River.[40]

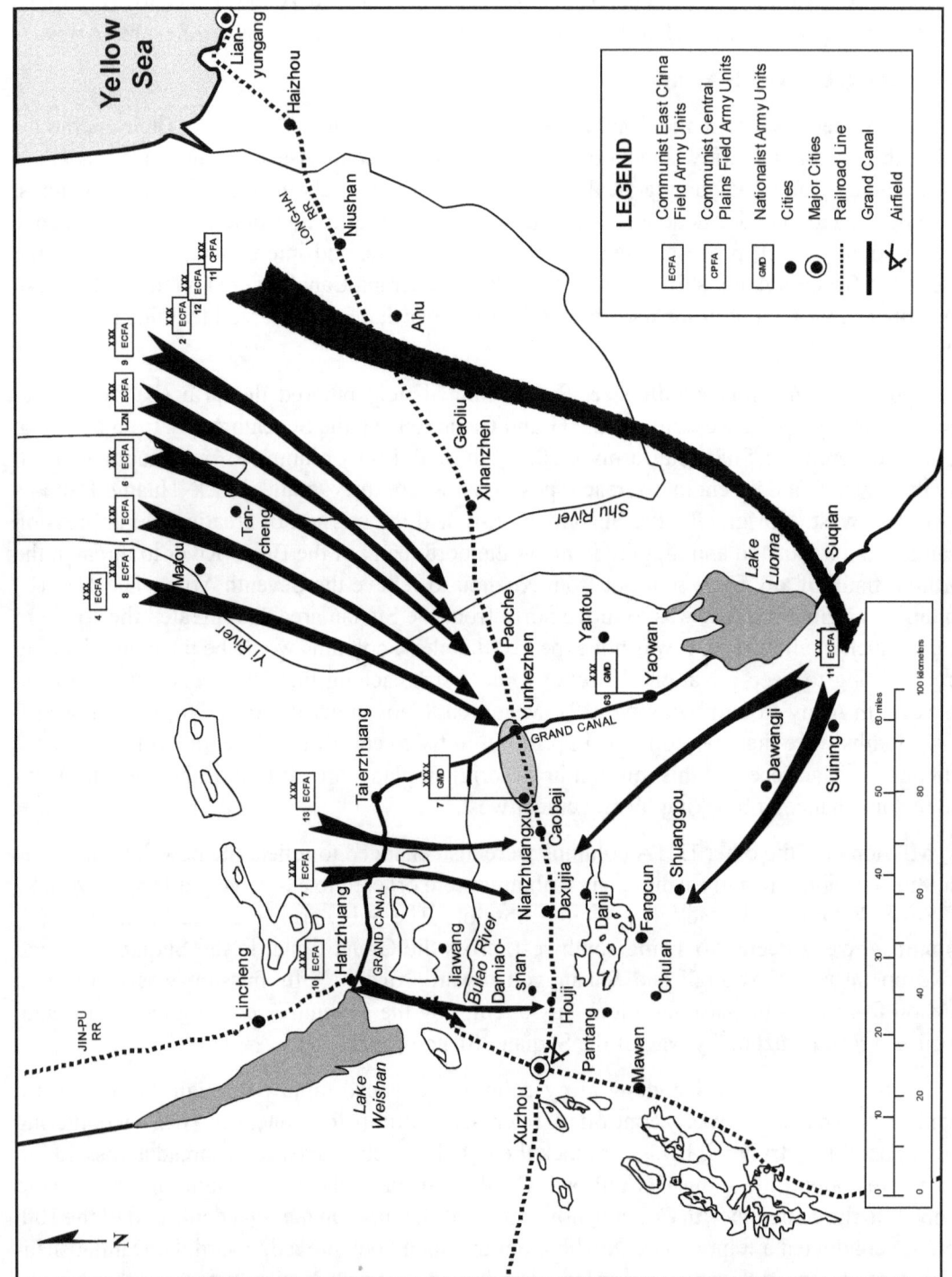

Map 2. The ECFA's plan to encircle the Seventh Army, 8 November 1948.

Before the campaign had begun, all ECFA columns had trained their engineers to construct floating bridges. This was to prepare for operations in areas crossed by many rivers and waterways. The Bulao River, however, posed a special challenge because of its size. In the area where the 7th Column was to cross the Bulao, for example, the river had been swollen by autumn rains to a width of nearly 200 meters and a depth of about 3 meters.[41] The column had brought a few rubber boats with it and about 10 wooden boats were found locally, but these proved inadequate for getting the column across the river. To speed the crossing, makeshift rafts were constructed using dried stalks, and a few hardy soldiers swam across the icy river with the aid of large dried gourds.[42]

Still, during 9 November only a few companies were able to cross to the southern shore. The rest of the column had to wait while column and division engineers constructed floating bridges made from dry sorghum stalks and cornstalks. The first step in building these bridges was the painstaking process of gathering dried stalks and binding them into tight bundles. Then bundles were tied into larger bundles to provide the buoyancy needed to support the necessary weight. Next the engineers tied the large bundles together so the current would not tear them apart. Finally, the bundles were stretched across the river and fastened to support posts on the side to make them more stable. Two of these bridges were constructed on 9 November, and that night the column's main body started across. By noon, 10 November most of the 7th Column had crossed the Bulao.[43]

During the afternoon of 10 November the 13th Column's lead division, the 38th, crossed the Long-Hai railroad east of Caobaji, surrounded the town, and began preparing to attack the 44th Division (C Corps) units that had taken up positions inside.[44] The 38th Division had suffered heavy losses during fighting to defend the Yunhezhen perimeter on 9 November and had reached Caobaji just hours earlier.[45] Also, during the afternoon of 10 November, the 7th Column's three divisions, advancing abreast on a 10-km front, reached the Long-Hai railroad in the area centered on Daxujia.[46] While part of the column pressed ahead toward Danji, the 20th Division encircled the last rear guard battalion of Li Mi's Thirteenth Army at Dagengzhuang, a village 3 km west of Caobaji. 10th Column units, because of a longer distance to cover and rougher terrain in their sector, did not reach the Bulao River until the evening of 10 November. However, since their route of advance lay close to the river's headwaters, their river crossing was not the problem it had been for the 7th and 13th Columns. That very night 10th Column units were able to reach the Long-Hai railroad in the Damiaoshan area and push to within 20 km of Xuzhou at Houji. With these actions, in only one day the Shandong army created a 30-km gap between the Seventh Army and the Xuzhou defense perimeter.

C Corps' 44th Division was the westernmost unit in the Seventh Army. To increase the distance between the Seventh Army and Xuzhou and eliminate a Nationalist strongpoint, at dusk on 10 November the 13th Column launched an attack against Caobaji using its 38th Division. Because this town had been the location of Li Mi's Thirteenth Army headquarters, in addition to the surrounding wall and moat that had provided the town's defense in earlier eras, there was an elaborate network of pillboxes, bunkers, and barbed-wire barriers.[47] Around midnight sappers succeeded in blowing a hole in the town wall near the north gate, and Communist soldiers rushed into the town. However, because this force had focused on pushing forward and had not kept enough soldiers back to shore up the shoulders of the penetration, the defenders were able to seal off the breakthrough point and cut off the troops who had entered the town.[48] Near dawn a regiment of the 13th Column's 39th Division attacked the southern gate area, but its attack was also blocked.[49] The situation remained a standoff until noon when another 38th Division regiment arrived outside the north gate and joined the battle. This regiment pushed through the hole in the wall and quickly linked up with the unit that had been trapped inside. Around noon the Nationalist artillery position was overrun, and organized resistance ended soon after. By 1400 11 November the battle for Caobaji was over.[50]

While the fighting at Caobaji was in progress, two regiments of the 7th Column's 20th Division and a regiment from the 13th Column's 38th Division were attacking the Nationalist force at Dagengzhuang. This fighting also ended on the afternoon of 11 November with the defeat of the Nationalist forces.

Action by the Shandong army on 10 November effectively cut the Seventh Army's route to Xuzhou. On 11 November the victories at Caobaji and Dagengzhuang confirmed the reality of the Seventh Army's isolation. That same day Su Yu began deploying the Shandong army along a line east of Xuzhou in anticipation of a Nationalist effort to link up with the Seventh Army. The 7th Column was ordered to move west from Daxujia and take up positions south of the 10th Column. The 11th (E) Column was told to move west from Danji and take up positions south of the 7th Column.[51] These three columns faced west to block any Nationalist relief force trying to reach the Seventh Army. To ensure unity of command and unity of effort, Song Shilun, commander, 10th Column, commanded all three columns. Behind them the 13th Column faced east to block any attempt by Huang Baitao to keep moving west.

From 8 to 11 November, as the Shandong army operations were taking place, east of the Seventh Army the ECFA's main body and the Subei army were rushing to catch and encircle this force. Because Su Yu knew the Seventh Army could only evade the ECFA by moving to the west, southwest, or south, he directed most of his columns east of the Grand Canal to move southwest on the south side of the Long-Hai railroad. The 4th, 8th, and 6th Columns were ordered to head toward the key canal crossing point of Yunhezhen. The 4th Column was to move directly toward Yunhezhen from the northeast to interfere with the Seventh Army crossing the Grand Canal. The 8th Column was to go south and turn right to move toward Yunhezhen along the north side of the Long-Hai railroad. The 6th Column was to cross the Long-Hai railroad west of Wayao and move toward Yunhezhen south of the railroad. The 9th, 1st, and Luzhongnan Columns were to head southwest toward Yaowan. The Subei army—the 2d, 12th, and 11th (C) Columns—was ordered to make a wide sweeping movement that swung south through the Suqian area and turned northwest. These movements were designed to encircle the Seventh Army and place the ECFA in position to respond to future developments and opportunities.

On the evening of 8 November, the 4th Column's lead elements reached the Nationalist defensive perimeter northeast of Yunhezhen, but their attacks failed to break through. On the morning of 9 November the entire column went into action against the C Corps' 44th Division and XXV Corps' 108th Division, but the Nationalist line still held. During the day Nationalist troops, equipment, and supplies continued to move across the steel bridge and head west.

By the afternoon of 9 November the XXV Corps had crossed the Grand Canal, and the C Corps commander was dealing with how to withdraw his last unit, the 44th Division, from the east bank. His concern was that the XXV Corps unit responsible for destroying the bridge would blow it up prematurely and trap his men on the east bank. By directly threatening that he would take Huang Baitao with him to Nanjing after the battle and personally file court-martial charges against the officers in charge if the bridge was blown before the 44th Division made it across, the corps commander kept the bridge open through the afternoon.[52] Because of his efforts, nearly one full regiment of the 44th Division was able to cross. However, shortly after the corps commander left the scene, a cart loaded with ammunition exploded as it was approaching the east end of the bridge. Night was falling, and the commander in charge of the demolition unit had become extremely jittery. Thinking the explosion meant a PLA plainclothes unit had arrived, he ordered the bridge blown.[53] Justified or not, this decision left two regiments of the 44th Division, the last rear guard for the crossing, stranded with no chance of escape.

The Nationalist success in holding off the 4th Column at Yunhezhen was a source of frustration to Su Yu. To bypass this Nationalist obstacle and get his forces moving around the Seventh Army's flanks, on 9 November he ordered the 4th Column to start preparing to transfer its positions in Yunhezhen to the 8th Column and cross the Grand Canal to the northwest. On the evening of 9 November a 4th Column advance party established a crossing point at a small village 12 km northwest of Yunhezhen. During the night, as the 8th Column arrived to take its place, the 4th Column began marching toward it. On 10 November the 4th Column crossed the canal and pushed west to overtake the Seventh Army and move in front of it.[54]

While crossing the canal, for the first time the 4th Column encountered attacks by Nationalist aircraft. Damage was minimal and order was maintained. The greatest effect, according to reminiscences, was a large number of fish that were killed when bombs detonated in the water. As the fish floated to the surface soldiers picked them up, as the story goes, joking about "Jiang Jieshi sending us gifts to improve our meals."[55]

Through the night of 9 November the Nationalists continued to hold the west bank of the Grand Canal at Yunhezhen, gaining more time for the Seventh Army's main body to move to Nianzhuangxu. However, shortly after dawn on 10 November the rear guard withdrew from the west bank and 8th Column units began crossing the canal. While 8th Column advance elements pursued withdrawing Nationalists, ECFA engineers began repairing the damaged bridge. Soon they had constructed a level roadway using the bridge structure as a base, and large numbers of troops were rushing across.

On 9 November the 6th Column had also been approaching Yunhezhen from the east. But with the Nationalists blocking the Yunhezhen crossing, the 6th Column was ordered to bypass the town to the south. Early on 10 November the column began crossing the Grand Canal at a small village 7 km south of the Yunhezhen bridge with orders to move to the area south of Nianzhuangxu. By the evening of 11 November the column was assembling in this area with the 13th Column on its left and the 8th Column on its right.[56]

By nightfall on 11 November the Seventh Army's main body was surrounded. To its north and northeast was the 4th Column. The 8th Column was positioned on its east and southeast. The 6th Column was in position to the south and southwest. To its immediate west was the 13th Column, and beyond that column farther to the west were the 7th, 10, and 11th (E) Columns.

While the Seventh Army's main body was being encircled at Nianzhuangxu, the LXIII Corps was suffering a similar fate at Yaowan. As was discussed earlier, from 6 to 8 November this corps had been unable to establish a crossing point on the Grand Canal, and during the evening of 8 November the 9th Column had overtaken the LXIII Corps' rear guard at Yantou.

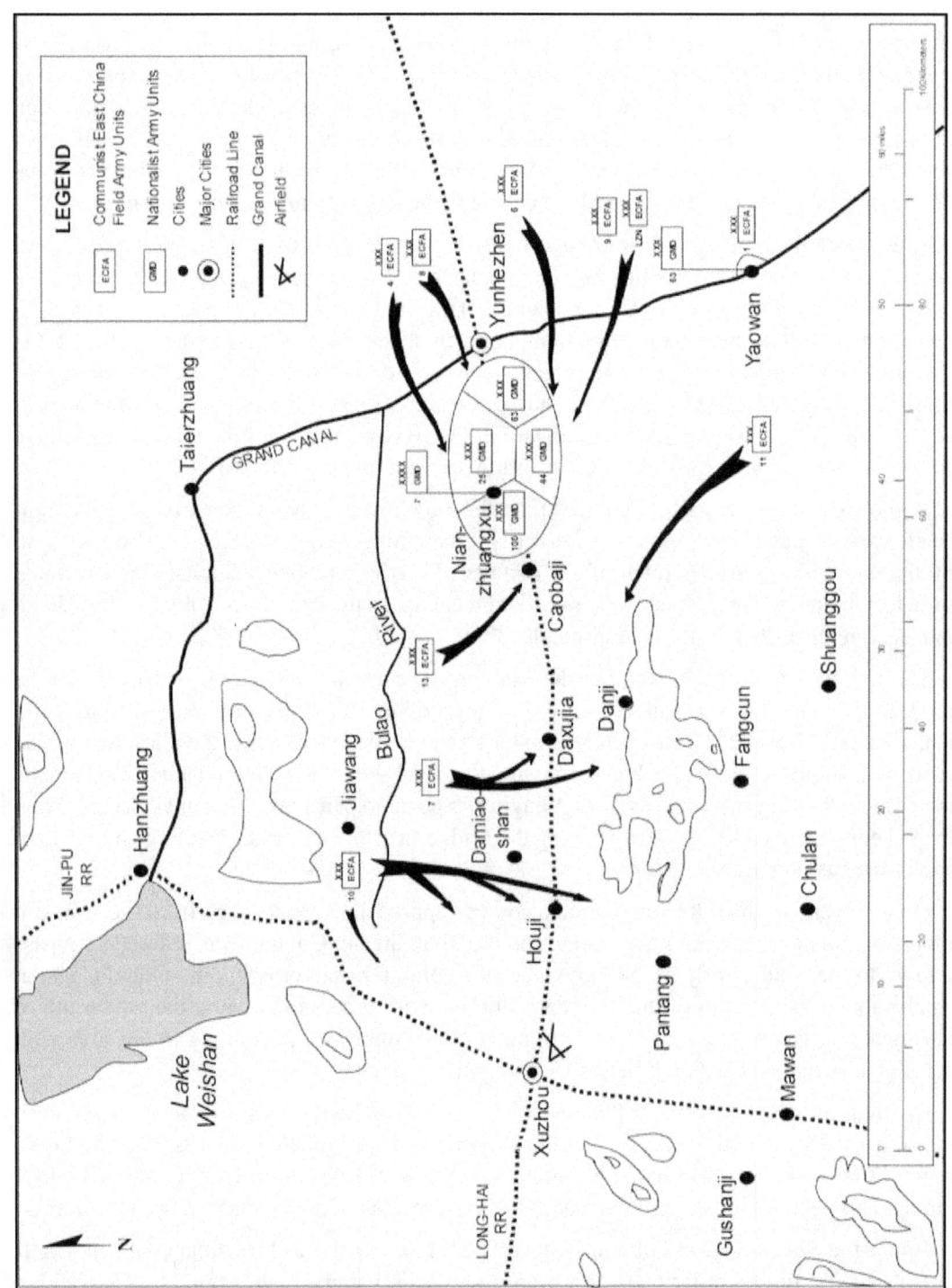

Map 3. Encirclement of the Seventh Army.

In fighting that included the celebrated "10-man-bridge" example of PLA ingenuity, initiative, and bravery under fire, the 9th Column inflicted heavy casualties on the rear guard and sent it fleeing toward Yaowan.[57] On the morning of 9 November the 9th Column continued to move toward Yaowan to engage the rest of the LXIII Corps, but as it was doing so, the ECFA headquarters suddenly changed its mission. Instead of going to Yaowan, the column was directed to cross the Grand Canal north of Yaowan and move toward Nianzhuangxu to increase the forces available to fight the Seventh Army's main body.[58] In its place, the 1st Column received the task of encircling and destroying the LXIII Corps. The 1st Column, which had been advancing close behind the 9th Column, had two 105mm howitzer companies from the Special Type (ST) Column attached to it and was therefore better equipped to attack Yaowan's fortified defenses. The fortifications included not only a town wall but a system of bunkers and pillboxes constructed by the Japanese army and Japanese-sponsored Chinese puppet forces during the War of Resistance Against Japan (1937-1945).[59]

By the evening of 9 November the 1st Column had extended its lines around the LXIII Corps' defensive perimeter. That night the column commander gave a status report to Su Yu by telephone and told Su about his plans for the attack. At this time the Luzhongnan Column was available at Yantou in case two columns were needed to overcome the LXIII Corps. However, Su asked the 1st Column commander if his column could destroy the LXIII Corps by itself, and he replied with an emphatic "yes." The Luzhongnan Column was not ordered forward.[60]

On 10 November the 1st Column cleared LXIII Corps units from their outposts beyond the town wall and made final plans for an all-out assault. At 1630 on 11 November, following an artillery barrage that six 105mm howitzers and 17 75mm pack howitzers fired against command posts and defensive positions, the column launched a general attack from three directions.[61] By 1730 assault teams using demolition charges had penetrated the eastern gate of the town wall, but it was 2100 before the attacking force on the north side made it through the wall. Street fighting continued for several hours, but around 0230, 12 November, the corps command post in the Catholic church was captured and resistance ceased. Before the fighting ended, however, corps commander Chen Zhang attempted to escape. Chen had only assumed command of the corps a month earlier after having been promoted. Before that he was the deputy commander, LXII Corps, in Tianjin.[62] With his command collapsing around him, Chen made his way through the darkness down a narrow alley that led to the Grand Canal. After reaching the canal, he picked up a board, hoping that he could use it to float downstream beyond the PLA positions and make his way back to Nationalist lines. Just as he was about to enter the water, a random bullet fired from the west bank of the canal struck him and he fell to the ground dead.[63]

With the LXIII Corps' defeat assured and close at hand, at 2400, 11 November, the ECFA ordered the Luzhongnan Column to cross the Grand Canal, move to the area north of Fangcun, and make contact with the 11th (E) Column to support the 6th Column.[64] On the afternoon of 13 November this order was changed, and the Luzhongnan Column was attached to the Subei army to support that force's mission of threatening the right flank and rear of any Nationalist relief force that would attempt to reach the Seventh Army.[65] On 13 November, with the fighting at Yaowan over, the 1st Column crossed the Grand Canal and began moving toward Fangcun to serve as a reserve.[66]

Because of its location on 8 November, the Subei army's 2d, 12th, and 11th (C) Columns did not play a role in isolating or encircling the Seventh Army. However, while the rest of the ECFA was achieving these objectives, the Subei army did accomplish the impressive feat of moving from the Ahu area to the west bank of the Grand Canal by way of Suqian. By the afternoon of 12 November the 2d Column was already northwest of Suining in pursuit of the Nationalist CVII Corps, and the 12th and 11th (C) Columns were close behind.[67] In four days these columns had moved more than 100 km through an area that had poor roads and was crossed by numerous waterways.

The ECFA's ability to recover from the situation of 7-8 November and encircle the Seventh Army 60 km from Xuzhou by 11 November was due to good leadership, high morale, and the ability to maneuver across country. It was also due to a series of Nationalist leadership failures. The defection of the Third Pacification Area, Liu Zhi's decision to order the Thirteenth Army to move into Xuzhou, and Huang Baitao's failure to ensure that a second bridge was constructed at Yunhezhen all made the ECFA's task easier. Other Nationalist command decisions further contributed to the ECFA's success.

One of the most important of these decisions was Li Mi's refusal to give Huang Baitao help when Huang asked for it. Huang was very upset by Liu Zhi's order directing the Thirteenth Army to move into Xuzhou. Looking at his army's condition as it crossed the Grand Canal, he saw a fatigued and disorganized force that could not possibly fill the void that would be created when the Thirteenth Army left its positions east and northeast of Xuzhou. In hopes that he could prevail upon Li Mi to slow the Thirteenth Army's movement and thereby protect his route of withdrawal, late on the evening of 8 November he went by jeep from his headquarters in Nianzhuangxu to see Li at Thirteenth Army headquarters in Caobaji. Huang wanted the Thirteenth Army to keep the area between the Bulao River and the Long-Hai railroad secure for two more days while his Seventh Army finished crossing the Grand Canal and resumed its move to the west.[68] Li expressed sympathy for Huang's problem but said he felt duty bound to execute Liu Zhi's order without delay. He informed Huang that his army headquarters and his VIII Corps would start moving west that night and that the IX Corps would pass responsibility for the area over to the Seventh Army the next morning and leave too.[69]

Given Li Mi's decision, Huang Baitao decided that his army should establish its intermediate assembly area after crossing the Grand Canal in the Caobaji-Daxujia area. Caobaji was 10 kilometers nearer to Xuzhou than Nianzhuangxu and had an elaborate system of fixed fortifications built by Thirteenth Army and VIII Corps engineers. Daxujia was another ten kilometers further west and close enough to Xuzhou so that the PLA would have difficulty maneuvering in between them. If the Seventh Army advanced that far, it might be impossible for the ECFA to encircle and destroy it.

Upon returning to his headquarters in Nianzhuangxu, Huang sent an urgent message to the LXIII Corps directing the corps to move to Caobaji instead of Nianzhuangxu after crossing the Grand Canal.[70] Early on the morning of 9 November he met with his other four corps commanders to discuss how they could move the army farther west. General agreement was reached on a movement plan and new corps assembly areas, but Liu Zhenxiang, commander, LXIV Corps, objected strongly to leaving their location. He felt his troops had worked hard preparing good defensive positions and that they might as well fight there as anywhere else. He also did not want to move farther away from Yaowan before the LXIII Corps had successfully crossed the canal.[71] The LXIV Corps and the LXIII Corps were both made up of officers and men from Guangdong province in south China, and Liu felt a special responsibility for his fellow southerners. He feared that the LXIII Corps could not reach Caobaji on its own and asked that a relief force be sent to help it cross the Grand Canal.

By this time Huang Baitao knew the LXIII Corps was in deep trouble because the corps commander had responded to his order to move toward Caobaji by saying he was going to defend in place until a relief force arrived and he needed airdrops of food and ammunition.[72] There was little, however, that Huang could do to aid the LXIII Corps. His first priority was to maintain the protective screen near the Yunhezhen bridge and move the XXV and C Corps to the west bank of the Grand Canal. Perhaps out of respect for Liu Zhenzhang's position, that morning he did not order the Seventh Army to start moving toward Caobaji and Daxujia. However, neither did he order that a relief force be organized and sent south to Yaowan.

During the day, Huang continued to monitor developments. Intelligence reports indicated that ECFA forces were moving west on his left flank and that ahead, on the army's right flank, they were already at the Bulao River. To the rear of his army, the 4th Column was attacking the defensive line at Yunhezhen and the 8th and 6th Columns were drawing closer. The LXIII Corps was surrounded at Yaowan. Huang realized that the speed of the ECFA advance was such that soon it would be able to bring the full combat power of its main body to bear. After weighing the risks of being caught on the move versus the danger of being encircled at Nianzhuangxu, the plight of the LXIII Corps at Yaowan, and the viewpoint of the LXIV Corps commander, Huang Baitao finally decided that his best option was to move farther west. Orders were issued to begin moving the next morning.[73]

This move never took place because of a decision the Nationalist High Command in Nanjing made. Since the start of the fighting, they had been anxiously following events by means of reports from units on the ground and aerial reconnaissance. Well aware of the PLA's ability to cause great damage to Nationalist units caught while on the move, they were worried that the Seventh Army's condition at this time made it particularly vulnerable to attack. When aerial reconnaissance on 9 November reported the movement of large numbers of Communist troops toward the Seventh Army from the north and east, they decided that the army should consolidate its positions in and around Nianzhuangxu and make a stand there. After this decision was reached on the evening of 9 November, the army chief of staff Gu Zhutong telephoned Liu Zhi in Xuzhou and directed him to order the Seventh Army to stay in Nianzhuangxu and await orders.[74] The next morning a handwritten order from Jiang Jieshi directing Huang Baitao to stay in Nianzhuangxu and fight was airdropped to Huang's command post from an airplane dispatched from Nanjing.[75] This act ensured that the Seventh Army would be isolated and encircled.

Nationalist Efforts to Retrieve the Situation

On 8 November the Nationalists took a major step toward trying to retrieve the situation when the Twelfth Army left the Queshan area under orders to go toward Xuzhou by way of Fuyang, Mencheng, and Suxian. Huang Wei received an order stating that he "could not delay his movement for any reason," so even though the LXXXV Corps had not yet reached the army assembly area, he set out with the X, XIV, and XVIII Corps.[76] The four corps' total troop strength was 120,000, and the Communists rated the XVIII Corps as one of the Nationalists' "five main forces."[77] The army was almost completely American equipped and possessed several hundred motor vehicles.[78] Each division had a 75mm pack howitzer battalion. In addition, the XVIII Corps controlled a 105mm artillery battalion as a corps asset, and its 118th Division contained an organic tank battalion.[79] Numerically speaking the Twelfth Army was equivalent to the CPFA, and in terms of potential firepower, it was notably superior to the CPFA. It represented a serious threat to Communist plans and would generate great concern as it drew closer to Suxian.

As mentioned earlier, also on 8 November Liu Zhi had ordered the Thirteenth Army into Xuzhou. Then on 9 November he decided to shift the Sixteenth Army from Mengcheng to Suxian. On the evening of 9 November the High Command decided to order Huang Baitao to defend in place at Nianzhuangxu. Implicit in this order was Nationalist determination not to abandon the Seventh Army. This position was confirmed the next morning at an 0930 meeting of the High Command in Nanjing.

The first priority of those attending this meeting, which included Jiang Jieshi, was to end the encirclement of the Seventh Army. This would be done in an offensive operation using interior lines and economy of force to reestablish control of the area between Xuzhou and the Grand Canal.[80] After the meeting, orders were sent to Liu Zhi in Xuzhou directing that the Second Army's main body and one corps of the Thirteenth Army be used in concert with the Seventh Army to squeeze the ECFA units west of Nianzhuangxu in a pincers and destroy them. After that objective was accomplished, they were to advance to the Grand Canal and relieve the LXIII Corps' encirclement at Yaowan.[81] While these operations were under way, the units attached directly to Bandit Suppression Headquarters and the rest of the Thirteenth Army were to defend Xuzhou. Sun Yuanliang's Sixteenth Army was to shift north from Suxian to the Fuliji-Jiagou area to block any attempt by CPFA units west of Xuzhou to swing south of the hill mass lying north of Fuliji and join the battle east of Xuzhou. Liu Ruming's force was to occupy the Suxian-Guzhen area and maintain security along the railroad.[82]

An important personnel action took place at this strategy session. Du Yuming was once again officially appointed to serve as Liu Zhi's chief deputy with responsibility for the overall direction of Nationalist armies in the field as commander, Xuzhou Forward Command Headquarters. Du had stayed in the northeastern port of Huludao until the Nationalist evacuation from northeastern China was almost complete and had flown to Beiping on the evening of 8 November. After a luncheon meeting the next day with Fu Zuoyi, commander, Nationalist forces in north China, he flew to Nanjing. Du first learned of the fighting around Xuzhou from Fu Zuoyi and was amazed to hear of the Third Pacification Area's defection and the Seventh Army's location.

Upon arriving in Nanjing the evening of 9 November Du immediately went to Gu Zhutong's home to find out what was happening. Gu's assessment made him apprehensive, and the strategy session held the next day increased his concern. Du believed that the decisions being made were not based on an understanding of actual battlefield conditions, and he feared being bound to a concept of operations that was inappropriate. After the meeting on 10 November he spoke to Gu alone and asked to be granted some flexibility: "As far as the strategy, tactics, and deployment of forces for breaking the encirclement of Huang Baitao are concerned, please allow me to deviate from what was decided at today's meeting."[83] Gu replied, "You can, you can. Do what you think is best. That will be fine."[84]

Du Yuming flew out of Nanjing late the night of 10 November and landed in Xuzhou at about 0100, 11 November. From the airfield he went straight to Bandit Suppression Headquarters where he was alarmed by what he found. The staff was confused and unsettled. Intelligence reports appeared to be worthless. The situation map on the wall showed strong enemy forces and heavy fighting in every quadrant around Xuzhou except for the southeast. Liu Zhi and his chief of staff, Li Shuzheng, were certain that the PLA's primary objective was Xuzhou, so they had not acted yet on the orders issued in Nanjing directing that Qiu Qingquan and Li Mi organize a force to move east toward Nianzhuangxu. In the opinion of Liu and his chief of staff, it was impossible to remove troops from the line anywhere around Xuzhou to create such a force.[85]

In large measure, weaknesses in their intelligence-collection systems caused the Nationalists' uncertainty and confusion. In the countryside the PLA had become very effective at capturing Nationalist agents and stopping the information flow they had formerly provided. The network of agents using radios to report Communist movements that had once existed around Xuzhou had been virtually eliminated. Aerial reconnaissance was of limited value because of the small number of aircraft available to cover a large area and the PLA's ability to conceal its movements by marching at night. As a result, the primary sources of intelligence coming in to Bandit Suppression Headquarters were reports that front-line units sent in. Based on experience, Du felt that the commanders of these units exaggerated the strength of the enemy forces they were facing, so he did not consider their reports as reliable bases for establishing enemy strengths or intentions.[86]

PLA deception operations also contributed to Nationalist misjudgments. The enemy order of battle the Second Army G2 established on 5 November had shown five ECFA columns—the 3d, 8th, 10th, 11th, and Liangguang—in southwest Shandong when only two columns were actually there.[87] The energetic attacks by these two columns and the two independent Ji-Lu-Yu Military Region divisions continued to keep the Second Army unclear about PLA strength west of Xuzhou. Loss of contact with the 181st Division added to the confusion. At the same time, the ECFA feint on the northeast side of Xuzhou caused the Nationalists to think a serious threat existed there.

Du Yuming felt that no matter what the reports from the field were, the PLA could not be conducting a broad attack. He believed that the main enemy effort must be in the east where a familiar pattern was taking shape—the isolation of a major Nationalist force and preparations to attack a relief force. Something told him that the attacks against the Second Army and the Nationalist lines northwest and northeast of Xuzhou were only vigorous diversionary attacks that posed no immediate danger to the city. He argued that large numbers of troops could be safely pulled out of those areas and used to form a force to relieve the Seventh Army.[88]

Liu Zhi and Li Shuzheng, however, were not convinced by Du Yuming's arguments, and they continued to oppose shifting the Second Army from the west side of Xuzhou to the east. This prompted Du to call Qiu Qingquan on the telephone to ask him directly for his latest intelligence reports. What he heard excited him. Qiu told him that there were indications that large elements of the forces in front of the Second Army were moving south. If these reports were accurate, Du thought, it might be possible to do something other than the obvious and, in the process, regain some initiative for the Nationalists. Thinking that the CPFA main body was moving south to block Huang Wei's Twelfth Army's movement to the northeast, Du proposed an operation to destroy that army. Instead of pulling troops from the west side of Xuzhou and sending them east to relieve the Seventh Army, which is what he was sure the PLA commanders expected him to do, he would first attack the CPFA and then relieve the Seventh Army.[89]

At mid-morning on 11 November Du Yuming presented this concept as the first of two options for Liu Zhi to consider. In this plan, the Thirteenth Army, with the LXXII Corps directly under Bandit Suppression Headquarters control in general reserve, would defend Xuzhou while the Second Army moved southwest, the Sixteenth Army moved west, and the Twelfth Army moved northeast to surround and destroy the CPFA in the Guoyang-Mengcheng area. After the CPFA was annihilated, these four armies would turn east and relieve the Seventh Army. Du felt that the current disposition of Nationalist forces on three sides of the suspected CPFA destination in the Guoyang area made this plan practicable. He also liked it because the Nationalists would be able to achieve clear superiority in troop strength over the CPFA. However, this plan carried with it the risk that the Seventh Army could not hold out long enough to be saved.[90]

Option two was a more conservative plan that corresponded to the High Command's directive of 10 November and responded directly to Jiang Jieshi's desire to free the Seventh Army. However, it differed from the plan agreed to at the previous day's strategy session in Nanjing in three ways. First, the size of the relief force was increased to include the entire Second and Thirteenth Armies. Second, the Sixteenth Army was to move into Xuzhou to defend the city instead of taking up positions in the Fuliji-Jiagou area. Third, the Twelfth Army would move to Xuzhou with all possible speed to join the battle against the ECFA. Du felt this plan would provide immediate psychological support for Seventh Army officers and men. It also ensured the security of Xuzhou. However, as Du cautioned, if the CPFA was able to slow the Twelfth Army's movement so it could not join the battles east of Xuzhou in a timely manner, the Xuzhou command might still not have enough combat power to defeat the ECFA.[91]

Liu Zhi and Li Shuzheng immediately rejected option one. They doubted Huang Baitao's ability to hold out long enough to make the plan work. They also feared the CPFA might not actually be in the Guoyang-Mengcheng area and that an operation focused in that direction might come up empty handed. If, they argued, in that case Huang Baitao's army was destroyed, Jiang Jieshi would certainly hold them responsible, and others in the army would harshly criticize their actions. Even if they destroyed a large portion of the CPFA, if during that period the Seventh Army was destroyed, they would have failed to achieve their primary mission.[92] There was also a very practical problem with this plan. Liu had no way to directly coordinate his armies' movements with those of the Twelfth Army. The Twelfth Army was not under Xuzhou Bandit Suppression Headquarters control and could only be given a different mission by going through army headquarters in Nanjing. This was a step that Liu was unwilling to take.

Liu and Li also objected to option two. They agreed that it fit Jiang Jieshi's directive, but they did not see how the Second Army could extricate itself from the fighting in the west. They also worried about how to stop the PLA units that they were sure would pursue the Second Army as it moved east. Unable to decide on anything, Liu and Li finally agreed to ask Qiu Qingquan to come to their headquarters to discuss the situation.[93]

Qiu Qingquan arrived at Xuzhou Bandit Suppression Headquarters around noon, 11 November. By now a major shift of CPFA units toward the south had been confirmed. (Unknown to the Nationalist generals, this was part of the CPFA's preparations for an operation to capture Suxian.) This news made Liu Zhi more agreeable to moving the Second Army to the east side of Xuzhou. However, he was concerned enough about the possibility of an attack against Xuzhou from the west to demand that the Second Army's LXXIV Corps be positioned in the Jiulishan hills northwest of the city. With pressure to act mounting by the minute, Du agreed to this modification of option two, and on the afternoon of 11 November the orders to shift units and set up the relief effort were issued. The Second Army, minus the LXXIV Corps, was to move to the eastern edge of Xuzhou south of the Thirteenth Army and prepare to advance east with the Thirteenth Army. The Sixteenth Army would move north from Suxian and, with the LXXII Corps attached, defend the airfield on the southeastern outskirts of the city and the approaches to the city from the south and west. Preparations for attacking to the east were to commence immediately and be completed on 12 November. This time line was met, and around 0900, 13 November, the Second and Thirteenth Armies launched the operation.[94]

Du Yuming's desire to make the relief force as strong as possible made good sense operationally and tactically. He sought to relieve the Seventh Army quickly, and the stronger the relief force, the more likely it was that this could be done. However, bringing the Sixteenth Army north to Xuzhou created a positional weakness of strategic significance. Just as moving the Thirteenth Army into Xuzhou had opened the way for the Shandong army to cut off the Seventh Army, shifting the Sixteenth Army guaranteed the success of the CPFA's operation to capture Suxian and isolate Xuzhou. The Nationalists understood this danger. On 9 November Liu Zhi had ordered the Sixteenth Army to move from Mencheng to Suxian to protect the Xu-Beng railroad. On 10 November the Nationalist strategy session in Nanjing had decided to keep this army just north of Suxian in the Fuliji-Jiagou area. On 11 November, however, Du Yuming and Liu Zhi decided to concentrate as many forces as possible in Xuzhou and make an all-out effort to link up with the Seventh Army. Once that army was saved there supposedly would be time to consider what to do next. Meanwhile, only one division and several battalions of rail security forces with a total strength of approximately 13,000 troops were left to defend Suxian and the surrounding area.

Notes

1. Sunzi, *The Art of War*, Samuel B. Griffith, trans. (New York: Oxford University Press, 1963) 85, 87.

2. Qiu Weida, "*Di qishisi jun de zai ci beijian*" [The Second Destruction of the LXXIV Corps], in *Huaihai zhanyi qinli ji* [A Record of Personal Experiences During the Huaihai Campaign], Zhongguo renmin zhengzhi xieshang huiyi quanguo weiyuanhui wenshi ziliao yanjiu weiyuanhui [The Historical Materials Research Committee of the National Committee of the Chinese People's Political Consultative Conference], eds. (Beijing: Wenshi ziliao chubanshe, 1983), 386, hereafter cited as *QLJ*.

3. Pan Yan, "*Huaihai zhanyi zhong de zhongyuan yezhanjun di yi zongdui*" [The CPFA's 1st Column in the Huai Hai Campaign], in *Huai Hai zhanyi* [The Huai Hai Campaign], Zhonggong zhongyang dangshi ziliao zhengji weiyuanhui [Chinese Communist Party Central Committee's Committee for the Collection of Party Historical Material], ed. (Beijing: Zhonggong dangshi ziliao chubanshe, 1988), vol. 2, 79-80, hereafter cited as *HHZY*.

4. Sun Jixian and Ding Qiusheng, "*Zongheng chicheng aozhan huai hai*" [Sweeping Freely Across Wide Expanses, Fiercely Fighting the Huai Hai Campaign], *HHZY*, vol. 2, 237.

5. Chen Shizhang, "*Di qi bingtuan de huimie*" [Destruction of the Seventh Army], *QLJ*, 191.

6. Liao Tiejun, "*Nianzhuangxu diqu zuozhan huiyi*" [Recollections of Fighting in the Nianzhuangxu Area], *QLJ*, 181.

7. Lei Xiumin, "*Di liushisan jun fumo gaishu*" [A General Description of the Annihilation of the LXIII Corps], *QLJ*, 216.

8. Liao Tiejun, 180.

9. Ibid.

10. Lei Xiumin, "*Di liushisan jun fumo gaishu*" [A General Description of the Annihilation of the LXIII Corps], *QLJ*, 216.

11. Liao Tiejun, 180.

12. Ibid., 180-81.

13. Wang Zejun, "*Di sishisi jun Nianzhuangxu beijianji*" [A Record of the Destruction of the XLIV Corps at Nianzhuangxu], *QLJ*, 196.

14. Ibid.

15. Li Yikuang, "*Huaihai zhanyi guomindangjun beijian gaishu*" [A General Description of the Nationalist Army's Destruction During the Huai Hai Campaign], *QLJ*, 68-69.

16. Ibid., 69.

17. Liao Tiejun, 181; Liu Zhenxiang, "*Di liushisi jun Nianzhuangxu fumo jiyao*" [A Summary of the LXIV Corps' Destruction at Nianzhuangxu], *QLJ*, 231.

18. Ibid.

19. Xiao Dexuan, "*Nianzhuangxu zhanyi qinliji*" [My Personal Experiences in the Nianzhuangxu Campaign], *QLJ*, 206.

20. Lei Xiumin, 217.

21. Ibid.

22. Li Jinxuan, "*Huaihai zhanyi pianduan huiyi*" [Fragmentary Recollections of the Huai Hai Campaign], *QLJ*, 293.

23. Xiao Dexuan, 207.

24. Liu Zhenxiang, 231.

25. Ibid., 232.

26. Li Tianrong and Li Youzhuang, "*Di liushisan jun Yaowanzhen beijian ji*" [A Record of the Destruction of the LXIII Corps at Yaowan], *QLJ*, 224.

27. Zhou Kaicheng, "*Huaihai zhanyi zhong de di ba jun*" [The VIII Corps in the Huaihai Campaign], *QLJ*, 244.

28. Xiong Shunyi, "*Sun Yuanliang bingtuan beijian jingguo*" [The Way the Destruction of Sun Yuanliang's Army Occurred], *QLJ*, 409.

29. US Army Field Manual 3-0, *Operations* (Washington, DC: US Government Printing Office, June 2001), 7-4.

30. "*Huadong yezhanjun Huaihai zhanyi yubei mingling*" [ECFA Warning Order for the Huai Hai Campaign], *HHZY*, vol. 1, 83.

31. He Jifeng, "*Yunhe qianxian qiyi*" [Revolt on the Grand Canal Frontline], *QLJ*, 140.

32. Ibid., 141.

33. Ibid.

34. Ibid., 141-42.

35. Ibid., 142-43.

36. Xu Changlin, "*Di qishiqi jun de qiyi ji qi canbu de beijian*" [The Revolt of the LXXVII Corps and the Destruction of Its Remaining Elements], *QLJ*, 176.

37. He Xiaohuan, Fu Jijun, and Shi Zhengxian, *Huaihai zhanyi shi* [*A History of the Huai Hai Campaign*] (Shanghai: Renmin chubanshe, 1983), 57, hereafter cited as *HHZYS*.

38. Ibid.

39. "*Su Yu, Tan Zhenlin, deng tiaozheng jian Huang Baitao bingtuan bushu zhi ge bingtuan, ge zongdui shouzhang de dianbao*" [Telegram From Su Yu, Tan Zhenlin, and Others to the Commanders of Every Army and Column Concerning Adjustments in the Deployment for Destroying Huang Baitao's Army], *HHZY*, vol. 1, 141.

40. Cheng Jun, "*Cong tupo yunhe dao gongzhan Dawangzhuang, Jiangudui*" [From Breaking Through at the Grand Canal to Taking Dawangzhuang and Jiangudui], *HHZY*, vol. 2, 275.

41. Ibid.

42. Ibid., 276.

43. Ibid. See page 273 for a description of how these floating bridges were constructed.

44. Zhuo Zhijian, "*Yongmeng qianjin fenzhan Huaihai*" [Boldly March Forward, Bravely Fight the Huai Hai Campaign], *HHZY*, vol. 2, 354.

45. Tan Jiping, "*Di sishisi shi zai Bayiji de fumie*" [The Annihilation of the 44th Division at Bayiji], *QLJ*, 235.

46. Cheng Jun, 276.

47. Zhou Zhijian, 354.

48. Ibid., 355.

49. Ibid., 356.

50. Ibid.

51. Hu Bingyun, "*Zai Huahai dazhan de riri yeye li*" [The Days and Nights of the Great Huai Hai Campaign Battles], *HHZY*, vol. 2, 334.

52. Tan Jiping, 236.

53. Ibid., 237.

54. Guo Huaruo, Mei Jiasheng, and Han Nianlong, "*Zhongyuan duo jizhan chuan xi dao jiangnan*" [The Many Fierce Battles on the Central Plains Send a Call to Arms South of the Yangzi], *HHZY*, vol. 2, 250.

55. Ibid.

56. Wang Bicheng and Jiang Weiqing, "*Huaihai juezhan zhong de huaye di liu zongdui*" [The ECFA's 6th Column in the Decisive Huai Hai Campaign], *HHZY*, vol. 2, 263.

57. Nie Fengzhi, "*Ganda ganpin yingyong fenzhan*" [Daring to Fight, Bravely Giving Our All], *HHZY*, vol. 2, 306. In the "10-man bridge" incident, to speed the division's advance, 10 soldiers jumped into chest-deep icy water and held a wooden ladder over their heads while hundreds of soldiers ran across. The ladder is part of the Huai Hai Campaign exhibit in the Military Museum in Beijing.

58. Ibid., 307.

59. Yeh Fei and Zhang Yixiang, "*Jizhi xunmeng jian wandi*" [Using Quick Wit, Speed, and Fierceness to Destroy the Stubborn Enemy], *HHZY*, vol. 2, 209.

60. Ibid.

61. Ibid., 210.

62. Ibid., 209.

63. Lei Xiumin, 220-21.

64. Qian Jun, "*Guanyu luzhongnanzongdui canjia Huaihai zhanyi de huiyi*" (Recollections of the Luzhongnan [LZN] Column's Participation in the Huai Hai Campaign),*QLJ*, 383.

65. Ibid.

66. "*Su Yu guanyu jianmie Huang Baitao zhuli hou youjian Qiu Qingquan, Li Mi bingtuan de bushu zhi Liu Bocheng, Chen Yi, Deng Xiaoping deng de dianbao*" [Telegram From Su Yu to Liu Bocheng, Chen Yi, Deng Xiaoping, and Others Concerning the Deployment for Drawing the Armies of Qiu Qingquan and Li Mi to Their Destruction After Annihilating Huang Baitao's Main Body], *HHZY*, vol. 1, 150.

67. Teng Haiqing, "*Zhuanzhan Huaihai de riri yeye*" [Fighting the Successive Battles of the Huai Hai Campaign, Day After Day and Night After Night], *HHZY*, vol. 2, 221.

68. Li Jinxuan, 293-94.

69. Ibid., 294.

70. Li Tianrong and Li Youzhuang, 225.

71. Liu Zhenxiang, 232.

72. Li Tianrong and Li Youzhuang, 225.

73. Li Shijie, "*Huang Baitao zai Nianzhuangxu zhihui mudu ji*" [An Eyewitness Account of Huang Baitao Commanding at Nianzhuengxu], *QLJ*, 187.

74. Du Yuming, "*Huaihai zhanyi shimo*" [The Huai Hai Campaign From Beginning to End], *QLJ*, 13.

75. Li Shijie, 187.

76. Huang Wei, "*Di shier bingtuan bei jian jiyao*" [A Summary of the Destruction of the Twelfth Army], *QLJ*, 486.

77. Wang Yuting, *Hu Lian pingzhuan* [An Appraisal of Hu Lian's Life] (Taibei: Zhuanji wenxue chubanshe, 1987), 103; "*Zongshu*" [Summary], *HHZY*, vol. 1, 23.

78. Wang Daoping, Zhou Hongyan, and Jiang Tiejun, *Zhenhan shijie de da juezhan* [A Great Decisive Battle Shaking the World] (Beijing: Jiefangjun chubanshe, 1990), 156.

79. Letter to the author from Deng Xiguang who at the time of the campaign was the operations officer, Xuzhou Forward Command Headquarters.

80. Guo Rugui, "*Huaihai zhanji zhong wo suo zhidao de Jiang jun guanjianxing juece*" [What I Know About Key Strategic Decisions Made by Jiang's Military During the Huai Huai Campaign], *Junshi lishi* (Military History), No. 6, 1988, 34.

81. Ibid.

82. Ibid.

83. Du Yuming, 16.

84. Ibid.

85. Ibid., 17.

86. Ibid., 17-18.

87. Guo Rugui, 33.

88. Du Yuming, 18.

89. Ibid.

90. Ibid.

91. Ibid., 18-19.

92. Ibid., 19.

93. Ibid.

94. Ibid., 19-20.

95. *Ming jiang Su Yu* [The Famous General Su Yu], Zhongguo geming bowuguan laozhanshi shiwen jibian weiyuanhui [Museum of the Chinese Revolution's Committee for Collecting and Compiling the Writings of Old Warriors], ed., (Beijing: Xinhua chubanshe, 1986), 392.

Chapter Six
Expanding Campaign Objectives

There has never been a protracted war that benefited a country.
—Sunzi, *The Art of War*

In war prize a quick victory, not extended operations.
—Sunzi, *The Art of War*

We are now fighting an all-out decisive battle with the enemy. During the past two decades of our revolutionary war, it was always the enemy who sought decisive battles with us. Today the situation has changed so that it is we who now concentrate our main forces to seek decisive engagements with the enemy.
—Zhu De, Huai Hai Campaign War Briefing, November 1948

Protracted war, according to Mao Zedong, was the only proper strategy for the Communists to follow in their war with the Nationalists when the enemy was "big and powerful" and the Red army was "small and weak."[1] Under such objective conditions, positional warfare and lengthy battles were to be avoided because they did not support force preservation and army building. Brief engagements and short battles characterized by swift attacks that annihilated enemy units while bringing relatively few friendly casualties were to be the accepted norm until a convergence of political, economic, social, and military factors caused the balance of forces to change. Until that change occurred, Mao said, one of the Red army's principles was to "Oppose protracted campaigns and a strategy of quick decision, and uphold the strategy of protracted war and campaigns of quick decisions."[2]

Even after the first two years of the civil war (1946-1948), with their armies in a stronger position than ever before, the Communists remained reluctant to directly challenge large Nationalist maneuver forces. In May 1948, Zhu De, in a talk to a gathering of East China Field Army (ECFA) commanders had this to say about the tactics to be employed against a force like the American-trained and -equipped V Corps, Second Army:

> We should try to find ways to eliminate the enemy's remaining army units. Once we do, the problem will be more than half solved. You should study especially how to cope with such main enemy units as the V Corps. I have thought out a method for you, namely, the method of catching big fish. When you have hooked a big fish, don't be so impatient as to try to pull it out of the water immediately. The reason is that the fish that has just swallowed the bait can still struggle hard and if you try to drag it out at this moment, the line will probably snap. So you'd better give it more line in the water until its energies are spent. In this way the big fish will end up in your hands. Similarly we should deal with the enemy's V Corps by the method of 'inducement.' When the corps comes to attack, we should retreat. When conditions are favourable for us, we should intercept it; otherwise we should not. In this way, the enemy troops will be exhausted by our manoeuvres and their ammunition will almost be depleted. Then we should rush a huge force to attack and annihilate them. You must make up your mind to catch one or two big fish like the V Corps.[3]

In late summer 1948 Zhu and other Communist military leaders were still holding to the view that, given the balance of forces in the central plains, it would be premature to be drawn into a decisive battle with the Nationalist forces there. In a briefing at People's Liberation Army (PLA) headquarters on 23 August, Zhu De stated that while the Nationalists were organizing "many large army formations" and seeking a decisive battle, the PLA would avoid such an encounter:

> We won't fight that battle, for the opportune time hasn't come yet. A premature decisive battle would not be to our advantage. Thus we now are only carrying out some manoeuvres against the enemy in the Central Plains. We will do our utmost to develop production to prepare the materiel conditions (mainly shells and explosives) so that, when conditions are ripe, we will wage a decisive battle with the Kuomintang troops in the Central Plains. By that time we will have to 'gnaw' at what seemingly can't be 'gnawed' at and 'remove' what seemingly can't be 'removed.'[4]

The sudden total collapse of the Nationalist forces in northeastern China in late October and early November changed this perception of what could be achieved on the central plains. Nationalist losses, coupled with incorporating many captured soldiers into the PLA, meant the overall balance of military forces across China had shifted to the point at which a strategy of protraction was no longer necessary. Now it was desirable to push for victory before Jiang Jieshi had time to replenish his losses and redeploy his armies. Looking at the war situation as a whole, Communist leaders began to consider expanding the Huai Hai Campaign's objectives into a decisive battle.

Su Yu's Strategic and Operational Analysis

Before the start of the Huai Hai Campaign, thoughts about a sequel to destroying the Seventh Army centered on attacking Huang Wei's Twelfth Army and Sun Yuanliang's Sixteenth Army. In a 5 November message to the Central Military Commission (CMC), Chen Yi and Deng Xiaoping stated that those armies would become their objective after they attacked Liu Ruming's Fourth Pacification Area.[5] A CMC message sent to Su Yu, other ECFA commanders, Chen, and Deng at 2000, 7 November also mentioned attacking these armies after the Seventh Army was eliminated, but it described such a scenario as occurring because of a Nationalist decision to keep its forces in Xuzhou where they would become vulnerable to being isolated:

> We estimate that the first series of battles will require approximately ten days. We will strive to destroy Huang Baitao's ten divisions (including the XLIV Corps), one or two of Li Mi's divisions, Feng Zhian's four divisions (including those that may possibly defect), and Liu Ruming's six divisions (including those that may possibly defect). Altogether this is some 21-22 divisions. If we can achieve this objective, the entire situation will change and you and Chen and Deng may find it possible to push close to the Jin-Pu railroad. At that time Jiang Jieshi will probably withdraw his forces that are in and around Xuzhou to the area south of Bengbu. If the enemy doesn't withdraw, we can then fight a second series of battles to destroy Huang Wei and Sun Yuanliang and completely isolate the enemy force in Xuzhou.[6]

Su Yu took this CMC thinking a step farther. For him, it was not enough to see whether the enemy would withdraw from Xuzhou and then decide on a course of action. As he looked ahead at both the operational and strategic levels, he concluded that it would be beneficial for the Communists if they could quickly destroy all of the Nationalist armies north of the Yangzi River. Around 0800 8 November he communicated a proposal to do just that to the CMC, Chen, Deng, and the Chinese Communist Party's (CCP's) East China Bureau and Central Plains Bureau. For Su, the issue of isolating the Nationalist armies in Xuzhou was not one to leave to the enemy to decide. He wanted to ensure that isolation by ECFA action. His greatest concern was whether the Communist base areas in northern and eastern China could support an extended large-scale campaign at this time. If they could, based on the analysis presented in his message, he wanted to have the ECFA start setting the stage for that larger campaign even as it fought to destroy the Seventh Army:

1. The recent continuous string of victories in every battlefield across the nation, especially the great victory in the Northeast and the complete liberation of that area, has rapidly brought about a momentous change in the war situation. Under these circumstances Bandit Jiang will probably adopt one of the following two courses of action:

A. He might add the troops now being evacuated from Huludao to his forces north of the Yangzi River and continue fighting with us north of the Yangzi River in an effort to gain time so he can strengthen his defenses along the Yangzi River, in the area south of the lower Yangzi, and throughout south China.

B. He might immediately abandon the Xuzhou, Bengbu, Xinyang, Huaian, and Huaiyin areas and pull the forces that he has north of the Yangzi River back to defend along the Yangzi, quickly strengthening river defenses to defend against our crossing to the south. The purpose would be to gain time so he could reorganize his forces and attempt to divide the rule of China with us along the Yangzi while he looks for opportunities to counterattack.

2. If Bandit Jiang adopts the first course of action, we will still have opportunities to carry out the large scale destruction of enemy units north of the Yangzi. If we're able to destroy large numbers of the enemy north of the Yangzi this will create more advantageous conditions for crossing the river later. Moreover, it will mean that after our main forces cross the Yangzi there will not be heavy fighting in Jiangsu, Zhejiang, Anhui, Jiangxi, and Fujian. (If we destroy enemy forces north of the Yangzi on a large scale the only heavy fighting will be in south China.) Also, none of these five provinces will suffer great destruction, and our army will be able to recover easily after liberating them. However, continued fighting north of the Yangzi will mean a heavier burden for the older liberated areas in northern and eastern China. This is a disadvantage.

If Bandit Jiang adopts the second course of action, the burden on the old liberated areas in northern and eastern China will be much lighter and they can recover quickly. However, our future crossing of the Yangzi River will be more difficult (The difficulties can be completely overcome.) and during the time we're crossing there will be some heavy fighting and even a number of seesaw battles in Jiangsu, Zhejiang, Anhui, and Jiangxi. In addition, south of the Yangzi conditions are less conducive to the large scale destruction of the enemy than they are north of the Yangzi. This is another disadvantage.

3. We do not know what level of support for the war effort can still be maintained by the old liberated areas. If they are capable of a higher level of support, then it is more advantageous to force the enemy to implement the first course of action. If you agree that forcing the enemy to adopt the first course of action is the correct approach, then after we destroy Huang's army in this phase of the campaign there is no need to send our main force to attack Huaian and Huaiyin. (The main enemy force in the Xinanzhen-Haizhou area has already withdrawn to the west.) Instead, we will move the main force toward the Xu-Gu [Xuzhou-Guzhen] railroad to keep the enemy in Xuzhou and the surrounding area. Then we will weaken individual units and gradually destroy them. (Or, perhaps we will destroy Sun's army or Huang Wei's army.) At the same time we will send part of the main force south of the Huai River to cut the Pu-Beng [Pukou-Bengbu] railroad, disrupt enemy dispositions, and isolate all enemy units in Xuzhou and Bengbu. In order to accomplish this, while the first phase of the campaign is underway we should send a force to destroy the Xu-Beng railroad to block and delay the southward movement of the enemy.

Please inform us what you think of our humble ideas.[7]

Campaign Visions of 9-13 November

The CMC quickly agreed that Su Yu's analysis was correct and decided to follow his recommmendation that the Nationalist forces in Xuzhou be kept from withdrawing to the south. On 9 November it approved Su's proposal and began taking action to achieve this new expanded objective. Two fundamental assumptions guided the planning that day: the Seventh Army would quickly disintegrate and the Second and Thirteenth Armies would soon abandon Xuzhou and flee south. In his message of 8 November, Su Yu had suggested sending his main force against the Xu-Gu railroad after the Seventh Army was destroyed "to keep the enemy in Xuzhou and the surrounding area." Given the ECFA columns' location on 9 November and their need to still fight the final battle of annihilation with the Seventh Army, the earliest that could happen was still several days in the future. Feeling that immediate action was needed and that the Central Plains Field Army's (CPFA's) current shaping operation west of Xuzhou was not essential to ECFA success, the CMC decided to give that mission to the CPFA. In its message of 1600, 9 November, the CMC also directed Su Yu to not only destroy the Seventh Army but also to quickly inflict as much damage as possible on the Thirteenth Army:

(1) The enemy in Xuzhou has the appearance of making a general withdrawal. Your calculations for swiftly deploying forces to cut the enemy's route of withdrawal in order to surround and destroy him are correct.

(2) The forces under the direct command of Chen and Deng, including the [CPFA] 1st, 3rd, 4th, and 9th columns should move directly on Suxian and cut the Su-Beng railroad. The 4th Column should not attack Qiu Qingquan in the Huangkou area, but should move rapidly to attack Suxian. After the 1st Column has defeated the 181st Division it should move immediately to

Suxian. The mission of the ECFA's 3rd Column and Liangguang Column is to maintain pressure on Qiu Qingquan, but they should take up positions in the Xiaoxian area and attack the Huangkou-Xuzhou rail line from the south. This will make it easier to coordinate with our forces at Suxian. If the enemy carries out a general withdrawal toward the south, then all six of these columns should be concentrated to attack him.

(3) Su [Yu], Chen [Shiju], and Zhang [Zhen] should order Tan [Zhenlin] and Wang [Jianan] to concentrate the 7th, 10th, and 13th columns and the 11th [E] Column that is moving from the south to the north and attack Li Mi's army with all their strength. They should use the technique of rapid movement to destroy all or a large part of that army and control and cut the railroad between Xuzhou and Yunhezhen. The main maneuver force can destroy Huang [Baitao]'s army.

(4) If the preceding things are done, we will be able to ruin the enemy's plan for a general withdrawal, his entire force will meet annihilation, and we will occupy Xuzhou. Now it's not a question of allowing the enemy to withdraw either south of the Huai River or south of the Yangzi River. Now it's a matter of in the first stage (that is, the currently ongoing Huai Hai Campaign) annihilating the enemy's main forces north of the Huai River and in the second stage (the future Yangzi River-Huai River Campaign) annihilating the remnants of these forces north of the Yangzi River.

(5) The enemy's command structure is in a panic and confused. We wish that you will resolutely implement the plans presented above. The more resolute and audacious we are, the easier our victory will be.[8]

A very brief message the CMC sent to Chen Yi, Deng Xiaoping, Su Yu, and the CCP's East China Bureau at about the same time as this message reiterated the need to isolate the Nationalist forces in Xuzhou. The message also brought up another important subject—the increased logistics requirements of an expanded campaign: "You should exert the greatest effort to destroy the enemy main force in the Xuzhou area. Do not allow it to scurry off to the south. . . . The East China, North China, and Central Plains areas must exert all of their strength to guarantee supplies for our army."[9]

Only a day after stating that the Nationalist armies in Xuzhou appeared to be preparing to abandon the city, the CMC changed its position. That assumption was no longer part of the planning process. The order to have the CPFA attack Suxian and occupy the central position, however, was not changed. That operational maneuver was still considered a critical part of setting the stage for a battle with those armies that would occur sometime in the future. This viewpoint was expressed clearly in the following message sent only to Chen Yi and Deng Xiaoping at 0300, 10 November:

1. Feng Zhian's entire force has defected. Because on 8 November Liu Zhi wasn't sure about the situation regarding Liu's force, at 0100 9 November he ordered Huang and Li's armies to withdraw to Xuzhou and set up a defense. Qiu's army is still in the Huangkou area. He does not have the mission of moving east to reinforce Huang and Li, and also has no intention of withdrawing to the south. Liu Zhi has ordered Sun Yuanliang to quickly move back to Suxian.

> The enemy is deploying to firmly defend Xuzhou, Huangkou, and Suxian.
>
> 2. You should concentrate all your forces (including the ECFA 3rd and Liangguang columns) to capture Suxian, destroy Sun Yuanliang, gain control of the Xu-Beng railroad, and cut off the enemy's route of withdrawal. The sooner the better. This is very important and we hope that it's accomplished. As far as Liu Ruming's force is concerned, don't pay any attention to it.[10]

Although the assumption about the imminent Nationalist retreat from Xuzhou had been quickly discarded, the assumption that the Seventh Army was on the verge of collapse remained strong. For several days it was an important element in decision making. A message the CMC sent to the CPFA and ECFA commanders at 1600, 11 November set forth a vision of future movements and operations based on the assumption that the Seventh Army would be annihilated by 15 November and that the ECFA would then replace the CPFA in the Suxian area. This message also expressed the CMC's supposition that by that date the CPFA would have destroyed the Sixteenth Army and occupied Suxian:

> (2) Given this [fluid] situation, once you have destroyed Huang Baitao and Sun Yuanliang's two armies and captured Suxian and the Xu-Beng railroad, then Xuzhou will be encircled and we can prepare for our second step, the destruction of Qiu and Li and the seizure of Xuzhou.
>
> (3) After Huang and Sun have been destroyed and Qiu and Li have been surrounded, the possibility is very great that Jiang Jieshi will order Qiu and Li to break out to the south or to the west and will order Huang Wei to coordinate with them. Because of this, after the destruction of Huang and Sun, all of the ECFA, except for a portion that will remain east of Xuzhou, should swiftly move to positions on both sides of the Xu-Beng railroad centered on Suxian. The CPFA and the ECFA 3rd and Liangguang columns should wait until after Su Yu and Tan Zhenlin's force reaches the Xu-Beng railroad and then move rapidly to the area between Yongcheng and Shangqiu. This will keep Huang Wei and Qiu and Li from establishing contact and will complete the strategic deployment for attacking Xuzhou. This deployment should be carried out immediately following the destruction of Huang and Sun's armies. The time for this to happen will probably be around 15 November.[11]

So confident was the CMC that the Seventh Army would soon be eliminated that in this same message it asked Su Yu to alter his plan to have the Subei army advance toward Xuzhou from the southeast. The CMC approved of Su's intention to have the Subei army swing south through Suining, but once there, the army was to stop and block the many soldiers from the Seventh Army that were expected to flee in that direction. The CMC wanted the Subei army to perform this task until the Seventh Army was completely destroyed and then move directly to Suxian to become part of the ECFA force replacing the CPFA in the central position.[12]

A 0300, 13 November a CMC message to CPFA and ECFA commanders showed no change in the vision of how the campaign would develop. The CPFA would destroy Sun Yuanliang's army and move to counter Huang Wei after the ECFA replaced it in the central position. The tone of the message was optimistic, but it also contained an incipient sense of urgency caused by Huang's Twelfth Army's move to the east. "If you are able in a day or two to destroy Sun Yuanliang and control the Xu-Beng railroad," the CMC told Liu Bocheng, Chen Yi, and Deng

Xiaoping, "then there will be ample time to counter Huang Wei."[13] For Su Yu the CMC raised the question, "Is it possible to have the Subei Army move west to Suxian earlier to link up with the CPFA so it will be easier for the CPFA to shift westward in a few days to Yongcheng to counter Huang Wei?"[14] Su was also reminded that "After Huang Baitao has been eliminated, it is important that the main body of the ECFA move swiftly to the Suxian area."[15]

The CPFA Occupies the Central Position

On the morning of 10 November Liu Bocheng and his staff arrived at Chen Yi and Deng Xiaoping's headquarters near Yongcheng after a rapid, arduous journey from southwestern Henan. Behind them, the 2d and 6th Columns were also moving east, trying to beat Huang Wei's Twelfth Army to the Guoyang-Suxian area. On 3 November Liu Bocheng had pointed out the vulnerability of the Xu-Beng railroad supply line and had suggested that an attack on Suxian would be an effective way to keep the Second and Thirteenth Armies from concentrating their combat power east of Xuzhou. Now, just a week later, the CPFA was preparing to attack Suxian in pursuit of a much larger goal—isolating and destroying those armies. At 1600, 10 November Liu Bocheng, Chen Yi, and Deng Xiaoping responded to their 9 November order by informing the CMC and Su Yu that "tomorrow night, the 11th, we will start our advance southward toward Suxian."[16]

At 0400, 11 November the CMC sent a message to Liu, Chen, and Deng reporting that when their forces reached Suxian they would encounter Sun Yuanliang's Sixteenth Army headquarters and its army assets, two corps headquarters and their corps assets, plus three divisions. The message further directed the CPFA to destroy that force as part of its strategic mission of encircling Xuzhou. With that accomplished, the CPFA would use Suxian as the center point for establishing control over the entire Xu-Beng railroad. Several defense lines were to be built to block the Nationalist forces that were expected to begin fleeing Xuzhou. Preparations were also to be made to help the ECFA wipe out those forces. The CMC also optimistically told Liu, Chen, and Deng to have their forces on alert to intercept Seventh Army remnants that would be trying to escape to the south.[17]

What would have happened if the Nationalists had not decided on 11 November to shift the Sixteenth Army from Suxian to Xuzhou is impossible to know. A few days later the Sixteenth Army helped defend Xuzhou against ECFA attacks. In this regard, the Nationalist move made tactical sense. However, by practically abandoning the campaign area's central position to the CPFA, the Nationalists were giving the Communists an important positional advantage at the operational level. It is not certain that the Sixteenth Army would have failed to hold Suxian. Furthermore, even if the army had been destroyed while defending Suxian, the CPFA's cost of fighting a major positional battle would have been high. This would have affected future Communist calculations about how to deal with other Nationalist forces on what was to become the southern front.

On the night of 11 November the CPFA set off on schedule. The 3d Column, augmented by the 9th Column's 27th Division and the column artillery battalions from the 1st and 9th Columns, was to encircle and capture Suxian.[18] The rest of the 9th Column and the Yu-Wan-Su independent divisions were to move past Suxian on the west and advance as far south as possible down the Xu-Beng railroad, destroying the track and all bridges along the way. To the left of the 3d Column three divisions of the 4th Column were to move past the southern end of the line

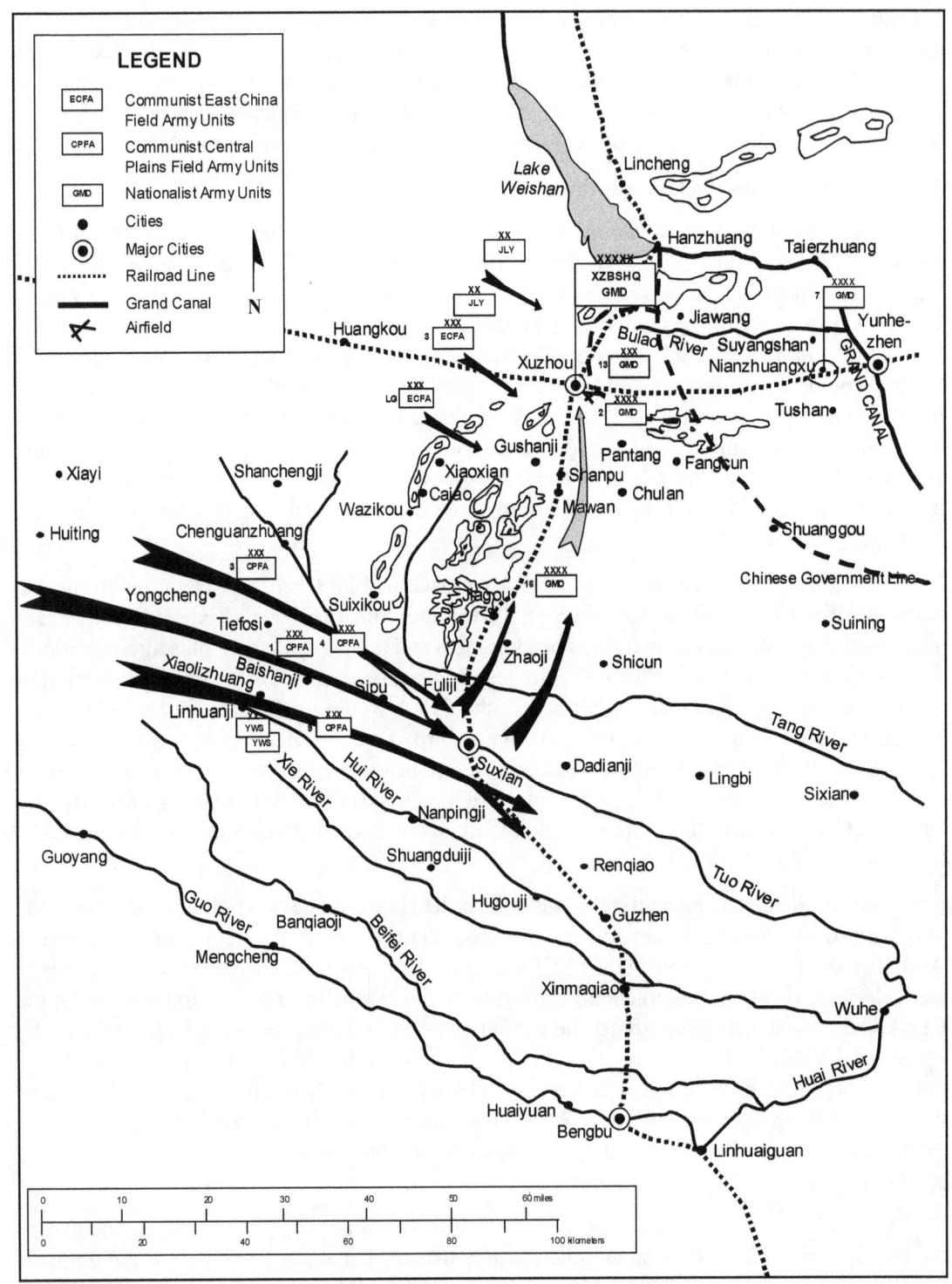

Map 1. The CPFA seizes the central position.

of hills that extended southwest from Xuzhou and attack Fuliji. The 1st Column, having just fought a battle in which it destroyed the Second Army's 181st Division near Shangqiu, was to serve as a reserve. To the north of these CPFA columns the ECFA 3d and Liangguang Columns were to move into the hills southwest of Xuzhou and threaten Xuzhou from that direction.

On 12 November the CPFA columns and the two ECFA columns attached to the CPFA advanced quickly against little opposition. The 3d Column swept through Nationalist screening forces and outposts and reached the Suxian area during the night. The 9th Column and the Yu-Wan-Su divisions also reached the Suxian area and continued on toward Guzhen. North of Suxian, the 4th Column captured Fuliji and in the Jiagou area north of Fuliji intercepted part of the Sixteenth Army's XLI Corps as the corps was moving toward Xuzhou. In a short, bitter battle the 4th Column killed, wounded, and captured more than 3,000 soldiers from the 122d Division and units attached to the corps headquarters.[19] The column also captured several artillery pieces and 16 trucks.[20] Still farther north, on the evening of 12 November the ECFA 3d and Liangguang Columns reached Xiaoxian and Wazikou.[21]

Because the Sixteenth Army's move to Xuzhou had implications for the battle east of Xuzhou, late on 12 November Liu Bocheng, Chen Yi, and Deng Xiaoping decided they must increase pressure against the Nationalist defenses south of Xuzhou to tie down as much of the Sixteenth and Second Armies as possible. The ECFA 3d and Liangguang Columns and the CPFA 4th Column received this mission. The ECFA 3d and Liangguang Columns were to establish a line through the hills east of Xiaoxian to Sanpu, a village only 15 km south of Xuzhou, and move north. The CPFA 4th Column was to push north from Jiagou along the Xu-Beng railroad and the road running parallel to the rail line. To ensure unity of effort as the three columns came together, on 13 November the ECFA 3rd and Liangguang Columns were placed under CPFA 4th Column commander Chen Geng's command.[22]

During the morning of 13 November the CPFA 3d Column encircled Suxian. Its first attack against the city was launched that evening, making only limited progress because of the formidable defenses. A high wall thick enough for two cars to drive abreast along the top surrounded the old city of Suxian, and a moat 35 feet wide and 10 feet deep was outside the wall. There were four city gates corresponding to the four points on the compass, and outside each gate a bridge crossed the moat. At both ends of each bridge an elaborate system of pillboxes with interlocking fields of fire had been constructed by the Japanese from 1938 to 1945 and reinforced later by the Nationalists. Outside the east side of the city near the railroad station was a large barracks complex surrounded by a wall and defended by pillboxes. This complex, nicknamed "Little Tokyo" because it had been built by the Japanese to house a large garrison, was an integral part of Suxian's defense and presented a major obstacle to an attack from that direction.

After evaluating what had happened during the attack the night of 13 November, on 14 November fire from artillery concealed in houses and explosive charges delivered by teams of sappers forced all Nationalist troops back inside the city walls. Planning then began for a general attack against the city.

This attack began at 1700, 15 November, with diversionary attacks against the northern and southern sides of Suxian.[23] Fifteen minutes later a 30-minute artillery preparation was fired against the eastern and western walls where the two main attacks were to take place. Then, under the cover of suppressing fire directed against the top of the wall, engineers put bridges across the moat, and sappers rushed across to set off explosive charges to break the wall. As the explosives went off they created steep slopes of shattered brick that assault teams used to reach the top of the wall and enter the city. After a night of fierce house-to-house fighting, at 0300, 16 November the Nationalist command post was captured and resistance ended.[24]

While the fighting around Suxian and south of Xuzhou was under way, the 9th Column and the Yu-Wan-Su divisions pushed south from Suxian along the Su-Beng railroad. By 16 November this force had moved close to Guzhen and was engaged in fighting with elements of Liu Ruming's Eighth Army. In just five days the CPFA had opened a 100-km gap between the Nationalist armies in Xuzhou and their base of supply in Bengbu. Operationally this was a significant move. If those armies could not withdraw to the Nationalist lines along the Huai River or be relieved, they would be lost. But the CPFA's situation was also a problem. According to earlier estimates and the vision of how the campaign would develop that had been held from 11 to 13 November, by this time the Seventh Army should have been destroyed and the ECFA should have been ready to relieve the CPFA in the central position. In actuality, the ECFA was not prepared to do this. On 13 November the CMC had decided to follow a new proposal Su Yu made and had adopted a different vision of how the campaign should develop. On 16 November the ECFA was still deeply engaged in combat east of Xuzhou trying to execute that vision, a vision that left the CPFA alone in the midst of six enemy armies—the Sixth and Eighth to the southeast; the Twelfth to the southwest; and the Second, Thirteenth, and Sixteenth to the north.

Su Yu's Sunzian Vision for Shaping the Campaign

During the first few days of the campaign the CMC, and apparently Su Yu too, envisioned that the campaign would take the form of a quick victory over the Seventh Army followed by the ECFA's rapid shift to the central position at Suxian. Once there the ECFA would continue to isolate the Nationalist armies in Xuzhou while the CPFA concentrated against Huang Wei's Twelfth Army. This would create conditions for subsequently destroying the armies of Qiu Qingquan and Li Mi and capturing Xuzhou.

Su Yu, however, soon developed an alternative vision of how the campaign should develop. In keeping with his interest in continuous operations or, at a minimum, short transitions between operations, he preferred not to break contact with the enemy after defeating the Seventh Army and then shift the ECFA's main body 80 km to the southwest. Since the campaign objectives had been expanded, as he had proposed on 8 November, to include destroying the Nationalist armies in Xuzhou, he wanted to engage those armies where he was. His vision was to engage the Second and Thirteenth Armies east of Xuzhou and after destroying a large part of them there finish the job in an attack to take the city.

Su Yu presented this vision and a concept of operations to the CMC and to Liu Bocheng, Chen Yi, Deng Xiaoping, and Su's senior ECFA commanders, in a message transmitted at 1700, 13 November. His proposal, as operational-level plans should, looked ahead in time, space, and events and presented a way to simultaneously progress toward several important objectives. One objective was the speedy annihilation of the Seventh Army, which was the primary objective of the original "little" Huai Hai Campaign. A second objective was to weaken the Second and Thirteenth Armies. Reducing these two armies' ability to generate combat power

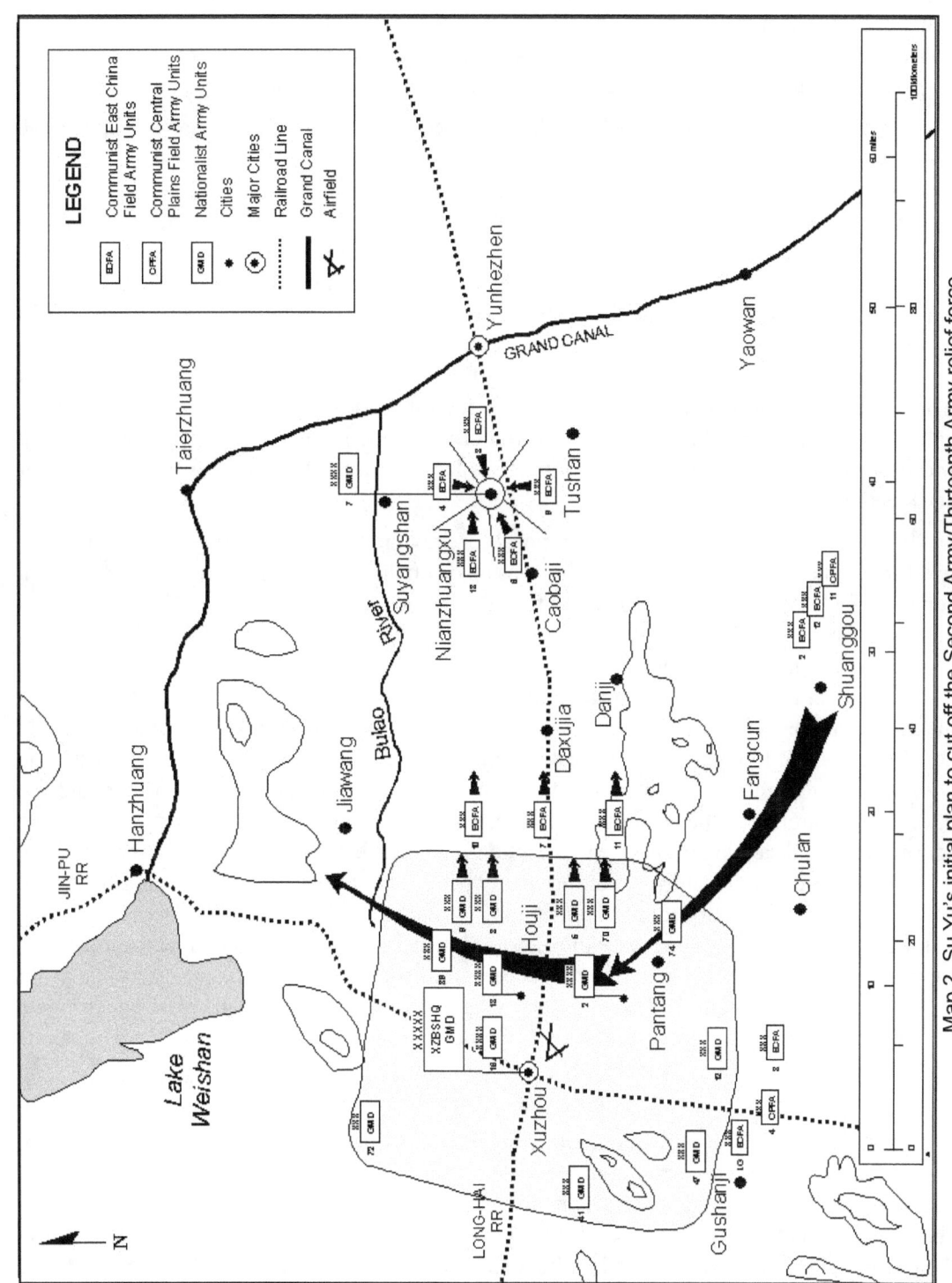

Map 2. Su Yu's initial plan to cut off the Second Army/Thirteenth Army relief force.

would, in turn, contribute to achieving two major objectives of the expanded "big" Huai Hai Campaign—destroying those armies and capturing Xuzhou. Su believed he would be able to shape events in such a way that while destroying the Seventh Army he could draw the Second Army/Thirteenth Army relief force into a position where it could be cut off from Xuzhou. This would set the stage for annihilating that force and assaulting Xuzhou.[25]

Sunzi would have been pleased had this plan been presented to him for approval because it embodied several key concepts contained in *The Art of War*. First, as had Su Yu's original proposal for the Huai Hai Campaign, the plan sought to take advantage of the *shi* (potential energy/momentum) that was present in the existing situation. It also followed Sunzi's idea that the best commanders are able to build on the existing *shi* and create an even stronger, more powerful, *shi*. Sunzi said, "The energy [*shi*] developed by good fighting men is as the momentum of a round stone rolled down a mountain thousands of feet in height."[26] For Su, the ECFA was like that rolling stone and the situation before him—the capabilities and locations of the forces involved, the terrain features, and the Nationalists' strong desire to relieve the Seventh Army—was like that mountain slope. Su knew his force had momentum and felt that conditions provided the opportunity to build even more. Energy, both physical and psychological, was flowing in a positive direction for him. Su wanted to strengthen that flow and direct it for his benefit.

It is not coincidental that Su Yu's proposal for drawing the Second Army/Thirteenth Army relief force into a position of vulnerability was made on the evening of the day this force began attacking ECFA blocking positions east of Xuzhou. Once Su became aware of the intensity of the Nationalist effort, he felt that this desire to save the Seventh Army represented energy that could be used against the Nationalists. Moving the enemy, not being moved by the enemy is an idea that lies at the heart of *The Art of War*. Sunzi speaks about how to draw one's enemy out of strong defenses when one wishes to fight: "All we need do is to attack some other place that he will be obliged to relieve."[27] He speaks of moving the enemy away from places where one does not wish to fight: "If we do not want to fight, the enemy cannot engage us, even though we have no more around us than a drawn line, because we divert him to a different objective."[28] He addresses using deception to shape enemy actions: "When able to attack, we must seem unable; . . . when we are near, we must make the enemy believe we are far away. . . . Hold out baits to entice the enemy. Feign disorder and crush him."[29] Tying these ideas together, Sunzi concludes, "Those skilled at making the enemy move do so by creating a situation to which he must conform; they entice him with something he is certain to take, and with lures of ostensible profit they await him in strength."[30] This is exactly what Su Yu wanted to do. His plan was to create the illusion that the relief force could reach the Seventh Army, lure it eastward, and attack its right flank and rear with the Subei army's full strength.

This luring and attacking reflected the Sunzian concept of using a fixing (*zheng*) force and maneuver (*qi*) force in combination. Other significant themes from *The Art of War* that were part of Su Yu's plan were pursuing numerical superiority at the point of *qi* force (Subei army) attack and using and manipulating human emotions. Su based his proposal on information about enemy and friendly force capabilities in keeping with Sunzi's statement: "He who knows the enemy and himself will never in a hundred battles be at risk; he who does not know the enemy but knows himself will sometimes win and sometimes lose; he who knows neither the enemy nor himself will be at risk in every battle."[31] He also wanted to attain objectives quickly as Sunzi had advocated. Su Yu believed that given the existing *shi*, simultaneously applying these Sunzian precepts would produce a major victory rapidly and set the stage for subsequent operations.

Su Yu's proposal contained several parts. He discussed how he was going to quickly reduce the Seventh Army's combat power. He anticipated that on the night of 13 November an attack by the 4th, 6th, and 13th Columns and part of the 9th Column would destroy the three corps in the western two-thirds of the Nianzhuangxu pocket. These were the XXV Corps in the north, C Corps in the west, and XLIV Corps in the south. Destroying the LXIV Corps and Seventh Army headquarters units would be left until the night of 14 November or 15 November. When the destruction of the LXIV Corps and Seventh Army headquarters troops was imminent, the holding force blocking the Second and Thirteenth Army's advance would feign weakness and withdraw eastward, allowing the Nationalists to advance. After the Nationalists had advanced in what Su assumed would be a rash, hasty manner as they tried to reach Nianzhuangzsu, the Subei army would strike from southeast of Xuzhou and swing around behind the Nationalist forces, cutting them off from Xuzhou. After accomplishing this objective, the Subei army would then attack the Second Army/Thirteenth Army relief force from the west while the blocking force (the 7th and 10th Columns reinforced by the 6th and 13th Columns) would attack from the east. After the 4th, 8th, and 9th Columns eliminated the Seventh Army's last elements, they would move southeast of Xuzhou and, together with the 1st Column and the ST tank force, form a powerful army that could either attack Xuzhou, aid the fight against the Second and Thirteenth Army forces trapped east of Xuzhou, or cooperate with the CPFA to attack Huang Wei.[32]

As if in anticipation that the CMC would approve this plan for engaging Nationalist forces, Su asked that the ECFA 3d Column be reattached to the ECFA to use in attacking Xuzhou.[33] He also expressed the view that the CPFA could handle the Twelfth Army by itself. He further stated that no matter which course of action was adopted, it would be beneficial to the campaign if operations were continuous. Su also mentioned several specific logistics problems that needed to be addressed:

> Due to the enemy's high level of concentration, we have had to increase artillery fire. Also, since we advanced into our present locations there have been difficulties in transporting grain and fodder. Because of this, we ask the CMC and the CCP East China Bureau to be ready to give us several basic loads of artillery ammunition and explosives. (We have already used one of the two loads we prepared and the follow-on supply from the military region has not reached us yet.) We also ask the East China Bureau to send the truck unit to strengthen our transport capability so we will be able to respond to operational opportunities.[34]

Within hours of receiving Su Yu's proposal, the CMC approved his plan. At 2300, 13 November the CMC sent the following message to Liu Bocheng, Chen Yi, Deng Xiaoping, and to Su Yu and his staff:

> (1) At present Qiu Qingquan is moving east as reinforcements. We ask Su [Yu], Chen [Shiju], and Zhang [Zhen] to consider what portion of each of Huang Baitao's corps has been destroyed and then, when Huang's force is about to be wiped out, allow Qiu Qingquan to advance as far east as Daxujia

and Caobaji where his army can be surrounded and not allowed to escape. Afterward, you can slowly annihilate that army.

(2) Liu[Bocheng], Chen [Yi], and Deng [Xiaoping]'s use of part of the force to take Suxian while the main body pursues Sun Yuanliang to the north is an excellent allocation of assets. If Qiu's army can be encircled and destroyed by us in a few days, Huang Wei will certainly move toward Xuzhou to reinforce the Nationalist position there. The CPFA, along with the ECFA 3rd and Liangguang columns, must prepare to fight Huang Wei by itself.[35]

Liu Bocheng, Chen Yi, and Deng Xiaoping's response to this concept came in a message sent at 1000, 14 November to the CMC, Su, and other ECFA and CPFA commanders. Liu, Chen, and Deng did not directly oppose Su Yu's plan, but they mentioned that without ECFA support their options for defending the central position were reduced. They stated that their preferred course of action was to attack Huang Wei's Twelfth Army because it was weary from a long march and was on the move without a base of supply. However, executing that option would require eight columns, and eight columns would not be available unless they could use the 4th (C), 3d (E), and Liangguang (E) Columns fighting south of Xuzhou. With five columns they could only block Huang Wei. If Huang Wei went to Bengbu instead of moving toward Suxian, there was little they could do. In conclusion they said, "Whatever we do must wait for developments on the ECFA's battlefield for a decision. We ask the CMC to check our plans. We ask Su, Chen, and Zhang to inform us daily about their battlefield situation."[36]

At 2300, 14 November the CMC sent out another message confirming its commitment to Su Yu's vision. This message, which was transmitted before the message from Liu, Chen, and Deng was received, was addressed to Liu, Chen, and Deng; Su Yu and other ECFA commanders; and the CCP's East China Bureau and Central Plains Bureau. One of its purposes was to call for a great mobilization effort to support "the largest campaign ever on the southern front."[37] Most of the message, however, was devoted to Su's concept of operations. The CMC expressed some apprehension about the ECFA blocking force's ability to maintain the gap between the Second Army/Thirteenth Army relief force and the Seventh Army. They asked Su to concentrate his forces and wipe out the XXV, XLIV, and C Corps in accordance with his plan of 13 November, leaving only the LXIV Corps and the Seventh Army headquarters as bait for drawing Qiu and Li's armies into a position where the Subei army would cut them off. The CPFA was given complete responsibility for conducting supporting shaping operations on the southern front: "We should employ the CPFA 1st, 2nd, 3rd, 4th, 6th, and 9th columns and the entire force of the Yu-Wan-Su regional army, taking the Su-Beng railroad as the pivot, to counter Huang Wei and enemy reinforcements that may be added in the south. The entire force of the ECFA will be dealing with the enemy forces that are along the Long-Hai railroad."[38]

Shortly after receiving Liu, Chen, and Deng's 1000, 14 November message, the CMC sent another message addressed to Liu, Chen, and Deng and to Su Yu and Tan Zhenlin. This message, which was transmitted at 0600, 15 November, attempted to address the concerns Liu, Chen, and Deng had about Su Yu's plan. It contained a broad review of the campaign's overall status and agreed to the need to reassess the situation after the Seventh Army was destroyed. Significantly, the message expressed a hint of doubt about Su Yu's plan being successful but also once again expressed support for it:

After we sent out our 2300 14 November message we received Liu, Chen, and

Deng's message of 1000 14 November. We are in basic agreement with you on basic policy. We must wait until after Huang Baitao's army is destroyed, and then, in accordance with the situation regarding the three armies of Qiu Qingquan, Li Mi, and Huang Wei, decide on a course of action.

Maybe our plan to lure Qiu and Li eastward and cut off their route to the rear can't be realized.

To sum up, everything must wait for Su [Yu] and Tan [Zhenlin] to wipe out Huang Baitao and for you to destroy the enemy at Suxian. Then we can decide our next operation on the basis of the changing situation. If, at that time, Qiu and Li withdraw into Xuzhou and Huang Wei moves to Bengbu, conditions for fighting in both places will be unfavorable. In that case it might be good for us to take the opportunity to rest for a short time. However, for now the ECFA still should be seeking to engage Qiu and Li after destroying Huang's army.[39]

Su Yu Attempts to Execute His Plan

Liu, Chen, and Deng's desire for a daily report on the ECFA's battlefield situation reflected their awareness that the campaign's overall development would be shaped by the ECFA's success or failure in executing Su Yu's plan. This was because what the ECFA was able to achieve and when it would do it largely determined the ECFA forces' future location and availability. Su had presented a grand vision and put forth an aggressive, imaginative plan for achieving a desirable outcome. However, because the Nationalists still retained the potential to generate significant combat power, the plan also entailed risks. In *On War*, Carl von Clausewitz describes the element of uncertainty that any plan faces: "War . . . is not the action of a living force upon a lifeless mass . . . but always the collision of two living forces. . . . [T]here is interaction. So long as I have not overthrown my opponent I am bound to fear he may overthrow me. Thus I am not in control."[40]

Sunzi also addresses the limits on a commander's ability to control events with this statement: "Invincibility depends on oneself; vulnerability lies with the enemy. Therefore the expert in battle can make himself invincible, but cannot guarantee for certain the vulnerability of the enemy. Hence it is said: Victory can be anticipated, But it cannot be forced."[41] The Liu-Chen-Deng message of 14 November shows an appreciation for the reality Clausewitz and Sunzi refer to. Liu, Chen, and Deng were concerned that Su Yu's plan might not work and that when the CPFA needed ECFA support it would not be available.

Su Yu certainly also understood that, as stated in FM 3-0, "Plans forecast, but do not predict."[42] He knew that the enemy has a voice in deciding what happens on a battlefield. However, given the flow of events before 13 November, he had good reason to believe he could "force" (shape or form) events and conditions and gain his envisioned great victory. The Seventh Army, having been tightly encircled, was clearly in a vulnerable position. The Second and Thirteenth Armies, given the Nationalist drive to relieve the Seventh Army, seemed susceptible to being drawn into a vulnerable position. Events, however, did not occur as anticipated, and Su Yu's plan was soon in trouble. Three major problems arose, all the result of enemy action. First, the Seventh Army, despite the loss of its LXIII Corps at Yaowan, was still a capable force. Second, the Nationalist relief force could not be lured into a vulnerable position. Third, the Subei army failed to penetrate behind the relief force. Due to these problems, the fighting east of Xuzhou became extended. As the days passed, other Nationalist army maneuvers created threats that eventually forced the CMC to abandon Su Yu's plan.

Sunzi states that "being invincible lies with the defense."[43] The Seventh Army was not invincible on the defense, but it stood its ground and fought far harder than Su Yu had expected. Several factors contributed to the Seventh Army's strong resistance. First, the Nationalist troop density was very high. The original Nationalist defense perimeter only encompassed a circular area about 7 km across, and within that area there were at least 75,000 soldiers. It was therefore not possible for the PLA to find infiltration routes along unit boundaries and penetrate weakly defended areas. Second, the prepared defenses in the Nianzhuangxu area were good. Nianzhuangxu had been the headquarters of the Thirteenth Army's IX Corps, and that corps had constructed a large number of pillboxes and other permanent fortifications. Also on 10 and 11 November the Seventh Army had worked feverishly to build additional defensive positions and connect the various small villages along and within the defense perimeter with a network of trenches. This created a defense in depth and made it possible to quickly reestablish a defense line if PLA units pushed into the outermost defensive positions.

Third, the natural setting favored the defense. Nianzhuangxu and the surrounding villages sat on a flat plain that offered no natural cover to the attacking forces. While the Nationalist forces could use village walls and moats, houses, and defensive works for cover and protection, ECFA soldiers had to advance across bare, open fields. Fourth, the Nationalists possessed significant fire power. In addition to the artillery available at division and corps levels, the army also had two artillery battalions, including a 105mm howitzer battalion, under its direct control. These two battalions were positioned near Seventh Army headquarters in Nianzhuangxu to provide additional fire support to any sector of the perimeter. Supplementing this ground artillery was aerial strafing and bombing by the Nationalist air force. Fifth, Nationalist morale was reasonably good. The army had advanced close enough to Xuzhou so that being relieved did not seem impossible. The sight of Nationalist planes attacking ECFA positions and dropping supplies was a constant reminder that they had not been abandoned. All these factors combined to produce an ability and a will to resist that surprised Su Yu and other ECFA commanders.

The strength of the Seventh Army's defenses became apparent as the pursuing ECFA columns approached the outer Nationalist defenses around Nianzhuangxu on 11 November. In keeping with their directives to be aggressive, ECFA commanders launched hasty attacks against what they assumed would be weak and ineffective Nationalist resistance. What they found was that withering Nationalist fire more than matched the attacking ECFA soldiers' enthusiasm around the Nationalist perimeter. Casualties mounted and the attacks ground to a halt. Finally, shocked commanders ordered their units to pull back while they considered what to do next. The chief of staff, 4th Column, which was advancing in the sector northeast and north of Nianzhuangxu, described the situation:

> When the vanguard of our column, which had been conducting a vigorous pursuit around the clock for five days, approached the enemy positions and began receiving fire we realized that the situation had changed. The pursuit operation had turned into an assault against fortified positions. The right and left flanks of the column were blocked . . . and reverses were suffered. The column commander immediately ordered a halt to the attacks and directed that units withdraw beyond the range of enemy guns. He also requested that each

division commander use the next three days to complete preparations for attacking field fortifications. Cadre were sent out by the column to each division to supervise their study of the situation. The column also stipulated that even after units had completed preparations for an attack they could not launch an attack without first obtaining approval from the column.[44]

Pressure to destroy the Seventh Army as rapidly as possible, however, did not allow three days to prepare for an attack. Under Su Yu's direction, at 2030, 12 November the ECFA 4th, 8th, 9th, 6th, and 13th Columns launched a coordinated attack against the Seventh Army perimeter.[45] In the south the 9th Column, one of three ECFA columns that had received special training in the techniques of attacking fortified positions, pushed forward to the XLIV Corps' main defense line, the railroad embankment that ran through its sector. To the west the 6th and 13th Columns had some success, driving C Corps units out of two villages. However, along the northern and eastern sides of the perimeter, the 4th and 8th Columns made little progress. On the whole, the results were disappointing, considering the number of casualties suffered.

Fighting on 13 November brought little change. In mid-morning part of the 9th Column pushed the last of the XLIV Corps units defending along the Long-Hai railroad embankment to the north of the embankment. From the embankment PLA soldiers could now look across open fields and see the village of Nianzhuangxu 2 km away. Further advance, however, proved impossible in the face of Nationalist artillery fire and bombing and strafing runs conducted by Nationalist aircraft flying out of Xuzhou.[46] Worse yet, the major attack on the night of 13 November that was supposed to destroy the three corps in the western portion of the pocket also failed to make any significant advances. Contrary to the expectations of 11, 12, and 13 November, when dawn broke on the morning of 14 November, the Seventh Army was still intact.

After the attacks carried out during the night of 13 November failed, Su Yu decided that changes needed to be made. To find out what was going wrong and devise ways to speed the Seventh Army's defeat, he called the six column commanders participating in the battle against the Seventh Army—the 4th, 8th, 9th, 6th, 13th, and ST—to meet with him at his forward headquarters at Tushan (10 km south of Nianzhuangxu) the evening of 14 November.[47]

This meeting addressed a number of issues, including command structure, strategy, tactics, and morale. To achieve greater unity of effort in attacks against the Seventh Army, Shandong army headquarters (Tan Zhenlin, commander; Wang Jinan, deputy commander) was to move to the Nianzhuangxu area and control the six columns involved.[48] This was made possible by shifting command responsibility for the blocking force east of Xuzhou—the 7th, 10th, and 11th (E) Columns—from Tan Zhenlin and Wang Jianan to the 10th Column commander.[49] A general strategy was adopted: "First attack the enemy's weak units and isolate his strong ones; then attack his command structure and disrupt his dispositions. Afterward concentrate forces and destroy him."[50] They also agreed on a series of measures to take at the tactical level to improve the effectiveness of ECFA attacks and reduce casualties.

One of the changes at the tactical level was adopting what could be called the indirect approach. Instead of attacking the strong points the Nationalists established in the villages, the ECFA decided to focus its attacks on the defensive lines between the villages. These attacks would cut Nationalist communication links, weaken their command and control structure, sap the defenders' morale, and create favorable conditions for assaults against the strong points.

Another step would increase ECFA artillery fire against Nationalist artillery and defensive positions before and during an attack. More emphasis was also placed on using trenches to counter the effect of Nationalist firepower. Trenches were to be dug as close to Nationalist lines as possible so assault units would be exposed to Nationalist observation and fire for the shortest possible time as they rushed toward Nationalist positions. Particular attention would be given to developing techniques for digging trenches under fire and to improving night-fighting tactics and procedures.[51]

On 15 November all attacks ceased as the ECFA examined how to adjust troop dispositions, organize artillery fire, replenish ammunition, and prepare for another general attack against the Seventh Army.[52] The plan for this attack had been established at the Tushan meeting, and every effort was made to incorporate the decisions reached at that meeting into the operation. Extra care went into observing Nationalist positions and developing avenues for attack. Assault trenches were pushed forward. Firepower was strengthened by adding more artillery pieces and the tank detachment.

On 16 November the Shandong army issued the order for a general attack to begin at 1730 on the evening of 17 November following a 30-minute artillery preparation.[53] The 8th, 9th, and 4th Columns were to launch three division-size attacks with supporting attacks around the perimeter of the rest of the pocket. The objective was to destroy what remained of the two weakest corps, the C and XLIV, and push into Nianzhuangxu, the location of Seventh Army and XXV Corps headquarters. The 8th Column attack toward Nianzhuangxu from the southeast was concentrated along the boundary between XLIV and LXIV Corps. The 4th Column attack coming from the opposite side of the pocket was concentrated along the boundary between the remnants of C Corps and XV Corps. On the 8th Column's left, the 9th Column attack was concentrated on the left flank of XLIV Corps near the boundary with LXIV Corps. The 6th Column was positioned southwest of Nianzhuangxu to capture Nationalist soldiers who might try to flee and to serve as a reserve to exploit any 9th Column breakthrough.[54]

Artillery support was key to the attack. After assuming command of the force encircling the Seventh Army on 15 November, Tan Zhenlin and Wang Jianan had asked Chen Ruiting, commander, ST Column, to devise a way to bring more firepower to the fight. In response Chen had developed "The Plan for Using Artillery Firepower in the Unified Attack on Nianzhuangxu." The central concept of the plan was to concentrate artillery to support the three columns that would launch the main attacks. To do this, three artillery groups were formed. The 1st Artillery Group consisted of two companies (eight US 105mm howitzers) from the ST Column and the 8th Column's artillery regiment (16 75mm pack howitzers). Its mission was to support the 8th Column's attack toward Nianzhuangxu from the southeast.

The 2d Artillery Group consisted of two companies (six Japanese howitzers) from the 3d Regiment, ST Column; the 9th Column's artillery regiment (16 75mm pack howitzer); and one company (three 75mm pack howitzers and one Japanese field gun) from the Shandong army's artillery regiment. Its mission was to support the 9th Column's attack toward Nianzhuangxu from the south. The 3d Artillery Group consisted of two companies (six US 105mm howitzers) from the 1st Battalion of the Shandong army's artillery regiment; three companies (nine 75mm pack howitzers) from the 3rd Battalion of the Shandong army's artillery regiment; one company (three 75mm pack howitzers) from the 3d Regiment, ST Column; and the 4th Column's artillery battalion (eight 75mm pack howitzers). Its mission was to support the 4th Column's attack toward Nianzhuangxu from the northwest.[55]

Chen Ruiting's artillery plan stipulated that each artillery group was to form a deep fire section and a close support section. The deep fire section would suppress Nationalist artillery fire and attack other deep targets. The close support section was to use direct fire against Nationalist defensive positions before the attack and against Nationalist points of resistance once the attack was under way. The plan also set up a firing schedule for registering the artillery and listed the signals to use for communication among units.[56]

The large-scale attack of 17 November achieved much but still did not meet expectations. The C and XLIV Corps were almost wiped out, but the XXV and LXIV Corps managed to extend their lines and keep the ECFA from penetrating the heart of Seventh Army's defenses. In the southern and southeastern sections, the 8th and 9th Column attacks stalled before reaching Nianzhuangxu. Once again the well-dug-in Nationalist defenses had proven to be a hard nut to crack.

Chen Ruiting placed much of the blame for the failure to achieve objectives on the artillery's inability to suppress fire from Nationalist bunkers. He saw a need for more precise reconnaissance, more thorough preparation, and closer coordination between the assaulting infantry and their supporting artillery.[57] To improve this coordination, the artillery providing direct-fire support was placed under the assault regiment commander's control.[58] Efforts were also made to improve infantry-tank coordination. Because the number of tanks available was small and they were dispersed to several columns, their impact was limited. In addition, due to the lack of training and experience in fighting together, once an attack began the tanks and infantry quickly became separated, further reducing the tanks' effectiveness.[59]

On 13 November Su Yu had predicted that the C, XLIV, and XXV Corps would be eliminated that night. On 18 November this objective had still not been achieved. Despite terrible living conditions and growing shortages of food, potable water, and ammunition, a week after being encircled, the Seventh Army still posed a problem for the ECFA and the CMC.

While the operation to destroy the Seventh Army was falling behind its projected time line, ECFA efforts to cut off the Second Army/Thirteenth Army relief force were also not achieving the anticipated results. On the evening of 15 November, despite the 13 November general attack's failure to achieve its objectives, Su had gone ahead with the operation to lure the Nationalist relief force to the east and attack into its rear area. That night the Shandong army's blocking (*zheng*) force—the 7th, 10th, and 11th [E] Columns—had begun withdrawing to a defense line just west of Daxujia.[60] The main attacking (*qi*) force, the Subei army's 2d, 12th, Luzhongnan, and 11th (C) Columns had also begun moving from Fangcun toward Pantang.[61] In addition, the ECFA's 3d Column and the Liangguang Column, which had been reattached to the ECFA and assigned to the Subei army that day, had begun moving to support the Subei army by advancing toward Pantang from the southwest.[62] However, neither the withdrawal nor the flank attack achieved the desired results. The relief force did not rush hastily to the east and the attempt to push through the Nationalist defenses southeast of Xuzhou and slice behind the relief force was repulsed.

Timing and chance played roles in the failure of the ECFA's first attempt to cut off the relief force. The timing problem was the lack of an interval between the start of the Shandong army's withdrawal and the Subei army's attack. Had the Subei army struck perhaps two days after the 7th, 10th, and 11th (E) Columns started to withdraw, the Nationalist relief force might well have moved far enough east for its attack to succeed. The Nationalist High Command had begun pressuring Liu Zhi and Du Yuming to order a rapid advance as soon as they had received aerial reconnaissance reports the morning of 16 November, describing the movement of large numbers of Communist troops and trucks to the east and northeast. Jiang Jieshi was extremely anxious to exploit the apparent victory and relieve the Seventh Army. However, at this time Du Yuming and Qiu Qingquan were taking units that were part of the existing relief force or could have been added to the relief force and shifting them to the area southeast of Xuzhou where fighting with the Subei army had broken out. By becoming involved in a battle with Nationalist forces at the same time that the 7th, 10th, and 11th (E) Columns were withdrawing, the Subei army reduced the ability and the desire of the Nationalist commanders on the ground to move hastily toward Nianzhuangxu.

Chance compounded the difficulties the timing of the Subei army's advance created. By coincidence, after being disappointed by the slight advances the Second and Thirteenth Armies had made in their attempts to break through the Shandong army defense line east of Xuzhou on 13 and 14 November, Du Yuming had decided the evening of 14 November to send the Second Army's LXXIV Corps down the Xuzhou-Fangcun road the morning of 16 November to turn the Shandong army's left flank. The LXXIV Corps had assembled near Pantang on 15 November and was preparing to start its operation when that evening a screening force from its 51st Division made contact with the Subei army's advance elements. A firefight ensued and by midnight the 51st Division found itself threatened with a double envelopment. The LXXIV Corps commander sent reinforcements forward and temporarily stabilized the situation, but the next morning Qiu Qingquan was concerned enough to order two divisions from the LXX Corps, which was to provide right flank security in the relief force, to the area. During the fighting that night the Nationalists had identified the presence of several columns from the Subei army and knew they faced a large force.[63]

Because the Subei army's advance posed a direct threat to the Xuzhou airfield, on 16 November Du Yuming and Liu Zhi had no choice but to focus their attention on blocking this force. In addition to redeploying most of the LXX Corps, they shifted the Sixteenth Army's XLI Corps from the area west and northwest of Xuzhou to the area on the Second Army's right flank. This move was made possible by attaching two understrength divisions, the 39th and 180th, to the Sixteenth Army and placing them in the defensive positions the XLI Corps' two divisions were vacating.[64] As it moved to the southern side of Xuzhou, the XLI Corps picked up two extra artillery battalions, one from the general reserve LXXII Corps and one from the Sixteenth Army's XLVII Corps.[65] After the Subei army launched a general attack at 1400 with four columns advancing abreast, Du and Liu also sent a reserve battalion of tanks to reinforce the LXXIV Corps.[66] With such an effort being expended in this battle, there was little energy left to push east toward Nianzhuangzu. With most of the LXX Corps removed from his right flank, the commander of the powerful V Corps was reluctant to advance, no matter how favorable the situation in front of him appeared to be. The Subei army's fighting, therefore, was actually counterproductive. It promoted concentration not dispersion. It encouraged caution, not the rash rush to the east that Su had envisioned happening when his *zheng* blocking force feigned weakness and began pulling back.

After realizing that the Subei army could not break through the Nationalist defenses at Pantang and that by continuing to fight there it was harming the attempt to lure Nationalist forces farther east from Xuzhou, during the night of 16 November Su Yu ordered the Subei Army to pull back toward Fangcun and Shuanggou. The Nationalists detected this movement by aerial reconnaissance the morning of 17 November. Coupled with the continued eastward withdrawal of the Shandong Army blocking force and reports from captured soldiers and local peasants that the Communists were running short of food and ammunition, this information led Liu Zhi and Du Yuming to believe that the Communists actually were in retreat.[67] Their response was to order a general advance that began on 17 November and continued the following day.

As the Nationalists followed the withdrawing ECFA units, Su Yu was setting the groundwork for a second attempt to implement his Sunzian plan. By now Liu Bocheng, Chen Yi, and Deng Xiaoping were apprehensive about the ECFA getting bogged down in fighting east of Xuzhou. In a message he sent to his field commanders and to Liu, Chen, Deng, and the CMC at 2100, 18 November, Su Yu sought to allay such worries and gain continued approval for his concept of how the ECFA should be shaping the development of the Huai Hai Campaign.

To do this, Su Yu began his message with a paragraph confidently describing the operation to be launched that night and the expected victory. One additional column, the 1st, had been added to the Subei army, bringing the *qi* (maneuver) force up to a strength of six columns. Su believed that with this addition the Subei army would be able to accomplish what it had failed to do three days earlier—cut off the Second Army/Thirteenth Army relief force and crush it in concert with the Shandong army's three-column *zheng* (fixing) force:

> Liu Zhi has concluded that our army is retreating and has ordered Qiu, Li [Mi], Sun, and Li (Yannian) to organize a pursuit. In addition, in order to entice Qiu and Li [Mi] to advance eastward to the area west of Daxujia, we have abandoned our defensive positions west of Daxujia. Now that the enemy has reached the place that I fixed in advance, I have decided that we will counterattack tonight. The 1st, 2nd, 3rd, Luzhongnan, 12th, and 11th (C) columns will cut off the route of withdrawal of the V Corps [Second Army] and the VIII Corps [Thirteenth Army] and will coordinate with the force in front of these two corps, the 7th, 10th, and 11th (E) columns, to destroy them.[68]

Su also gave an optimistic assessment of the progress made up to that time in the battle to destroy the Seventh Army: "As of today the LXIII, XLIV, and C Corps have been completely destroyed, one-half of the XXV and LXIV Corps have been annihilated, and the enemy is in great disarray."[69] He stated it was possible to wipe out what remained of the XXV and LXIV Corps and the army headquarters by 0700, 21 November, which would totally eliminate the Seventh Army and free up three columns for future action.[70] Su viewed the advance of Li Yannian's Sixth Army on his left flank a matter of "great concern," but he hoped the CPFA would gain time for him to carry out his plans by delaying or blocking all of the Nationalist armies moving north.[71] "If the ECFA has to take on that mission before Huang Baitao is completely eliminated and we are right in the middle of attacking Qiu and Li," he noted, "then I'm afraid the situation could become deadlocked."[72]

Nationalist Moves on the Southern Front

As discussed earlier, even before the CPFA occupied the central position of the Huai Hai Campaign area, in their 1000, 14 November message Liu Bocheng, Chen Yi, and Deng

Xiaoping expressed reservations about the CPFA's ability to hold the central position without ECFA assistance. Initially, their concern was due to the threat posed by Huang Wei's Twelfth Army that left Queshan on 8 November under orders to move across Henan and Anhui to Suxian and then up to Xuzhou. Then, as days went by, other Nationalist actions on the southern front added to their concerns. On 15 November, the day before the CPFA captured Suxian, the Nationalists carried out several organizational changes designed to improve their ability to project power along the Bengbu-Xuzhou corridor. In response to a request from Liu Zhi, Jiang Jieshi established the Bengbu Command Headquarters with Li Yannian, former commander, Ninth Pacification Area, as its commander. Two new armies, the Sixth and Eighth, were formed from several corps that were already in the Bengbu area and other corps that had been evacuated from northeastern China and shifted to Bengbu. In addition, this headquarters controlled a division at Suxian; a division at Lingbi; an assortment of logistics, signal, and engineer units; and the railroad protection units that manned security outposts and operated armored trains up and down the Xu-Beng railroad to forestall sabotage. These forces also represented a threat to the CPFA in its location in the central position.

Neither the Sixth Army nor the Eighth Army was as strong as the Twelfth Army. Like the Twelfth Army, the Sixth Army contained four corps, the XCVI, XCIX, XXXIX, and LIV, with Li Yannian, the army group commander, as its commander. Although these corps were all central government units, they were below strength and deficient in training. They also had very different backgrounds and no experience in conducting operations together. The XCVI Corps had been the garrison force providing security in the Bengbu area up through early November. The XCIX Corps, the strongest of the four, had only recently been detached from the Sixteenth Army and shifted to Bengbu when the Sixteenth Army had moved to Mengcheng. The XXXIX and LIV Corps had just arrived from Pukou after being evacuated by ship from Huludao as the Communists were driving the last Nationalist forces from the Northeast.[73] Since they had been part of the greatest Nationalist defeat up to that time in the civil war, their confidence and morale was low.

The Eighth Army was simply a redesignation of Liu Ruming's Fourth Pacification Area and had just two corps, the LV and the LXVIII. This force, like the Third Pacification Area, had its roots in Feng Yuxiang's old Northwest army, and the Third Pacification Area's defection had increased concerns about its reliability. In fact, a possible reason for creating the Bengbu Command was Jiang Jieshi and Liu Zhi's desire to increase outside control over Liu Ruming's units. Whatever the situation in this regard, Liu Ruming deeply resented having Li Yannian, who as commander, Ninth Pacification Area, had been his equal, appointed as his superior. The relationship between Liu and Li was strained from the beginning, and coordination between the Sixth and Eighth Armies suffered as a result.[74]

For all of their weaknesses, the Sixth and Eighth Armies had enough strength to increase Communist concerns about the southern front. In a message it sent to Liu Bocheng, Chen Yi, Deng Xiaoping, Su Yu, Tan Zhenlin, the CCP East China Bureau, the CCP Central Plains Bureau, and others at 1800, 16 November, the CMC acknowledged that the buildup of Nationalist forces on the southern front posed a growing challenge. When Huang Wei's army, Liu Ruming's army, and Li Yannian's army were added together, the CMC noted, "the total is 25 divisions, which is a large enemy force, and we must plan an appropriate way to deal with them."[75] As these three armies converged on the central position during the next few days, this question became more urgent and eventually sparked a debate among the Communist commanders about what that "appropriate way" should be.

As of 16 November, however, the CMC did not feel these forces were enough of a threat to warrant making a change in ECFA and CPFA missions. Its 1800, 16 November message stated that after wiping out the Seventh Army the ECFA should strive to destroy several divisions from Qiu and Li's armies. The CPFA, it was suggested, could send one part of its force toward Guzhen and another part to occupy Mengcheng. The purpose would be "to lengthen the time before Huang Wei could attack toward Suxian and also to threaten Bengbu."[76]

Two days later the CMC perspective was much the same. At 2400 18 November the CMC sent a message to Liu, Chen, Deng, Su, and Tan that addressed Nationalist advances on the southern front in some detail. (At this time the CMC was unaware of Liu Bocheng's decision to concentrate the CPFA for an attack against the Twelfth Army. That decision was contained in Liu's message of 0900, 19 November, which is quoted in part after this paragraph.) But the CMC did not express alarm about these developments. Instead, the CMC laid out three optimistic scenarios by which the CPFA could still counter all three of the Nationalist armies by itself. The 1st, 2d, and 6th Columns would establish blocking positions in front of the Twelfth Army and attack from both flanks to halt its advance. The 9th Column would block Liu Ruming's Eighth Army in light fighting and send agents to meet with Liu Ruming and his two corps commanders to encourage them to revolt against Jiang Jieshi. The 3rd and 4th Columns, plus the ECFA 1st Column, would engage and defeat Li Yannian.[77] (This suggested use of the ECFA 1st Column was probably based on its location. The column had crossed the Grand Canal at Yaowan on 13 November and was assembling in Fangcun on 17 November after a three-day road march. At the time it sent this message the CMC had not received Su Yu's message of 2100, 18 November. In that message Su Yu stated that the 1st Column had been attached to the Subei army and would be part of his *qi* force on 19 November.) The purpose of these proposed CPFA shaping operations, the CMC noted, would be to allow the ECFA to conduct a decisive operation east of Xuzhou:

> On the northern front, the revolt of He and Zhang was the first great victory. The complete annihilation of Huang [Baitao]'s army, which will occur in a few days, will be the second great victory. If we are able to meticulously organize the battle and wipe out four or five more of Qiu and Li's divisions and hit Qiu and Li so hard that they can't move, then that will be the third great victory.[78]

While the CMC was thinking along these lines, Liu Bocheng was concluding that the CPFA was not large enough to simultaneously counter three Nationalist armies advancing on different routes. On 17 November, the Sixth Army's XCIX Corps broke through CPFA defenses north of Guzhen and advanced 15 km. On 18 November Twelfth Army lead elements reached Mengcheng and in a fierce battle pushed through the CPFA defense line along the Guo River, forcing the CPFA 1st Column to withdraw to the north bank of the North Fei River 12 km north.[79] After considering the situation, in a message sent to the CMC at 0900, 19 November, Liu, joined by Chen and Deng, presented a plan to solve the dilemma before them. They were going to concentrate most of the CPFA against Huang Wei and let the ECFA counter Li Yannian:

> (4) We are having many difficulties coping with the large enemy forces

advancing on two routes with only the six columns that are now at our disposal. If we adopt a frontal defense, we must disperse our troops and cannot annihilate the enemy. Moreover, there is the danger that the enemy on one of the routes will be able to make it through to reinforce Xuzhou. If we could adopt mobile operations free of the mission to keep the Xuahou battlefield isolated, we could gradually destroy the enemy one by one, but this would have an impact on Su Yu's operations. If we tie down Huang Wei and attack Li Yannian, we would need at least five columns to fight Li and there is no assurance that one or two columns could defend against Huang Wei. Given our present posture, if Li Yannian advances rapidly along the east side of the Jin-Pu railroad there is little we can do. Therefore, we will continue to have the 9th Column contend with Li and Liu [Ruming] while we concentrate five columns to first destroy one or two corps in Huang Wei's army and then assist the ECFA in dealing with Li Yannian.

(5) The execution of this plan will mean that Su Yu, Chen Shiju, and Zhang Zhen will need to prepare a way to handle Li Yannian beforehand. We ask the CMC to tell us quickly if this is or is not the proper approach and ask Su, Chen, and Zhang to give us their thoughts.[80]

PLA Commanders Debate Alternative Courses of Action

Passing responsibility for handling Li Yannian from the CPFA to the ECFA ran counter to the concept of operations Su Yu and the CMC had been following since 13 November. However, Liu Bocheng, Chen Yi, and Deng Xiaoping felt they had little choice but to do this. As the message quoted previously indicates, the CPFA could not hold all of the central position against Nationalist advances on the southern front.

Shortly after sending this message, Liu, Chen, and Deng received Su Yu's message of 2100, 18 November outlining his second attempt to execute his plan for continuing operations east of Xuzhou and the CMC's message of 2400, 18 November. Realizing that Su was still pursuing a course of action that could result in the ECFA being tied down east of Xuzhou and that the CMC still thought the CPFA could hold the southern front by itself, they quickly composed a more strongly worded message and sent it to the CMC and Su Yu at 1700, 19 November. In the message they laid out their concerns in detail and called for a complete rethinking of how the campaign should develop. Basically, they suggested abandoning Su Yu's vision, a vision the CMC had adopted several days earlier:

The CMC message of 2400 18 November and the Su, Chen, Zhang message of 2100 18 November have both been read.

(1) The reasons for our decision to attack Huang Wei first were laid out in detail in our 0900 19 November message.

(2) As we observe the fighting east of Xuzhou, we see that six ECFA columns that are comparatively capable of attacking fortified positions have been used in the battle to destroy Huang Baitao and that after continuing for 12 days and nights the combat is still not over. Looking at the remainder of the forces, among which there are only 2-3 columns that are relatively good at attacking fortified positions, when the fatigue that they must be feeling is added in, the

edge of the knife is already dull. To use those forces to annihilate Qiu and Li, who are stronger than Huang, will by no means be easy.

We think that the Xu-Hai operation must be viewed from the perspective of 3-5 months. It must be divided into 3-4 campaign stages. At each stage there will need to be a period for rest and the integration of prisoners in order to guarantee victory. Because of this, under present circumstances, especially in this situation where Li Yannian and Huang Wei are advancing to the north, the best course of action is to do as follows. First, exert every effort to quickly annihilate Huang Baitao and then concentrate the [ECFA's] main body to the east and south of Xuzhou where they can keep watch on the three armies of Qiu, Li, and Sun and capture some rest for ten days to half a month. At the same time, shift five or three columns that haven't been employed yet for use on the southern front where they can coordinate with us to destroy Huang Wei and Li Yannian. This is the safest approach.

If we don't do this, take our own difficulties too lightly, and, under these circumstances where there is no guarantee that the large enemy forces advancing northward on two routes can be stopped, immediately proceed to fight Qiu and Li, then, not only is there no assurance of victory, it is possible that we will lose the initiative. (Among our six columns, all except the 4th have six regiments, and the 9th only has five. On average our columns number less than 20,000 soldiers. Our artillery is very weak, so it can only be used in one place at a time.)

What should be done? Please think about this.[81]

In this message Liu, Chen, and Deng pointed out a simple fact—there were not enough resources to pursue all desired objectives simultaneously. The CPFA could not defend the central position alone and needed immediate ECFA support. If the ECFA continued to engage the Nationalist armies east of Xuzhou in battle and failed to provide that support, there was the real danger that the overall initiative in the campaign would pass to the Nationalists. Su Yu, in his message of 2100, 18 November, had raised this possibility by stating that if he had to engage Li Yannian while fighting Qiu and Li the situation might become deadlocked. The solution that Liu Bocheng, joined by Chen and Deng, proposed was to slow operational tempo to reduce the risk of losing the initiative.

Operational tempo, the rate of military action, is a key element in determining which side possesses the initiative because the side that can consistently act faster than its opponent can react will have the initiative. A tempo advantage can create valuable operational opportunities and facilitate the exploitation of those opportunities because it makes it possible to take action against an enemy who is not fully prepared or may be completely unprepared to respond effectively. By implication, a slower operational tempo therefore means that certain opportunities will be missed or will never occur because the time factor is not being exploited to the fullest extent possible.

As has been discussed, Su Yu was an advocate of trying to elevate operational tempo. His plans for the Huai Hai Campaign sought a high tempo of operations by including surprise; multiple, large-scale simultaneous attacks; and rapid deep maneuver in his operational design.

He wanted to quickly establish a situation in which the Nationalists would be unable to respond in a timely, effective way to his actions. He wanted to maintain pressure on the enemy through continuous operations. Once the campaign began, Su Yu used bold execution at the tactical level to attain a high tempo. The following excerpt from a message Su Yu sent to all ECFA army, column, division, and regimental commanders at 1000, 9 November shows his desire that forces in the field do two things to increase operational tempo—avoid unnecessary combat and give subordinate commanders maximum freedom to display initiative:

> At this moment the 4th, 8th, and 11th [E] columns are attacking Huang's XXV, C, and XLIV corps. Huang's disposition is in disorder and the other [Nationalist] armies are also moving. If we are able to attack courageously in this situation where the enemy disposition is not yet set, we will be more able to create favorable opportunities for disrupting the deployment of the 'Xuzhou Command' and destroying large numbers of the enemy. For this reason, each of our units should not be distracted by small numbers of the enemy, but should attack boldly and bravely, taking advantage of this time when the enemy is panic stricken, confused, and suffering from low morale to destroy him while he is on the move. If we are able to inflict heavy losses on the enemy north of the Yangzi, then not only will we completely change the situation in the central plains, we will open the way to having favorable conditions for our army to execute a crossing of the Yangzi. The ECFA Front Committee makes the following special requests of you:
>
> 1. Each unit must overcome weariness and hardship, must not be distracted by small enemy units, and must not be stopped by rivers or streams. Each unit must resolutely carry out the policy of pursuing the enemy wherever he goes until he is caught and destroyed.
> 2. The enemy has left his fortifications. His organization is in disarray and his morale is low. He is confused. . . . We must be fierce and not allow the enemy to catch his breath. Then we can utterly destroy him.
> 4. During this great war of liberation every member of our forces should gloriously complete their individual mission. Don't fear breakdowns in organization, casualties, difficulties, weariness, or hunger. At the front, as you capture prisoners use them as replacements and as you use them as replacements continue to fight, thus maintaining numbers required for combat, replenishing our strength for battle, and carrying forward the spirit of continuous, protracted combat. At this time political work should display special vigor.
> 5. Because enemy positions are not set and are changing several times each day, in addition to sending out strong reconnaissance units and lightly armed scouts to boldly probe deep into the enemy rear, each unit should, within the overall intent of the operation, act firmly according to their situation so that no opportunities are lost.[82]

Complementing Su Yu's push for a high-tempo pursuit of the Seventh Army was the CMC's order on 9 November that the CPFA take Suxian and occupy the central position. This was followed by Su Yu's proposal of 13 November to encircle part of the Second and Thirteenth Armies and fight them at the same time the ECFA was fighting the Seventh Army. The simultaneous conduct of operations is a major way to increase operational tempo, and as of 15 November the ECFA-CPFA combination was executing three large operations. The risks associated with doing this were assumed to be low because the Seventh Army's disintegration was thought to be imminent. After that collapse happened, as was expected, on the night of 15 November, there would be ample time for the ECFA to send whatever troops might be needed to help the CPFA defend the southern front.

From the beginning, Liu Bocheng, Chen Yi, and Deng Xiaoping had expressed reservations about committing the ECFA to a difficult sequel operation while it was engaged in destroying the Seventh Army. Since then the Seventh Army's strong resistance had caused their concerns to increase day by day. After the initial phase of the campaign when a high tempo of ECFA and CPFA operations had produced much Nationalist uncertainty and disorganization and had led to significant gains, the battlefields had become more stable and the fighting more positional. By the end of the first week of the campaign, the time when audacious maneuver could easily produce great benefits had passed. Liu, Chen, and Deng felt this different battlefield environment required a slower, more methodical course of action.

The CMC was also sensing that a new situation was developing. In a message it sent to Liu Bocheng; Chen Yi; Deng Xiapoing; Su Yu; Tan Zhenlin; and the CCP's East China, Central Plains, and North China Bureaus on 14 November, the CMC estimated that the Huai Hai Campaign would possibly last as long as two months.[83] Two days later in another message to the same addressees, it doubled this estimate and announced the formation of a General Front Committee to help direct the campaign:

> The CPFA and ECFA should prepare to conduct operations in your present locations for the next 3-5 months (including periods for rest, reorganization, and replenishment). The number of people to be fed, including prisoners, will be approximately 800,000 men.
>
> Victory in this campaign will not only settle the situation north of the Yangzi, it will basically decide the situation in the entire country. We hope that this perspective will be the starting point for all planning. Those leaders responsible for overall planning, Liu Bocheng, Chen Yi, Deng Xiaoping, Su Yu, and Tan Zhenlin, will organize a General Front Committee. When possible, five person meetings will be conducted to discuss important questions. For regular activities, Liu, Chen, and Deng will form a standing committee and they will handle everything as the occasion requires. Comrade Xiaoping will serve as the Secretary of the General Front Committee.[84]

Establishing the General Front Committee implemented, in a way, the request Su Yu had made on 31 October to have Chen Yi and Deng Xiaoping exercise overall command of the Huai Hai Campaign. That request had the appearance of a pro forma acknowledgment that Chen Yi was still his superior because, given the distance between the CPFA and ECFA headquarters and the way message traffic between them was routed through the CMC in Xiabaipo, it was impossible for Chen Yi to provide direction to ECFA forces in the field. The CMC, which in terms of communication time was closer to Su Yu than Chen Yi, also recognized its inability to keep abreast of battlefield conditions and issue timely, appropriate orders when it told Su Yu on 7 November: "We completely agree with your plan for attacking.... Don't change your plan.

... In executing this plan, use your judgment and act quickly. Don't be asking for instructions. However, report your views on the situation to us every day or every second or third day."[85]

On 16 November, however, with the need for greater coordination between the ECFA and CPFA already apparent in the concerns about Su Yu's vision that Liu Bocheng, Chen Yi, and Deng Xiaoping had expressed and a long campaign looming ahead, the CMC placed the leading field commanders and political commissars of the two field armies into his new committee. Whereas on 31 October Su Yu had not mentioned Liu Bocheng as joining Chen Yi and Deng Xiaoping in exercising overall command because Liu was far away in western Henan, Liu was included in the General Front Committee due to his command position and presence at CPFA headquarters. Tan Zhenlin's positions as political commissar and acting commander, Shandong army, and deputy political commissar, ECFA, made him a logical choice as a second member from the ECFA. For day-to-day operations, establishing this new committee meant little. No new headquarters organization was created. There was no designated General Front Committee staff. The five committee members only met together once during the campaign and that was in mid-December, well after the outcome of the campaign had been decided. However, by establishing the committee, the CMC showed its adherence to the principle of unity of command and emphasized that the Huai Hai Campaign was a joint ECFA-CPFA endeavor.

Exactly what new role the CMC envisioned the General Front Committee playing in the planning process that the committee members were not already performing is unclear because during the next several days there was not a common committee position on how the campaign should develop. After the General Front Committee was created, the CMC initially continued to support Su Yu's vision for subsequent operations despite Liu Bocheng, Chen Yi, and Deng Xiaoping's concerns about that vision. While the General Front Committee's standing committee advocated shifting units away from the fight east of Xuzhou, Su Yu and Tan Zhenlin, with CMC approval, continued to seek battle with the Second, Thirteenth, and Sixteenth Armies and continued to ask that all ECFA columns be assigned to that battle.

In a message sent at 1700, 19 November to Liu Bocheng, Chen Yi, Deng Xiaoping, Su Yu, and Tan Zhenlin, the CMC approved Su Yu's second attempt to isolate part of the Second and Thirteenth Armies. A word of caution was issued to Su about getting overcommitted in this fight, but he was told to continue with his planned operation. Liu, Chen, and Deng were advised that the CPFA would have to conduct its southern front shaping operations alone:

> We have just received Su Yu's message sent at 2100 18 November. We know that the entire ECFA is engaged on the northern front fighting Huang, Qiu, and Li and at present is unable to divide its forces and help the CPFA fight the enemy on the southern front. We should at present carry out operations following Su's deployment. We ask Liu, Chen, and Deng to deal appropriately with the enemy on the southern front. However, we ask Su Yu to be careful not to become too heavily involved in fighting with Qiu and Li. It's best to first destroy a part of their force.[86]

Within minutes after this message was transmitted, the CMC received Liu, Chen, and Deng's message of 0900, 19 November. After what must have been a frantic burst of activity, at 1900, 19 November the CMC sent a message to Liu, Chen, Deng, Su, and Tan that addressed the issues Liu, Chen, and Deng had raised and modified its directive to Su Yu. With this message, for the first time the CMC gave the ECFA clear responsibility for helping the CPFA hold the central position. The CMC, however, did not completely end Su Yu's operations east of Xuzhou at this time. The shift of forces to meet Li Yannian was couched in terms of creating conditions for Su to continue his fight with the Second and Thirteenth Armies:

> [Liu, Chen, and Deng's] message of 0900 19 November has been read.
>
> This afternoon we received Su Yu's message sent at 2100 18 November which described his use of the entire ECFA to fight Qiu, Li, and Sun. (We also advocated this several days earlier.) Since he was already deployed to do this, we responded with a message this afternoon saying that he could execute as planned. We also gave the entire responsibility for countering Huang Wei, Liu Ruming, and Li Yannian on the southern front to Liu, Chen, and Deng.
>
> Now we have received Liu, Chen, and Deng's telegram sent at 0900 19 November and know that Liu, Chen, and Deng are using their main body to counter Huang Wei, one column to counter Liu Ruming, and have no force to place against Li Yannian. Given this kind of situation, Su Yu must, in the near future, for a short time limit his fighting with Qiu, Li, and Sun to the range of destroying 4-5 divisions so he can pull out the troop strength to take on Li Yannian. Excluding that part of Tan Zhenlin's five columns that is needed to dispose of Huang Baitao's remnants, his force should immediately move west to counter Li Yannian either through destruction or interdiction. Only in this way will the threat to Su Yu's flank be removed and his ability to continue destroying Qiu, Li, and Sun be guaranteed. We ask Su Yu, Chen Shiju, and Zhang Zhen to arrange this carefully and skillfully. This is our sincerest hope.[87]

Clearly, Liu Bocheng, Chen Yi, and Deng Xiaoping's message of 0900, 19 November significantly affected the debate on future courses of action. Their message of 1700, 19 November did even more to shift the campaign's main effort away from the ECFA's battle east of Xuzhou. The CMC response to this message was sent at 2000, 20 November. It reiterated the directive sent the day before asking Su Yu to immediately send most of Tan Zhenlin's force at Nianzhuangxu west to counter Li Yannian. It also confirmed the CPFA mission to concentrate its forces to attack Huang Wei's army:

> According to the 1700 19 November message from Liu, Chen, and Deng, it has been decided that the CPFA will attack Huang Wei. You must assume the complete responsibility for handling Li Yannian. The CPFA is unable to send any troops. Besides the 11th (C) Column and the 13th Column that have already been dispatched, you should swiftly shift the main force made up of the 4th, 6th, 8th, and 9th columns (leave a force to fight the LXIV Corps) to meet Li Yannian. Command responsibility for fighting Li Yannian will be assumed by Tan Zhenlin and Wang Jianan. We hope that Tan and Wang will quickly move their command post to an appropriate location in the area between Dadianji, Chulan, and Shuanggou.[88]

Before receiving this CMC message of 20 November, Su Yu was already reacting to the Liu, Chen, Deng messages of 19 November and the CMC message sent that date. In a message sent at 2100, 20 November he stated that his attempt to cut off part of the Nationalist relief force the night of 18-19 November had failed and that this objective could not be achieved. "Originally I had planned to use the situation in which the Seventh Army had not yet been destroyed and Qiu and Li were energetically pushing east as a relief force to cut off, surround, and destroy part of that force (2-3 divisions), but now that is impossible."[89] In a new assessment of the overall situation, Su agreed with Liu, Chen, and Deng's desire to have the ECFA shift location from east of Xuzhou to the central position and support the CPFA. He estimated that after two more night attacks the Seventh Army's last remnants (three and one-half regiments of the LXIV Corps) would be destroyed and that once that happened the main Nationalist effort would become retaking the central position. Su expressed his determination to keep that from occurring:

> After Huang Baitao has been completely destroyed, we calculate that there is an extremely high probability of the following happening. Qiu and Li's armies will pull back into Xuzhou, go on the defensive, and at the opportune time coordinate with Huang Wei and Li Yannian in an operation in which they will all advance toward the Suxian center point from opposite directions, north, south and southwest, to reopen the Jin-Pu railroad connection. . . . We completely agree with Liu, Chen, and Deng's directive to take 4-5 of our columns, which if the need arises could be increased by another three, and have them coordinate with the CPFA to destroy Huang Wei and Li Yannian. . . . If the enemy forces located in Xuzhou, Bengbu, and Mengcheng advance toward the Suxian center point in an attempt to establish a south-north link, and Liu, Chen, and Deng, with the ECFA 2d and 11th columns, use all their strength to wipe out Huang Wei, then we will use all of our forces to guarantee Liu, Chen, and Deng's victory in the battle to destroy Huang Wei by assuming responsibility for blocking the enemy reinforcements coming from either Bengbu or Xuzhou.[90]

In this way a new vision supplanted Su Yu's vision of how the campaign would develop. Instead of leading the ECFA into a sequel in which it would be fighting against the main Nationalist force, Su was now going to direct the ECFA in shaping operations in support of the CPFA. The new main effort was to be the battle with the Twelfth Army led by Liu Bocheng.

The Seventh Army's Final Destruction

Once the new campaign vision was adopted, Su Yu wanted to finish the fight against the Seventh Army as soon as possible. The general attack on the night of 17 November had destroyed the XLIV and C Corps as effective units. Still, the XXV Corps continued to hold Nianzhuangxu, and the LXIV Corps controlled several villages east and north of XXV Corps positions. The general attack launched the night of 19 November as part of Su Yu's last attempt to cut off part of the Second and Thirteenth Armies inflicted further serious losses. Most of the XXV Corps was eliminated, and Huang Baitao and the XXV Corps commander were forced to abandon their command posts in Nianzhuangxu. As dawn broke on 20 November they fled east with approximately 1,000 soldiers to the nearby village of Dayuanshang, the site of the LXIV Corps headquarters. This corps, which now stood at less than half strength, was basically all that remained of the Seventh Army on 20 November.

After a day to reorganize following the general attack the night of 19 November, on the evening of 21 November the 4th, 8th, and 9th Columns launched another general attack.

Following a heavy artillery bombardment, the 4th Column moved against villages north of Dayuanshang, the 8th Column moved against villages to the east, and the 9th Column conducted a direct assault on Dayuanshang. Around 0600, 22 November 9th Column units penetrated the Dayuanshang defenses, and by 1000 the battle for Dayuanshang was over.[91] By then, the Seventh Army had been reduced to a few remnants holding several tiny hamlets north of Dayuanshang. Late in the afternoon, with darkness falling, Huang Baitao decided there was nothing to do but abandon the fight and try to escape through enemy lines. That evening as Huang and a small group of aides were moving west, they came under fire and Huang was wounded. Realizing he could not avoid capture, he took his own life.[92] The Seventh Army and its commander were no more.

During the next day or two, between 2-3,000 Seventh Army soldiers made their way across country to Nationalist lines east of Xuzhou.[93] Behind them lay 25,000 of their fellow soldiers who had been killed in action. There were also approximately 80,000 prisoners, including several thousand wounded, in ECFA custody.[94] This was an enormous loss for the Nationalists because many of these prisoners would become soldiers in the ECFA as the Communists implemented their principle of obtaining manpower at the front. This phenomenon produced an accelerating change in the force ratio between the two armies. A ratio that favored the Nationalists at the start of the campaign was already starting to move in favor of the Communists. This development had enormous implications for subsequent operations.

Notes

1. Mao Zedong, "Problems of Strategy in China's Revolutionary War," *Selected Works of Mao Tse-tung* (Peking: Foreign Languages Press, 1967), vol. 1, 199, hereafter cited as *SWM*.

2. Ibid.

3. Zhu De, "The Present Situation and the Building of Our Army," *Selected Works of Zhu De* (Beijing: Foreign Languages Press, 1986), 244-45, hereafter cited as *SWZD*.

4. Zhu De, "Four Talks at the War Briefing Meetings Held by the Operations Bureau of the Chinese People's Liberation Army Headquarters, *SWZD*, 249-250.

5. "*Chen Yi, Deng Xiaoping guanyu xian da Liu Ruming bu zhi zhongyang junwei de dianbao*" [Telegram From Chen Yi and Deng Xiaoping to the CMC Concerning First Striking Liu Ruming's Force], in *Huaihai zhanyi* [The Huai Hai Campaign], Zhonggong zhongyang dangshi ziliao zhengji weiyuanhui [Chinese Communist Party Central Committee's Committee for the Collection of Party Historical Material], eds. (Beijing: Zhonggong dangshi ziliao chubanshe, 1988), vol. 1, 124, hereafter cited as *HHZY*.

6. "*Zhongyang junwei yuji diyizhang jian di ershiyi, er ge shi dierzhang da Huang Wei, Sun Yuanliang zhi Su Yu, Chen Shiju, Zhang Zhen deng de dianbao*" (Telegram From the CMC to Su Yu, Chen Shiju, Zhang Zhen, and Others [Including Chen Yi and Deng Xiaoping] Concerning the CMC Estimate That During the First Phase of the Campaign 21-22 Enemy Divisions Would Be Destroyed and That the Second Phase Would Be an Attack on Huang Wei and Sun Yuanliang), *HHZY*, vol. 1, 129.

7. "*Su Yu, Zhang Zhen guanyu di keneng caiqu de fangzhen ji wo zhi duice zhi zhongyang junwei deng dianbao*" [Telegram From Su Yu and Zhang Zhen to the CMC and Others Concerning the Policies the Enemy Might Adopt and Our Response], *HHZY*, vol. 1, 131-32.

8. "*Zhongyang junwei guanyu pohuai diren zong tuique jihua jian di yu Huaihe yi bei zhi Chen Yi, Deng Xiaoping deng de dianbao*" (Telegram From the CMC to Chen Yi, Deng Xiaoping, and Others [Including Su Yu] Concerning How to Wreck the Enemy's Plan for a General Withdrawal and Destroy the Enemy North of the Huai River) *HHZY*, vol. 1, 136-37.

9. "*Zhongyang junwei guanyu wu shi Xuzhou diren nan cuan zhi Su Yu, Zhang Zhen de dianbao*" ("Telegram From the CMC to Su Yu and Zhang Zhen Concerning Not Enabling the Enemy in Xuzhou to Scurry Off to the South"), *HHZY*, vol. 1, 138.

10. "*Zhongyang junwei guanyu jizhong quanli suzhan Suxian duan di tuilu zhi Chen Yi, Deng Xiaoping de dian bao*" [Telegram From the CMC to Chen Yi and Deng Xiaoping Concerning the Concentration of Their Entire Force to Quickly Occupy Suxian and Cut the Enemy's Route of Withdrawal], *HHZY*, vol. 1, 139.

11. "*Zhongyang junwei guanyu weijian Huang Baitao bingtuan ji erhou de zuozhan bushu zhi Liu Bocheng, Chen Yi, Deng Xiaoping deng de dianbao*" (Telegram from the CMC to Liu Bocheng, Chen Yi, Deng Xiaoping, and Others [Including Su Yu] Concerning the Encirclement and Destruction of Huang Baitao's Army and the Operational Deployment for What Will Follow), *HHZY*, vol. 1, 147.

12. Ibid.

13. "*Zhongyang junwei guanyu zhunbei duifu Huang Wei bingtuan zhi Liu Bocheng, Chen Yi, Deng Xiaoping deng de dianbao*" (Telegram From the CMC to Liu Bocheng, Chen Yi, Deng Xiaoping, and Others [Including Su Yu] Concerning Preparations for Handling Huang Wei's Army), *HHZY*, vol. 1, 148.

14. Ibid.

15. Ibid.

16. "*Liu Bocheng, Chen Yi, Deng Xiaoping guanyu zhongye zhuli nanjin Suxian zhi zhongyang junwei deng de dianbao*" (Telegram From Liu Bocheng, Chen Yi, and Deng Xiaoping to the CMC and Others [Including Su Yu] Concerning the Main Body of the CPFA Advancing South to Suxian), *HHZY*, vol. 1, 143.

17. "*Zhongyang junwei guanyu jianmie Sun Yuanliang bingtuan kongzhi Xu Beng xian zhi Liu Bocheng, Chen Yi, Deng Xiaoping de dianbao*" [Telegram From the CMC to Liu Bocheng, Chen Yi, and Deng Xiaoping Concerning the Destruction of Sun Yuanliang's Army and the Establishment of Control Over the Xu-Beng Railroad], *HHZY*, vol. 1, 144.

18. Chen Xilian, "*Jieduan Xu Beng xian huizhan Shuangduiji*" [Cutting the Xu-Beng Railroad and Fighting the Decisive Battle of Shuangduiji], *HHZY*, vol. 2, 107.

19. Liu Youguang, "*Huaihai zhanyi zhong de zhongye sizong*" [The CPFA 4th Column in the Huai Hai Campaign], HHZY, vol. 2, 129.

20. Ibid.

21. Sun Jixian and Ding Qiusheng, "*Zongheng chicheng, aozhan Huaihai*" [Sweeping Freely Across Wide Expanses, Fiercely Fighting the Huai Hai Campaign], *HHZY*, vol. 2, 237.

22. Liu Youguang, 129.

23. Chen Xilian, 110.

24. Ibid., 111.

25. "*Su Yu guanyu jianmie Huang Baitao zhuli hou youjian Qiu Qingquan, Li Mi bingtuan de bushu zhi Liu Bocheng, Chen Yi, Deng Xiaoping deng de dianbao*" (Telegram From Su Yu to Liu Bocheng, Chen Yi, Deng Xiaoping, and Others [Including the CMC and CCP East China Bureau] Concerning the Deployment for Luring and Destroying Qiu Qingquan and Li Mi's Armies After Wiping Out Huang Baitao's Main Body), *HHZY*, vol. 1, 149-51.

26. Sunzi, *The Art of War*, Lionel Giles, trans. (Singapore: Graham Brash (Pte) Ltd, 1988), 41.

27. Ibid., 45.

28. Sunzi, *The Art of War*, Roger T. Ames, trans. (New York: Ballantine Books, 1993), 125.

29. Sunzi, Giles, 6.

30. Sunzi, *The Art of War*, Samuel B. Griffith, trans. (New York: Oxford University Press, 1963), 93.

31. Sunzi, Ames, 113.

32. "*Su Yu guanyu jianmie Huang Baitao zhuli hou youjian Qiu Qingquan, Li Mi, bingtuan de bushu zhi Liu Bocheng, Chen Yi, Deng Xiaoping deng de dianbao*" (Telegram From Su Yu to Liu Bocheng, Chen Yi, Deng Xiaoping, and Others [Including the CMC and CCP East China Bureau] Concerning the Deployment for Luring and Destroying Qiu Qingquan and Li Mi's Armies After Wiping Out Huang Baitao's Main Body), *HHZY*, vol. 1, 149-50.

33. Ibid., 150.

34. Ibid., 150-51.

35. "*Zhongyang junwei guanyu zhongye zhunbei duli duifu Huang Wei bingtuan zhi Liu Bocheng, Chen Yi, Deng Xiaoping deng de dianbao*" (Telegram from the CMC to Liu Bocheng, Chen Yi, Deng Xiaopiing, and Others [Including Su Yu] Concerning the Preparation of the CPFA to Handle Huang Wei's Army by Itself), *HHZY*, vol. 1, 152.

36. "*Liu Bocheng, Chen Yi, Deng Xiaoping guanyu jianji Huang Wei bingtuan zhi zuozhan fangan zhi zhongyang junwei deng de dianbao*" (Telegram From Liu Bocheng, Chen Yi, and Deng Xiaoping to

the CMC and Others [Including Su Yu] Concerning the Operational Policy for Destroying Huang Wei's Army), *HHZY*, vol. 1, 154.

37. "*Zhongyang junwei guanyu jian Huang Wei, Liu Ruming, Qiu Qingquan, Li Mi zhudi de bushu zhi Liu Bocheng, Chen Yi, Deng Xiaoping de dianbao*" (Telegram From the CMC to Liu Bocheng, Chen Yi, and Deng Xiaoping [and Su Yu] Concerning the Destruction of the Multiple Enemy Armies of Huang Wei, Liu Ruming, Qiu Qingquan, and Li Mi), *HHZY*, vol. 1, 155-56.

38. Ibid., 156.

39. "*Zhongyang junwei guanyu jueding xiabu zuozhan fangzhen wenti zhi Liu Bocheng, Chen Yi, Deng Xiaoping deng de dianbao*" ("Telegram From the CMC to Liu Bocheng, Chen Yi, Deng Xiaoping, and Others [Including Su Yu] Concerning the Question of Policy for Deciding the Next Operation"), *HHZY*, vol. 1, 159-60.

40. Carl von Clausewitz, *On War*, Michael Howard and Peter Paret, trans. (Princeton, NJ: Princeton University Press, 1976), 77.

41. Sunzi, Ames, 115.

42. US Army Field Manual 3-0, *Operations* (Washington, DC: US Government Printing Office, June 2001), 6-1.

43. Sunzi, Ames, 115.

44. Guo Huaruo, Mei Jiasheng, and Han Nianlong, "*Zhongyuan duo jizhan chuan xi dao jiangnan*" [The Many Fierce Battles on the Central Plains Send a Call to Arms South of the Yangzi], *HHZY*, vol. 2, 250.

45. Nie Fengzhi, "*Ganda ganpin yingyong fenzhan*" [Daring to Fight, Bravely Giving Our All], *HHZY*, vol. 2, 308.

46. Ibid., 309.

47. *HHZY*, vol. 1, 325.

48. Ibid.

49. Li Mancun, "*Huaihai zhanyi zhong de huadong yezhanjun di shi zongdui*" [The ECFA's 10th Column in the Huai Hai Campaign], *HHZY*, vol. 2, 323.

50. Wang Yiping, "*Huaye ba zong zai huaihai zhanyi zhong de riri yeye*" [The Days and Nights of the ECFA's 8th Column During the Huai Hai Campaign], *HHZY*, vol. 2, 292.

51. Ibid., 293.

52. He Xiaohuan, Fu Jijun, and Shi Zhengxian, *Huaihai zhanyi shi* [*A History of the Huai Hai Campaign*] (Shanghai: *Renmin chubanshe*, 1983), 93, hereafter cited as *HHZYS*.

53. Ibid., 94.

54. Ibid.

55. Chen Ruiting, "*Wei hu tian yi*" ("Adding Wings to a Tiger"), *HHZY*, vol. 2, 412-13.

56. Ibid., 413.

57. Ibid.

58. Ibid.

59. Wang Bicheng and Jiang Weiqing, "*Huaihai juezhan zhong de huaye di liu zongdui*" [The ECFA's 6th Column in the Decisive Huai Hai Campaign], *HHZY*, vol. 2, 266.

60. *HHZYS*, 75.

61. Ibid., 74.

62. Sun Jixian and Ding Qiusheng, "*Zongheng chicheng, aozhan Huaihai*" [Sweeping Freely Across Wide Expanses, Fiercely Fighting the Huai Hai Campaign], *HHZY*, vol. 2, 238.

63. Qiu Weida, "*Di qishisi jun de zaici beijian*" [The Second Destruction of the LXXIV Corps], in *Huaihai zhanyi qinli ji* [A Record of Personal Experiences During the Huaihai Campaign, Zhongguo renmin zhengzhi xieshang huiyi quanguo weiyuanhui wenshi ziliao yanjiu weiyuanhui [The Historical Materials Research Committee of the National Committee of the Chinese People's Political Consultative Conference], eds. (Beijing: Wenshi ziliao chubanshe, 1983), hereafter cited as *QLJ*, 388.

64. Xiong Shunyi, "*Sun Yuanliang bingtuan beijian jingguo*" [The Way the Destruction of Sun Yuanliang's Army Occurred], *QLJ*, 414.

65. Ibid. 415.

66. Qiu Weida, 389.

67. Du Yuming, "*Huaihai zhanyi shimo*" [The Huai Hai Campaign From Beginning to End], *QLJ*, 24.

68. "*Su Yu, Chen Shiju, Zhang Zhen guanyu huaye quanjun da beixian zhudi zhi Tan Zhenlin, Wang Jinan, Li Yingxi de dianbao*" (Telegram From Su Yu, Chen Shiju, and Zhang Zhen to Tan Zhenlin, Wang Jianan, and Li Yingxi [and also to Liu, Chen, and Deng and the CMC] Concerning the Entire ECFA Fighting the Various Enemy Forces on the Northern Front), *HHZY*, vol. 1, 166.

69. Ibid.

70. Ibid., 166-67.

71. Ibid., 167.

72. Ibid.

73. Li Yikuang, "*Huaihai zhanyi guomindangjun beijian gaishu*" [A General Description of the Nationalist Army's Destruction During the Huai Hai Campaign], *QLJ*, 66.

74. Meng Hengchang, "*Di ba bingtuan zai Huaihai nanxian zuozhan jiyao*" ("A Summary of Eighth Army Operations on the Huai Hai Campaign's Southern Front"), *QLJ*, 473. See also Li Yikuang, "*Huaihai zhanyi nanxian guomindangjun zengyuan beixian jingguo*" [The Experience of the Nationalist Armies on the Southern Front Reinforcing the Northern Front During the Huai Hai Campaign], *QLJ*, 466.

75. "*Zhongyang junwei guanyu chengli zongqianwei zhi Liu Bocheng, Chen Yi, Deng Xiaoping deng de dianbao*" (Telegram From the CMC to Liu Bocheng, Chen Yi, and Deng Xiaoping [and Su Yu and Tan Zhenlin] Concerning the Establishment of the General Front Committee), *HHZY*, vol. 1, 164-65.

76. Ibid., 164.

77. "*Zhongyang junwei guanyu jianji nanxian diren de bushu zhi Liu Bocheng, Chen Yi, Deng Xiaoping deng de dianbao*" (Telegram From the CMC to Liu Bocheng, Chen Yi, Deng Xiaoping, and Others [Including Su Yu] Concerning the Deployment for Attacking the Enemy on the Southern Front), *HHZY*, vol. 1, 168-69.

78. Ibid., 168.

79. Huang Wei, "*Di shier bingtuan beijian jiyao*" [A Summary of the Destruction of the Twelfth Army], *QLJ*, 486.

80. "*Liu Bocheng, Chen Yi, Deng Xiaoping guanyu jianji Huang Wei, Li Yannian bingtuan zhi fangan zhi zhongyang junwei deng de dianbao*" (Telegram From Liu Bocheng, Chen Yi, and Deng

Xiaoping to the CMC [and also Su Yu] Concerning the Policy for an Attack to Destroy the Armies of Huang Wei and Li Yannian), *HHZY*, vol. 1, 171.

81. "*Liu Bocheng, Chen Yi, Deng Xiaoping guanyu juexin xian da Huang Wei bingtuan zhi zhongyang junwei deng de dianbao*" (Telegram from Liu Bocheng, Chen Yi, and Deng Xiaoping to the CMC [and also Su Yu] Concerning the Decision to Attack Huang Wei First) *HHZY*, vol. 1, 175-76.

82. "*Huadong yezhanjun qianwei guanyu quanjian Huang Baitao bingtuan de zhengzhi dongyuan ling*" [Order From the ECFA Front Committee for Political Mobilization to Completely Destroy Huang Baitao's Army], *HHZY*, vol. 1, 134-35.

83. "*Zhongyang junwei guanyu jian Huang Wei, Liu Ruming, Qiu Qingquan, Li Mi zhudi de bushu zhi Liu Bocheng, Chen Yi, Deng Xiaoping de dianbao*" (Telegram From the CMC to Liu Bocheng, Chen Yi, and Deng Xiaoping [and Su Yu] Concerning the Destruction of the Multiple Enemy Armies of Huang Wei, Liu Ruming, Qiu Qingquan, and Li Mi), *HHZY*, vol. 1, 156.

84. "*Zhongyang junwei guanyu chengli zongqianwei zhi Liu Bocheng, Chen Yi, Deng Xiaoping deng de dianbao*" (Telegram From the CMC to Liu Bocheng, Chen Yi, and Deng Xiaoping [and Su Yu and Tan Zhenlin] Concerning the Establishment of the General Front Committee), *HHZY*, 165.

85. "*Zhongyang junwei yuji di yi zhang jiandi ershiyi, er ge shi di er zhang da Huang Wei, Sun Yuanliang zhi Su Yu, Chen Shiju, Zhang Zhen deng de dianbao*" (Telegram From the CMC to Su Yu, Chen Shiju, Zhang Zhen, and Others [Including Chen Yi and Deng Xiaoping] Estimating That in the First Phase of the Campaign 21-22 Enemy Divisions Would be Destroyed and That the Second Phase Would be an Attack on Huang Wei and Sun Yuanliang), *HHZY*, vol. 1, 129.

86. "*Zhongyang junwei guanyu zhongye duli yingfu nanxian zhi di zhi Liu Bocheng, Chen Yi, Deng Xiaoping deng de dianbao*" (Telegram From the CMC to Liu Bocheng, Chen Yi, Deng Xiaoping, and Others [Including Su Yu] Concerning the CPFA Countering the Enemy on the Southern Front by Itself), *HHZY*, vol. 1, 174.

87. "*Zhongyang junwei guanyu zhongye jianji Huang Wei bingtuan, huaye duifu Li Yannian bingtuan zhi Liu Bocheng, Chen Yi, Deng Xiaoping deng de dianbao*" (Telegram From the CMC to Liu Bocheng, Chen Yi, Deng Xiaoping, and Others [Including Su Yu] Concerning the CPFA Attacking Huang Wei's Army and the ECFA Handling Li Yannian), *HHZY*, vol. 1, 177-78.

88. "*Zhongyang junwei guanyu duifu Li Yannian bingtuan you huaye wanquan fuze zhi Su Yu, Chen Shiju, Zhang Zhen de dianbao*" (Telegram From the CMC to Su Yu, Chen Shiju, and Zhang Zhen [and also Liu, Chen, and Deng] Concerning the ECFA Assuming Complete Responsibility for Handling Li Yannian), *HHZY*, vol. 1, 179.

89. "*Su Yu, Chen Shiju, Zhang Zhen guanyu xietong zhongye jianji, Huang Wei, Li Yannian bingtuan de bushu zhi Liu Bocheng, Chen Yi, Deng Xiaoping de dianbao*" (Telegram From Su Yu, Chen Shiju, and Zhang Zhen to Liu Bocheng, Chen Yi, and Deng Xiaoping [and also the CMC] Concerning the Deployment for Cooperating With the CPFA in Attacking the Armies of Huang Wei and Li Yannian), *HHZY*, vol. 1, 180-81.

90. Ibid.

91. *HHZYS*, 101.

92. Ibid.

93. Li Yikuang, "*Huaihai zhanyi guomindangjun beijian gaishu*" [A General Description of the Nationalist Army's Destruction During the Huai Hai Campaign], *QLJ*, 71.

94. These casualty and prisoner of war numbers are estimates based on statistics presented in *HHZY*, vol. 1, 337.

Chapter Seven
Contesting the Central Position

The victorious army wins first, then seeks battle;
the army destined to defeat enters battle in search of victory.

—Sunzi, *The Art of War*

If one knows where and when a battle will be fought, one can march a thousand miles to join the battle. But if one does not know either the place or the day of battle, one's left flank will be unable to aid one's right, or one's right, the left; one's front will be unable to aid one's rear, or one's rear, the front. This is true even if the separation between the forces is only several tens of li or even only a few li.

—Sunzi, *The Art of War*

By being able to use many to attack a few,
we place those we fight against in grave difficulty.

—Sunzi, *The Art of War*

When the Central Military Commission (CMC) withdrew its support from Su Yu's plan to achieve the expanded objectives of the "big" Huai Hai Campaign through continuous East China Field Army (ECFA) operations east of Xuzhou, the campaign's focus was set squarely on the central position around Suxian. As discussed earlier, this area had been an important element in Huai Hai Campaign planning before the campaign started and had become even more so after the campaign was enlarged. Control over this area was seen as key to isolating the Nationalist armies in Xuzhou and destroying them. For this reason the CMC had ordered the Central Plains Field Army (CPFA) to seize Suxian and as long a segment of the Xu-Beng railroad as possible. This is also why, before adopting Su Yu's plan to envelop and encircle much of the Second and Thirteenth Armies east of Xuzhou, the CMC had envisioned that after the Seventh Army was destroyed several ECFA columns would shift rapidly to locations around Suxian. The CMC's acceptance of Su Yu's vision did not in any way signify that it was reducing the value it placed on the central position. It merely indicated CMC agreement with Su Yu's assumption that the CPFA could successfully block the advance of all the Nationalist armies on the southern front. When that assumption proved to be incorrect, the CMC quickly changed course, abandoning Su Yu's vision and adopting a course of action designed to ensure that Communist forces maintained control over the central position.

The CMC's intent to hold the central position was stated strongly in the conclusion of its message of 2400, 18 November that, as was noted earlier, also contained a statement supporting Su Yu's operations east of Xuzhou. This was a clear expression of commander's intent that, by referring to a "gradual" elimination of the three armies in Xuzhou, raised the possibility that a slower-paced campaign was possible:

> All that we need do is to destroy about half of each of the southern front armies and make it impossible for them to advance. Then the northern armies will become like turtles in a bottle and we can gradually wipe them out.
>
> You should exert all of your strength to keep control over part of the Xu-Beng railroad in our hands. You must be sure to keep the southern enemy forces

separated from the northern enemy forces and make it impossible for them to link up.[1]

Five days later, with the Seventh Army eliminated and ECFA columns moving from east of Xuzhou into the central position, the CMC continued to emphasize the area's critical importance. It also continued to present its view that holding that area would allow the Communists to stretch out the campaign if they so desired. On 23 November the CMC sent two messages to ECFA and CPFA field commanders and the regional Chinese Communist Party (CCP) bureaus giving its appraisal of the strategic and operational situations after achieving one major operational goal, destroying the Seventh Army. Both messages manifested a shift away from Su Yu's emphasis on continuous and simultaneous operations. The first message mentions having a rest period, waiting for opportunities, and conducting a long-term defense of the central position. The second speaks of a campaign lasting 3 to 5 months with several operational phases in which enemy forces would be destroyed in sequence. In both cases, the implication was that the operational tempo would slow. Such a change was acceptable because the CMC felt that Communist forces held the initiative and had time on their side.

Message 1

(2) We stand in accord with Liu, Chen, and Deng in agreeing with Su Yu's deployment as presented in his message of 1800 21 November. No matter whether Huang Wei, Liu Ruming, or Li Yannian advance or stop, these dispositions are all good. If the enemy advances, then we can destroy most of Li and Liu's forces and part of Huang Wei's forces. If the enemy stops, then we can gain a short rest period.

(3) At present we do not want to consider seeking other operational opportunities. Now we must grab hold of the Xuzhou enemy's two weak points, his isolation and his difficult food situation, keep the enemy forces in Xuzhou and Bengbu separated, and wait for opportunities to destroy enemy forces.

(5) If, after ten days, there are still no opportunities for fighting in either the Xuzhou or Bengbu areas, as long as it does not obstruct our general plan of cutting Xuzhou off from Bengbu and destroying Liu Zhi's main force, then the idea of dispatching a force to capture Huaian and Huaiyin can be considered.

(7) In order to carry out the long-term separation of Xuzhou from Bengbu and keep the enemy in Xuzhou pinned down, the ECFA should construct strong defensive works between Xuzhou and Bengbu with Suxian serving as the center point.

(8) We look forward to your comments on implementing these things.[2]

Message 2

(1) Congratulations on your great victory of wiping out the ten divisions of Huang Baitao's army.

(2) During the 16 days from 7 November through 22 November you eliminated 18 divisions from Liu Zhi's command (including the 3 divisions that were part of He and Zhang's revolt).... Before the start of the campaign we already calculated that it would be possible to annihilate 18 enemy divisions, but at that time we still did not dare estimate that we could cut Xuzhou

off from Bengbu and completely isolate the enemy force in Xuzhou.

(3) . . . Besides those divisions that have been destroyed, the enemy still has approximately 50 remaining. This enemy force can be destroyed, but we must prepare for a campaign 3-5 months in length. We must prepare to go through several operational phases (You have already completed the first operational phase.) in order to achieve complete victory in the campaign. We must prepare an army and labor force of around 1,300,000; 3-5 months of food, fodder, and ammunition; and medical treatment for 100,000-120,000 wounded. We must ensure that during whatever time is required to finish the entire campaign, for every unit in the army more than half of that time will be spent resting, reorganizing, and replenishing. We must keep soldier morale and spirits high. As for troop strength, we must implement the policy of 'as we fight, fill in the ranks; as we fill in the ranks, fight.'

(4) There is only one situation that could possibly cause you to leave your present situation and seek other operational opportunities. That situation would be one in which the southern front armies of Huang Wei, Liu Ruming, and Li Yannian temporarily stop instead of advancing, so they haven't yet suffered serious losses from attacks by you, and in order to save Qiu, Li, and Sun's armies, Jiang Jieshi completely changes his Yangzi River defenses . . . and shifts all possible forces to Bengbu for a push north to open the Xu-Beng railroad and connect with the enemy in Xuzhou. If Jiang Jieshi does this he will be abandoning the Ping-Han railroad and laying Wuhan and the middle reaches of the Yangzi bare before our army. This would be very dangerous for the Guomindang.

Whether or not the enemy will shift his forces in this way, and whether or not there is enough time to do it will become apparent. As far as we are concerned, the most advantageous approach is to use the present situation and destroy the enemy forces that lie before us one by one. We should energetically strive to achieve this. If we are able to destroy large parts of the armies the enemy has on the southern front during the second phase of the campaign, then even if the enemy does shift [all those other forces to Bengbu], we will be able to fulfill our original plan.[3]

Nationalist Strategy to Retake the Central Position

Time was on the Communists side because of the entropy inherent in the isolated Nationalist armies in Xuzhou. Sunzi states, "An army without its baggage-train is lost; without provisions it is lost; without bases of supply it is lost."[4] Nationalist commanders understood this reality very well, and soon after the CPFA took Suxian the Nationalists developed a plan to retake the central position. The Twelfth Army, which was at that time near Fuyang in southern Henan, was to continue moving toward Mengcheng and Suxian while the two newly organized armies based in Bengbu moved north. The Sixth Army was to move toward Suxian from the southeast along the Xu-Beng railroad to complement the Twelfth Army's advance from the southwest. The Eighth Army was to support the Sixth Army by providing rear area security. Upon reaching Suxian, the Twelfth and Sixth Armies were to continue moving toward Xuzhou while the Eighth Army protected the reopened Xu-Beng railroad.[5]

Had this plan been executed quickly, it might have worked. However, CPFA delaying tactics, poor roads, bad weather, and other sources of friction combined to slow all three armies' movement. On the day the Seventh Army was destroyed, the Sixth Army had only advanced a short distance north of Renqiao on the Su-Beng railroad.[6] Meanwhile the Twelfth Army was just crossing the Beifei River northeast of Mengcheng.[7] At this point the Twelfth Army was approximately 60 km from the Sixth Army. Suxian, their common objective, lay 50 km ahead of the Twelfth Army and 30 km ahead of the Sixth Army.

The Twelfth Army's position was particularly precarious and its commander knew it. One major cause of concern for Huang Wei was logistics. As his army had moved across Henan, it had effectively dropped its line of communication to the rear. It was impractical to transport new supplies for the army all the way from Queshan, and in any case Communist guerrilla activity in central Henan made such an effort impossible. After reaching Mencheng on 18 November the army had established contact with supply depots in Bengbu and some much-needed supplies were brought up the Bengbu-Mengcheng road.[8] However, this road was not a line of communication capable of supporting four corps in heavy combat. Another cause for concern was intelligence reports indicating the presence of large enemy forces to his front and on his left flank. Especially troubling was the capture of soldiers from the 6th Column because this indicated that the force the Twelfth Army had been fighting two weeks earlier in western Henan had beaten them to Mengcheng. Huang was also worried about the terrain obstacles he faced between Mengcheng and Suxian. Several rivers ran perpendicular to his route, and they were filled with water due to recent unusually heavy rains. Looking at the situation, Huang decided that continuing to push directly toward Suxian was too risky. As his army was reorganizing and replenishing after reaching Mengcheng, he proposed a different course of action to his superiors in Nanjing.

Huang Wei's concept was to move southeasterly using the Guo River to help screen his left flank until he reached Huaiyuan, a town 10 km west of Bengbu. There he would cross the Guo River, link up with the Sixth and Eighth armies along the railroad, and move against Suxian with them.[9] Huang thought such a maneuver would likely catch the enemy by surprise and be a more secure way to proceed. He estimated that the time required to do this would take no longer than it would to fight his way through to Suxian on the most direct route.

While waiting for the response from Nanjing, Huang Wei used the time to bring in supplies and arrange his army for whatever lay ahead. The pause also allowed the LXXXV Corps, which had departed Queshan several days after the rest of the army, to come closer to catching up. On 20 November Nationalist headquarters in Nanjing rejected Huang's proposal and ordered him to advance directly to Suxian with all possible speed. The next day the Twelfth Army set out from Mengcheng just as the LXXXV Corps was reaching the city.[10]

As the Twelfth Army had approached Mengcheng on 18 November, Huang Wei had ordered each of the three corps to establish bridgeheads on the north side of the Guo River. This they had done. In the center of the Mengcheng city area was the XVIII Corps, the Twelfth Army's most powerful corps. The X Corps was west of the city and the XIV Corps was to the east.[11] On 21 November these three corps advanced from these positions in a line abreast with the LXXXV corps, the designated army reserve, following behind. On 21 November the advance carried to the Beifei River. On 22 November the army pushed its way across this river and also crossed the Xie River. On the evening of 23 November it reached the Hui River, the last major terrain obstacle between the army and Suxian. The morning of 24 November the XVIII and X Corps put units across the river, expanded their bridgeheads, and prepared to push on to Suxian only 20 km away.[12]

The Seventh Army's final destruction did not alter the concept of operations for the Nationalist armies on the southern front. It did, however, change the orientation of the armies in Xuzhou. No longer committed to a relief effort to save Huang Baitao's force, they could now concentrate on ensuring their own survival. What form such actions would take was the main topic on the agenda of a meeting of the Nationalist High Command held at the presidential office building in Nanjing the morning of 23 November. Early that morning Liu Zhi and Du Yuming flew from Xuzhou to Nanjing to attend this important strategy session, which Jiang Jieshi also attended. All in attendance agreed that the immediate objective should be to retake Suxian and reestablish a ground link to Xuzhou along the Xu-Beng railroad. The Twelfth, Sixth, and Eighth Armies were already engaged in operations intended to reach Suxian, and it was decided that those operations should continue. They also decided that as soon as possible the Xuzhou force should launch its own attack toward Suxian to create, with the Sixth, Eighth and Twelfth Armies, a three-pronged attack on this single point. The intent was to have these armies crush the Communist forces that were located between them and thereby reestablish communications between Xuzhou and Bengbu.[13]

After the meeting, Du Yuming felt hopeful about this plan, especially if Jiang Jieshi made good on his promise to add two to three more corps to the force fighting north of Bengbu.[14] When he and Liu Zhi flew back to Xuzhou that afternoon, he had the pilot fly over the Twelfth Army so he could talk by radio with Huang Wei. Huang expressed concern about the heavy resistance his army had been facing and his casualties, but Du told him to be optimistic. Du informed Huang about the meeting he had just attended and assured him that a comprehensive strategy had been approved. If he followed the orders he would soon receive, everything would work out.[15]

After reaching Xuzhou, Du and Liu decided that the Second and Sixteenth Armies would attack to the south and the Thirteenth would defend Xuzhou. On 24 November forces shifted positions as required and completed preparations for the operation. On 25 November the attack began, with the Second Army to the east of the Xu-Beng railroad and the Sixteenth Army to the west.[16]

Communist Strategy to Hold the Central Position

While Nationalist strategy for retaking the central position was to attack on external lines from three directions—north, southeast, and southwest—the Communists decided to use the flexibility provided by internal lines to mount their defense. Having successfully blocked the Nationalist attempt to relieve the Seventh Army, the Communists believed they could hold those armies to the north of the central position and conduct counteroffensives in the south. This was the essence of Su Yu's proposal for future operations contained in his message of 2100, 20 November. Applying the principle of economy of force, he suggested that eight columns, a force smaller than the Nationalist group army in Xuzhou, be deployed in an arc south of the city and that seven columns be sent to the southern front.

Su's message presented two courses of action to aid the CPFA. One course was to have the ECFA 6th Column replace the CPFA 9th Column in the defensive line southeast of Suxian,

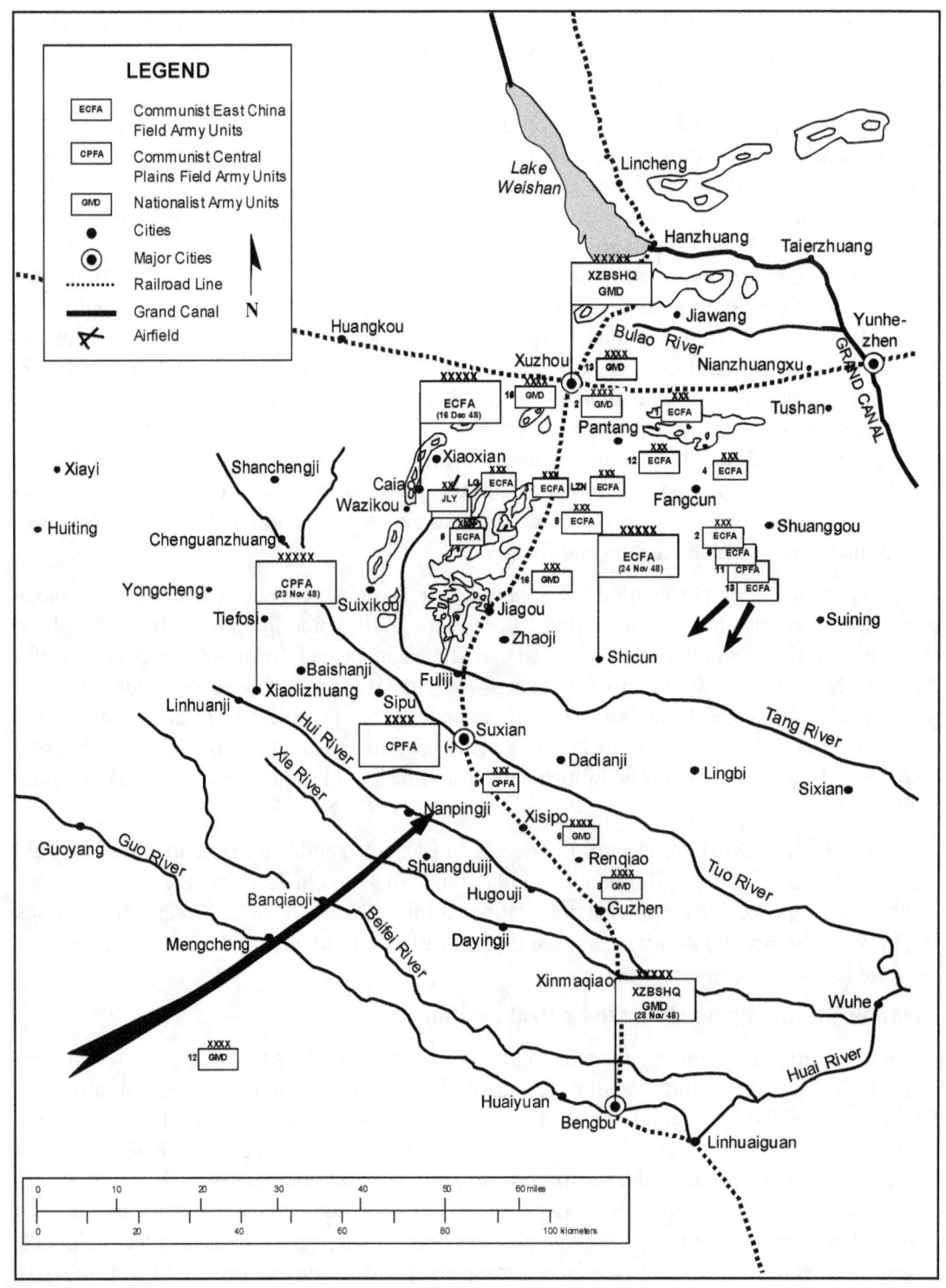

Map 1. Holding the central position.

freeing it for use against Huang Wei. The other was to have the ECFA 2d and 11th (C) Columns, under the command of Wei Guoqing and Ji Luo, prepare to go under CPFA operational control and move west to join the fight against Huang Wei if they were needed. But as Su's expression of how the ECFA's shaping operations might develop shows, he was hoping that such a shift of forces would not be necessary and that he could concentrate a large force for offensive action: "If we do not need to send forces to participate in the battle with Huang Wei, then, besides holding Qiu, Li, and Sun in the north, we can concentrate the 2d, 7th, 8th, 9th, 11th (C) and 13th columns to destroy Li Yannian's army."[17]

At the same time that Su Yu was drafting this proposal, he was already taking action to implement it. To prepare for the coming defensive battle south of Xuzhou, on 20 November the 3d Column, which had been engaged in the attempt of Su's *qi* force to break through the Nationalist lines at Pantang, was ordered to move west and start constructing a defense in depth astride the Xu-Beng railroad.[18] Also, to give the ECFA a presence on the southern front, "the 2d, 6th, 11th (C), and 13th columns started advancing to the south along different routes under the command of Wei [Guoqing] and Ji [Luo]."[19] Before the Nationalists had agreed on a concept of operations and developed a plan to achieve their next operational objectives, the ECFA was already preparing to thwart their moves.

The times on the messages sent during this period and the content of those messages provide a glimpse into the problems the Communists faced—coordinating large forces moving across a broad area—because of slow communications. Transmitting Chinese characters by radiotelegraph was painstaking and time consuming. The standard method was to use a codebook listing several thousand characters in a format that assigned four Arabic numbers to each character. Since messages were a series of numbers, any errors made in entering numbers would produce errors in the messages when they were received. The need to encode and decode messages complicated the process further. Time was also spent assessing information, evaluating alternative courses of action, developing plans, and formulating orders. Given the requirements for careful work and the small size of the staffs to handle the work, it was inevitable that on occasion messages with differing, or even contrary, thoughts and directives were moving through the command, control, and communications network from one headquarters to another at the same time. (For instance, at this time the CPFA operations section only had 10 staff officers assigned.[20])

The CMC practice of giving field army commanders the freedom and flexibility to display initiative within agreed-upon strategic and operational objectives significantly reduced the potential for shortcomings within the communication system to cause harmful delays and create confusion in planning and executing operations. This "Moltkean" approach to command and control helped avoid the first of what Sunzi described as the "ways in which a ruler can bring misfortune upon his army: 'When ignorant that the Army should not advance, to order an advance or ignorant that it should not retire, to order a retirement.'"[21] It also made the matter of having messages with different concepts and plans crossing paths of less consequence than it could have been. For example, in its 2000, 20 November message to Su Yu the CMC directed Su to quickly dispatch the 4th, 6th, 8th, and 9th Columns to the south and have Tan Zhenlin command them. At virtually the same time Su Yu was sending a message to the CMC containing the following sentence that was just quoted: "This evening the 2d, 6th, 11th (C), and 13th Columns started advancing to the south along different routes under the command of Wei

[Guoqing] and Ji [Luo]."²² This was not the same group of columns or the same commander the CMC had asked for, but it met the CMC's intent—to have the ECFA send columns quickly to bolster the southern front. This arrangement also gained Liu, Chen, and Deng's approval as was expressed in their message of 1500, 21 November:

> We completely agree with the deployment laid out in your message of 2100 20 November. We have decided that during the night of 21 November we will withdraw to another line and draw the enemy forward. This is setting the stage for destroying Huang Wei's army south of Nanpingji.
>
> We hope that Wei Guoqing and Ji Luo will be able to lead 4-5 columns to reach the Suxian-Dadianji line by nightfall on 23 November and be ready to use 3 columns to clamp down on Liu Ruming and Li Yannian and commit more than 2 columns to the fight against Huang Wei.²³

Since Su's action met its intent and Liu, Chen, and Deng had approved what he had done, rather than request that Su Yu adhere to the details of its 2000, 20 November directive, the CMC allowed Su Yu's deployment to stand and the campaign went on from there. Again, when Su assigned the 4th and 8th Columns to the defensive line south of Xuzhou and made Tan Zhenlin the overall commander of that blocking force, the CMC accepted his decisions.

At 1800, 21 November Su Yu sent a message laying out more specific ECFA deployments and command relationships for the upcoming shaping operations to Liu, Chen, and Deng; the CMC; the East China Military Region (ECMR); Tan Zhenlin; and other ECFA commanders. The 1st, 3d, 12th, Luzhongnan, and Liangguang Columns and the two Ji-Lu-Yu Military District divisions were assigned to the blocking force front line. The 4th, 8th, and 9th Columns, having suffered heavy casualties in the battle at Nianzhuangxu, were assigned to the second line of defense. All were placed under command of Tan Zhenlin and his Shandong army headquarters. On the southern front the 2d Column, not the 6th, was directed to replace the CPFA 9th Column. All other columns, including the 11th (C) Column, were to be used to fight Li Yannian. Su suggested to Liu Bocheng that "for ease of coordination" it would be best if the CPFA "destroyed Huang Wei to the south of the Nanpingji-Sundingji line." Reflecting his offensive aggressiveness, Su stated his desire to maintain control of his ECFA columns to use against Li Yannian: "During the first phase of the [southern front] campaign I will concentrate forces to destroy Li Yannian's army. Because of this, except for having the 2d Column take over the [blocking] mission of the CPFA's 9th Column, for the present I will be unable to send forces to directly coordinate with the CPFA operations."²⁴

In this message Su Yu also announced his intention to move his headquarters to a new location that was more centrally located and closer to the southern front. Since 7 November his headquarters had been in Matou, a village 35 km north-northwest of Xinanzhen.²⁵ Now he was going to move 140 km southwest to Shicun, a village 40 km east-northeast of Suxian. In his message he estimated that he would be on the road for two nights and would reach Shicun the evening of 23 November.²⁶ Actually, he did not reach there and set up his headquarters until the next day.²⁷ At the same time Su Yu was moving, Liu Bocheng, Chen Yi, and Deng Xiaoping were also shifting the locations of their headquarters. Since 4 November they had been in Boxian, which was almost 150 km west of Suxian. On 23 November they established their headquarters in Xiaolizhuang, a small village only 30 km due west of Suxian and about the same distance away from Nanpingji, the place where they planned to fight the decisive battle to destroy the Twelfth Army.[28]

Liu Bocheng's Sunzian Plan for Attacking the Twelfth Army

CMC approval of the deployment of forces and concept of operations contained in Su Yu's message of 1800, 21 November was issued in a message sent to Liu Bocheng, Chen Yi, Deng Xiaoping, Su Yu, Tan Zhenlin, Wei Guoqing, the CCP's East China Bureau, and others at 2100, 23 November. The message shows that at this time the CMC was not certain the Nationalist armies on the southern front would continue to move toward the north. Another CMC message sent on 23 November contains the same perspective. Liu Bocheng, however, was certain his army would soon be engaged in a major battle with Huang Wei's force. During the day on 23 November he, along with Chen Yi and Deng Xiaoping, developed a Sunzian plan to shape that battle and destroy Huang Wei's army. At 2200 that evening they transmitted this plan to Su Yu, Chen Shiju, Zhang Zhen, and the CMC.

On 22 November Liu Bocheng, Chen Yi, and Deng Xiaoping had expressed their approval of Su Yu's plan to have the ECFA do nothing more to aid the CPFA than send the 2d Column to take the place of the CPFA 9th Column on the defensive line southeast of Suxian. In this plan, the 11th (C) Column would move into position east of the 2d Column and when ordered, "attack eastward to keep Li Yannian from linking up with Huang Wei's army."[29] In Liu Bocheng's plan of 23 November, however, the 11th (C) Column would attack *west* against Huang Wei's army, not east against Li Yannian's army. In addition, Liu wanted the ECFA to send "at least four columns to join an operation to destroy Huang Wei." In the estimation of Liu Bocheng, Chen Yi, and Deng Xiaoping, destroying all or part of the Twelfth Army would be of greater benefit than destroying the Sixth and Eighth Armies:

> (1) Today (23 Nov), from 0900 to dusk, with the support of more than 20 tanks, the enemy's XVIII Corps fiercely attacked our Nanpingji defenses. During the day, despite suffering fairly heavy casualties, we didn't give up a single defensive position. However, early this afternoon more than a regiment of enemy troops pushed across the Hui River some five kilometers east of Nanpingji.
>
> (2) We have decided to abandon Nanpingji and withdraw more than five kilometers, arranging our positions in the shape of a bag. We plan to entice the XVIII Corps to cross the Hui River and then spread out using the 4th and 9th columns to attract this enemy force. This will make use of the Hui River as a way to cut links between this force and the three enemy corps that will be south of the river. At the same time tomorrow (24 Nov) night, we will have the 1st, 2d, 3rd, 6th, and 11th (C) columns attack the enemy force located south of the Hui River in an effort to cut off and destroy 2-3 divisions.
>
> (3) Because the 9th Column must cooperate with the 4th Column to grab hold of the enemy's main force, the XVIII Corps, we have decided to have the 11th (C) Column attack from east to west, which will aid in cutting the enemy apart. At the same time we are ordering the 2d (E) Column to construct defensive works north and south of Xisipo Station to block a possible westward move by Li Yannian and Liu Ruming to aid the Twelfth Army.
>
> (4) This is a very opportune moment to destroy Huang Wei because Li

Yannian and Liu Ruming haven't been advancing. Therefore, our idea is that, in addition to the 11th (C) Column, we ask Su, Chen, and Zhang to use 2-3 columns to defend against Li and Liu and send at least 4 columns to join in an operation to destroy Huang Wei. If we destroy all of Huang Wei's army or a large part of it, this will be more beneficial than destroying Li and Liu. If the CMC approves, this is what we will do. We also ask Su, Chen, and Zheng to quickly give us their thoughts.[30]

In this message Liu Bocheng presented a proposal that, like Su Yu's plan of 13 November for shaping the battles east of Xuzhou, was deeply imbued with ideas that appear in Sunzi's *The Art of War*. There was the element of deception, of having a *zheng* (fixing/holding) force that is directly engaged with the enemy voluntarily abandon its positions to lure an enemy force into a vulnerable position. According to Sunzi, "Warfare is the art (*tao*) of deceit. Therefore, when able, seem to be unable; when ready, seem unready; when nearby, seem far away."[31] Liu planned to have the 4th and 9th Columns feign an inability to hold in place to draw the XVIII Corps into his bag.

This act of deception was expected to work because it tapped into the *shi* (energy/momentum) inherent in the Twelfth Army's drive toward Suxian. It was also in accordance with Sunzi's advice on how to shape human behavior: "If the enemy seeks some advantage, entice him with it."[32] Then, after the XVIII Corps had reached the desired place, Liu intended to loose his *qi* (maneuver) force to slice into the enemy rear. The plan even followed Sunzi's advice about the tactics for opposing a river crossing: "When an invading force crosses a river in its onward march, . . . it will be best to let half the army get across, and then deliver your attack."[33] Like Sunzi and Su Yu, Liu Bocheng wanted to use information superiority and the initiative to shape the battlefield to his advantage and then act. In this he was pursuing the Sunzian ideal of the proficient commander who "moves the enemy, and is not moved by him."[34]

At this time Liu Bocheng was facing both threats and opportunities on a rapidly changing battlefield. Along the Su-Beng railroad the Sixth Army's XCIX Corps was nearing Xisipo, and its XXXIX Corps had reached Renqiaozhan. The Twelfth Army had outflanked the CPFA positions at Nanpingji the morning of 23 November, forcing Liu to withdraw several km toward Suxian. On 21 November Liu had planned to hold the Twelfth Army south of Nanpingji (see his 1500, 21 November message). Now he was worried that Huang Wei might not move directly toward Suxian but instead slide east and reach the Su-Beng railroad in the area the XCIX Corps controlled. Such a development would ruin all plans for isolating the Twelfth Army and lead to further problems on the southern front. It could not be permitted. Time was of the essence, so Liu, along with Chen Yi and Deng Xiaoping, decided that before receiving CMC approval of Liu's plan to encircle the Twelfth Army they would take operational control of the ECFA columns that the plan called for and execute it.

This is another example of what was described earlier as a Moltkean approach to command and control within the PLA. As discussed previously, the CMC, in the pattern of the 19th-century commander, Prussian General Staff, Helmuth von Moltke the Elder, granted senior field commanders the responsibility and the authority to take the initiative and act on their own when circumstances required it. This principle of decentralized execution was expressed in several messages during the campaign. On 1 November a CMC message to Chen Yi, Deng Xiaoping, Su Yu, and others stated, "Our army's operation southwest of Xuzhou will be selected from among the three options presented by Chen [Yi] and Deng [Xiaoping] as the situation dictates."[35] A 3 November message from the CMC to Chen Yi and Deng Xiaoping, with information copies sent to Liu Bocheng and Su Yu, said, "Actual attack missions should be determined by you on the basis of the situation you face."[36] The CMC message to Su Yu and other ECFA commanders on 7 November, the eve of the planned start date of the campaign, contained this statement, "In executing this plan, use your judgment and act quickly. Don't be asking for instructions. However, report your views on the situation to us every day or every second or third day."[37] When the CMC established the General Front Committee for the campaign on 16 November it made this point once again, "Liu, Chen, and Deng will form a standing committee and they will handle everything as the situation requires."[38]

This was the authority that Liu Bocheng, Chen Yi, and Deng Xiaoping used when, at 1000, 24 November they transmitted the following message to Su Yu and the CMC. In the message they expressed their concerns and the need for quick action:

1. The enemy unit attacking us yesterday, 23 November, at Nanpingji was the 118th Division [of the XVIII Corps]. According to an assistant company commander who was captured, that division has suffered heavy casualties and two regiments are already combat ineffective.

2. Last night, 23 November, and early this morning, 24 November, besides controlling an area two to two and one-half kilometers west of Nanpingji and ten kilometers south of Nanpingji and both sides of the Hui River, the enemy main body is moving east toward Li Yannian and Liu Ruming. It is possible that they will cross the [Hui] River in the section east of Nanpingji and Qixanji and place their rear against the Jin-Pu railroad.

3. Our main body will attack tonight, 24 November, according to our original plan, but on the line running from Suxian to Qixianji and south of Qixianji, we only have the CPFA 9th and 11th columns. Our troop strength on the eastern side is comparatively weak. Because of this, we ask Su[Yu], Chen [Shiju], and Zhang [Zhen] to rush at least three columns to the Xisipo Station-Hugouji-Qixianji area tonight. Furthermore, a column should be sent south of Qixianji to keep Huang Wei from linking up with Li and Liu. Also preparations should be made to have a large, strong force attack westward south of the Hui River and destroy the enemy while moving to the west.

4. Please give us a reply saying how this will be carried out.[39]

The CMC message approving Liu Bocheng's plan was sent to Liu, Chen Yi, and Deng Xiaoping and also to Su Yu, Chen Shiju, and Zhang Zhen before this message of 1000, 24 November had been fully processed at PLA headquarters. Transmitted at 1500, 24 November, it acknowledged receipt of the 2200, 23 November message that contained Liu's plan and expressed total concurrence with Liu, Chen, and Deng's decision to make an attack on the Twelfth Army the main effort on the southern front. Again, following the "Moltkean" practice, the message also granted authority to Liu, Chen Yi, and Deng Xiaoping to do what they thought best. The effect was to not only approve the plan presented in the 2200, 23 November message but also to preapprove the orders Liu, Chen, and Deng issued in their 1000, 24 November message:

Your message of 2200 23 November has been received.

(1) We completely agree that Huang Wei should be attacked first.

(2) We hope that Su, Chen, and Zhang will follow the deployment set forth by Liu, Chen, and Deng and dispatch the necessary forces to participate in the attack on Huang Wei.

(3) In urgent situations everything will be handled by Liu, Chen, and Deng on the spot. Do not ask for guidance.[40]

Su Yu's deployment of forces to implement Liu Bocheng's plan was presented in a message sent to Liu, Chen, and Deng and also to the CMC, Wei Guoqing and Ji Luo, and Tan Zhenlin and Wang Jianan at 0900, 25 November. The message acknowledged the receipt of Liu, Chen, and Deng's 1000, 24 November message, so Su Yu knew that Liu Bocheng, Chen Yi, and Deng Xiaoping wanted three ECFA columns to reach the area southwest of Suxian on the night of 24 November. But, as Su Yu stated, that would be impossible. Until the night of 26 November the CPFA would have to try to encircle the Twelfth Army by itself:

> The [Liu-Chen-Deng] message of 1000 24 November and the CMC message of 1500 24 November have been read. We endorse completely the operational policy of first concentrating our strength and destroying Huang Wei. We have disposed our forces as follows:
>
> (1) Today the 6th Column, except for one division which will relieve the 2d (C) Column's 6th division of its responsibility for controlling Suxian, will advance to the Hugouji-Guanyintang line and then push eastward with all possible energy. It will construct defensive positions to firmly block any possible effort by the Li and Liu armies to move westward south of the Guzhen [Hui] River to aid Huang Wei. To its west this column will establish and maintain contact with the 11th (C) Column.
>
> The 2d Column will continue to control a line west and north of Caijiaqiao, Wangjiadazhuangzi, Gujiadian, Xisipo, Zhangjiaqiao, and Gaokouji and also the railroad to block any advance by Li and Liu's armies to the northwest along the railroad. Moreover, it will make every effort to extend the defensive works toward the southeast so that the armies of Li and Liu are far from Huang Wei and Suxian. This column will establish contact with the 6th Column.
>
> The 13th Column and the Jiang-Huai regional force, after taking Lingbi, will move as follows: The 13th Column will go to the area south of Sanpu and Dadian to join in the blocking of Li and Liu's armies. The two Jiang Huai divisions will advance to Tuoheji and conduct flanking attacks against the armies of Li and Liu.
>
> All of the forces mentioned above will be under the command of Wei Guoqing and Ji Luo. They will determine the specific disposition of these units.
>
> (2) Besides the 11th (C) Column, which is already under CPFA command for the attack on Huang Wei, we will only additionally dispatch the 7th and 11th (E) columns to participate in the operation against Huang Wei. Not until tomorrow evening can those two columns reach the area south and southwest of Suxian. The 10th Column will also be able to reach the area east of Suxian tomorrow to serve as a reserve. After a short period of rest and reorganization,

it will prepare to join in the battle of annihilation against Huang Wei.

I look for your instructions on how these columns should be used.

(3) The 1st, 3rd, 4th, 8th, 19th, 12th, Luzhongnan, and Liangguang columns will stay on the northern front to perform the mission of blocking a possible move by the armies of Qiu, Li, and Sun to aid Huang Wei by going to the south or to the southwest along the Xuzhou-Xiaoxian road. This force is all under the command of Tan Zhenlin and Wang Jianan.[41]

Encircling the Twelfth Army

While the Communist commanders were developing their plans and concentrating their forces to destroy the Twelfth Army, Huang Wei's army continued fighting toward Suxian. The morning of 24 November, with the XVIII Corps in the lead, the Twelfth Army began pushing north of the Hui River. However, progress was slow, and intelligence reports indicated that a dangerous situation was developing. XVIII Corps plainclothes intelligence personnel operating ahead of the corps had reported large numbers of Communist soldiers moving toward the Twelfth Army along the Mengcheng-Suxian road. Division reconnaissance teams were encountering overlapping "fish-scale" defensive positions built in depth along the corps' flanks. On the army's left flank, the X Corps reported a large enemy force moving from the west toward the corps' left flank and rear. Soldiers arriving from Mengcheng had brought news that the city had fallen into Communist hands.[42] Faced with stiff resistance, loss of any supply line to the rear, indications that he was moving into a sack-shaped area lined with defensive works, and other evidence of enemy intentions to surround him, at mid-day Huang Wei called his corps commanders together to discuss the situation.[43] A decision was reached to not abandon the attempt to reach Suxian but to go by way of Guzhen.[44] This would allow them to join with the Sixth and Eighth Armies and regain a supply line to support the advance to Suxian. That afternoon Huang issued orders for those units north of the Hui River to withdraw to the south bank and for the entire army to begin preparing to move toward Guzhen.[45]

The general outline of the Twelfth Army plan for shifting the army to Guzhen was, according to XVIII Corps commander Yang Botao as follows:

> (1) The XIV Corps, which was located southeast of Nanpingji, was to quickly move to the area along the Hui River west of Dongpingji and occupy defensive positions facing north along the south bank of the Hui River. There it would be on guard to block any southward advance by the Communists, thus providing a protective screen for the movement of the army.
>
> (2) The LXXXV Corps was to concentrate most of its forces in and around Nanpingji and defend the northwest approaches to the town so that the XVIII and X corps could shift positions [from north of the Hui River]. After these two corps had passed through Nanpingji, the corps was to move eastward toward Guzhen.
>
> (3) The X Corps was to break contact with the enemy and use the protection provided by the LXXXV and XIV Corps to move to the area west of Guzhen.
>
> (4) The XVIII corps was to immediately break contact with the enemy and move to an area west of Guzhen.

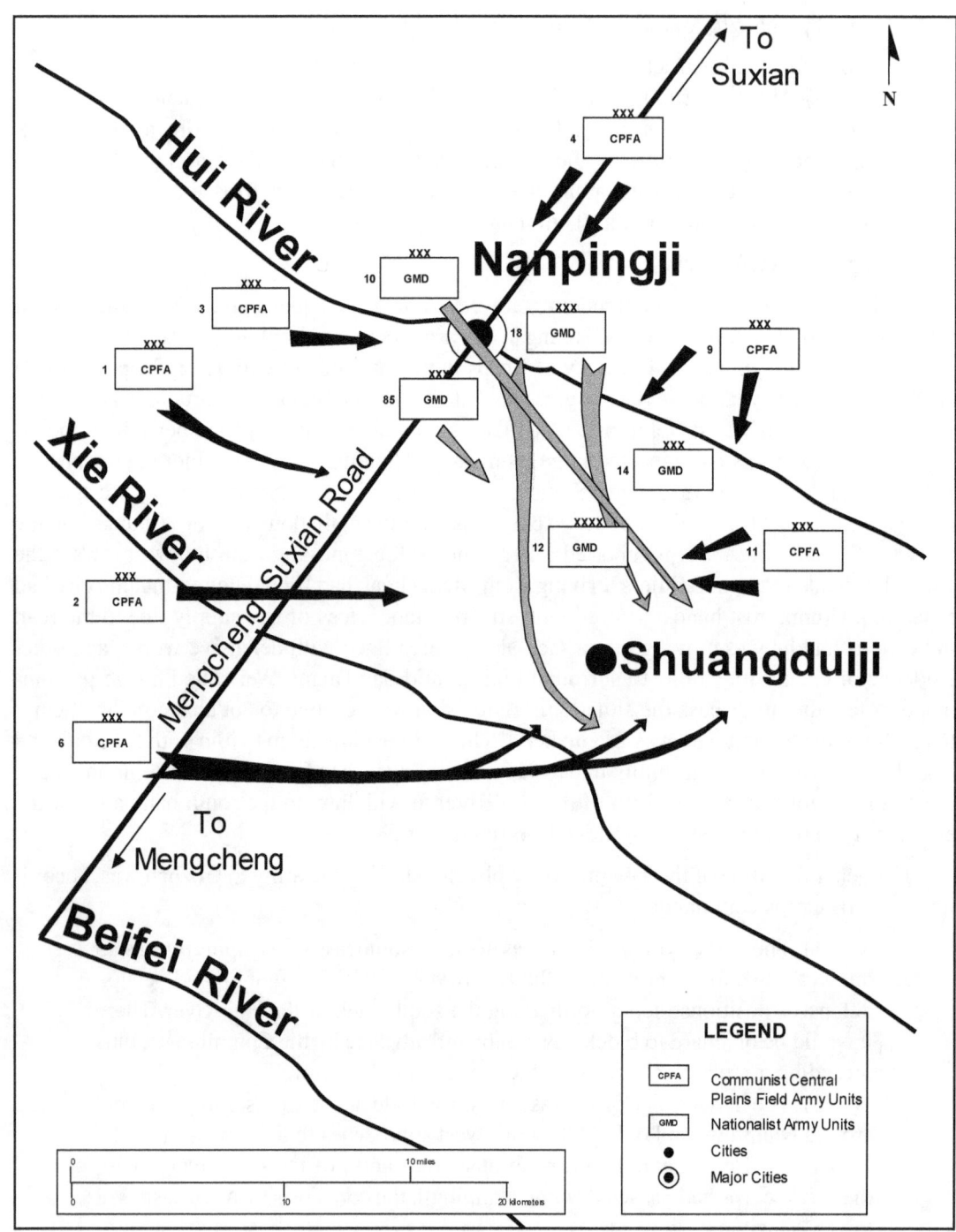

Map 2. Encirclement of the Twelfth Army.

(5) The army headquarters was to follow the XVIII corps.[46]

Huang Wei hoped to execute a rolling advance in which his four corps would alternate between attacking to the front and providing protective screens along the flanks and rear of the large army formation.[47] For a while this seemed achievable. Despite the fact that during the night of 24 November the CPFA launched its planned attack, the X and XVIII Corps units were able to withdraw south of the Hui River, and on 25 November they reached the area around Shuangduiji. The XIV Corps also successfully withdrew from the Hui River line to an area east of Shuangduiji. However, during the day the LXXXV Corps, which was defending the army's rear came under heavy attack from pursuing Communist columns. Communist units infiltrated between Nationalist positions and created chaos and confusion as they destroyed trucks, equipment, and supplies. Finally, Huang Wei was forced to send XVIII Corps elements back to restore the situation.[48] They accomplished this mission, but the resulting loss of forward momentum allowed the CPFA 6th Column to reach the army's front and begin to build blocking positions. At 0500, 26 November Liu Bocheng, Chen Yi, and Deng Xiaoping reported triumphantly to the CMC that the Twelfth Army was encircled:

> As of this morning, Huang Wei's army has been completely surrounded by us in the area between Nanpingji, Qixianji, Shaoweizi, Shuangduiji and Lugouji. We have blocked the attempt by the enemy to break out in the space between Shaoweizi and Shuangduiji. We have already ordered all columns to gradually squeeze the pocket until this enemy force is completely destroyed. We ask the CMC to direct New China Radio to intensify its political propaganda work aimed at the enemy.[49]

At the time this message was being transmitted, the Twelfth Army was preparing to resume its push toward Guzhen. Working through the night, Huang Wei had organized his army as follows: the LXXXV Corps was positioned on the right flank, west of Shuangduiji; the X Corps was in the center, east of Shuangduiji; the XIV Corps was on the left flank, northeast of Shuangduiji; and the XVIII Corps was providing rear security north of Shuangduiji. The plan was that after the three corps in front had reached and secured their intermediate objectives, the XVIII Corps would pass through the center and extend the advance to the southeast.[50] At dawn's first light the three columns in the lead element set out, but after advancing only a short distance to a line a few kilometers southeast of Shuangduiji, stiff CPFA resistance brought them to a stop. Given the continuing attacks against his army's flanks and rear, it was clear to Huang that he was encircled. This was confirmed in the afternoon when observers in reconnaissance aircraft flying out of Nanjing reported seeing Communist troops digging trenches all around his force.[51]

Huang Wei's first inclination after realizing that his army was encircled was to launch a major attack the next day to push through the Communist defensive positions before they were strengthened further.[52] Late in the afternoon he received orders from Nanjing directing that he do that very thing. The orders further informed Huang that Li Yannian had already been directed to launch an attack west toward Hugouji to support his attack. What Huang was supposed to do was "attack to the east with all the strength of his army, defeat the enemy in front of him, and link up with Li Yannian's army."[53]

Early on the evening of 26 November Huang Wei called a meeting of his corps and division commanders to plan for the next morning's attack. To make the attack as strong as possible, Huang decided to use four divisions—the 18th Division, X Corps; the 10th and 118th Divisions, XVIII Corps; and the 110th Division, LXXXV Corps.[54]

Selecting the 110th Division to participate in the attack proved to be a bad choice for Huang Wei. Division commander Liao Yunzhou had joined the CCP in March 1927 during the Northern Expedition and had served as an underground party member within the Nationalist army ever since. Through the years the party occasionally was able to send agents secretly to the division to help Liao's organizational work.[55] In summer 1947 the CCP gave him permission to establish an underground party committee within the division. Soon after, Liao began asking when he should lead the division to revolt, but Deng Xiaoping told him to "wait patiently in order to have the greatest effect at the most opportune time."[56]

In July 1948 Liu Bocheng and Deng Xiaoping passed word to Liao that the time to defect might be near and that he should prepare for such action. Now, on his own initiative, Liao decided that Deng's "opportune time" had arrived. During the meeting with Huang Wei, he volunteered the 110th Division to be one of the four divisions to participate in the attack. In addition, to facilitate the division's defection, he convinced Huang to change his concept of having four divisions attack abreast to one in which the divisions would attack in column with the 110th Division in the lead.[57] Once free to do so, he quickly went to his division's position on the perimeter of the Twelfth Army's pocket and drafted a message to send across the lines to the commander, 6th Column, telling him the Twelfth Army was preparing to launch a large attack against his positions the next morning and that the 110th Division wanted to defect.[58]

Around 0300, 27 November the messenger returned and took Liao across the lines to meet with 6th Column commander Wang Jinshan and his staff. Wang expressed great gratitude for the Twelfth Army plans that Liao had given them and told Liao they had been sent on to Liu Bocheng. Wang also set the conditions under which the 110th Division defection would take place. Gaoliang stalks would be set out to mark the routes to follow. Officers and soldiers would have a piece of white cloth or a towel on their left arms. When the two forces met, three rounds of artillery would be fired as a sign they were in contact. The goal was to have the entire division across the lines before daybreak.[59]

Returning to his division, Liao first informed his fellow Communist conspirators and then other officers who were known to be sympathetic to the Communist cause about what was going to happen. Security measures were put in place to ensure that word of their plans did not leak out as the division assembled for its scheduled attack. Then the Communist officers, and the other officers they trusted to join them, announced to their units what they said was good news. In the midst of a hopeless situation the division commander had arranged a way to save their lives. He would surrender the whole division immediately. Everyone was to put on the white cloth as directed and start moving out. An invitation was issued to those who did not want to go to say so.[60] Not surprisingly, as Liao later noted, no one spoke up, and off the division went.[61]

As the 110th Division was defecting, it was not clear to Huang Wei what was happening. The division had walked away in darkness, and at daybreak Liao had begun reporting to Huang by walkie-talkie that he was advancing easily against little resistance.[62] After 0900, with the division completely through the Communist lines, Liao still had the proper ground panels laid out to indicate to observers flying overhead that everything was proceeding well.⁶³ Reports from the follow-on divisions behind the 110th, however, indicated that things were not going well. They were encountering fierce resistance and going nowhere. With confusion compounding the effect of Communist defensive fire, the breakout attempt failed with hardly any forward progress being made. Meanwhile, on the Twelfth Army's flanks and rear, Communist attacks were compressing the pocket.

Liu Bocheng saw the situation at Shuangduiji at this time as extremely favorable and getting better. The 110th Division's defection and the number of prisoners being taken indicated to him that the Twelfth Army was about to disintegrate. As the following message sent to the CMC at 1700 27 November indicates, he was assuming the battle would be over the next day. Already he was directing that ECFA columns return to ECFA control for use in operations against Li Yannian:

> (1) As of the present moment we have already compressed Huang Wei's army into a little over ten villages around Shuangduiji. As the attacks have moved along, we have been taking prisoners. This morning Liao Yunzhou (commander of the 110th division of the LXXXV Corps) led his force to revolt on the battlefield. (Don't publicize this for 3 days.) The XVIII Corps and other units now densely packed into Shuangduiji like the spines of a hedgehog have already had men surrendering to us in certain areas. At the latest, the battle with the entire force will be completed tomorrow.
>
> (2) We have already told Su, Chen, and Zhang to immediately begin deploying to destroy Li Yannian and Liu Ruming. We have also already directly ordered that the 11th (E) and 7th (E) columns be returned to Wei and Ji's command. Moreover, we have already directly ordered the 7th Column to move rapidly tonight (27 November) to the area between Guzhen and Bengbu to cut the route of withdrawal for all enemy forces north of Guzhen. We have also told Wang and Ji to order the 6th Column to attack from Hugou toward Guzhen. Afterward, the 7th Column and the 11th (E) Column (but not the 11th (C) Column) will return to the control of Su, Chen, and Zhang. Concerning the arrangements for surrounding and destroying Li and Liu, they will be the responsibility of Su and Chen.
>
> (3) Each column of the CPFA (including the 11th (C) Column), after they have completed the task of finishing off Huang Wei tomorrow, must have a certain number of days to handle post-battle matters. We ask the CMC to tell us what our future strategic orientation will be.⁶⁴

Intimidating the Sixth and Eighth Armies

Three hours before Liu Bocheng, Chen Yi, and Deng Xiaoping sent out the preceding message, at 1400, 27 November Su Yu had already transmitted his plan for surrounding the Sixth Army's XCIX Corps and XXXIX Corps in the Renqiaoji area and cutting the Su-Beng railroad south of Guzhen.⁶⁵ This deep thrust toward Bengbu was intended to net as many Nationalist forces as possible before they could retreat to safety. It was also designed to hold the LIV Corps, which Su expected would try to relieve the XCIX and XXXIX Corps after they were surrounded, as far from them as possible. In his message, Su stated he had already received intelligence reports indicating that the XCIX and XXXIX Corps were withdrawing toward Guzhen, but he was still confident that his forces, which were to begin moving that night, would be able to surround and destroy them.[66]

Su Yu did not achieve this objective. After Lingbi had fallen to the 13th Column-Jiang Huai Military District force on 25 November, Li Yannian had become very concerned about the growing threat on his right flank posed by the ECFA columns moving south from the Xuzhou area. His XCIX and XXXIX Corps were at the tip of a very long thin salient along the Su-Beng railroad. Behind him was the Eighth Army, a force in which he had little confidence. As a result, on the evening of 26 November he sent these two corps back south, a movement that, as Su Yu's reference to it in his message of 1400, 27 November indicates, the Communists quickly realized.[67] Despite what the Nationalist High Command told Huang Baitao about the Sixth Army supporting his breakout attempt on 27 November by attacking west from Renqiaoji, the attack did not take place. Instead, the Sixth Army continued to move south on 27 November.

Li Yannian's actions saved his army. On 28 November ECFA units could only catch up with the tail end of the Nationalist forces moving south. Some Nationalist soldiers were killed and captured. A number of trucks and the supplies they were transporting were captured or destroyed. Basically, however, the Sixth and Eighth Armies reached Bengbu intact. There they were deployed in a defensive line along the Huai River, leaving the Twelfth Army deeply isolated 60 km to their northwest.

Holding the Line on the Northern Front

By encircling the Twelfth Army and forcing the Sixth and Eighth Armies to withdraw to Bengbu from 25 to 28 November the CPFA and ECFA eliminated the two southern prongs in the Nationalist plan to regain the central position. Meanwhile, the eight ECFA columns deployed south of Xuzhou to hold the northern side of the central position were fighting to block the third prong. This was the key shaping operation of this phase of the campaign. PLA commanders were concerned that if the three armies in Xuzhou, the strongest Nationalist force on the campaign battlefield, were able to move south to Suxian and beyond, they would directly threaten the CPFA's rear and could possibly break the Twelfth Army's encirclement.[68]

To keep any of Liu Zhiming's Group Army from making such a breakthrough, Tan Zhenlin adopted a linear area defense. Five columns and the two independent Ju-Lu-Yu Military Region divisions were deployed along a 50-km arc that ran from the Xiaoxian area southwest of Xuzhou to the Long-Hai railroad area in the east. The units' positions, left to right, were the Ji-Lu-Yu divisions near Xiaoxian, the Liangguang Column, the 3d Column in the center, the Luzhongnan Column, the 12th Column, and finally the 1st Column on the extreme east end of the line. These columns were directed to construct three lines of defensive works in their sectors and set up interlocking fields of fire.[69]

Behind these columns, as reserves, were the three columns that had suffered the most casualties in fighting east of Xuzhou, the 9th on the left, the 8th in the center, and the 4th on the right. Tan organized the columns into three army-sized groupings to promote unity of effort. The "western route blocking army" consisted of the Ji-Lu-Yu divisions, the Liangguang Column, and the 9th Column under the 9th Column commander's overall command. In the center the "frontal blocking army" contained the 3d Column, the Luzhongnan Column, and the 8th Column under the direct control of Tan and his Shandong army headquarters. On the right the "eastern route blocking army," consisting of the 12th Column, 1st Column, and 4th Column, was under the 4th Column commander's command.[70] Tan's objective was to firmly hold this line for 20 days to one month to give the CPFA time to destroy the Twelfth Army.[71]

Liu Zhi and Du Yuming faced an unenviable task in trying to overcome the defenses Tan Zhenlin had established and reach Suxian. The frontal attacks the Thirteenth and Second Armies conducted in their attempt to reach Nianzhuangxu and relieve the Seventh Army had failed. In that difficult battle the two armies had expended large quantities of ammunition and suffered approximately 15,000 killed and many thousand wounded.[72] According to the commander, Thirteenth Army, VIII Corps, units committed to that effort had suffered about 30-percent casualties.[73] Now Du replaced the Thirteenth Army with the Sixteenth Army as an attacking force but again called on the Second Army. He knew he lacked the element of surprise, but he hoped an advantage in firepower would enable him to destroy the prepared defenses and advance south.

On 25 November the Sixteenth and Second Armies launched their offensive, employing four corps abreast supported by aerial strafing, tanks, and artillery. During the day, the Nationalists occupied the ECFA's first defensive line in several places and captured a number of hills. However, the average advance for the Second Army was only a disappointing 3 km.[74] Gains on 26 and 27 November were no better, which lead Qiu Qingquan and Sun Yuanliang to appeal to Du Yuming to either give them more firepower or stop attacking.[75] With infantry losses running high, they felt that continuing to carry out frontal assaults that gained little ground would soon put them in a position whereby they would be unable to conduct any offensive operations at all. Du agreed with them in principle but said that shortages in bombs and artillery ammunition made it impossible to give them all the fire support they wanted. All he could do was direct that they continue their efforts to break through.[76]

Whether the Nationalists could have broken through the ECFA defenses south of Xuzhou is unclear. On 28 November their armies were into their third week of almost continuous combat. Casualties had been heavy, and ammunition, fuel, and food consumption had been high. Qiu Qingquan and Sun Yuanliang's concerns about their ability to continue their attacks were undoubtedly valid, but the ECFA was also feeling the strain of continuous operations. On 20 November Su Yu had reported to the CMC that ECFA casualties in the fighting east of Xuzhou had reached nearly 40,000, with the 8th and 9th Columns having more than 5,000 casualties each and the 4th Column having more than 4,000.[77] Most of the columns that were now on the front line had also suffered significant losses in earlier fighting. The 1st Column had more than 3,000 casualties, and the 3d and Luzhongnan Columns had more than 2,000 casualties each.[78] Added to these losses were those incurred during the Nationalist attacks of 25-28 November.

By 26 November the Liangguang Column had suffered so many casualties and was in such a battle-weary state that the commander, 9th Column, pulled it from the front and replaced it with his own columns.[79] On 28 November Tan Zhenlin decided the Luzhongnan Column needed to be taken out of the line and sent to the area east of Fuliji for rest and reorganization.[80] 8th Column elements went into its place. This costly battle of attrition was taking a heavy toll on both sides. The question was, could the Nationalists, given their slow rate of forward progress, continue attacking long enough to wear down the Communists and reach their objective?

This would have been hard to do because the Nationalists, being an isolated force, could not replace their losses as the Communists could. On 21 November Su Yu had ordered the

Bohai Column, which had been performing garrison duty in Jinan, to go south to the Xuzhou area as rapidly as possible.[81] Traveling the first 140 km of their journey by train to Yanzhou and then marching 150 km, the column reached the northeast side of Xuzhou on 26 November and was immediately put on the line next to the 1st Column to increase pressure on that sector of the Xuzhou defenses.[82] The Communists also continued, during the battle, to use Nationalist soldiers who had surrendered or been captured as replacements.

Using enemy soldiers as one's own was not new in Chinese history. Sunzi had advocated the practice in *The Art of War* in keeping with his preference for preservation over destruction. Sunzi wanted to capture, not kill the enemy: "It is better to capture an army entire than to destroy it, to capture a regiment, a detachment or a company entire than to destroy them."[83] Once they were captured, Sunzi saw no better place for these soldiers and their equipment than in one's own force:

> Therefore in chariot fighting, when ten or more chariots have been taken, those should be rewarded who took the first. Our own flags should be substituted for those of the enemy, and the chariots mingled and used in conjunction with ours. The captured soldiers should be kindly treated and kept. This is called using the conquered foe to augment one's own strength.[84]

The Communists had long relied on turning warlord or Nationalist soldiers into Communist soldiers as a way to increase their army's size. This was easier than taking a peasant out of the field and turning him into a soldier. The practice was embedded in PLA operational principles as part of principle nine where it states specifically: "replenish our strength with all of the arms and most of the personnel captured from the enemy." During the Huai Hai Campaign, using Nationalist soldiers as replacements received command emphasis right from the start. As the following excerpt from a message the CMC sent to the ECFA and CPFA commanders on 7 November indicates, this was to be a major way to keep forces up to strength:

> In order to fight consecutive operations and destroy a large number of the enemy, you should follow the method used in the Jinan Campaign, keeping troop strength robust and morale high by having every combat unit replace losses as they fight and fight as they replace losses. This is very important.

> To accomplish this, the trained replacement units in the rear should be shifted to positions near the battlefield, so that the new soldiers and captured soldiers who have already been properly trained can rapidly replenish the forces. At the same time, take all of those captured during this campaign, quickly give them training, and replenish the forces.[85]

Other messages sent during the campaign reveal a continuing command focus on this practice. Su Yu's message of 1000, 9 November sent to all ECFA army, column, division, and regimental commanders stated: "At the front, as you take prisoners, use them as replacements, and as you use them as replacements, continue to fight, thus maintaining the numbers required for combat, replenishing our strength for battle, and carrying forward the spirit of continuous, protracted combat."[86] In his message of 2100, 18 November to his field commanders Su Yu said, "You should immediately use your prisoners as replacements to maintain sufficient strength for continuous operations."[87] Tan Zhenlin's message to his column commanders upon assuming command of the blocking force south of Xuzhou included a similar request to "Firmly grasp the work of integrating liberated soldiers into your units."[88]

The pace of integrating captured Nationalist soldiers into ECFA units quickened as the Huai Hai Campaign progressed. Large ECFA losses created the need. The changing characteristics of the Nationalist soldiers being taken prisoner created the conditions that made it possible. The political commissar, 4th Column, later recounted how, at the time, the political cadres responsible for reeducating the Nationalist soldiers began to realize that many of the soldiers were poor peasants who had only recently been dragooned into the army. Given their backgrounds, they could be swayed easily by the Communist political message and would readily agree to enter the PLA. As a result, the 4th Column asked for and received permission from ECFA headquarters to process its prisoners quickly and put as many of them into the column as the column commander saw fit. But this was not done haphazardly. Not all Nationalist soldiers could be transformed into PLA fighters because of political considerations or other reasons. The 4th Column developed a systematic program involving several steps to carry out this transformational process. The steps were "capture, divide (clearly distinguish between ordinary soldiers and officers and the small number of hooligans and army riffraff); educate; place in the ranks; commit to combat; and evaluate (the granting of awards and promotions.)"[89]

Ceremonies were held when captured soldiers entered the PLA and received their weapons. When time permitted, sessions telling about the misery of life under the Nationalists were convened. Old PLA fighters were assigned to help the new arrivals. As a result of this program, 13,000 captured Nationalist soldiers were brought into the 4th Column between 6 November and 15 December.[90] How many thousands of these were in the column when it was fighting south of Xuzhou after 25 November is unknown, but there must have been many because in the latter stages of the battle to destroy the Seventh Army the column commander had begun to plan attacks specifically with capturing soldiers to replace his losses in mind.[91] With eight ECFA columns using former Nationalist soldiers as replacements, it is easy to see how their total number could have been quite large. Ironically, they may have been numerous enough to have tipped the balance in the Communists' favor in the attrition battle south of Xuzhou.

Communist Visions and Operational Concepts, 27 November-1 December

After receiving the optimistic report on the fight to destroy Huang Wei's army that Liu Bocheng, Chen Yi, and Deng Xiaoping had sent at 1700, 27 November and Su Yu's message of 1400, 27 November expressing his confidence that he would soon destroy two of Li Yannian's corps, the CMC responded at 0400, 28 November with a grand vision of developing opportunities and future operations. Worth noting is that at this point, with the CPFA having only fought the Twelfth Army for a few days and an easy, quick victory anticipated, the CMC was still thinking this army should spend two weeks resting, reorganizing, and replenishing before resuming operations. The message also shows the CMC's desire to maintain maximum pressure on the Nationalists. Although destroying the three Nationalist armies in Xuzhou was to be the next main effort, the CMC also wanted Communist forces to be in position on the Yangzi's north bank opposite Nanjing (at Pukou) as soon as possible:

(1) Both the Liu-Chen-Deng message sent 1700 27 November and the Su-Chen-Zhang message sent 1400 27 November have been read.

(2) If today (28 November), Liu, Chen, and Deng are able to completely take care of Huang Wei's army, and Su, Chen, and Zhang are able to surround

the various units from Li Yannian and Liu Ruming's armies that are located north of Bengbu and destroy them during the next several days, then the entire Huai Hai Campaign will have undergone a decisive change. The second phase of the campaign would be over.

(3) The third phase of the campaign will be to finish off the enemy forces in Xuzhou and Bengbu and capture both cities.

(4) After completely destroying Huang Wei and all the units Li Yanian and Liu Ruming have north of Bengbu, the entire army should rest and reorganize for a short period. The length of time will be determined by conditions. Most likely, approximately two weeks will be required. Afterwards, the main force will be used to take Xuzhou while a fairly large force will be used to take Bengbu, Pukou, Hefei, and other cities located in the area bounded by the Huai River on the north, the Yangzi River on the south, the Grand Canal on the east, and Chao Lake on the west. This force will press right up against the Yangzi.

(5) Presently, the ECFA altogether has 16 columns of different sizes, the 1st, 2d, 3rd, 4th, 6th, 7th, 8th, 9th, 10th, 11th, 12th, 13th, Bohai, Luzhongnan, Liangguang, and Special Type [ST]. The CPFA has 7 columns, the 1st, 2d, 3rd, 4th, 6th, 9th, and the Wang [Bingzhang]-Zhang[Linzhi] 11th. (The Wang-Zhang column should return to CPFA control.) After the second phase of the campaign has concluded, and before the short period of rest and reorganization has begun, please immediately consider the question of troop deployment for the next phase of operations and give us your ideas on how many troops will be needed to attack Xuzhou and how many will be needed to take Bengbu and Pukou.

(6) If Li and Liu's main body can be destroyed north of Bengbu, then there will be very few enemy troops in Bengbu or along the Beng-Pu [Bengbu-Pukou] railroad. It seems that there is the possibility here to build on a victory and seize both Bengbu and part, or all, of the Beng-Pu railroad. If this possibility arises, then we should have at least two or three columns go south of the Huai River at an early date to carry out this mission. Even if Bengbu cannot be taken immediately, we still should, at an early date, cut the communication link between Bengbu and Pukou so that the reinforcements that the enemy could shift from other places will have no way to reach Bengbu. Once the columns that would execute this mission have cut communications between Bengbu and Pukou, they can rest and reorganize along the Beng-Pu railroad. Then, they can attack Bengbu.[92]

At 2200, 28November the CMC sent Liu Bocheng, Chen Yi, Deng Xiaoping, Su Yu, and Tan Zhenlin a message that followed up on this vision of quickly advancing into the area south of the Huai River and capturing Bengbu. Reflecting the CMC's desire that this movement across the Huai River take place soon, the CMC identified the ECFA columns that were in the Guzhen area not far from Bengbu as the units that could execute such an operation. While these columns would be moving south, the CPFA would move north to fight the Nationalist armies in Xuzhou supported by the ECFA columns under Tan Zhenlin:

(1) We ask Su, Chen, and Zhang, after they have destroyed the enemy in

the Guzhen-Caolaoji area, to consider exploiting this victory by sending five columns, the 2d, 6th, 7th, 11th, and 13th south of the Huai River to cut the Beng-Pu railroad and surround Bengbu, all the while looking for an opportunity to seize Bengbu. The 10th Column would stay at Suxian to rest and reorganize. Afterwards, the columns led by Tan [Zhenlin], Wang [Jinan], and Li [Yingxi] and the 10th Column would be used in coordination with the CPFA to take care of the enemy in Xuzhou. We look forward to your telling us whether or not this could be done and what difficulties there would be in a river crossing operation across the Huai so we can make a final decision.

(2) After Huang Wei is finished off, we must consider the possibility of the enemy in Xuzhou taking flight toward the two Huai cities [Huaian and Huaiyin] or toward Wuhan. Because of this, even though, on the one hand, the CPFA and the ECFA columns under Tan, Wang, and Li should try to take two weeks for rest and reorganization, on the other hand, they should quickly handle the post-battle work so they can counter the unexpected from an advantageous position. We ask that you take heed of this matter and get a good handle on it.[93]

During the hours when the CMC was preparing and transmitting these messages laying out its vision of future possibilities, events on the Shuangduiji battlefield were undercutting the foundation on which that vision was built. Far from disintegrating the night of 27 November, the Twelfth Army managed to mount a strong defense that grew stronger on 28 November. At 1700, 28 November Liu Bocheng, Chen Yi, and Deng Xiaoping had to inform the CMC that the battle to destroy the Twelfth Army not only would not be over that day as they had expected, it would take at least 10 more days:

(1) After last night's (27 November) fighting, we have already compressed the enemy into a long, narrow small area 7.5 kilometers long and 2.5 kilometers wide. The enemy has fiercely attacked our 6th Column's positions several times using large numbers of aircraft and tanks in an attempt to open a route for escaping toward the southeast. All attacks have been repulsed and more than 300 soldiers have been taken prisoner. We have been pressing on the pocket from the west, east, and north, in a southerly direction. Our troops are fiercely courageous, but [last evening] because of the murky weather and nightfall the units became disorganized. Also, the enemy, after the failure of the break out attempt, relied on the positions they already had to mount a firm defense. As a result, before dawn this morning we stopped attacking.

(3) At present, in light of the enemy's tenacious defense, we are waiting for ammunition to arrive. Then, on the night of 29 November we will start attacking to annihilate the enemy. Our method of fighting will be to concentrate firepower against points in sequence, taking them out one by one.

(4) From the time that we began the blocking battle at Guoyang on 19 November, up to this morning (28 November), total casualties for our six columns have not exceeded 6,000. Morale is very high. With the addition of the ECFA 7th Column and artillery we can surely destroy this enemy. However, finishing the task will require ten days or so. Originally, on the basis of conditions

existing at the time of the enemy's full-scale break out attempt and the revolt of Liao, we calculated that combat would soon be over. Those conditions have already changed.

(5) Because the enemy is mounting a strong defense, we will keep the ECFA 7th Column as a general reserve.[94]

This message caused a dramatic shift in CMC thought. The vision of establishing a reserve force and concentrating on attacking Huang Wei replaced the vision of quickly sending several ECFA columns south of the Huai River. Destroying the Twelfth Army was central to maintaining the initiative in the campaign. Once that happened, more than 100,000 Communist soldiers would be free for use elsewhere, and the isolation of the Nationalist armies in Xuzhou would be greatly deepened. At 0600, 29 November the CMC outlined its revised campaign vision in the following message addressed to Liu, Chen, and Deng and also sent to Su Yu and Tan Zhenlin:

(1) Your 1700 28 November message has been read. Looking at the enemy's strong defense, your plan to concentrate firepower and destroy the enemy in detail step by step over a period of ten or more days is safe and reliable.

(2) Finishing off Huang Wei's army is the key to finishing off all 66 enemy divisions in the Xuzhou and Bengbu areas. You must consider what the enemy's last ditch struggle will be like. You must ensure that you have extra strength at hand sufficient to meet unexpected situations. Because of this, after Su, Chen, and Zhang have destroyed the enemy in the Guzhen-Caolaoji area they should immediately bring the 2nd, 6th, 10th, 11th, and 13th columns together to rest and serve as a general reserve for the destruction of Huang Wei. As for the matter of crossing south of the Huai River, we will wait until after Huang Wei is destroyed to discuss that again.

(3) We hope that Tan, Wang, and Li can firmly block the armies of Qiu, Li, and Sun and not allow them to reach Suxian. What is the situation on the northern front? Please inform us.[95]

Su Yu's response to the previous three messages, his analysis of the emerging situation the Communists faced, and his suggestions for how to proceed came in a message he sent to the CMC; Liu, Chen, and Deng; and the CCP's East China Bureau at 1500, 29 November. The CMC's message of 2200, 28 November had mentioned the possibility of the Nationalists abandoning Xuzhou after the Twelfth Army was destroyed. In his message, Su reported signs that such a development might be imminent, and he also indicated he thought the direction the Nationalists would take when they abandoned Xuzhou would be toward the south or southeast. Su told the CMC that he was moving the 2d, 6th, 10th, and 11th (E) Columns into positions southeast and northeast of Suxian where they would become a reserve for the fight against Huang Wei and would be ready to counter any attempt by the Nationalist armies in Xuzhou to flee toward the southeast.

Su Yu also presented another Sunzian vision in which, if the situation presented itself, he would try to entice those armies to move into an area between Xuzhou and Shuanggou and destroy them there. If the Nationalists did not abandon Xuzhou but drew back toward the city and defended in place, Su wanted the mission of destroying them given to the ECFA alone. His primary justification was that keeping the ECFA together would facilitate the exercise of command. He also pointed out that sending the CPFA south of the Huai River was more appropriate than sending part of the ECFA because the CPFA already had links to people in that area established during the Liu-Deng army's strategic leap to the Dabie Mountains in late summer 1947 and the battles that followed. The excerpt from Su's message presented below shows his careful analysis of the situation before him and again illustrates how, as an operational commander, he continually asked and answered the questions that lay at the heart of operational art.

> Liu, Chen, and Deng's message of 1700 28 November, and the CMC's messages of 2200 28 November and 0600 29 November have all been read. In addition to expressing complete agreement with the directives in the CPFA message of 1700 28 November and the CMC message of 0600 29 November, I am adding the following ideas:
>
> (1) Huang Wei, having no hope of being relieved by a force moving north from Bengbu, seems to be drawing back and concentrating to firmly defend while waiting for the force in Xuzhou to move south to relieve him.
>
> Liu [Ruming] and Li [Yannian] . . . have already withdrawn to Bengbu and the area just to the north of Bengbu. The opportunity to destroy them while they were moving has passed.
>
> The Xuzhou 'suppression headquarters' has already changed its command location. Most of the personnel have flown to Nanjing. On this basis, I estimate that the armies of Qiu, Li, and Sun will either use all of their strength in an attack toward the south to reinforce Huang Wei and then withdraw southward with him, or they will take advantage of this situation where one major force is still engaged in fighting Huang Wei and another in pursuing Li and Liu . . . to seize an opening and either go south or go toward the two Huai cities. If they do not do this, then after Huang Wei is taken care of, Qiu, Li, and Sun will be in a difficult situation that will be even more conducive to our destroying them one by one.
>
> (2) In accordance with commands, I'm adjusting deployments.
> The two Jiang Huai divisions will be sent south of the Huai River and will coordinate with the force sent there in October to conduct operations to destroy the Pu-Beng railroad so the enemy cannot reinforce Bengbu.
>
> The 13th Column will control the Guzhen-Caolaoji area to block any attempts by the enemy forces in Bengbu to advance northward or westward to aid Huang Wei.
>
> All other southern front forces except for the 11th [C] (Wang-Zhang), 7th, and ST columns that are attached to the CPFA for the fight against Huang Wei, that is, the 2nd, 6th, 10th, and 11th [E] columns, will assemble in the area between Suxian, Lingbi, and Guzhen and the area northeast of Suxian. There they will await opportunities and prepare to add needed troop strength at the right time for the final destruction of Huang Wei. At the same time, these columns will also prepare to entice the Qiu, Li, and Sun armies to come down the east side of the railroad until they reach the north banks of the Tang River. There they will attack in conjunction with the northern front columns and this attack from two sides will destroy the enemy between Xuzhou and the area west of Jiagou.

If the enemy breaks out toward the southeast, I can also maneuver in time to cut him off.

Before Huang Wei has been fundamentally taken care of, the primary focus has to be on blocking the Xuzhou force in order to guarantee the destruction of Huang Wei. Only after the greater part of Huang Wei's force has been destroyed can we look for opportunities to lure the enemy southward so we can more easily concentrate and destroy his main force outside of Xuzhou. (The degree of resistance to the enemy advance will be decided by looking at how conditions in the CPFA's operation against Huang Wei are developing.) When the time has arrived, not only will the ECFA's main force participate, but if troop strength is insufficient, part of the CPFA can join in, adding strength to eliminating Qiu, Liu, and Sun. If we're able to destroy Huang Wei on schedule, and at the same time, or later, also wipe out Qiu and Li, then the battle for the Central Plains will be basically decided. Therefore, with our CPFA and ECFA where they are now in terms of the campaign as a whole, it is appropriate for us to adopt a plan to use all their strength to gain the consecutive destruction of Huang, Li, and Qiu.

(3) If Huang Wei is finished off quickly and the armies of Qiu, Li, and Sun are still concentrated in Xuzhou, then, after a short period for rest and replenishment, the CPFA and the ECFA can divide forces between south and north and take Xuzhou and Bengbu. Regarding the assignment of missions, the Xuzhou enemy force of Qiu, Li, and Sun has 21 divisions and numbers between 250,000 and 300,000. The Bengbu force of Li and Liu has 15 divisions and almost 150,000 soldiers. To facilitate the command of operations and the use of the forces, don't split the organizational structure. We suggest that the entire ECFA take on the task of destroying the enemy in Xuzhou, and that it's more appropriate for the CPFA to seize Hefei and the Beng-Pu railroad and work at opening up the area south of the Huai River. Moreover, the CPFA already has ties with the work going on in the Dabie Mountains and central and southern Anhui. What we will actually do depends upon future developments and will be decided by the CMC.[96]

On 29 November the CMC and Su Yu were both thinking that if and when the Nationalist forces abandoned Xuzhou their most likely route would be an attempt to flee southeast through Shuanggou toward the two Huai cities of Huaian and Huaiyin. This was based in large part on where the strongest attacks against the ECFA blocking force had been conducted to date and on intelligence showing the location of Nationalist army units. At 1000, 1600, and 2130 on 29 November Tan Zhenlin; Wang Jianan, deputy commander, Shandong army; and Li Yingxi, chief of staff, Shandong army, sent messages to Su Yu and the CMC repeatedly stating their view that the center of mass of the armies in Xuzhou was toward the east and that Qiu, Li, and Sun were about to flee to the southeast.[97] In these messages they proposed that to quickly and firmly encircle these armies and keep them from fleeing, "it was necessary to add two more main force columns to the defense of the line from Shuanggou to Danji."[98]

After receiving these reports and recommendations from commanders in the field and after receiving intelligence from agents (perhaps Guo Rugui) in Nanjing, at 1700, 30 November the

CMC sent a message to Liu, Chen, and Deng, and also to Su Yu and Tan Zhenlin suggesting that three more columns be sent to the Shuanggou area. The tone of the message, however, did not reflect a sense of urgency. Apparently, the CMC still did not feel the Nationalist armies in Xuzhou were about to abandon Xuzhou:

> (1) All of the messages sent by Su, Chen, and Zhang and Tan, Wang, and Li on 29 November have been received. All of the calculations and ideas are very good.
>
> (2) After the enemy on the Guzhen-Caolaoji line has been taken care of, sending the two Jiang Huai divisions south of the Huai River and using the 13th Column to control Guzhen and Caolaoji is very appropriate. We hope that this will be done.
>
> (3) As for the 2d, 6th, 10th, and 11th (E) columns, two of those four columns should be positioned north of Guzhen to rest and prepare to be used at any time by Liu, Chen, and Deng. They will be a general reserve for finishing off Huang Wei. This is a good plan. Could the other two columns go to the Shuanggou-Dawangzhuang line as Tan, Wang, and Li suggested and coordinate with the 1st Column to block the possible break out attempt by Qiu [Qingquan] and Li [Mi] toward the two Huai cities? We ask Liu, Chen, and Deng and Su, Chen, and Zhang to decide what to do on the basis of conditions.
>
> (4) The 7th Column artillery has already been given to Liu, Chen, and Deng to use. This won't be discussed further. The entire Special Type [ST] Column should be committed to the fight against Huang Wei so as to strengthen our firepower.
>
> (5) Where is the Bohai Column? It seems that that column should also be used in the Shuanggou area to counter Qiu and Li's main force.
>
> (6) Liu, Chen, and Deng's radio transmitter should quickly make a connection with Tan, Wang, and Li's transmitter.
>
> (7) Our current inclination is that after Huang Wei is destroyed we will concentrate the entire strength of the ECFA and CPFA to finish off Qiu, Li, and Sun. Afterwards, we will rest and reorganize for a period of time and then carry out the Jiang-Huai [advance south of the Huai River to the Yangzi] campaign together.[99]

If, at 1700, 30 November the CMC did not feel an urgent need to shift forces to counter a possible Nationalist attempt to flee Xuzhou, several hours later the situation was different. At 0200, 1 December the CMC ordered three columns to immediately shift to the area east and southeast of Xuzhou. The CMC had finally decided the Nationalists would be trying to escape by moving in either of those directions. As this message shows, they wanted preparations to block such a move to begin quickly:

> Foreign news agencies have revealed that the enemy forces in Xuzhou have a plan to flee to Lianyungang. We estimate that when Huang Wei's army is near destruction and Qiu, Li, and Sun have given up hope of fleeing to the south, it is most likely that their direction of flight will be toward either the two Huai cities or Lianyungang. Because of this, you should immediately make preparations as follows: (1) order the Bohai Column to quickly concentrate in the

Daxujia-Danji area; (2) from among the 2nd, 6th, 10th, and 11th (E) columns, immediately send two columns to the Shuanggou-Suining line; (3) warn all of the military districts and sub-districts in southern Shandong and in the area between Huaian/Huaiyin and Haizhou to make arrangements regarding the local militia so that when the time comes they can act. We look for your word on how you are deploying your forces.[100]

The Nationalists Decide to Abandon Xuzhou

This CMC message and the other messages sent from 29 to 30 November reflect the Communists' customary attempt to anticipate possible future Nationalist actions and to begin preparing countermoves even before the Nationalists acted. Up to this point in the campaign, Communist commanders had already correctly anticipated a number of Nationalist moves. A good intelligence system provided information superiority that greatly aided them in doing so. It is, therefore, surprising that at the very moment the CMC was ordering more columns to the eastern side of Xuzhou to block a Nationalist breakout toward the east or southeast, Du Yuming's army group was marching away from Xuzhou toward the west.

The complete story on why, in this case, the Communists were so wrong in anticipating what the Nationalists were going to do remains to be determined. Obviously, there was an intelligence failure within an intelligence system that not only usually provided Communist commanders with an accurate picture of enemy dispositions and movements within their operational areas but often gave them information on Nationalist intentions. This was a significant advantage that was missing in this instance. But the Communists' failure to correctly determine what the Nationalist armies in Xuzhou were doing and what they intended to do was also the result of effective Nationalist operational security and deception. In large measure, credit for giving the Nationalist armies in Xuzhou a chance to escape the fate Su Yu and others planned for them must go to Du Yuming.

Du Yuming's leading role in the Nationalist decision to abandon Xuzhou goes back to 28 November, which was a pivotal day for Nationalist decision making. On this day, in an attempt to strengthen the command structure at Bengbu, Jiang Jieshi ordered Liu Zhi's Bandit Suppression Headquarters to move from Xuzhou to Bengbu. There Liu was to establish a command headquarters to command and control the Sixth and Eighth Armies.[101] Jiang also assigned the LIV Corps to the Sixth Army to improve the ability of the forces in the Bengbu to move north when called on to do so. Moving Liu Zhi out of Xuzhou increased the independence of Du Yuming's forward command headquarters, which remained in Xuzhou, and basically made him responsible for the fate of the three armies he controlled. It was in this position of responsibility that he flew to Nanjing the morning of 28 November to attend another major strategy session Jiang Jieshi had convened.

Du arrived in Nanjing before noon and went straight to the presidential building. Soon Army Chief of Staff Gu Zhutong arrived, and since there was time before the meeting started, he invited Du into a reception room for a private discussion about the crisis the Nationalists were facing. The plan for regaining the central position adopted on 23 November had clearly failed. The Xuzhou armies were not pushing through Tan Zhenlin's blocking force. Li Yannian and Liu Ruming were withdrawing toward Bengbu. The Twelfth Army was encircled and, worse yet, on 27 November had shown itself incapable of breaking out of that encirclement on its own. Something had to be done to turn the situation around. Du frankly told Gu that the single solution was to add troops to the only place they could be added, the Bengbu front. He expressed his frustration over Jiang Jieshi's failure to add the several extra corps he had promised to shift to the Bengbu front at their meeting on 23 November and asked angrily, "Why wasn't even one added? Now we are riding a tiger and can't get off."[102]

After Gu Zhutong explained that Jiang Jeshi had wanted to shift several corps to Bengbu but that every possible corps was already committed somewhere else, Du replied, "If Jiang already knew that he was unable to pull troops from elsewhere to fight a decisive battle, then from the very start he should not have decided to fight and let Huang Wei fall into this tight encirclement with no way out. Now the only approach for saving Huang Wei is to concentrate all possible forces and fight a decisive battle with the enemy. Otherwise, Huang Wei is finished, Xuzhou will be lost, and Nanjing will be in danger."[103] Gu then told Du that Jiang had decided to "abandon Xuzhou and come out to fight" and went on to ask, "Can you safely get out of Xuzhou?"[104] This question troubled Du deeply because, in his view, if additional forces were not brought in to reinforce the Bengbu front, Huang Wei would be destroyed, and after that so would all of the armies in Xuzhou. After a long silence, he finally said:

> In this difficult situation, the problem of leaving Xuzhou is not a big one. However, if we pull out of Xuzhou, there can be no thought of fighting. If we are to fight, then we can't leave Xuzhou. To abandon Xuzhou and come out to fight will just be taking the three armies in Xuzhou and immediately sending them to the enemy. The only approach is to have Huang Wei hold in place to tie down the enemy while the Xuzhou force leaves Xuzhou and goes by way of Yongcheng to the Mengcheng-Guoyang-Fuyang area. Once there, with the Huai River behind us, we can turn toward the enemy and fight to break the encirclement of Huang Wei.[105]

After listening to Du's idea, Gu agreed that there really was no other alternative. Hearing this, Du asked Gu to please not raise this option in the coming meeting. Du's request, as Gu well knew, was based on his distrust of Guo Rugui. In spring 1948 Du had told Gu directly of his suspicions that Guo Rugui was in contact with the Communists and had asked Gu not to appoint him chief of the High Command's operation section.[106] At the time, Gu had told Du that his concerns were unfounded, but Du had never felt at ease with Guo in that position and had always tried to keep him in the dark about his plans until the last possible moment. When Gu and Guo had flown to Xuzhou to see why the Second and Thirteenth Armies were moving so slowly in their push toward Nianzhuangxu, Du had told Gu of his plan to send the LXXIV Corps on a flanking attack, a plan that inadvertently probably saved the relief force from being cut off and isolated, but he had kept that information from Guo.[107] Now he wanted to be sure Guo did not learn that he was thinking of moving out of Xuzhou toward the west. Respecting Du's wishes, Gu said, "After the meeting I'll talk to the old man, and you can tell him this alone."[108]

The strategy meeting began, as always, with a report from Guo Rugui. The proposed plan that he laid out was for the armies in Xuzhou to push toward the southeast through Shuanggou and then turn south to Wuhe on the Huai River. There they would move west and join with Li Yannian in an attack to relieve Huang Wei.[109] Some of those in attendance raised the issue of the route being unsuitable for a large, partially motorized force because it was marshy, crossed by many waterways, and had poor roads, but according to Guo Ruigui, Du at the time "*falsely said*" that this was the best route to take (author's italics).[110] It was at this point in the discussion that Gu decided to tell Jiang Jieshi that Du wanted to share a few words with him in private. Jiang agreed, and while the general strategy meeting continued without them, he and Du went to an adjoining small meeting room. There Du presented his concept for abandoning Xuzhou that Gu had approved earlier. Jiang also agreed that this was the best approach, and they returned to the meeting. With time of the essence, Jiang quickly asked if anyone had any more comments or ideas. When none were offered, he declared the meeting over. For those who had attended, it appeared that Guo Rugui's proposal was to become Du Yuming's course of action.

Following the meeting, Du Yuming flew back to Xuzhou to initiate the planning and preparation process for leaving Xuzhou. That afternoon Gu Zhutong also boarded an airplane and flew to the air above Shuangduji to talk to Huang Wei by radio. Part of the new Nationalist plan was to have the Twelfth Army defend in place, and Gu wanted to explain to Huang how Twelfth Army's actions fit into a broader strategy. Gu asked Huang to mount a tenacious defense and try to expand the size of the pocket. The Twelfth Army's food and ammunition requirements, Gu assured him, would be met by airdrop.[111]

The evening of 28 November, Du Yuming met with his three army commanders to discuss the decision to abandon Xuzhou. All agreed with Du's concept of moving west and then turning south and his determination not to engage in battles along the way. Once out of Xuzhou, continuing to move would be their protection. They knew that if caught and surrounded, they would be in grave difficulty.

The plan Du developed called for a continuation of large-scale assaults on the 29th and 30th to mislead the Communists. Then on the evening of 30 November the withdrawal was to begin and continue through the night. Small units would be left behind to cover the withdrawal and keep the enemy from discovering what was happening as long as possible. By the evening of 3 December the entire force was supposed to assemble in Yongcheng to prepare for the advance toward Guoyang and Mengcheng.[112] Every unit was to bring food for seven days, fuel to drive trucks and other motor vehicles 500 km and as much ammunition as possible. It was assumed that there would be no resupply before reaching Fuyang, which lay 200 km away.[113]

On 29 and 30 November the Nationalist feints to the east and southeast of Xuzhou achieved the results that Du Yuming had hoped for. Su Yu was particularly concerned about the location of Du's most powerful corps, the Second Army's V Corps, and what it was doing. In his 1500, 29 November message to the CMC Su noted that "the V Corps and the [Thirteenth Army's] IX Corps have both concentrated east of Xuzhou and not yet moved."[114] When, on 30 November, "the V Corps attacked with full force against the Eastern Route Blocking Army's positions," this helped confirm in his mind, that the Nationalist attempt to break out of Xuzhou had begun and that the breakout was directed toward the east or southeast.[115]

Whether intelligence reports from Guo Rugui or others in Nanjing contributed to the CMC's similar belief that the Nationalists would try to break out from Xuzhou toward the east or southeast is unclear. If this was so, it would be another way Du Yuming's secrecy and deceptiveness contributed to his army group successfully evacuating Xuzhou. On 1 December he did, as he had told Gu Zhutong he would, get his force out of Xuzhou. The challenge he now faced was moving that force safely to the Huai River and out of danger.

Encircling Du Yuming's Army Group

The ECFA's after-action report for the Huai Hai Campaign notes that when the Nationalists destroyed the warehouses at the Xuzhou airfield on 30 November, it was clear they were about to abandon Xuzhou but "the direction of their flight had still not been determined."[116] Not until noon on 1 December when it was confirmed that the Second Army was west of Xuzhou did Su Yu decide that Du Yuming was indeed fleeing in that direction.[117] Then he moved swiftly, ordering his main force columns to pursue Du's force and the military districts and subdistricts southwest of Xuzhou to do all in their power to obstruct and delay Du's advance. Except for the 6th Column, which was to remain on the southern front to defend against any Nationalist forces moving north from Bengbu, and the 7th and 13th Columns, which were to continue to fight with the CPFA against Huang Wei, all other columns were to stop Du Yuming's movement and encircle him.[118] Local militias were ordered to take control of all boats and crossing points along the Guo and Sha Rivers. They were also ordered to send radio reports to ECFA headquarters indicating when Nationalist forces reached their area. The information would then be used to direct the movements of the main force columns.[119]

At approximately 1500, 1 December Su Yu informed the CMC and Liu Bocheng, Chen Yi, and Deng Xiaoping about Du Yuming's movement to the west and the measures he had taken in response. His plan had columns moving to attack the rear and left flank of Du's force and also racing to get in front of Du to set up blocking positions. The Bohai Column was ordered to follow the Long-Hai railroad into Xuzhou from the east, leave one division in the city to establish control, and continue west in pursuit of Du. The 12th, 1st, and 4th Columns, the eastern route blocking army, were ordered to move west from their positions southeast of Xuzhou, cross the Xu-Beng railroad 12-15 km south of Xuzhou and pass through gaps in the line of hills running southwest from Xuzhou to reach Xiaoxian. Once there, they were to attack against the rear and flank of Du's force as the situation dictated.

Columns that had been in the central and western route blocking armies—the 3d, 8th, 9th, and Luzhongnan Columns—were directed to move as quickly as possible around the southern end of the hills southwest of Xuzhou and then go west toward Suixikou, Wazikou, Changshoulou, and Zulaolou to get in front of Du's force. The 10th Column was ordered to move from its position 20 km north-northeast of Suxian through Suxian to Yongcheng. The Subei army headquarters was to go with the 2d Column from Guzhen to Yongcheng to set up a second blocking line. The 11th Column was to move from its position southwest of Guzhen to Guoyang and Bozhou by way of the Guzhen-Guoyang Road and establish a third blocking line. For the moment, the Liangguang Column and the two Ji-Lu-Yu divisions were to stay in their positions southwest of Xuzhou.[120] Su Yu wanted to keep Du Yuming's army group from escaping to the south, but he also wanted to make it impossible for it to turn back to Xuzhou. Furthermore, he hoped that after his columns encircled Du's force they could penetrate between his armies and corps and cut it to pieces before Du realized what was happening and organize a coherent defense in place.

Du Yuming had a head start in what was now a race to Yongcheng, an advantage that was achieved through surprise. But that surprise was gained by drastically limiting the time available to plan a large, complex operation and virtually eliminating the time to prepare for it. This was a calculated risk. Du was asking his armies to conduct realistic feints in one direction on 30 November and then, under the cover of darkness and protected by rear guard forces, withdraw

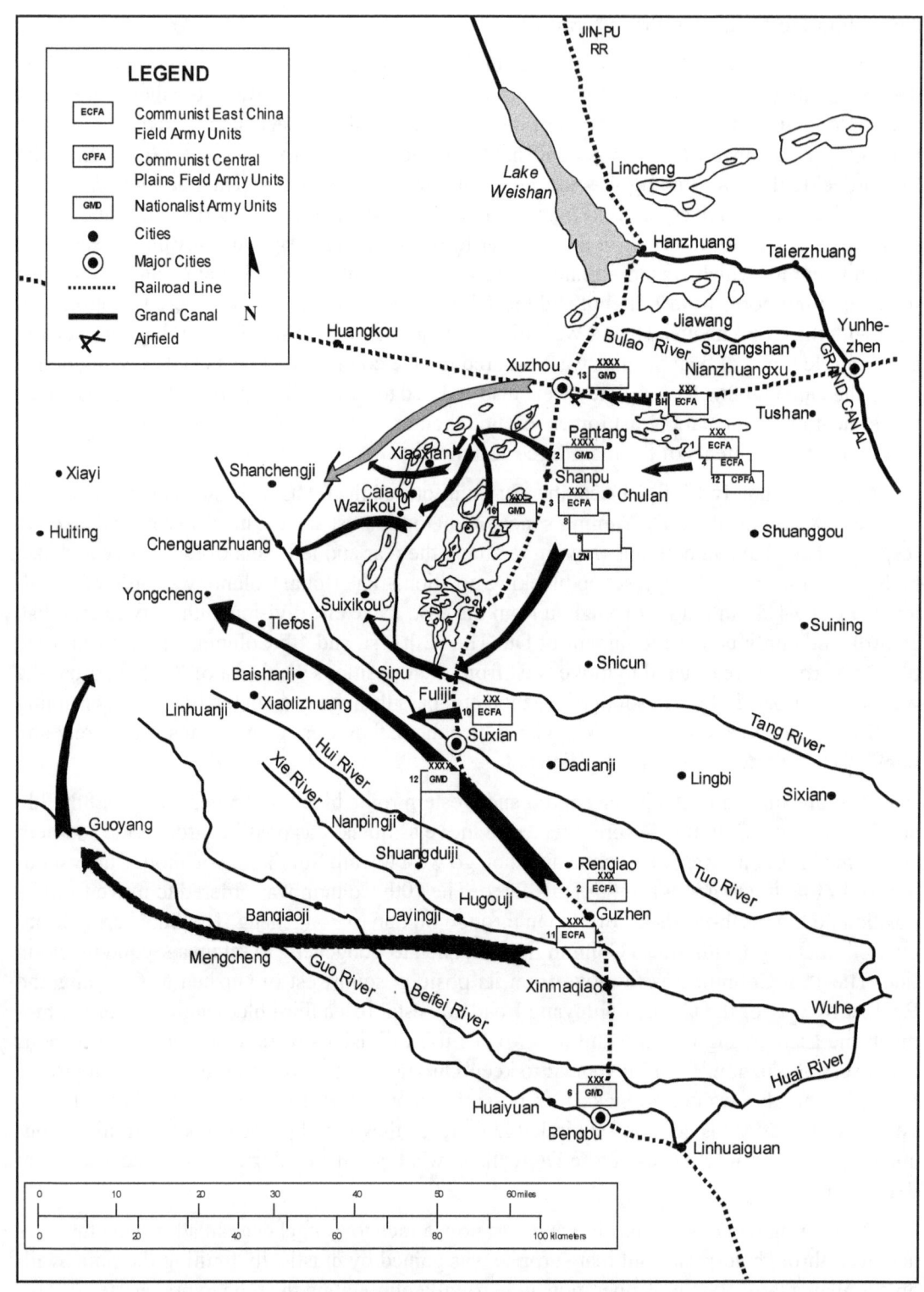

Map 3. Pursuing Du Yuming's army group.

in the opposite direction. This would have been a difficult transition to make under the best of circumstances. To try it with hardly any preparation, an inadequate communication network for exercising command and control, and a battle-fatigued force of 250,000 was going to be very hard. Du, however, felt there was no alternative. He rightly feared that if more time was spent planning and preparing to implement his vision, the operational plan would be compromised. He knew that if that happened Su Yu would be able to make preparations against him, and his force surely would be doomed. Now if he could keep on schedule and reach Yongcheng on 3 December, there was a chance that much of his force could be saved.

In *On War*, Clausewitz emphasizes the impact of what he calls "friction" on military operations. He defines friction as the "countless minor incidents . . . that combine to lower the general level of performance."[121] It is "the force that makes the apparently easy so difficult."[122] It is a concept that distinguishes "real war from war on paper."[123] As such, friction is something that generals must understand, not to make them hesitant because they realize its presence and unpredictable effects but to make them realistic in their expectations of what is possible. In the words of Clausewitz, "The good general must know friction in order to overcome it whenever possible, and in order not to expect a standard of achievement in his operations which this very friction makes impossible."[124]

Whether Du Yuming was asking his force to do something that friction made impossible is not clear, but certainly friction's drag was felt in many ways and places as the operation progressed. Divisions that were to establish security along the route his force was to take moved out late. Divisions that were to hold rear guard positions and maintain the deception left their areas of responsibility early. Units made wrong turns and went down wrong roads, leading to jumbling units within divisions and corps. Army vehicles—tanks, armored cars, trucks, and jeeps—competed for space on highways clogged with tired soldiers, panic-stricken civilians, and an assortment of wagons and carts pulled by draft animals. When Du Yuming's headquarter staff began moving early the morning of 1 December, he had no idea where any of the three armies were located because he had no communication links to the commanders.[125] All he knew was what he could see, a panorama of confusion as his army struggled to move west away from Xuzhou as quickly as friction allowed.

The afternoon of 1 December Du established direct contact with Qiu Qingquan, but it was not until late morning on 2 December that he received a status report on the Thirteenth Army from Li Mi.[126] According to Du's plan, the army group was to continue moving through the night of 2 December so it would reach Yongcheng the evening of 3 December. However, several factors combined to cause Du to order a halt before nightfall. First, Qiu and Li told him their armies needed to stop to reorganize and rest. Second, Du had not yet heard from Sun Yuanliang, so he was unsure of the Sixteenth Army's situation. Third, during the afternoon aerial reconnaissance flights from Nanjing had reported large Communist formations in the Suixikou area moving west toward Yongcheng. Worried that continuing to move while there was so much confusion and disorder would possibly expose his army to penetrating thrusts by pursuing Communist forces, Du decided to stop in place and prepare to resume the march toward Yongcheng the next morning.[127]

Around 0800 the morning of 3 December, Sun Yuanliang reported to Du that his Sixteenth Army had arrived in its designated area west of the Thirteenth Army and apologized for not having reached there the night before. He explained that after two days without rest his troops had been too tired to move, but now he was prepared to advance toward Yongcheng. By 1000 Du had his army group on the move.[128] The Second Army was in the van. The Thirteenth Army was screening the left and left rear. The Sixteenth Army was screening the right flank and the right rear.

Shortly before noon events took a fateful turn when a handwritten order from Jiang Jieshi was airdropped from an airplane that had flown up from Nanjing. The order changed Du's mission from saving his force to relieving Huang Wei. Instead of moving southwest toward Yongcheng, he was now directed to move southeast toward Suixikou and Shuangduiji. This new concept of operations was based on an optimistic interpretation of Communist moves. Jiang had decided that the withdrawal of most Communist forces from the Guzhen area and the movement of a large body of Communist troops toward Yongcheng was a retreat caused by Du's breakout from Xuzhou. To take advantage of this new situation, he had ordered the Sixth Army to begin advancing north from Bengbu to relieve the Twelfth Army. Now he was ordering Du to strengthen the effort to relieve Huang Wei by moving on Shuangduiji from the northwest.[129]

Du Yuming did not share Jiang Jieshi's optimism and was very upset by this change from the concept he and Jiang had agreed to on 28 November. His planning and preparations had been based on the vision that his army group would not fight after leaving Xuzhou. Now Jiang was asking him to engage tens of thousands of Communist troops moving in his direction, troops that Du believed were not trying to evade him but were moving to attack him.

The first thought that crossed Du's mind when he read this order was Sunzi's admonition that when the general is in the field "*jun ming you suo bushou*" (there are commands from the ruler not to be obeyed).[130] He wanted to ignore the order and keep moving toward Yongcheng. However, after considering the matter, he decided he did not want to take full responsibility for a decision that might mean the difference between the Twelfth Army being saved or lost. If continuing to follow his plan of first going south to the Huai River enabled his force to relieve Huang Wei, his disobedience might be excused. But if his plan failed and the Twelfth Army was destroyed, he would be blamed for losing the campaign and would be harshly punished for not following orders. After weighing his options for several minutes, Du decided to order his force to halt and have his army commanders meet for a council of war.

Li Mi was unable to attend the meeting but he sent two of his deputies. Qiu Qingquan and Sun Yuanliang came in person. Du showed them Jiang's order and gave his views on the merits of either staying with their current plan or following the new order. After much discussion, Qiu and Sun both stated they felt obligated to follow Jiang's order. Qiu Qingquan also volunteered to have his Second Army continue leading the way with the Thirteenth and Sixteenth Armies providing flank and rear security. With his army commanders committed to doing as Jiang had directed, Du issued orders changing the orientation of the army group's advance. On the morning of 4 December, they would begin moving toward Suixikou.

During the evening of 3 December, Du received additional orders by radio from the High Command in Nanjing. He was particularly disturbed when he read the estimate that there were only about 40,000 Communist soldiers in the Suixikou area and the following paragraph directing him to attack them quickly:

> Your force should swiftly and with determination destroy the Communist

force in the Suixikou-Mazhuang area during the next 2-3 days. This is the only good opportunity to destroy a solitary Communist force. If you delay, Communist armies from all over will swarm around you and you will again lose the initiative. Absolutely do not lose this opportunity. By all means, do not move toward Yongcheng again, taking a roundabout way to avoid battle.[131]

This was a direct order not to consider following his original plan, and its insinuation that by moving toward Yongcheng Du was trying to avoid battle like a coward left him feeling insulted. As he read the order and the unrealistic course of action it contained, he saw the handiwork of Guo Rugui and felt his army group was now exposed to destruction. Years later he described how, at that moment, his heart was filled with regret for stopping and thus allowing his armies to fall into such grave danger:

> After receiving this order I felt again that Jiang Jieshi had changed his mind because he was influenced by the ideas of that little devil Guo Rugui. I regretted that on 28 November I had not clearly expressed my views about Guo Rugui to Jiang and had not gotten the agreement of Gu Zhutong . . . and others to support my plan of withdrawal from beginning to end. Now Jiang had listened to Guo's manipulation and had used first, a hand written order, and second, an order transmitted by radio, to send us to attack the PLA. By doing so he had placed the Nationalist army in danger of being completely wiped out. I also regretted my timidity and lack of resolution in the morning. I should not have halted the armies and called a council of war. A day of movement had been lost. Now it was too late to escape and fighting was hopeless. . . . All I could do was . . . be 'loyal' to the end.[132]

Du Yuming's pessimism was justified. Halting the night of 2 December, a decision he later viewed as an error, and again on 3 December had taken away the time-space advantage his force had possessed at noon on 1 December.[133] At 1100, 3 December in a message sent to his army and column commanders and also to the CMC, Liu Bocheng, Chen Yi, and Deng Xiaoping, Su Yu described a situation in which his columns had already basically surrounded Du's force. The 9th Column and 8th Column were astride the Xuzhou-Yongcheng Road northeast of Yongcheng and were building defensive works. East of these two columns the Luzhongnan Column was also building defenses. Su expected the 2d and 10th Columns to reach the Qinglongji-Dahuicun area, which was east of the Luzhongnan Column's position and southeast of Du's army group, that evening. Meanwhile other columns were moving close to the rear and flanks of Du's force. In this message Su gave responsibility for directing the arrangement of columns to Tan Zhenlin, who would perform this task from his headquarters 13 km west of Suixikou until other commanders arrived. Su also announced that he was relocating his own headquarters from Shicun to an area near Suixikou and that he would be there the next evening, 4 December. All columns were directed to report to higher headquarters as soon as possible what they saw as the emerging shape of enemy actions and the unit designations of the enemy forces with which they were in contact. They were also ordered to establish full radio and telephone communication links as soon as possible.[134]

At dawn on 4 December, Su Yu's position was significantly stronger than it had been 24 hours earlier. On 3 December his columns had conducted hasty harassing attacks as they overtook various parts of Du's force. On 4 December Su was ready to conduct a coordinated operation designed to implement his strategy of blocking the forward advance of Du's army group while attacking Du's flanks and rear. To do this he had the following array of forces ready to defend or attack as required. Moving counterclockwise around the Nationalist perimeter, beginning in the southwest, the 8th Column was preparing to defend northeast of Yongcheng. Next, the 10th and Luzhongnan Clumns were in defensive positions south and southwest of Qinglongji with the 2d Column moving into position behind the 10th Column. The 3d Column was in Zulaoji preparing to attack to the west as was the 4th Column in Zhangshoulou. On the north side of the pocket, ready to advance south, were the 1st Column in Yuanxu and the Liangguang Column and the two Ji-Lu-Yu Military District divisions in the Hongheji area. The 9th Column was now west of Mengji and was ready to attack toward the east.[135] In addition to these columns, the 11th (E) Column was north of Guoyang moving toward Yongcheng, the 12th Column was positioned in Wazikou to control that area and serve as a general reserve, and the Bohai Column was in a reserve position behind the 1st Column.[136]

Due to this formidable force deployed against him, Du Yuming's attack on 4 December made little progress. The Second Army managed to advance 2-3 km, but as it did so, the rear of Du's pocket was being compressed. At the beginning of the day Du's force occupied an area that was basically a square 10 km on a side. By nightfall, that area had become an 8-km by 10-km rectangle, as gains in the south were less than the territory lost in the north.

On 5 December Su Yu made some adjustments in deploying his columns with the 2d Column replacing the 10th Column on the south side of the Nationalist pocket. He also established a new command structure. Three army-level organizations were established. The forces on the north side of the Nationalist pocket—the 1st, 4th, 9th, Liangguang, and Bohai Columns, the two Ji-Lu-Yu divisions, and part of the ST Column—were placed under Tan Zhenlin and Wang Jianan's command and ordered to attack from north to south.[137] The 3d, 10th, and Luzhongnan Columns were placed under command of 10th Column commander Song Shilun and his political commissar, Liu Peishan. Their mission was to defend southeast of the pocket and, if conditions were right, to attack to the northwest.[138] Wei Guoqing and Ji Luo commanded the 8th, 2d, and 11th (E) Columns and were assigned to defend to the southwest of the pocket and, if the opportunity arose, attack to the northeast.[139]

Du Yuming's Second Army continued to try to move to the southeast on 5 and 6 December but again made little forward progress. Meanwhile, on the north side of the pocket Tan Zhenlin's columns maintained their slow but steady advance. Tan made much of that advance against Sun Yuanliang's Sixteenth Army, and on the afternoon of 6 December Sun gained Qiu Qingquan's agreement to make a joint appeal to Du to change his strategy. After hearing their complaints, Du asked them to accompany him to Li Mi's command post where they discussed what they should do. Sun strongly advocated that each army immediately attempt to break out. Qiu and Li also argued that their situation was untenable and supported Sun's suggestion that each army should punch a small opening in the enemy lines opposite its sector and then dash for Fuyang. This would be going against their orders to move to Suixikou and Shuangduiji, but all three commanders saw this as the only course of action with any reasonable possibility of success. To justify this act of independence, they all referred to Sunzi's statement that a general can ignore certain orders from the ruler when he is in the field.[140]

Du Yuming was reluctant to go along with the request to order a breakout. He told Qiu, Li, and Sun he wished they had taken their current position three days earlier. "Then," he said, "we could have returned with our entire force and would have been able to face the old man."[141] In the end, however, Du agreed to order a breakout under two conditions. First, each army was to conduct a detailed reconnaissance of enemy positions opposite it and be very careful in selecting the place where it would penetrate enemy lines. Second, heavy weapons and vehicles were not to be abandoned unless there was absolutely no way to continue moving with them.[142]

After their meeting ended around 1500, Du and the army commanders returned to their respective command posts and began preparing to break out that night. Sun Yuanliang, the most enthusiastic proponent of this course of action, assembled his corps and divisions commanders and told them they should be ready to launch their breakout attack no later than 1800.[143] Then, contrary to Du's orders, Sun failed to conduct reconnaissance and assess the viability of a breakout attempt, and he also directed that his heavy weapons be destroyed.[144] Furthermore, he dropped his communication links with Du Yuming's headquarters. This meant Du was unable to inform Sun that after evaluating the strength of Communist defenses, Li Mi and Qiu Qingquan had decided not to try to break out.[145]

Not surprisingly, the result was a disaster. The Sixteenth Army attacked as Sun had ordered, but since it was the only Nationalist force attacking, it was soon overwhelmed as the Communist defenders concentrated their fire against it. Of its 40,000 soldiers, some 10,000 straggled back into the pocket where the next day Du directed that they be organized into a division and attached to the LXXII Corps. Almost all of the remaining 30,000 were either killed or captured, with only a few, like the army commander Sun Yuanliang, being able to disguise themselves as ordinary peasants and make their way across Henan to Nationalist lines north of Wuhan.[146]

The Sixteenth Army's destruction on 6 December was a heavy blow to Du Yuming. Not only had 30,000 soldiers been lost, so, too, had a large quantity of weapons and supplies. Discouraged by this event and his army group's continuing inability to make meaningful progress toward the south, on 7 December Du sent a message to Jiang Jieshi describing his situation and proposing a way out. My army group, Du told Jiang, is "tightly surrounded . . . and has no chance whatsoever of breaking Huang Wei's encirclement."[147] The only hope, he added, lay in the High Command committing more forces to the campaign.

The Nationalists Advance Again on the Southern Front

Du Yuming's request that more troops be added to the southern front echoed requests he had made on 23 and 28 November. The problem the Nationalists had, and this was one that had received much attention during their August strategy meeting in Nanjing, was the lack of a large strategic reserve. When Du had complained to Gu Zhutong on 28 November about Jiang Jieshi's failure to reinforce the Bengbu front, Gu had told him Jiang had wanted to do that but could find no units that were not already committed somewhere. On 8 December Jiang stated this reality directly in his reply to Du's 7 December plea: "At present there are no troops that can be added. I hope that you will not continue to have illusions about more troops being committed. You should quickly supervise each army so their attacks make forward progress and you can break the encirclement of Huang's army."[148]

If the Nationalists had had a reserve to commit to the campaign, the days following Du Yuming's withdrawal from Xuzhou would have been a good time to have done so. Continuous fighting on three battlefields was stretching yhe ECFA and CPFA very thin. Su Yu's response to Du's leaving Xuzhou had been to order a major economy-of-force operation on the Bengbu

221

front. All ECFA columns that had been in that area, except for the 6th, were shifted to the Suixikou-Yongcheng area to be used in Su's effort to block and encircle Du's army group. The result was that even without adding a corps or two to their forces at Bengbu, the Nationalists suddenly had numerical superiority on this front. On 2 December Jiang Jieshi moved quickly to take advantage of this new opportunity, ordering the Sixth and Eighth Armies, to undertake another operation to link up with the Twelfth Army.

The Sixth and Eighth Armies had already failed an earlier attempt to do this from 20 to 26 November. Since then the LIV Corps had been added to the Sixth Army, but one of that corps' three divisions was committed to manning a portion of the defensive line near Bengbu and was not available for the operation. Another addition was the assignment of an independent division, the 296th, to the Sixth Army, and Jiang also decided to commit the prized armor regiment his son, Jiang Weiguo, commanded to this effort.[149] The question was, would three more infantry divisions and an armor regiment generate enough additional combat power to achieve what the Sixth and Eighth Armies had been unable to accomplish a little over a week earlier?

The morning of 3 December, at approximately the same time Jiang's written orders to Du Yuming directing him to move toward Shuangduiji were being sent, the Sixth Army began its operation to reach Shuangduiji. The XXXIX Corps and XCIX Corps crossed the Fei River from positions north of Bengbu, and east of Bengbu the LIV Corps crossed the Huai River at Linhuaiguan. Behind the XCIX Corps came the Eighth Army's LV Corps with the mission of advancing north to the Xie River and then moving northwest along the south side of the Xie River to provide right flank and rear security to the Sixth Army. Meanwhile the Eighth Army's other corps, the LXXVIII, began moving west from Bengbu along the Guo River to protect the Sixth Army's left flank. Opposition was light for the LIV Corps advancing east of the Su-Beng railroad, and by 5 December it was approaching Xinmaqiao near where the Su-Beng railroad crossed the Xie River. The XXXIX and XCIX Corps encountered heavier opposition and their progress was slower. By 6 December the LIV Corps had moved abreast of these two corps, and from that point forward all three corps advanced in one line with the LIV Corps on the right, the XCIX Corps in the center, and the XXXIX Corps on the left.[150] To the left of the XXXIX Corps was the 296th Division, which had come north from Huaiyuan after the XXXIV Corps had cleared the northern bank of the Xie River in that area.

The Sixth and Eighth Armies' advance caused immediate concern within the CMC and the General Front Committee. In a message sent to Liu, Chen, Deng, Su, and Tan at 1600, 4 December the CMC stated, "Li Yannian's force has already crossed the Fei River and is advancing toward Baojiaji. How are you going to counter this enemy? We look forward to Liu, Deng, and Chen telling us by radio."[151]

Also on 4 December, at 2200 the CMC transmitted the following message to Liu, Chen, and Deng and also to Su Yu and his staff that again raised this issue:

> (1) Li Yannian is now using seven divisions (they include units of the LIV Corps) north of the Huai River. A part of his force has already reached Caolaoji. We hope that you will order the 6th [E] Column to strengthen its blocking action so that the enemy will not be able to advance too far north and threaten our annihilation of Huang Wei.
>
> (2) Liu, Chen, and Deng are already using the 13th Column to attack

Huang Wei, so for the moment that column cannot be shifted.

(3) After Huang Wei is finished off, the 6th and 13th columns and the entire strength of the CPFA can be used to fight Qiu, Li, and Sun.[152]

At 0500, 5 December the CMC sent yet another message to Liu, Chen, and Deng and also to Su Yu and his staff. This was a clear directive to shift more forces to the Bengbu front:

> In order to guard against the threat posed by the enemy force advancing from Bengbu toward your battlefield, you should order the 6th Column and other troops that you can use (for example the two local divisions from northern Jiangsu that were formerly preparing to go south of the Huai River), to build strong defensive positions in depth. This point can absolutely not be neglected.[153]

To counter the broad, multiple corps advance of Li Yannian's army, at this time the 6th Column had spread itself out along a 35-km front. On 6 December Su Yu decided that this frontage was too great for the column to cover and that a Sixth Army breakthrough was a real possibility. In a message to Liu Bocheng, Chen Yi, Deng Xiaoping, and the CMC, he proposed that the CPFA 2d Column; the five regiments of the Yu-Wan-Su Military District; the 11th Division, Bohai Column; and the two regiments from the Yu Xi Military District be shifted to the Bengbu front to assist the 6th Column. Liu, Chen, and Deng agreed with Su's analysis and the course of action he proposed and immediately ordered the units he had listed to move to aid the 6th Column.[154]

The 6th Column was in this difficult position as the result of Su Yu's decision on 1 December to use all possible columns to block Du's army group as it moved out of Xuzhou. On that day and for several days thereafter Su was extremely worried that Du's force would be able to escape his clutches. Ensuring that did not happen was his highest priority, and this led him to accept risk on the southern front. Perhaps when assessing the risk of leaving only one column north of Bengbu he had underestimated the speed and vigor with which the Nationalists would respond to his economy-of-force operation. In any case, on 6 December Su acted to rectify the situation by asking that additional forces be sent south to assist the 6th Column in its fight against Li Yannian.

The seriousness of the 6th Column's situation can be seen in a personal letter that Chen Yi wrote to the commander and political commissar of the column on 7 December. In his letter, Chen asked them to clench their teeth and grit it out. They had to be prepared to sacrifice "more than half of the column" to ensure the success of the fight to destroy Huang Wei. Chen also told them to keep their spirits up because reinforcements would soon be there.[155]

The CPFA 2d Column was the first reinforcing unit to arrive. It was deployed along the Nationalist force's right flank. On 9 December the Bohai Column's 11th Division and the military district divisions reached the area in front of Li Yannian's army and went under 6th Column control. Even after the addition of these forces, Li Yannian was still able to continue moving forward, but his rate of advance was only 1-3 km per day. On 15 December, the day on which the last Twelfth Army elements were destroyed, the Sixth Army was still 30 km from Shuangduiji.[156]

The Hard Fight to Destroy the Twelfth Army

While the supporting operations to keep the Nationalist armies from reaching the Shuangduiji area were under way, the Communist main effort continued to be to destroy Huang Wei's force. On 27 November Liu Bocheng had predicted the battle to destroy the Twelfth Army would be over the next day. On 28 November he estimated it would take at least 10 days to achieve the objective. Even this estimate proved to be overly optimistic due to the Twelfth Army's tenacious defense and two CPFA weaknesses, a lack of experience in conducting positional warfare against a large, well-entrenched enemy and limited firepower.

As discussed earlier, the CPFA lacked firepower because it had lost so much artillery during the march to the Dabie Mountains in late summer 1947.[157] This artillery shortage meant the CPFA had to rely on ECFA artillery to develop the combat power necessary to overcome Twelfth Army defenses. It also seems to have contributed to an attitude within the CPFA that infantrymen armed with an offensive spirit could compensate to a large extent for the lack of artillery. This attitude can be seen by comparing remarks ECFA chief of staff Chen Shiju and Liu Bocheng made at an after-action evaluation session CPFA commanders at the battalion level and above attended several weeks following Luoyang's capture in March 1948.

By the time of this battle, the ECFA already had extensive experience in artillery-infantry coordination, and the ECFA columns that joined CPFA columns in the battle for Luoyang used artillery effectively to destroy Nationalist defenses and reduce infantry casualties. In his review of events, Chen heaped praise on the ECFA artillery's contribution to the victory to such an extent that many in the audience began to wonder about the CPFA's ability to win battles like this on its own.[158] Liu Bocheng sensed this and was so disturbed that, even though night had already fallen when Chen had finished speaking, he kept all the officers there and presented a rebuttal that criticized the psychology of relying on artillery for everything.[159] In words designed to reassure his infantrymen of their importance and their ability to generate destructive force, he reminded them of the effects that soldiers throwing hand grenades produced.[160]

Chen Shiju's emphasis on artillery and Liu Bocheng's emphasis on infantry reflect what might be described as a difference in culture between the CPFA and the ECFA. Chen Yi became aware of this "cultural" difference after he went to work in the Central Plains Military Region (CPMR) and the CPFA in May 1948. He was troubled by the way it affected how the two armies' commanders and soldiers looked at each other. The reality was that the ECFA, because it had more and better artillery than the CPFA and had a small armor force while the CPFA had none, was conducting combined arms training and carrying out combined arms operations while the CPFA was still relying primarily on infantry action. For this reason, there were those within the ECFA who considered the CPFA to be less skilled and competent than they were and, in dealings with CPFA personnel, were displaying what CPFA commanders and soldiers perceived to be "arrogance."[161] On 24 July 1948 Chen raised this issue in a telegram he sent to Su Yu, Chen Shiju, and the CMC. He suggested that measures to address this problem needed to be implemented as part of the training and reorganization sessions to be conducted during the upcoming rainy season.[162] This was done, but at the time of the Huai Hai Campaign, what might be called sensitivity training was still given to ECFA columns before they joined operations with CPFA columns.[163]

What role CPFA reliance on infantry and infantry spirit to overcome enemy defenses played in the heavy casualties CPFA columns suffered on 28-29 November is unclear. To a certain extent, those casualties occurred, just as the high casualties ECFA columns experienced in the first days of fighting the Seventh Army at Nianzhuangxu had occurred, because it took time for commanders to realize the enemy had established a defense in place and that the hasty attacks appropriate for pursuit or exploitation operations were no longer going to be successful. However, many CPFA commanders' faith in the ability of courageous infantry to defeat defensive steel certainly contributed to those losses. Even after the losses of 28-29 November, there were commanders who still expressed a willingness to keep throwing soldiers into the fight, with such comments as "Our lives belong to the people. Let's just put them on the line and be done with it."[164] These commanders viewed heavy losses as inevitable and responded to mounting casualties by asking, "Can one fight a war without casualties?"[165]

The General Front Committee, however, felt that continuing to suffer losses at the rates seen on 28-29 November was unacceptable. The evening of 29 November they issued a tactical directive telling all commanders that because the enemy was now defending in place while awaiting relief, they needed to adopt a careful, step-by-step approach when planning and preparing attacks. A new strategy was laid out. The pocket was to be squeezed gradually by taking enemy positions one by one through deliberate, well-planned actions.[166]

The General Front Committee's directive was the result of it recognizing the battlefield conditions it was facing required a change in tactics and fighting style. At the same time the highest echelons of command were realizing this, CPFA soldiers engaged in combat were reaching the same conclusion. Furthermore, those soldiers were developing new tactics and techniques for coping with what for them was a new experience—extended combat with a well-armed enemy entrenched on flat terrain.

Events in the CPFA's 9th Column during this period show how a confluence of senior leader desire to preserve forces, and rank and file interest in saving lives combined to quickly change the face of the Shuangduiji battlefield. On 29 November, after receiving the General Front Committee's directive, the 9th Column commander issued an order that every unit was to cherish its soldiers' lives. Commanders were told to stop using morale-promoting political slogans like "*pin lao ming*" ("dare to die") as the basis for their tactical thought. They were to seriously study tactics and appreciate why "intelligence needed to be added to bravery" when trying to crack the enemy's "tough nut."[167] Interestingly, within this column, soldiers on the front line had already initiated a change in this direction two days earlier. This was the 27th Division's discovery of the value of digging approach trenches before conducting an assault.

The 27th Division's idea to dig approach trenches came from an incident that occurred on the afternoon of 27 November. At that time, several 27th Division soldiers dug into the ground for protection after Nationalist fire stopped their regiment's assault on the small village of Xiaozhangzhuang, and they were caught in the open. Unable to advance or withdraw, they dug deep enough so that, despite intense Nationalist fire, they were able to maintain their positions close to the Nationalist trenches throughout the night and the next day. This event was a revelation to regiment and division commanders, and it changed their tactical thinking. Suddenly, as the 9th Column commander later described it, they saw that the key to successfully attacking their well-dug-in enemy was to "reduce the distance to be crossed while under enemy fire."[168] At the same time they realized that digging approach trenches was the way to achieve that objective.

The General Front Committee's 29 November directive stated that future CPFA attacks were to be carefully planned, deliberate operations that had limited objectives and followed the principle of "take a village, hold a village."[169] Digging approach trenches fit this tactical concept well, and with the 27th Division's commander as a strong advocate, it was made an integral part of the 9th Column's new plan for attacking Xiaozhangzhuang. Greater emphasis was also placed on using firepower to destroy enemy defenses. In the end the plan focused on three points:

> (1) Approach trenches should reach as close to the enemy as possible, so that the assault troops will be able to quickly leap into the enemy's outer trenches.
>
> (2) All of the division's firepower will be concentrated in order to develop the powerful effects of gunfire and explosives. The column will guarantee the supply of ammunition.
>
> (3) Concurrent with the military attacks on the fortifications there will be a political attack on the enemy's spirit and will.[170]

Soon after the 27th Division's plan of attack was completed the night of 29 November, the digging of trenches began. Company commanders led the way, crawling forward with rice bags on their backs that were filled with ashes to use to mark the path the trench would take. Behind them came a line of crawling soldiers, all carrying spades and using the white ashes as a guide. After the lead officer had moved forward about 250 meters to a point 70 to 100 meters from the Nationalist lines, he gave a silent signal and the digging started. By dawn on 30 November three approach trenches were well on their way to being finished, and during the day they were deepened until soldiers could stand up without being seen.[171]

While the trenches were being dug, the division's heaviest weapons—five mountain howitzers, more than 30 mortars, 12 heavy machine guns, and several explosive launching tubes—were placed in position to support the infantry assault. At 1700, 1 December the attack began, and, unlike the attacks on 27, 28, and 29 November, it ended with taking Xiaozhangzhuang 12 hours later. At a relatively low cost in casualties, during the battle the 27th Division killed or captured 1,200 soldiers and seized more than 30 machine guns and five mortars.[172]

This victory and the methods used to achieve it quickly gained the General Front Committee's attention and earned praise from Deng Xiaoping as an example of the kind of battlefield creativity that could hasten Huang Wei's defeat.[173] Other columns sent unit commanders to study the 27th Division's experience in achieving "a rather large victory at a rather small cost."[174] The most important innovation, it was seen, was digging trenches, and many slogans were quickly developed to help drill that lesson deep into the tactical thought of commanders and soldiers alike. The rhymes of those slogans are lost in translation, but their meaning comes through in the following examples:

> Use trenches to take trenches, use strongholds to take strongholds.
>
> More sweat flowing means less blood running. Make earthworks well and our losses in annihilating the enemy will be low.
>
> Whoever digs in front makes a great contribution.
>
> The faster we dig, the sooner the enemy will collapse.[175]

While the CPFA's own experience was turning it toward the extensive use of trenches, the ECFA's experience at Nianzhuangxu was also influencing this change in fighting method. After direct telephone communication was established between the CPFA (General Front Committee) headquarters at Xiaolizhuang and Su Yu's ECFA headquarters at Shicun on 1 December, Chen Yi called Su Yu and asked for a detailed explanation of how the ECFA had destroyed the Seventh Army.[176] Su Yu's answer emphasized what the CPFA was already learning—digging trenches was the way to put assault forces in positions from which they could successfully attack Nationalist defenses.[177] The CMC made this same point in a message sent to Liu, Chen, and Deng at 1600, 4 December:

> The experience gained fighting both Huang Baitao and Huang Wei proves the following. An enemy with strong combat power cannot be annihilated by relying on the method of hasty attacks. We must use the techniques of cutting the enemy into segments, conducting reconnaissance, digging trenches up close to the enemy, concentrating troops and firepower, and coordinating the infantry and the artillery, every one of these techniques. Only then can we destroy him.[178]

Simply applying these various techniques in a carefully planned and well-prepared attack, however, was no guarantee of success. Nationalist combat engineers and infantry were adept at constructing field fortifications, and once the order to defend in place had been issued, the Twelfth Army had quickly created formidable defenses in depth. Strongpoints were established in villages and linked by trenches. In places, trucks and other motor vehicles were lined up and filled with dirt to create defensive lines. The Nationalists also used bombardment and spoiling attacks to disrupt Communist preparations for attacks. During the day artillery fire, aerial bombing, and ground attacks supported by tanks destroyed Communist trenches and defense works. At night illumination shells and large fires made by burning piles of wood and grass cast light on Communist soldiers digging in no man's land and enabled the Nationalists to fire on them or send ground units to attack them.[179] Initially, Nationalist spoiling attacks were quite successful because Communist preparations for attacking did not include preparations for mounting a defense if the Nationalists attacked first.[180]

Further complicating CPFA efforts to destroy the Twelfth Army was the boost in morale Twelfth Army officers and soldiers received on 1 December when the well-respected deputy commander, Twelfth Army, Hu Lian, arrived in Shuangduiji.[181] Hu had not been with the Twelfth Army on its march across Henan because before the army left Queshan he had requested leave to go to Wuhan to visit his acutely ill father and receive treatment for a serious dental problem.[182] After learning the Twelfth Army had been surrounded, however, he immediately flew to Nanjing and asked Jiang Jieshi to let him rejoin his troops. Jiang was happy to oblige, and after a makeshift airstrip was prepared just east of Shuangduiji, Hu flew into the pocket in a light aircraft.[183] His arrival had a dramatic effect because it represented tangible evidence of a link to Nationalist lines to the south and the High Command's commitment to this surrounded force. After reaching Shuangduiji, Hu met with all corps and division commanders and visited every division's front-line position to see conditions for himself. Everywhere he went he explained Jiang Jieshi's strategy of having the Twelfth Army mount a strong defense while other armies were sent to its relief.[184] His optimism brought a ray of hope that lifted spirits and kept the army fighting hard.

Hu Lian's presence could not, however, alter the objective reality of the Twelfth Army's situation. As a surrounded force fighting a battle of attrition, it was growing weaker with each passing day. Local Nationalist successes could not keep the overall balance between the

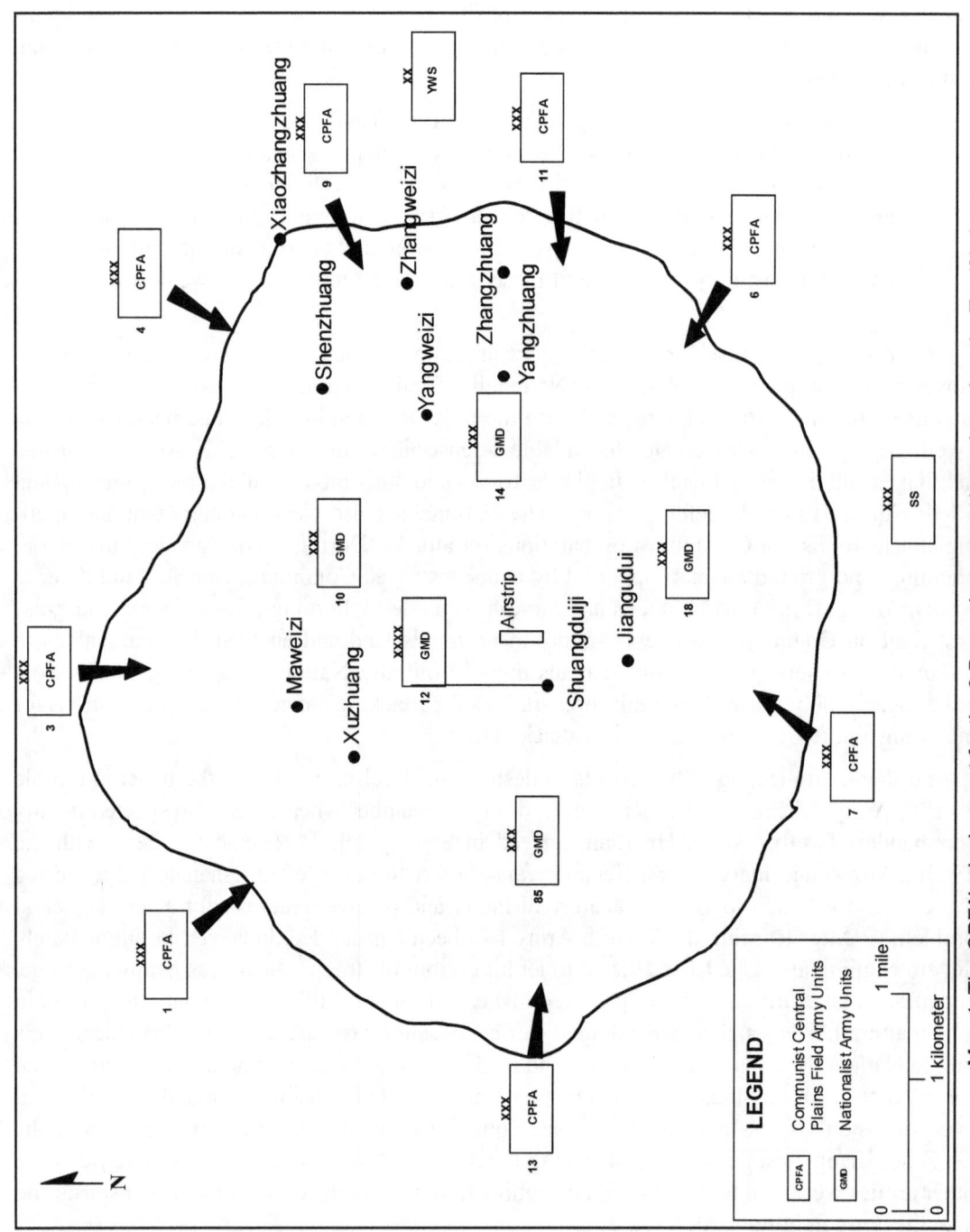

Map 4. The CPFA's deployment for the 6 December general attack against the Twelfth Army.

Nationalists and the Communists from continuing to shift in the Communists' favor. In light of this changing balance and because of their desire to gain a clear numerical superiority in the Huai Hai Campaign as a whole as soon as possible, on 3 December Liu Bocheng, Chen Yi, and Deng Xiaoping decided to change CPFA strategy. As the following message they sent to the CMC at 1600, 3 December indicates, given their estimate that the Twelfth Army only had six mobile, fully capable regiments remaining, it was time to shift from small-scale, local attacks to seeking victory by employing the reserves in a general attack:

> During the past three days all of our units have strengthened their work of digging trenches close to the enemy and have conducted local attacks. We have only completely wiped out the 341st Regiment of the X Corps' 114th Division (less one battalion). The enemy has selected several strong regiments and, with several, or even more than ten tanks in support, has concentrated power and destroyed our preparations for attacks. Every time, they have been beaten back with heavy losses.
>
> Up till now, we have only captured 5,000 enemy soldiers, but we calculate that enemy killed and wounded cannot be less than 20,000. Adding in the 5,500 from the revolt of Liao's division, the enemy has already lost about 30,000 men. According to evidence from several sources, since the breakout attempt, most of the XVIII Corps' 49th Division has been wiped out. The corps' powerful 118th Division is already largely wrecked. In that corps, only the 11th Division can still be called intact. In the X Corps, two of the 18th Division's regiments have largely been destroyed and the remnants have become two battalions. Only the third regiment is still complete. The X Corps' 114th Division has already lost a regiment and casualties in the 75th Division are very heavy. The LXXXV Corps' 23rd Division has had about 2,000 casualties and its 216th Division is made up of new troops. The XIV Corps' two divisions have also been hit hard.
>
> To sum up the situation, we estimate that the enemy has no more than six regiments that are still capable of trying to break out. As a result, we have decided to immediately use the ECFA 7th and 13th columns (the reserve) in an attack. Our fighting method will be based on the Nianzhuang experience, that is, having attacks converge against a single point from several directions. Because the enemy is tightly compressed and is resisting stubbornly, we will still need several days to finish him off. During the past several days our casualties have not been light, but our determination to destroy the enemy remains strong.[185]

When this message was sent, Liu, Chen, and Deng estimated that two days would be required to bring up the reserves, conduct reconnaissance, dig approach trenches, and replenish ammunition stocks. Their plan, therefore, was to launch the general attack the evening of 5 December. However, because preparations took longer than expected, they delayed the start of the attack until 1630, 6 December.[186] This time remained firm, even though all of the preparatory work was not fully completed. For example, the ECFA 7th Column, one of the reserve columns, had still not finished digging its approach trenches when it began its attack.[187]

To carry out the general attack, Liu, Chen, and Deng organized their columns into three army-sized groups that were designated the eastern, western, and southern groups. The eastern group consisted of the CPFA 4th, 9th, and 11th Columns and the Yu-Wan-Su Military District division under command of 4th Column commander Chen Geng and his political commissar, Xie Fuzhi. The western group consisted of the ECFA 13th Column and the CPFA 1st and 3d Columns under command of 3d Column commander Chen Xilian. The southern group contained the CPFA 6th Column, the ECFA 7th Column, and the 12th Division from the Southern Shaanxi Military District under command of 6th Column commander Wang Jinshan and his political commissar, Du Yide.[188] To increase the firepower available to these three groups, one artillery regiment (six companies) from the ST Column was brought in and divided among them.[189]

The order to launch the attack, which is presented below, was issued by telephone at 1105, 5 December to the three attacking groups' commanders.[190] Strong emphasis was placed on establishing and maintaining a high tempo of operations. Pressure was to be applied continuously around the Nationalist perimeter to make it difficult for Huang Wei to respond effectively with his weakened force. Pauses, delays, hesitation, anything that might cause a loss of momentum were to be avoided at all cost. Opportunities were to be seized quickly. Swift, appropriate responses were to minimize the possible negative effects of setbacks. The initiative was to be held by attacking until the Twelfth Army was destroyed:

Order Issued at 1105 5 December.

(1) After our operations of the past half month, the enemy Huang Wei's army has already lost at least one-third of its overall strength. Losses in the combat units stand at at least forty percent. His most powerful force, the XVIII Corps, is already shattered. This is the great result of every one of our units fighting bravely.

(2) In accordance with overall operational requirements and the actual conditions before us, we issue this order with the following five points:

(a) Tomorrow afternoon (6 November) at 1630 the entire line will launch a general attack on the enemy. No delays will be permitted for any reason.

(b) The Chen [Geng]-Xie [Fuzhi] group must destroy the enemy in the Shenzhuang-Zhangweizi-Zhangzhuang area. The [Chen] Xilian group must destroy the enemy in the Sanguanmiao-Maweizi-Yuwangmiao-Xuzhuang area. The Wang [Jinshan]-Du [Yide] group must destroy the enemy in the Yuwangmiao-Zhaozhuang area south of Shuangduiji and the Qianzhouzhuang-Zhouzhuang-Songzhuang area west of Shuangduiji. All groups must also establish control in these above-mentioned places. Afterwards, they will launch a general attack on Shuangduiji and completely wipe out the enemy.

(c) After the general attack begins, there should be continuous attacks until the missions assigned above have been completed. Stopping or asking for a delay will not be permitted.

(d) No unit should hesitate to make the greatest sacrifice in order to guarantee the completion of these missions. They must also take action promptly under their own initiative to help adjacent units seize victory.

(e) As for those who waver in front of enemy positions and thereby cause opportunities for victory to be lost, every army and column commander has the authority to exercise strict disciplinary measures. They should not be lenient.

(3) This order will be transmitted orally to companies.[191]

Although not stated in this order, the attack's main effort was to be in the east where Chen Geng's group was to take Shenzhuang, Zhangweizi, and Zhangzhuang and move on to capture Yangweizi and Yangzhuang.[192] The objective was to ruin the Nationalist defensive system by penetrating far enough into the pocket so the airstrip and the area where Twelfth Army headquarters was located were exposed to Communist fire. The attacks the western and southern groups conducted were to support this main effort by tying down Nationalist forces that might otherwise shift to the east side of the pocket.

At 1530, 6 December the artillery preparation for the general attack began. At 1700 the infantry began its assault.[193] Results did not live up to expectations.

Fundamentally, the problem was that changing an army's way of fighting takes time, and the CPFA had not had much time to train and prepare its commanders and soldiers to conduct the kind of operations in which they were now engaged. For example on the first day, the eastern group (9th and 11th Columns) attacking Zhangweizi encountered a long list of difficulties. A major one was poor artillery-infantry coordination. When the ECFA ST Column's artillery units had first begun assisting the CPFA in attacking the Twelfth Army pocket, they commonly had to teach the CPFA infantry commanders about something as basic as the preparatory work needed to make artillery fire effective.[194]

Not surprisingly then, the complexities of coordinating artillery fire with infantry movement had not been mastered by 6 December. Another difficulty was coordinating infantry assaults. Assaults from different directions on a single objective did not occur simultaneously, so the defenders were able to shift troops and fires to block them. Also, the space between the assault teams was too great for them to be mutually supporting, and the distance they had to cover (80 to 200 meters) while exposed to enemy fire proved to be too far still. Furthermore, the attacking forces had no answer for how to deal with flamethrowers, which proved to be formidable weapons in the defense.[195]

After the 6 December attack on Zhangweizi failed to take the village, these problems were thoroughly analyzed and solutions were proposed. Once agreed upon, the following changes were incorporated into preparing for the next attack, scheduled for 1700, 7 December. Fire support was strengthened by moving artillery firing positions forward and by adding several guns. A four-gun battery of mountain howitzers was brought in and given the mission of counterbattery fire against Nationalist artillery emplaced far behind the front line. The artillery providing direct fire support to the assaulting infantry was positioned so its impact area was fan shaped. This meant that both the infantry that continued to move forward after penetrating the Nationalist defenses and the soldiers defending the shoulders of the breach against enemy counterattacks had artillery support. Extending the approach trenches forward to points around 50 meters from the Nationalist lines reduced the distance the assault forces had to cross before reaching the Nationalist trenches. Also the assaulting infantry's firepower was increased. Every squad in the first assault wave was given a light machine gun. Two so-called "dagger" squads in each platoon received submachine guns and carbines to use to kill the soldiers carrying flamethrowers. Attention was also given to strengthening the assault troops' fighting spirit and determination. They were reminded of the importance of the battle and exhorted to show great courage, especially if their company commander or platoon leader was lost.[196]

Perhaps because of these adjustments, the attack that began at 1700, 7 December succeeded in taking Zhangweizi. Around 0400, 8 December the Nationalist defenders abandoned their positions and withdrew to Yangweizi. Around dawn, the Nationalists sent a regiment-sized unit supported by six tanks out of Yangweizi in an attempt to retake Zhangweizi, but the attack was beaten back. It had taken two days of hard fighting, but the CPFA's eastern group had succeeded in taking and holding an important link in the Nationalist defense line and had further compressed the Twelfth Army's pocket.[197] Around the Twelfth Army perimeter similar developments were occurring. Even if the CPFA attacks were at first not succeeding, they were continuing, and as they went on, they were steadily eroding the Twelfth Army's strength.

Faced with the pressure of the CPFA's general attack, inadequate aerial resupply, no way to treat his wounded properly, word that Du Yuming's force was tightly encircled northeast of Yongcheng, and reports that Li Yannian was having trouble advancing toward him, on 7 December Huang Wei sent Hu Lian back to Nanjing to explain to the High Command the increasingly desperate situation his force was in and to seek new guidance on what he should do.[198] At first Jiang Jieshi told Hu he was transferring the XX and XXVIII Corps and other units to Bengbu to reinforce Li Yannian's effort to reach Shuangduiji and the Twelfth Army should continue to defend in place until it was relieved.[199] However, after reports of Communist advances on 7-8 November reached Nanjing, Jiang changed his mind, and before Hu left Nanjing on 9 December to return to Shuangduiji, Jiang told him that Huang Wei had permission to break out of his encirclement. Hu asked that aerial bombing missions be increased and an adequate supply of food and ammunition be airdropped before any breakout operation. Jiang assured him he would personally see to it that this was done.[200]

According to Huang Wei, when Hu Lian returned to Shuangduiji his message from Jiang Jieshi was "You can break out. Do not concern yourself with Du Yuming and don't count on any support from Li Yannian."[201] This disturbed Huang because it made him feel that the High Command no longer had an overarching strategy for fighting the campaign.[202] He didn't see how the Twelfth Army could possibly break out without a significant increase in support from the air force and a strong advance by Li Yannian's army.[203] He was also concerned that if he did break out, Du Yuming would be left in a much more difficult situation.[204] After considering these various factors and their own circumstances, Huang and Hu both agreed not to begin planning for a breakout or even to let others know of Jiang's decision to allow them to break out.[205] They wanted to help Du Yuming by continuing to fight on. They also were waiting for a clearer picture of just how much support the air force would be able to give them.

While the Nationalist High Command and the commanders in the field were struggling to stem the tide of events running against them, the Communists were also feeling the need to take steps to ensure they maintained the initiative. They had reasons for concern. One was the heavy casualties in the general attack against Huang Wei and the Twelfth Army's continued strong resistance. For example, after two days of fighting to try to take Shenzhuang, the eastern group's 4th Column was forced to reduce the number of companies in certain regiments from nine to six and the number of battalions from three to two to maintain viable units at the front.[206]

Also, the column had to adopt the practice of *lifu lipu*, (immediately upon capture, immediately fill in) for changing captured Nationalist soldiers into PLA soldiers.[207] Second, the force engaging Li Yannian was only able to slow his advance, not stop it. Third, those ECFA units that were not engaged in fighting Li Yannian and Huang Wei were committed to the operation to contain and destroy Du Yuming's army group. With their troops spread out and fighting on three battlefields, Communist commanders faced a shortage of soldiers almost as great as the Nationalists.

As Su Yu looked at this situation, he was troubled by intelligence reports that not only were the Nationalists shifting the XX and XXVIII Corps to the Bengbu front, they were preparing to transport the 40,000-man, American-equipped II Corps down the Yangzi River by boat from Hubei for use on the Bengbu front and were gathering ships in Shanghai to bring soldiers from the Beiping-Tianjin area south to fight on this front.[208] In Su's estimation, if the fighting to destroy the Twelfth Army and Du's army group dragged on, the Nationalists might be able to gain a clearly dominant position in the south. If that happened, they could relieve the Twelfth Army and perhaps even relieve Du's force. Su's proposal for forestalling the development of this potential threat was to pull several ECFA columns out of the fight against Du and employ them against Huang.[209] The purpose would be to eliminate the Twelfth Army quickly and free the CPFA to counter any foreseeable Nationalist threat coming from the Bengbu area.[210]

Su Yu submitted this proposal for his economy-of-force operation to Liu Bocheng, Chen Yi, Deng Xiaoping, and the CMC on 9 December. The morning of 10 December, Liu, Chen, and Deng agreed to Su's concept and asked how he would maintain the encirclement of Du's force and what units he would send south to fight Huang Wei.[211] Su's reply came at 1300, 10 December. His strategy for keeping Du's army group in check was to mount a defense on the south side of the pocket while continuing to attack on the north. The forces he was sending to the Shuangduiji battlefield included his powerful 3d Column, two weaker columns, and additional artillery from the ST Column. This force was under command of Su's chief of staff, Chen Shiju, a commander who was well known for his love of artillery:

> Your telephonic message call has been received. We have decided to pull out three columns, the 3rd, 11th (E), and the Luzhongnan (these three columns actually amount to two column's worth of combat power) add some artillery, and send them south tonight to join in the battle to destroy Huang Wei. This force will be under the command of Chen Shiju on the way south. Please assign their operational missions.
>
> As for our battle with Du [Yuming], Qiu [Qingquan], and Li [Mi], the 2d, 8th, 10th, and 12th columns are defending against the enemy advancing toward the south. Those four columns are only able to carry out local attacks. The three columns on the north, the 1st, 4th, and 9th, on the other hand, are still actively attacking so the enemy has no chance to catch his breath.[212]

To promote mutual respect and close relations between ECFA and CPFA units, Chen Yi sent messages to the ECFA column commanders Su Yu was sending south to remind them they were representing the ECFA. He specifically requested they do three things to foster unity with the CPFA. They should be the first to reach their attack objectives, thereby greatly assisting their CPFA "brothers in arms." They should humbly learn from their brothers in arms and take the initiative in building unity with them. Every item that was captured, from large things like weapons, ammunition, and soldiers down to things as small as personal items used in daily life and pieces of paper were to be turned over to their brothers in arms. No one was to be permitted to hold back anything for their own use.[213] Chen's directive was passed to all division and regiment commanders with the guidance that everyone should be made to understand that the coming operation was not only about defeating the enemy, but it was also an opportunity to create a stronger ECFA-CPFA relationship.[214]

While the ECFA's 3d, 11th, and Luzhongnan Columns marched south toward Shuangduiji, the Communist columns surrounding the Twelfth Army continued to press their attacks. On 11 December the CPFA 4th Column captured the XIV Corps headquarters at Yangweizi and killed the corps commander.[215] On 12 December, with the Twelfth Army pocket reduced to a circular area with a diameter of only about 3 km, Liu Bocheng and Chen Yi sent Huang Wei a letter detailing the hopelessness of his situation and warning him that if he did not surrender he would be destroyed.[216] Huang ignored the warning and kept his army fighting, but the gains the Communists made the nights of 12 and 13 December made it clear to both him and Hu Lian that the end was near. Especially damaging to the Twelfth Army's defenses was losing the prehistoric mound at Jiangudui to the ECFA 7th Column the night of 13 December.[217]

The area around Shuangduiji, which literally means "pair (*shuang*) of mounds (*dui*) village (*ji*)," had a number of large cone-shaped mounds prehistoric people had built. The diameters of the mounds were around 40 meters, and they were about 20 meters high. On the flat plain they provided good vantage points for observing enemy positions and movements and for directing artillery. The Nationalists used several mounds in creating their defenses, and none was more important than the Jiangudui mound. It anchored a defensive line that ran east to west about 1 km south of the makeshift airfield and Twelfth Army headquarters. By taking it, the Communists could see directly into the heart of the pocket and bring observed artillery fire down on it.[218]

On 14 December with Communist artillery fire becoming more accurate as a result of their capture of Jiangudui, his own artillery out of ammunition, food in short supply, and his effective troop strength at a new low, Huang Wei knew it was either break out or be wiped out. Not wanting to wait to be destroyed, he decided to break out.[219] He radioed Nanjing that he would launch a breakout operation 15 December and then ordered the planning and preparation to begin.[220] Huang was not optimistic about the results of the operation, but he felt that "with luck" a portion of his army could be saved.[221] That, he thought, would be better than losing everything by staying in place.

On paper the Twelfth Army's breakout plan had order and coherence. The plan was based on the assumption that the strongest Communist forces were on the southern and southeastern sides of the pocket. Therefore, the plan called for what was left of the army to break out in the other directions, with some units going west, some north, and some east. Once they had broken through the Communist front lines and advanced into the Communist rear, all units were to swing to the south and head for Bengbu.[222] Weapons light enough to be carried by hand were to be brought along. All artillery pieces and most communication equipment were to be destroyed. Several thousand seriously wounded troops were to be left behind, some in trenches that had been dug to protect them but most simply lying on open ground. Tanks that were still operable were to be used to lead the breakout. The operation was to begin at dusk 15 December.[223]

When Liu Bocheng and Chen Yi had sent their letter to Huang Wei on 12 December demanding he surrender, they were well aware that the battle to destroy the Twelfth Army was nearing its climax. On 13 December they decided that because of the Twelfth Army's weakening condition and the shrinking pocket, it would not be necessary to use the ECFA 11th and Luzhongnan Columns in the battle. They ordered the Luzhongnan Column to assemble north of Shuangduiji and serve as a general reserve.[224] They directed the 11th Column to turn around and head back north to rejoin the fight against Du Yuming.[225] The ECFA 3d Column and the ST Column artillery that came with it, however, were assigned important roles in a general attack that was to begin late the afternoon of 14 December.

Along with the decision to use the 3d Column came a major reorganization of the forces attacking the Twelfth Army. On 13 December the 3d Column and the newly arrived ECFA ST Column artillery were placed in the southern group of columns, and the ECFA 13th Column was shifted from the western group to this group.[226] Chen Shiju became commander of this group, and it was designated the main effort in the 14 December general attack.[227] At this time the southern group consisted of three ECFA infantry columns, the 3d, 7th, and 13th Columns; several batteries of ECFA ST Column artillery; and the CPFA 6th Column.

The afternoon attack on 14 December began with the largest artillery preparation of the Shuangduiji battle. On the southern side of the pocket the artillery fire began at 1550 and continued for 2 hours.[228] At 1750 the infantry began their assaults. During the night and into the morning of 15 December the Twelfth Army continued to defend, but as Communist artillery fire destroyed more communication trenches and telephone lines, it became increasingly difficult for Huang Wei and the corps commanders to exercise command and control. When the time came, late in the afternoon, to execute the breakout operation, confusion reigned. The orderliness of the plan, as written, disintegrated into what was basically a rush by small groups of soldiers seeking escape. Within hours the surrounding Communist forces swept up almost all the Twelfth Army remnants, and the battle was over. Among those captured were Huang Wei and his X, XVIII, and LXXXV Corps commanders.[229] Ironically, Hu Lian, who had twice voluntarily flown into the Shuangduiji pocket, was able to make his way out of the tiger's mouth and safely return to Nanjing.

Notes

1. "*Zhongyang junwei guanyu jianji nanxian diren de bushu zhi Liu Bocheng, Chen Yi, Deng Xiaoping deng de dianbao*" (Telegram From the CMC to Liu Bocheng, Chen Yi, Deng Xiaoping, and Others [Including Su Yu] Concerning the Deployment for Attacking the Enemy on the Southern Front], in *Huaihai zhanyi* [The Huai Hai Campaign], Zhonggong zhongyang dangshi ziliao zhengji weiyuanhui [Chinese Communist Party Central Committee's Committee for the Collection of Party Historical Material], eds., (Beijing: Zhonggong dangshi ziliao chubanshe, 1988vol. 1, 169,), hereafter cited as *HHZY*.

2. "*Zhongyang junwei guanyu geduan Xu, Beng jianji Liu Zhi jituan de zong fangzhen zhi Liu Bocheng, Chen Yi, Deng Xiaoping deng de dianbao*" (Telegram From the CMC to Liu Bocheng, Chen Yi, and Deng Xiaoping and Others [Including Su Yu] Concerning the General Policy for Separating Xuzhou and Bengbu and Annihilating Liu Zhi's Army Group), *HHZY*, vol. 1, 190-91.

3. "*Zhongyang junwei guanyu zhunbei lianxu zuozhan sange yue zhi wu ge yue, zhengqu zhanyi quansheng zhi Liu Bocheng, Chen Yi, Deng Xiaoping deng de dianbao*" (Telegram From the CMC to Liu Bocheng, Chen Yi, Deng Xiaoping, and Others [Including Su Yu and the CCP's Central Plains and East China Bureaus] Concerning Preparations for Conducting Continuous Operations for 3-5 Months and Gaining Complete Victory in the Campaign), *HHZY*, vol. 1, 193-95.

4. Sunzi, *The Art of War*, Lionel Giles, trans. (Singapore: Graham Brash [Pte] Ltd., 1988), 60.

5. Huang Wei, "Di shier bingtuan bei jian jiyao" [A Summary of the Destruction of the Twelfth Army], in *Huaihai zhanyi qinli ji* [A Record of Personal Experiences During the Huaihai Campaign], Zhongguo renmin zhengzhi xieshang huiyi quanguo weiyuanhui wenshi ziliao yanjiu weiyuanhui [The Historical Materials Research Committee of the National Committee of the Chinese People's Political Consultative Conference], eds. (Beijing: Wenshi ziliao chubanshe, 1983), 486, hereafter cited as *QLJ*.

6. Li Da, "*Huigu Huaihai zhanyi zhong de zhongyuan yezhanjun*" [Recollections of the CPFA in the Huai Hai Campaign], *HHZY*, vol. 2, 8.

7. Huang Wei, *QLJ*, 486.

8. Yang Botao, "*Di shiba jun cong jingong dao beijian*" [The XVIII Corps From Its Advance in the Attack to Its Destruction], *QLJ*, 513.

9. Huang Wei, *QLJ*, 486.

10. Ibid.

11. Yang Botao, 512-13.

12. He Xiaohuan, Fu Jijun, and Shi Zhengxian, *Huaihai zhanyi shi* [A History of the Huai Hai Campaign] (Shanghai: Renmin chubanshe, 1983), 57, 114, hereafter cited as *HHZYS*.

13. Du Yuming, "*Huaihai zhanyi shimo*" [The Huai Hai Campaign from Beginning to End], in *QLJ*, 27.

14. Ibid.

15. Ibid.

16. Ibid.

17. "*Su Yu, Chen Shiju, Zhang Zhen guanyu xietong zhongye jianji Huang Wei, Li Yannian bingtuan de bushu zhi Liu Bocheng, Chen Yi, Deng Xiaoping de dianbao*" (Telegram From Su Yu, Chen Shiju, and Zhang Zhen to Liu Bocheng, Chen Yi, and Deng Xiaoping [and also the CMC] Concerning the Deployment for Cooperating With the CPFA in Attacking the Armies of Huang Wei and Li Yannian), *HHZY*, vol. 1, 181.

18. Sun Jixian and Ding Qiusheng, "*Zongheng chicheng, aozhan Huaihai*" [Sweeping Freely Across Wide Expanses, Fiercely Fighting the Huai Hai Campaign], *HHZY*, vol. 2, 239.

19. "*Su Yu, Chen Shiju, Zhang Zhen guanyu xietong zhongye jianji Huang Wei, Li Yannian bingtuan de bushu zhi Liu Bocheng, Chen Yi, Deng Xiaoping de dianbao*" (Telegram From Su Yu, Chen Shiju, and Zhang Zhen to Liu Bocheng, Chen Yi, and Deng Xiaoping [and also the CMC] Concerning the Deployment for Cooperating With the CPFA in Attacking the Armies of Huang Wei and Li Yannian), *HHZY*, vol. 1, 182.

20. Deng Maomao, *Deng Xiaoping: My Father* (New York: Basic Books, 1995), 398.

21. Sunzi, *The Art of War*, Samuel B. Griffith, trans. (New York: Oxford University Press, 1963), 81.

22. "*Su Yu, Chen Shiju, Zhang Zhen guanyu xietong zhongye jianji Huang Wei, Li Yannian bingtuan de bushu zhi Liu Bocheng, Chen Yi, Deng Xiaoping de dianbao*" (Telegram From Su Yu, Chen Shiju, and Zhang Zhen to Liu Bocheng, Chen Yi, and Deng Xiaoping [and also the CMC] Concerning the Deployment for Cooperating With the CPFA in Attacking the Armies of Huang Wei and Li Yannian), *HHZY*, vol. 1, 182.

23. "*Liu Bocheng, Chen Yi, Deng Xiaoping guanyu huaye chou bing canjia da Huang Wei bingtuan zhi Su Yu, Chen Shiju, Zhang Zhen deng de dianbao*" (Telegram From Liu Bocheng, Chen Yi, and Deng Xiaoping to Su Yu, Chen Shiju, and Zhang Zhen [and also the CMC] Concerning the ECFA Pulling Out Troops to Join the Attack on Huang Wei's Army), *HHZY*, vol. 1, 185.

24. "*Su Yu, Chen Shiju, Zhang Zhen guanyu jianji Li Yannian bingtuan de bushu zhi Liu Bocheng, Chen Yi, Deng Xiaoping deng de dianbao*" (Telegram From Su Yu, Chen Shiju, and Zhang Zhen to Liu Bocheng, Chen Yi, Deng Xiaoping and Others [Including the CMC] Concerning the Deployment for Attacking Li Yannian's Army), *HHZY*, vol. 1, 187.

25. *Zhongguo renmin geming junshi bowuguan* [The Military Museum of the Chinese People's Revolution], Zhongguo renmin jiefangjun zhanshi tuji [Maps of the Chinese People's Liberation Army's War History] (Beijing: Zhongguo ditu chubanshe, 1990), 210.

26. "*Su Yu, Chen Shiju, Zhang Zhen guanyu jianji Li Yannian bingtuan de bushu zhi Liu Bocheng, Chen Yi, Deng Xiaoping deng de dianbao*" (Telegram From Su Yu, Chen Shiju, and Zhang Zhen to Liu Bocheng, Chen Yi, Deng Xiaoping, and Others [Including the CMC] Concerning the Deployment for Attacking Li Yannian's Army), *HHZY*, vol. 1, 187.

27. Zhongguo renmin geming junshi bowuguan [The Military Museum of the Chinese People's Revolution], 209.

28. Ibid.

29. "*Su Yu, Chen Shiju, Zhang Zhen guanyu jianji Li Yannian bingtuan de bushu zhi Liu Bocheng, Chen Yi, Deng Xiaoping deng de dianbao*" (Telegram From Su Yu, Chen Shiju, and Zhang Zhen to Liu Bocheng, Chen Yi, Deng Xiaoping, and Others [Including the CMC] Concerning the Deployment for Attacking Li Yannian's Army), *HHZY*, vol. 1, 187.

30. "*Liu Bocheng, Chen Yi, Deng Xiaoping guanyu jianji Huang Wei bingtuan de bushu zhi Su Yu, Chen Shiju, Zhang Zhen de dianbao*" (Telegram From Liu Bocheng, Chen Yi, Deng Xiaoping to Su Yu, Chen Shiju, and Zhang Zhen [and also the CMC] Concerning the Deployment for Attacking Huang Wei's Army), *HHZY*, vol. 1, 189.

31. Sunzi, *The Art of War*, Roger T. Ames, trans. (New York: Ballantine Books, 1993), 104.

32. Ibid.

33. Sunzi, Giles, 81.

34. Sunzi, Ames, 123.

35. "*Zhongyang junwei guanyu Huaihai zhanyi tongyi zhihui wenti zhi Chen Yi, Deng Xiaoping, Su

Yu de dianbao" [Telegram From the CMC to Chen Yi, Deng Xiaoping, and Su Yu Concerning the Question of Unity of Command for the Huai Hai Campaign], *HHZY*, vol. 1, 107.

36. "Zhongyang junwei guanyu an dangmian qingkuang jueding juti gongji renwu zhi Chen Yi, Deng Xiaoping de dianbao" (Telegram from the CMC to Chen Yi and Deng Xiaoping [and also Su Yu and Liu Bocheng] Concerning Determining Actual Attack Missions on the Basis of the Situation You Face), in *HHZY*, vol. 1, 116.

37. "*Zhongyang junwei yuji di yi zhang jiandi ershiyi, er ge shi di er zhang da Huang Wei, Sun Yuanliang zhi Su Yu, Chen Shiju, Zhang Zhen deng de dianbao*" [Telegram From the CMC to Su Yu, Chen Shiju, Zhang Zhen, and Others Estimating That in the First Phase of the Campaign 21-22 Enemy Divisions Would be Destroyed and That the Second Phase Would be an Attack on Huang Wei and Sun Yuanliang], *HHZY*, vol. 1, 129.

38. "*Zhongyang junwei guanyu chengli zongqianwei zhi Liu Bocheng, Chen Yi, Deng Xiaoping deng de dianbao*" (Telegram From the CMC to Liu Bocheng, Chen Yi, Deng Xiaoping [and Su Yu and Tan Zhenlin] Concerning the Establishment of the General Front Committee), *HHZY*, vol. 1, 165.

39. "*Liu Bocheng, Chen Yi, Deng Xiaoping guanyu zhongye an yuan jihua chuji zhi Su Yu, Chen Shiju, Zhang Zhen deng de dianbao*" (Telegram From Liu Bocheng, Chen Yi, and Deng Xiaoping to Su Yu, Chen Shiju, Zhang Zhen, and Others [Including the CMC] Concerning the CPFA Attacking in Accord With Its Original Plan), *HHZY*, vol. 1, 196.

40. "*Zhongyang junwei wanquan tongyi xian da Huang Wei bingtuan zhi Liu Bocheng, Chen Yi, Deng Xiaoping de dianbao*" (Telegram From the CMC to Liu Bocheng, Chen Yi, and Deng Xiaoping [and also Su Yu] Agreeing Completely to First Attack Huang Wei), *HHZY*, vol. 1, 197.

41. "*Su Yu, Chen Shiju, Zhang Zhen guanyu peihe zhongye jianmie Huang Wei bingtuan de bushu zhi Liu Bocheng, Chen Yi, Deng Xiaoping de dianbao*" (Telegram From Su Yu, Chen Shiju, and Zhang Zhen to Liu Bocheng, Chen Yi, Deng Xiaoping [and also the CMC, Wei Guoqing, and Tan Zhenlin] Concerning the Deployment for Coordinating With the CPFA to Destroy Huang Wei's Army), *HHZY*, vol. 1, 200-201.

42. Yang Botao, *QLJ*, 515.

43. *HHZYS*, 115.

44. Ibid.

45. Ibid. This order of events differs from Liu Bocheng's statement in his 1000, 24 November message to the CMC that the Twelfth Army was already moving east that morning. What information led him to that conclusion is unclear.

46. Yang Botao, *QLJ*, 516.

47. *HHZYS*, 115-16.

48. *Xubeng Huizhan zhi bu* [The Xu-Beng Battle Section], Sanjun daxue zhanshi bianzuan weiyuanhui [The Armed Forces University War History Compilation Committee], eds. (Taibei: Sanjun daxue, [n.d.]), 61.

49. "*Liu Bocheng, Chen Yi, Deng Xiaoping guanyu yi wanquan baowei Huang Wei bingtuan zhi zhongyang junwei de dianbao*" [Telegram From Liu Bocheng, Chen Yi, and Deng Xiaoping to the CMC Concerning Their Having Already Completely Surrounded Huang Wei's Army], *HHZY*, vol. 1, 203.

50. *HHZYS*, 152.

51. Liao Yunzhou, "*Di yiyiling shi zhanchang qiyi shimo*" [The Revolt of the 110th Division on the Battlefield From Beginning to End], *QLJ*, 563.

52. Ibid., 561.

53. *HHZYS*, 152.

54. Ibid., 153.

55. *Zhongguo renmin jiefangjun quanguo jiefang zhanjeng shi* [The History of the Chinese PLA's War to Liberate the Entire Country], Wang Miaosheng, ed. (Beijing: Junshi kexue chubanshe, 1997), vol. 4, 310-11, hereafter cited as *QJZS*.

56. Liao Yunzhou, "*Di yiyiling shi zhanchang qiyi shimo*" [The Revolt of the 110th Division on the Battlefield From Beginning to End], *QLJ*, 555.

57. Ibid., 563-64.

58. Ibid, 563.

59. Ibid., 564.

60. Ibid., 566.

61. Ibid. Liao Yunzhou makes it clear that no one would have been permitted to stay behind. Even the wounded who could not walk were carried with the division. As for the offer of free choice in deciding whether to go or stay, Liao says this, "Actually, that was only a way to place a weight on their mind. I calculated that even if there were those who did not want to go, none of them would dare say so."

62. Ibid., 567.

63. Ibid.

64. "*Liu Bocheng, Chen Yi, Deng Xiaoping guanyu qingshi jiejue Huang Wei bingtuan hou de zhanlue fangxiang wenti zhi zhongyang junwei deng de dianbao*" (Telegram From Liu Bocheng, Chen Yi, and Deng Xiaoping to the CMC and Others [Including Su Yu] Asking for Guidance Concerning the Strategic Direction to be Taken After Finishing Off Huang Wei's Army), *HHZY*, vol. 1, 206.

65. "*Su Yu, Chen Shiju, Zhang Zhen guanyu weijian Li Yannian bingtuan de bushu zhi Liu Bocheng, Chen Yi, Deng Xiaoping deng de dianbao*" (Telegram From Su Yu, Chen Shiju, and Zhang Zhen to Liu Bocheng, Chen Yi, Deng Xiaoping, and Others [Including the CMC, the CCP East China Region Bureau, and Tan Zhenlin] Concerning the Deployment for Encircling and Destroying Li Yannian's Army), *HHZY*, vol. 1, 205.

66. Ibid.

67. *HHZYS*, 125.

68. *Su Yu zhuan* [A Biography of Su Yu], Su Yu zhuan bianxiezu [The Group for Compiling A Biography of Su Yu], ed. (Beijing: Dangdai zhongguo chubanshe, 2000), 760, hereafter cited as *SYZ*.

69. *QJZS*, vol. 4, 323.

70. Ibid.

71. Ibid.

72. This number of deaths is an estimate based on statistics presented in *HHZY*, vol. 1, 337.

73. Zhou Kaicheng, "*Huaihai zhanyi zhong de di bajun*" [The VIII Corps in the Huai Hai Campaign], *QLJ*, 248.

74. Du Yuming, *QLJ*, 28.

75. Ibid.

76. Ibid.

77. "*Su Yu, Chen Shiju, Zhang Zhen guanyu xietong zhongye jianji Huang Wei, Li Yannian bingtuan de bushu zhi Liu Bocheng, Chen Yi, Deng Xiaoping de dianbao*" (Telegram From Su Yu, Chen Shiju, and Zhang Zhen to Liu Bocheng, Chen Yi, and Deng Xiaoping [and also the CMC] Concerning the Deployment for Cooperating With the CPFA in Attacking the Armies of Huang Wei and Li Yannian), in *HHZY*, vol. 1, 180.

78. Ibid.

79. Nie Fengzhi, "*Ganda ganpin yingyong fenzhan*" [Daring to Fight, Bravely Giving Our All], *HHZY*, vol. 2, 314.

80. Qian Jun, "*Guanyu luzhongnanzongdui canjia Huaihai zhanyi de huiyi*" (Recollections of the Luzhongnan [LZN] Column's Participation in the Huai Hai Campaign), *QLJ*, 385.

81. Ou Yangping, "*Zhandou zai Huiaihai zhanchangshang de bohai zongdui*" [The Bohai Column's Combat on the Huaihai Battlefields], *QLJ*, 389.

82. Ibid.

83. Sunzi, Giles, 17.

84. Ibid., 16.

85. "*Zhongyang junwei yuji diyizhang jian di ershiyi, er ge shi dierzhang da Huang Wei, Sun Yuanliang zhi Su Yu, Chen Shiju, Zhang Zhen deng de dianbao*" (Telegram From the CMC to Su Yu, Chen Shiju, Zhang Zhen, and Others [Including ChenYi and Deng Xiaoping] Concerning the CMC Estimate That During the First Phase of the Campaign 21-22 Enemy Divisions Would Be Destroyed and That the Second Phase Would Be an Attack on Huang Wei and Sun Yuanliang), *HHZY*, vol. 1, 129-30.

86. "*Huadong yezhanjun qianwei guanyu quanjian Huang Baitao bingtuan de zhengzhi dongyuan ling*" [Order From the ECFA Front Committee for Political Mobilization to Completely Destroy Huang Baitao's Army], *HHZY*, vol. 1, 135.

87. "*Su Yu, Chen Shiju, Zhang Zhen guanyu huaye quanjun da beixian zhudi zhi Tan Zhenlin, Wang Jinan, Li Yingxi de dianbao*" (Telegram From Su Yu, Chen Shiju, and Zhang Zhen to Tan Zhenlin, Wang Jianan, and Li Yingxi [and also to Liu, Chen, and Deng, and the CMC] Concerning the Entire ECFA Fighting the Various Enemy Forces on the Northern Front), *HHZY*, vol. 1, 167.

88. *QJZS*, vol. 4, 323.

89. Guo Huaruo, Mei Jiasheng, and Han Nianlong, "*Zhongyuan duo jizhan chuan xi dao jingnan*" [The Many Fierce Battles on the Central Plains Send a Call to Arms South of the Yangzi], *HHZY*, vol. 2, 253.

90. Ibid.

91. Ibid., 252.

92. "*Zhongyang junwei guanyu zhanyi di san jieduan jiejue Xu-Beng zhi di zhi Liu Bocheng, Chen Yi, Deng Xiaoping de dianbao*" (Telegram From the CMC to Liu Bocheng Chen Yi, Deng Xiaoping [and also to Su Yu and Tan Zhenlin] Concerning Finishing Off the Enemy Forces in Xuzhou and Bengbu During the Third Phase of the Campaign), *HHZY*, vol. 1, 207-208.

93. "*Zhongyang junwei guanyu jianmie Huang Wei bingtuan hou fang Xu di keneng taopao zhi Liu Bocheng, Chen Yi, Deng Xiaoping deng de dianbao*" (Telegram From the CMC to Liu Bocheng, Chen Yi, Deng Xiaoping, and Others [Including Su Yu and Tan Zhenlin] Concerning Defending Against the Possibility of the Enemy Forces in Xuzhou Taking Flight After Huang Wei's Army Has Been Destroyed), *HHZY*, vol. 1, 211.

94. "*Liu Bocheng, Chen Yi, Deng Xiaopping guanyu caiqu jizhong huoli xian da yi dian de zhanfa zhi zhongyang junwei deng de dianbao*" (Telegram From Liu Bocheng, Chen Yi, and Deng Xiaoping to the CMC and Others [Including Su Yu] Concerning the Adoption of the Fighting Method in Which Firepower is Concentrated to First Attack One Point), *HHZY*, vol. 1, 209-210.

95. "*Zhongyang junwei guanyu jianmie Huang Wei bingtuan xu zhangwo zong yubeidui zhi Liu Bocheng, Chen Yi, Deng Xiaoping de dianbao*" (Telegram From the CMC to Liu Bocheng, Chen Yi, and Deng Xiaoping [and also to Su Yu and Tan Zhenlin] Concerning the Need to Have in Hand a General Reserve When Fighting to Destroy Huang Wei's Army), *HHZY*, vol. 1, 212.

96. "*Su Yu, Tan Zhenlin deng dui xujian Huang Wei bingtuan ji Xuzhou zhi di de buchong yijian zhi zhongyang junwei deng de dianbao*" (Telegram From Su Yu, Tan Zhenlin, and Others [Chen Shiju, the ECFA Chief of Staff and Zhang Zhen, the ECFA Deputy Chief of Staff] to the CMC [and also to Liu, Chen, and Deng] Presenting Ideas for the Consecutive Destruction of Huang Wei's Army and the Enemy in Xuzhou), *HHZY*, vol. 1, 213-15.

97. *QJZS*, vol. 4, 331.

98. Ibid., 332.

99. "*Zhongyang junwei guanyu huaye zhunbei yi liangge zongdui wei gongjian Huang Wei bingtuan de zong yubeidui zhi Liu Bocheng, Chen Yi, Deng Xiaoping deng de dianbao*" (Telegram From the CMC to Liu Bocheng, Chen Yi, Deng Xiaoping, and Others [Including Su Yu and Tan Zhenlin] Concerning the ECFA Preparing to Use Two Columns as a General Reserve for the Annihilation of Huang Wei's Army), *HHZY*, vol. 1, 216-17.

100. "*Fangzhi dijun xiang liang Huai huo Lianyungang taopao*" (Prevent the Enemy Armies From Fleeing Toward the Two Huai Cities [Huaian and Huayin] or Lianyungang), in *Mao Zedong junshi wenji* [A Collection of Mao Zedong's Military Documents] (Beijing: Junshi kexue chubanshe, 1993), vol. 5, 300, hereafter cited as *MZDMD*.

101. *HHZYS*, 127.

102. Du Yuming, *QLJ*, 28.

103. Ibid.

104. Ibid.

105. Ibid.

106. Ibid, 24.

107. Ibid., 23.

108. Ibid., 29.

109. Ibid.

110. Guo Rugui, "*Huaihai zhanyi qijian guomindangjun tongshuaibu de zhengchao he juece*" [Wrangling and Decision Making Within the Nationalist High Command During the Time of the Huai Hai Campaign], *QLJ*, 59.

111. Huang Wei, *QLJ*, 488.

112. Du Yuming, *QLJ*, 31.

113. Ibid., 32.

114. "*Su Yu, Tan Zhenlin deng dui xujian Huang Wei bingtuan ji Xuzhou zhi di de buchong yijian zhi zhongyang junwei deng de dianbao*" (Telegram From Su Yu, Tan Zhenlin, and Others [Chen Shiju, the ECFA Chief of Staff and Zhang Zhen, the ECFA Deputy Chief of Staff] to the CMC [and also to Liu,

Chen, and Deng] Presenting Ideas for the Consecutive Destruction of Huang Wei's Army and the Enemy in Xuzhou), *HHZY*, vol. 1, 213.

115. *QJZS*, vol. 4, 325.

116. "*Huadong yezhanjun silingbu guanyu Huaihai zhanyi jingguo gaishu*" [The ECFA Headquarters' General Description of What Happened During the Huai Hai Campaign], *HHZY*, vol. 1, 298.

117. Ibid.

118. Ibid.

119. *QJZS*, vol. 4, 335.

120. *HHZYS*, 134-35. See also "*Huadong yezhanjun silingbu guanyu Huaihai zhanyi jingguo gaishu*" [The ECFA Headquarters' General Description of What Happened During the Huai Hai Campaign], *HHZY*, vol. 1, 299.

121. Carl von Clausewitz, *On War*, Michael Howard and Peter Paret, trans. (Princeton, NJ: Princeton University Press, 1976), 119.

122. Ibid., 121.

123. Ibid., 119.

124. Ibid., 120.

125. Du Yuming, *QLJ*, 32.

126. Ibid., 33.

127. Ibid.

128. Ibid.

129. *HHZYS*, 137.

130. Du Yuming, *QLJ*, 34. For the quote from Sunzi's *The Art of War*, see Sunzi, Ames, 134-35.

131. Ibid., 35.

132. Ibid., 35-36.

133. Ibid., 33.

134. "*Su Yu, Chen Shiju, Zhang Zhen guanyu jianmie Du Yuming jituan de bushu zhi ge bingtuan, ge zongdui shouzhang de dianbao*" (Telegram From Su Yu, Chen Shiju, and Zhang Zhen to Every Army and Column Commander [and also to the CMC and Liu, Chen, and Deng] Concerning the Deployment for the Destruction of Du Yuming's Army Group), *HHZY*, vol. 1, 226-27.

135. "*Huadong yezhanjun silingbu guanyu Huaihai zhanyi jingguo gaishu*" [The ECFA Headquarters' General Description of What Happened During the Huai Hai Campaign], *HHZY*, vol. 1, 300.

136. Ibid.; *HHZYS*, 142.

137. Ibid., 143.

138. Ibid.

139. Ibid., 144.

140. Du Yuming, *QLJ*, 37.

141. Ibid.

142. Ibid., 38.

143. Xiong Shunyi, "*Sun Yuanliang bingtuan beijian jingguo*" [The Way the Destruction of Sun Yuanliang's Army Occurred], *QLJ*, 425.

144. Du Yuming, *QLJ*, 39.

145. Ibid., 38.

146. Ibid., 39.

147. Ibid., 40.

148. Ibid.

149. Li Yikuang, "*Huaihai zhanyi nanxian guomindangjun zengyuan beixian jingguo*" [The Experiences of the Nationalist Armies on the Southern Front Reinforcing the Northern Front During the Huai Hai Campaign], *QLJ*, 465.

150. *Xubeng Huizhan zhi bu* (The Xu-Beng Battle Section), 56.

151. "*Zhongyang junwei guanyu da qiangdi bixu yong qianggong fangfa zhi Liu Bocheng, Chen Yi, Deng Xiaoping de dianbao*" (Telegram From the CMC to Liu Bocheng, Chen Yi, and Deng Xiaoping [and also Su Yu and Tan Zhenlin] Concerning the Need to Adopt the Strong Attack Method When Attacking a Strong Enemy), *HHZY*, vol. 1, 230.

152. "*Liuzong ying jiaqiang zuji Li Yannian beijin*" [The 6th Column Should Strongly Block Li Yannian's Advance to the North], *MZDMD*, vol. 5, 323.

153. "*Wei fangzhi Bengbu diren weixie ying gouzhu duoceng jianqiang fangyu zhendi*" [In Order to Guard Against the Threat Posed by the Bengbu Enemy, We Should Construct Strong Defensive Positions in Depth], *MZDMD*, vol. 5, 325.

154. *QJZS*, vol. 4, 329.

155. Ibid.

156. Ibid., 330.

157. *Chen Yi zhuan* [Chen Yi's Biography], "*Dangdai zhongguo renwu zhuanji congshu*" bianjibu (Editorial Department for the Modern Chinese Biography Series), ed. (Beijing: Dangdai zhongguo chubanshe, 1991), 440.

158. Ibid., 430.

159. Ibid.

160. Ibid.

161. Ibid., 429.

162. Ibid., 430.

163. Zhou Zhijian, "*Yongmeng qianjin fenzhan Huaihai*" [Boldly March Forward, Bravely Fight the Huai Hai Campaign], *HHZY*, vol. 2, 360.

164. Qin Jiwei, "*Zhongye jiuzong zai Huaihai zhanchangshang*" [The CPFA 9th Column on the Huai Hai Battlefields, *HHZY*, vol. 2, 161.

165. Ibid.

166. Ibid.

167. Ibid.

168. Ibid.

169. "*Di er yezhanjun silingbu guanyu jianmie Huang Wei bingtuan zuozhan jingguo deng wenti*

de zongjie" (A Summary by Second Field Army [the Name of the CPFA After the Huai Hai Campaign] Headquarters of What Happened During the Operation to Destroy Huang Wei's Army and Other Questions) *HHZY*, vol. 1, 313.

170. Qin Jiwei, *HHZY*, vol. 2, 161.

171. Ibid.

172. Ibid.

173. Ibid.

174. Ibid., 163.

175. Ibid.

176. S*YZ*, 763.

177. Ibid.

178. "*Zhongyang junwei guanyu da qiangdi bixu yong qianggong fangfa zhi Liu Bocheng, Chen Yi, Deng Xiaoping de dianbao*" (Telegram From the CMC to Liu Bocheng, Chen Yi, Deng Xiaoping [and also to Su Yu, Tan Zhenlin, and Others] Concerning the Need to Adopt the Strong Attack Method to Attack Strong Enemy Forces), *HHZY*, vol. 1, 229.

179. Chen Xilian, "*Jieduan Xu Beng xian, huizhan Shuangduiji*" [Cutting the Xu-Beng Railroad and Fighting the Decisive Battle of Shuangduiji], *HHZY*, vol. 2, 117-18.

180. Ibid., 119.

181. Huang Wei, *QLJ*, 490.

182. Ibid.

183. Yang Botao, *QLJ*, 522.

184. Ibid.

185. "*Liu Bocheng, Chen Yi, Deng Xiaoping guanyu weijian Huang Wei bingtuan de qingkuang zhi zhongyang junwei deng de dianbao*" [Telegram From Liu Bocheng, Chen Yi, and Deng Xiaoping to the CMC and Others Concerning the Situation in the Fight to Destroy Huang Wei's Army], *HHZY*, vol. 1, 228.

186. "*Di er yezhanjun silingbu guanyu jianmie Huang Wei bingtuan zuozhan jingguo deng wenti de zongjie*" (A Summary by Second Field Army [the Name of the CPFA After the Huai Hai Campaign] Headquarters of What Happened During the Operation to Destroy Huang Wei's Army and Other Questions) *HHZY*, vol. 1, 314.

187. Du Yide, "*Huiyi zhongye liuzong canjia weijian Huang Wei bingtuan zhi zhan*" [Recollection of the CPFA 6th Column's Participation in the Battles to Encircle and Destroy Huang Wei's Army], *HHZY*, vol. 2, 151.

188. *HHZYS*, 161.

189. Chen Ruiting, "*Wei hu tian yi*" [Adding Wings to a Tiger], *HHZY*, vol. 2, 414.

190. "*Liu Bocheng, Chen Yi, Deng Xiaoping fabu zonggong Huang Wei bingtuan de mingling*" [The Order for a General Attack on Huang Wei's Army Issued by Liu Bocheng, Chen Yi, and Deng Xiaoping], *HHZY*, vol. 1, 232.

191. Ibid.

192. "*Di er yezhanjun silingbu guanyu jianmie Huang Wei bingtuan zuozhan jingguo deng wenti de zongjie*" (A Summary by Second Field Army [the Name of the CPFA After the Huai Hai Campaign]

Headquarters of What Happened During the Operation to Destroy Huang Wei's Army and Other Questions), *HHZY*, vol. 1, 314.

193. Liu Xing and Pei Zhigeng, "*Zai zhandouzhong duanlian chengzhang*" [Tempering Oneself and Maturing in Battle], *HHZY*, vol. 2, 176.

194. Chen Ruiting, *HHZY*, vol. 2, 414-15.

195. Liu Xing and Pei Zhigeng, *HHZY*, vol. 2, 176.

196. Ibid., 176-77

197. Ibid., 177-78.

198. Huang Wei, *QLJ*, 491.

199. Yang Botao, *QLJ*, 523.

200. Ibid.

201. Huang Wei, *QLJ*, 491.

202. Ibid.

203. Yang Botao, *QLJ*, 524.

204. Ibid.

205. Ibid.

206. Liu Youguang, "*Huaihai zhanyi zhong de zhongye sizong*" [The CPFA 4th Column in the Huai Hai Campaign], *HHZY*, vol. 2, 139.

207. Ibid.

208. *QJZS*, vol. 4, 316.

209. Ibid., 317.

210. Ibid.

211. *HHZYS*, 163.

212. "*Su Yu, Tan Zhenlin deng guanyu zengdiao sange zongdui canjia da Huang Wei bingtuan zhi Liu Bocheng, Chen Yi, Deng Xiaoping deng de dianbao*" (Telegram From Su Yu, Tan Zhenlin, and Others to Liu Bocheng, Chen Yi, Deng Xiaoping, and Others [Including the CMC and the CCP East China Bureau] Concerning the Transfer of Three Additional Columns to the Fight Against Huang Wei's Army), *HHZY*, vol. 1, 234.

213. Sun Jixian and Ding Qiusheng, "*Zongheng chicheng, aozhan Huaihai*" [Sweeping Freely Across Wide Expanses, Fiercely Fighting the Huai Hai Campaign], HHZY, vol. 2, 243.

214. Ibid.

215. Liu Youguang, *HHZY*, vol. 2, 139-140.

216. "*Liu Bocheng, Chen Yi cu Huang Wei liji touxiang shu*" [Letter From Liu Bocheng and Chen Yi Urging Huang Wei to Immediately Surrender], *HHZY*, vol. 1, 236.

217. Cheng Jun, "*Cong tupo yunhe dao gongzhan Dawangzhuang, Jiangudui*" [From Breaking Through at the Grand Canal to Taking Dawangzhuang and Jiangudui], *HHZY*, vol. 2, 284.

218. Du Yide, *HHZY*, vol. 2, 155.

219. Yang Botao, *QLJ*, 529.

220. Huang Wei, *QLJ*, 492.

221. Ibid.
222. Yang Botao, *QLJ*, 530-31.
223. Ibid., 531.
224. *HHZYS*, 164.
225. Hu Bingyun, "*Zai Huaihai dazhan de riri yeye li*" [The Days and Nights of the Great Huai Hai Campaign Battle], *HHZY*, vol. 2, 340.
226. Chen Xilian, *HHZY*, vol. 2, 123.
227. Ibid., 124.
228. Sun Jixian and Ding Qiusheng, *HHZY*, vol. 2, 244.
229. Huang Wei, *QLJ*, 493.

Chapter Eight
End Moves in the Campaign

Those skilled in war subdue the enemy's army without battle
They capture his cities without assaulting them.

—Sunzi, *The Art of War*

Annihilating the Twelfth Army was a major victory for the Communists at the operational level. It made their hold on the central position absolute and, in doing so, set the conditions for achieving the main objective of the expanded Huai Hai Campaign—destroying Du Yuming's army group. This force had been encircled since 4 December and had lost the Sixteenth Army during a failed breakout attempt on 6 December. It had been losing soldiers steadily as it continued to follow Jiang Jieshi's orders to attack toward the southeast to relieve the Twelfth Army and fought to defend itself from East China Field Army (ECFA) attacks against the other sides of the pocket. Its stocks of food and ammunition were running low. Clearly, on 15 December, this force was much weaker than it had been when it had left Xuzhou. The surrounding Communist forces, on the other hand, due to the Twelfth Army's destruction, were about to become stronger.

Du Yuming was unaware of what was happening on the Shuangduiji battlefield. He was shocked, therefore, when on the evening of 16 December he received a message from Liu Zhi saying, "Yesterday evening Huang Wei's army conducted a breakout operation. Li Yannian's army is withdrawing south of the Huai River."[1] Du's immediate reaction was to wonder why he had not been ordered to break out at the same time. The question of whether the Central Plains Field Army (CPFA) would join with the ECFA to attack his force had been a matter of concern in his command.[2] Now, he thought, with Huang Wei's army having broken out and the Sixth and Eighth Armies in the process of withdrawing, it was likely that the Communists would add to the forces arrayed against him.[3] He also understood that his force was becoming even more isolated. After the Sixth and Eighth Armies retired south of the Huai River, the distance between Du's force and the main Nationalist defense line would be 140 km. After receiving Liu's message he ordered his two armies to cease their attacks to the southeast, to strengthen their field fortifications, and to prepare to defend in place. He also sent a message to the High Command asking for guidance and repeating his 7 December plea that it commit more troops to the campaign.[4]

Nationalist Planning to Save Du Yuming's Army Group

On 17 December, Jiang Jieshi responded to Du Yuming's message by directing him to send a representative to Nanjing for consultation and planning. The next morning an airplane arrived at the makeshift airstrip near Du's headquarters at Chenguanzhuang and took Du's chief of staff for operations, Shu Shicun, back to Nanjing.[5] In the meantime, Du had received another message from Liu Zhi informing him that "As far as the breakout of Huang Wei's army is concerned, only Hu Lian has reached Bengbu. The whereabouts of the rest of the force is unknown."[6] This news confirmed Du's belief that trying to break out was futile.[7]

When Shu Shicun flew back from Nanjing to Chenguanzhuang early the afternoon of 19 December he brought with him a lengthy handwritten letter from Jiang Jieshi to Du Yuming. In the letter, Jiang placed responsibility for the failure of the Twelfth Army's breakout operation on Huang Wei, blaming him for trying to break out at night instead of during the day when the air force could have provided support. Jiang informed Du that, try as he could, it was impossible for him to shift forces from other parts of China to the Bengbu area and fight to relieve him. "The only approach," he stated, "is to concentrate all your strength and with air force support rupture enemy defenses on one side and then break out."[8] Jiang was prepared to lose half of Du's force if the other half could be saved and brought south.[9]

To help develop the breakout plan and improve coordination between Du Yuming's planning staff and air force headquarters in Nanjing, Dong Mingde, deputy chief of staff for operations, air force headquarters, accompanied Shu Shicun back to Chenguanzhuang. Jiang Jieshi wanted Du's force to break out as soon as possible, so planning began that evening and carried on late into the night. Based on aerial photographs of Communist positions that Dong brought, a decision was made to attack toward the west.[10] The Second and Thirteenth Armies were to advance abreast with the Thirteenth on the right and the Second on the left. Just before the ground forces launched their attack, the air force was to fly 100 sorties, dropping tear gas bombs onto the Communist defense line.[11] The first Nationalist assault wave was to be equipped with gas masks, and it was assumed that with the defenders temporarily incapacitated by gas, they could quickly breach the Communist defenses.[12] Once that happened, the second assault wave would push through. After the force had broken out, the air force was to maintain a combat patrol of fighter aircraft over Du's force to provide support when and where needed.[13] Du personally paid great attention to the methods the troops on the ground would use to identify themselves as friendly forces to the pilots above. He did not want the air force firing on his soldiers.[14] The operation was set to begin after three full days of airdrops had brought food and ammunition stocks up to the desired levels.[15]

Although he participated actively in the planning process for the breakout operation, Du Yuming was pessimistic about his army group's chances of successfully making it through Communist lines and crossing approximately 150 km of open country with the Communists in pursuit. After retiring to his room the night of 19 December, he sat down and wrote a personal letter to Jiang Jieshi. Du told him he thought an attempt to break out would end in disaster and asked Jiang to reconsider. Du suggested two alternatives. One was to have Jiang move forces from Xian and Wuhan, even abandoning Wuhan if necessary, and concentrate those forces for a decisive battle with the People's Liberation Army (PLA). The second was to have Du's force defend in place and hope that time would bring positive political developments. Only as a last resort, Du said, should a breakout operation be attempted. Du felt there was little hope of dissuading Jiang from ordering a breakout operation, but he also felt he had to make one final appeal.[16]

Du intended to have Shu Shicun take his letter to Nanjing on 20 December when Su and Dong were scheduled to fly back with the completed breakout plan. However, as they were preparing to leave, heavy snow began to fall and their aircraft was grounded. For more than a week, wind, snow, rain, and a low ceiling kept their airplane on the ground. This bad weather also stopped airdrops of food, ammunition, medicine, and other supplies into the Chenguanzhuang pocket, which caused the Nationalist supply situation to become even more critical. Meanwhile the ECFA bided its time. Instead of continuing, or even intensifying, its attacks against the surrounded Nationalist forces, as it was fully capable of doing, it stopped attacking and focused on conducting a political offensive designed to weaken the will and sap the spirits of Du's armies.

An Operational Pause for Strategic Purposes

This operational pause was ordered by the Central Military Commission (CMC) as part of its grand strategy for conducting the civil war. As was described and discussed in earlier chapters, the Huai Hai Campaign was originally conceived as a way to achieve the operational objective of occupying northern Jiangsu. Achieving this objective would place additional human and materiel resources in Communist hands. It would also establish favorable conditions for future military operations. Later the primary campaign objective was changed to destroying the Seventh Army. This objective fit the Communist overarching attrition strategy that sought to steadily, systematically annihilate Nationalist forces. After the campaign had begun, following Su Yu's suggestion, the campaign's main objective had been expanded to become destroying all Nationalist armies in the central plains. This reflected a new strategic vision born in the Communist victories in northeastern China in October and November. After destroying the large Nationalist armies in the Northeast, Communist leaders had decided to try to destroy the other Nationalist army groups that were fighting north of the Yangzi River. If this were done, those forces could not be shifted south to man a defensive line along the Yangzi River, and conquering southern China would be easier.

In accordance with this new strategic vision, at roughly the same time the CMC approved Su Yu's proposal to expand the Huai Hai Campaign, it began developing a campaign plan to keep Fu Zuoyi's 500,000-man force in the Beiping-Tianjin area and annihilate it there. The concept for this campaign, called the Ping Jin (Beiping-Tianjin) Campaign, was simple—trap Fu's force by blocking possible routes of withdrawal from the Beiping-Tianjin area and then either attack his force or negotiate his surrender. A major problem was that until the Northeast China Field Army (NECFA) reached the campaign area the Communists would not be able to block Fu's movement south by sea. To keep Jiang Jieshi from becoming alarmed and ordering Fu to do exactly that, when the CMC, in late November, ordered the North China Field Army (NCFA) to start cutting Fu's line of communication northwest of Beijing, large attacks on Nationalist forces were not permitted. Meanwhile, the NECFA was secretly moving as rapidly as possible toward Tianjin and its port of Tanggu to get into position to cut Fu's access to the sea.

In early December the CMC began to feel that Communist successes in the Huai Hai Campaign might also cause Jiang Jieshi to shift Fu Zuoyi's forces to the Yangzi River valley. A message the CMC sent to NECFA commander Lin Biao, political commissar Luo Ronghuan, and chief of staff Liu Yalou at 0200, 11 December indicated that by this time the CMC was less concerned about what was going to happen to the Twelfth Army and Du Yuming's army group than it was about what was going to happen regarding Fu Zuoyi. In this message the CMC shows no doubt about the fate of Huang Wei and Du Yuming's armies: "The 34 divisions southwest of Xuzhou can be completely destroyed in about 10 days."[17] But the message expressed concern that Jiang could still decide to send the many ships concentrated in Shanghai north to evacuate Fu's soldiers from Beiping, Tianjin, and Tanggu.[18]

To keep the destruction of Du Yuming's army group from being the catalyst that pushed Jiang Jieshi to adopt a new strategy and completely redeploy his forces, later on 11 December the CMC decided to order Su Yu not to move quickly to annihilate Du. In a message sent that day to Lin Biao, Luo Ronghuan, and others, the CMC, in its role of providing overall strategic guidance and direction to Communist forces, clearly linked the conduct of the Huai Hai Campaign to the Ping Jin Campaign. The former was to be shaped to support the latter:

8. In order not to make Jiang Jieshi decide to quickly ship his troops in the Beiping-Tianjin area south by sea, we are preparing to order Liu Bocheng, Deng Xiaoping, Chen Yi, and Su Yu to, after wiping out Huang Wei's army, spare what is left of the armies commanded by Du Yuming, those under Qiu Qingquan, Li Mi and Sun Yuanliang (about half of which have already been destroyed), and for two weeks make no dispositions for their final annihilation.

9. To prevent the enemy [Fu Zuoyi] from fleeing toward Qingdao, we are preparing to order our troops in Shandong to mass certain forces to control the section of the Yellow River near Jinan and to make preparations along the Qingdao-Jinan railroad.

10. There is little or no possibility that the enemy will flee towards Xuzhou, Zhengzhou, Xian, or Suiyuan.

11. The main or the only concern is that the enemy might flee by sea. Therefore, in the coming two weeks the general method should be to encircle without attacking or to cut off without encircling.

12. This plan is beyond the enemy's range of expectation. It will be very difficult for him to discern what is happening before you complete your final dispositions.[19]

The morning of 14 December, with the final destruction of Huang Wei's force imminent, the CMC implemented this concept by directing Su Yu to cease attacking Du Yuming: "We suggest that each of your columns now encircling and attacking Du[Yuming], Qiu [Qingquan], and Li[Mi] rest in place for several days. Only conduct defensive operations; do not attack."[20]

Two days later, at 2400, 16 December, the CMC sent Su Yu a message that elaborated its thinking. The ECFA units surrounding Du Yuming were to rest and reorganize for 10 days while CPFA forces were brought in. Then they could attack. In the meantime, to lower Nationalist soldiers' morale, the CMC wanted Su's columns to conduct a political offensive:

(1) Huang Wei's army has been wiped out. All of Li Yannian's army has withdrawn to defenses on the south bank of the Huai River.

(2) All of our units encircling Du Yuming can take approximately 10 days for rest and reorganization. Moreover, the entire strength of the CPFA should be concentrated. Then launch an attack.

(3) Ceaselessly carry out a political offensive against Du, Qiu, and Li. In addition to what your units are doing, we ask you to draft some colloquial broadcast scripts. Change their content every three or four days in accordance with changes in actual battlefield conditions. Then send them to us by radio so that we can revise our broadcasts.[21]

The CMC and the General Front Committee Look Ahead

As these messages indicate, several days before the Twelfth Army's annihilation the CMC already viewed the destruction of that army and Du Yuming's army group as a foregone conclusion. The CMC's decision to have the ECFA support a strategic deception plan by ceasing offensive action against Du was a manifestation of that attitude. So, too, was the following message the CMC sent to Liu Bocheng, Deng Xiaoping, Chen Yi, Su Yu, and Tan Zhenlin on

12 December. In this message the CMC requested that the five of them meet to discuss arrangements for having the ECFA and the CPFA rest, reorganize, and replenish supplies after Du Yuming's force was destroyed. The CMC also wanted them to consider possible future operations, especially crossing the Yangzi River. Once the General Front Committee had reached a consensus, the CMC wanted Liu Bocheng to bring its recommendations to CMC headquarters at Xibaipo for more discussions:

> (1) We request that after Huang Wei's army is destroyed, Comrade Bocheng come to CMC Headquarters to discuss strategic concepts. We estimate that Huang Wei can be completely wiped out within a few days. A longer period will be required before we can wipe out Qiu and Li. We ask that after Huang Wei is destroyed Liu, Chen, Deng, Su, and Tan, all five comrades, convene a meeting of the General Front Committee. The purpose is for you to reach a consensus on plans for rest and reorganization after Qiu and Li have been destroyed, plans for subsequent operations, and plans for the future crossing of the Yangzi River so that the views of the General Front Committee can be presented to the CMC.
>
> If Su Yu and Tan Zhenlin are unable to take time from their main work [commanding forces in the field against Du Yuming] to go to the location of the General Front Committee [CPFA headquarters], then we ask Bocheng to go to Su and Tan's command posts so he can meet with them in person, gain an understanding of conditions in the ECFA, and ask for their opinions. Then he can come to the CMC. We hope that Bocheng can reach the CMC sometime between 20 and 25 December.
>
> (2) Our thoughts on operational concepts for subsequent operations are, more or less, as follows:
>
>   a. After the complete destruction of Huang, Qiu, and Li, the ECFA and the CPFA will rest and reorganize for two months. (This period will be divided into four periods, each half a month long.) Furthermore, the two armies will roughly finish preparing the items needed for a Yangzi River crossing operation (rainwear, money, artillery ammunition, therapeutic medicine, steam powered boats, etc.) They will also finish the first steps in the political education of the troops.
>
>   b. If the enemy forces now positioned between the Yangzi River and the Huai River do not withdraw south of the Yangzi River, the two armies will join in a 1-2 month campaign to wipe out enemy forces between the Huai River and the Yangzi River . . . and establish control over the north bank of the Yangzi River.
>
>   c. After this, another period of appropriate length will be spent completing all of the final preparations for crossing the Yangzi River. Then the river crossing operation will be executed, probably some time in May or June of next year.[22]

Liu, Chen, and Deng felt that fulfilling the CMC's request for the General Front Committee to meet as a group was important. To meet with Su and Tan and not take them away from their command work for very long, after the Twelfth Army was destroyed, the three decided to travel to Su Yu's ECFA headquarters at Caiao for a meeting. After completing tasks that had to be done following the Shuangduiji battle, they left Xiaolizhuang the evening of 16 December and arrived in Caiao the next morning. At about the same time Tan Zhenlin arrived from his Shandong army headquarters.[23] This was the first and only time that all five General Front Committee members would meet together during the campaign. Su briefly described the situation at Chenguanzhuang, but the main topics of discussion were how to cross the Yangzi River and unit reorganization.[24] During a brief break, they posed outside their meeting place for a picture and then resumed the meeting. That evening Liu Bocheng, accompanied by Chen Yi, left for Xibaipo.[25] Deng Xiaoping went back to Xiaolizhuang, and Tan Zhenlin returned to his headquarters. Su Yu remained in place, directing the political offensive against Du Yuming, keeping his force ready to block any attempt by Du to break out and preparing the ECFA to resume combat.

The Political Offensive Against Du Yuming's Army Group

Since the beginning of the Communists' struggle against the Nationalists, political work, which involved spreading the Communist message and attempting to convince enemy officers and soldiers they should join the Communist ranks, was an integral part of Communist military operations. It was the basis for Communist operational principle number 9 that stated that the PLA's main source of manpower was at the front and that most of the captured enemy personnel (80 to 90 percent of the men and a small number of junior officers) could be incorporated into their units.[26] Communist leaders believed their cause was just and that when explained to enemy soldiers it would convince many of them to come over to their side.

The Communists carried out political work both clandestinely and openly. During the Huai Hai Campaign clandestine political work paid off handsomely when Zhang Kexia and He Jifeng led most of the Third Pacification Area to defect at the beginning of the campaign. It also produced the Liao Yunzhou-orchestrated 110th Division's defection that doomed Huang Wei's attempt to break through the encircling forces at Shuangduiji on 27 November. But open political work also produced significant results, both in terms of the number of soldiers who were induced to surrender and those who became Communist soldiers after surrendering. It was viewed as being especially effective when conducted over time against surrounded Nationalist units.

Open political work had been conducted against Du Yuming's army group since its encirclement on 3-4 December. Several thousand Nationalist soldiers had surrendered in the nearly two weeks that had passed since then. However, the intensity of political work, or what might be referred to as psychological operations, increased after 16 December. As part of the new political campaign, on 17 December a radio broadcast urged Du Yuming and his subordinates to surrender. As the following excerpt from this broadcast indicates, the Communists' appeal to surrender asked Du and others to face reality and stop fighting, not only to save their lives but also the lives of many others:

> General Du Yuming, General Qiu Qingquan, General Li Mi and all corps, division and regiment commanders of the two armies under Generals Qiu Qingquan and Li Mi:
>
> You are now at the end of your rope. Huang Wei's army was completely wiped out on the night of the 15th. Li Yannian's army has turned about and fled

south. It is hopeless for you to think of joining them. Are you hoping to break through? How can you break through when the People's Liberation Army is all around? During the last few days you have tried to break through, but what was the result? Your planes and tanks are useless. We have more planes and tanks than you, that is, artillery and explosives which people call our home-made planes and tanks. Aren't they ten times more formidable than your foreign-made planes and tanks? Your army that Sun Yuanliang commanded has already been wiped out. What remains is your two armies, and more than half the men in them have been wounded or captured. You brought along many miscellaneous personnel from various organizations and many young students from Xuzhou and forced them into your army, but how can these people fight? For more than ten days, you have been surrounded layer after layer and have received blow after blow. Your position has shrunk greatly so that you're in a tiny place little more than five kilometers square. So many people are crowded together that a single shell from us can kill a lot of you. Your wounded soldiers and the families who have followed the army are complaining to high heaven. Your soldiers and many of your officers have no stomach for any more fighting. You all . . . should understand and sympathize with the feelings of your subordinates and families, hold their lives dear, find a way out for them as early as possible, and stop sending them to a senseless death.

Now that Huang Wei's army has been completely wiped out and Li Yannian's army has fled towards Bengbu, we are able to concentrate an attacking force several times your strength. This time we have fought for only 40 days, and you have already lost 10 divisions under Huang Baitao, 11 under Huang Wei, 4 under Sun Yuanliang, 4 under Feng Zhian, 2 under Sun Liangcheng, 1 under Liu Ruming, 1 division in Suxian and another in Lingbi—altogether you have lost 34 whole divisions. . . . You have seen with your own eyes the fate of the 3 armies under Huang Baitao, Huang Wei, and Sun Yuanliang. . . . You should . . . immediately order all your troops to lay down their arms and cease resistance. Our army will guarantee the life and personal safety of your high-ranking officers, and all officers and men. This is your only way out. Think it over! If you feel this is the right thing to do, then do it. If you still want to fight another round, then continue fighting. But in the end, you will be finished off anyway.

Headquarters of the Central Plains
People's Liberation Army

Headquarters of the Eastern China
People's Liberation Army[27]

Radio broadcasts such as this were only a small part of the political offensive against Du Yuming's force. The following excerpt from a message the ECFA Political Department sent to the political departments in armies, columns, and divisions shows the wide variety of methods employed to influence the minds of the Nationalists and soldiers at the front:

Important concrete methods [for political work].
1. Front line shouting toward the enemy.

a. First exert every effort to determine the enemy's unit designation, composition, and internal situation. After this, make the actual decision as to the content of what will be shouted toward the enemy.

b. Cadre should take the lead in organizing key educational personnel as appropriate. Using newly captured soldiers (officers are good, also) from the same home area to shout is very effective. So, too, is having liberated personnel shout about their present situation.

c. Pay attention to selecting an opportune moment for shouting. By all means avoid the enemy's officer supervisory units.

d. To enable the enemy to hear clearly, megaphones can be used, shouting can be spread out to different places, or those shouting can move nearer to the enemy positions. Sentences must be spoken slowly and clearly.

e. Individual units have sung songs for the enemy or established a telephone link. These methods can also be adopted as appropriate.

2. Distribution of propaganda items.

a. There should not be too many different kinds, and they should clearly be meaningful. Columns should unify the printing of the actual propaganda items going to the enemy across from them.

b. Small units can be used to penetrate enemy positions and distribute these items. They can be placed on routes traveled by the enemy. Prisoners can pass them out. Kites can spread them around. Rice and steamed buns can be sent. (Do not send too many.) Propaganda shells can be fired. (The 4th Column is making 30-50 60mm mortar propaganda shells every day.)

3. Using prisoners to call for surrender.

a. Take the captured officers, and soldiers and dependents who have been captured, run them through a brief education course, and then send them back to make oral appeals to surrender or have them carry back written calls to surrender. The 68th Regiment used prisoners to cause 110 men to come over in one night.

b. Be careful not to reveal secrets.

c. Establish methods for liaison. Guarantee the safety of prisoners.

4. Put up large size slogans. Use old flags, doors, or mats for putting up big characters. These slogans can be changed frequently.[28]

Shifting the army from conducting armed attacks to political work was not a simple task. Front-line soldiers had to be convinced that shouting, singing, and placing hot buns in no man's land was meaningful and useful. They easily became frustrated when they did not see quick results from all the time and effort spent organizing, preparing, and executing the activities described in the preceding quote. This is why the ECFA Political Department asked subordinate political departments to explain the need for patience. Let soldiers know, the message quoted above stated, that "at present it is impossible to bring about the surrender of a large body of enemy troops, but having small detachments disintegrate across a wide area is good, too."[29] The message also presented examples of impermissible behavior that had occurred as a result of unrealistically high expectations and impatience: "One unit that didn't get any response from their shouting began to dislike doing it. Another unit that received no response from their propaganda shell fired off a real one. These kinds of behavior are improper."[30]

During the first several days of the political offensive, from 16-24 December, the number of Nationalist soldiers who went over to the Communists totaled approximately 2,500, including 16 officers with the rank of second lieutenant or above.[31] As days passed and conditions within the Nationalist pocket worsened, the number of those surrendering steadily increased. Growing hunger was a major contributor to this phenomenon. Du Yuming's force had begun to experience a food shortage shortly after being encircled because, in accordance with Du's assumption that they would move quickly to link up with a base of supply, they had not brought a large amount of food with them from Xuzhou. After the force was surrounded, the amount of food that was airdropped in a single day never even once matched the force's daily requirements.

As Du's chief of staff for operations, Wen Qiang, noted, "on the best day, the food that was airdropped was only enough to feed 10,000 soldiers."[32] The food would be divided to give 30,000 soldiers one meal in a day, but that was still far below what was needed.[33] Yet, it was something. After the airdrops were halted by bad weather on 20 December, the food shortage quickly became a crisis. Soldiers killed and ate army horses for food and ate wild grass, tree bark, and winter wheat sprouts to satisfy their hunger.[34] Another problem was that fuel for cooking and keeping warm was running out. After all the trees in the pocket were chopped down and every house had been taken apart searching for wood, soldiers even dug up graves and burned coffins.[35] Looking around, Wen Qiang felt the pocket had become "hell on earth."[36] It was only natural that the passage of time created the desire to escape this hell in more and more soldiers.

With the morale of Du's force declining and the number of Nationalist soldiers surrendering on the rise, the CMC began to think that perhaps it would be possible to eliminate Du Yuming's force without a final climactic battle. The afternoon of 28 December the CMC sent a message to Su Yu and Tan Zhenlin directing them to increase the tempo of the ECFA's political offensive and try to bring about the complete internal collapse of Du Yuming's armies. It was hoped that something similar to what had happened at the surrounded city of Changchun in Northeast China could be repeated. There the surrender of one corps had led Nationalist commander Zheng Dongguo to surrender his entire command to the NECFA on 19 October. However, this CMC message also made it clear that while expanding the political offensive, the ECFA should still be preparing for other eventualities:

> Now the situation of Du Yuming's force is worse than that of Zheng Dongguo's force at Changchun. Hunger and cold are pressing against them. The surrender of large groups is increasing daily. If the speed and scale of the enemy's internal disintegration is tending to increase, perhaps in ten or twenty days the result will be the same as at Changchun. You should now exert the utmost efforts to strengthen the political offensive. Using the name of every possible position (yours, each column and division commander, and the commands of officers who have surrendered), write letters to enemy commanders at all levels and openly disseminate them in order to stir up the great mass of soldiers. Do this work openly. There are three possibilities before you:
> 1. Eliminate the enemy with a strong attack.
> 2. Eliminate the enemy partially through his own disintegration and partially through a strong attack.

3. The enemy's disintegration will develop to the point of complete, mass surrender.

Please pay close attention to enemy developments and keep us informed. Liu and Chen have arrived.[37]

The ECFA and CPFA Make Ready to Resume Combat

While conducting the political offensive against Du Yuming's force, the ECFA was also energetically carrying out a program to rest its soldiers, reorganize units, and replenish supplies. Some columns did this while on the line around the Chenguanzhuang pocket. Others did it in their positions as reserves behind the front lines. To the south the CPFA was resting and reorganizing in a triangular area bounded by Suxian on the east, Mengcheng to the southwest, and Guoyang to the northwest, except for five regiments from the Yu-Wan-Su Military District that were on watch along the Fei River north of Bengbu. Its mission was to serve as a general reserve, preparing to either reinforce the ECFA in fighting with Du Yuming or block any new effort by Li Yannian and Liu Ruming to advance north from Bengbu.[38]

After 40 days of continuous operations, the troops in both field armies needed a respite from combat and marching. They were tired; they had endured much. As a way to reward his soldiers for their efforts, on 16 December Su Yu asked the CMC for permission to give each ECFA soldier one-half kilogram of pork and five packs of cigarettes. Those soldiers who did not smoke would receive items of equivalent value. On 17 December the CMC agreed to Su's request and also extended this extra ration to CPFA soldiers.[39]

The unit reorganization that took place during the period was also important. Casualties had been heavy, especially in the lower command ranks, and a major effort was needed to restore combat units to full strength. During the fighting up through 15 December, the ECFA had suffered 73,300 casualties.[40] Only 12,700 of those casualties had returned to their units, meaning that more than 60,000 soldiers and leading cadre who had started the campaign needed to be replaced just to stay even.[41]

To replace the cadre in units of regimental size and smaller, the ECFA drew on many sources. More than 1,000 cadre were taken from column headquarters staffs, political departments, logistics departments, and units directly under column command. Training regiment cadre were assigned to combat units. Ordinary soldiers who had distinguished themselves were promoted. There were even cases where Seventh Army soldiers taken during the fighting at Nianzhuangxu served as platoon and company commanders.[42] In addition, 1,500 low-level cadre were brought in from military districts in Shandong province.[43]

Replacements for the rank-and-file soldier came from two sources. One source was the militia units in each military district. In mid-December 24,000 soldiers from military districts in eastern China were brought into the ECFA.[44] The other source was continuously infusing captured Nationalist soldiers. As of 16 December the total number of Nationalist soldiers the ECFA captured exceeded 100,000.[45] A large percentage of these entered the ECFA because in late December, despite the losses and relatively small number of militia soldiers who had entered the force, the ECFA's strength stood at 460,000, which was 40,000 more than when the campaign started.[46]

Due to the large number of former Nationalist soldiers who had been placed in the ranks and because the civil war was about to enter a new phase, with the old ECFA veterans about to be sent to places far from their homes in Shandong and Jiangsu, the rest and reorganization period included a political education campaign. The campaign extolled the Chinese Communist Party's (CCP's) virtues and explained the benefits that all ordinary Chinese would gain when the Communist revolution was completed. It explained not only why it was important to achieve total victory in the Huai Hai Campaign but also why it was necessary for the soldiers to fight to completely overthrow the Nationalist government. The campaign aimed at motivating soldiers and preparing them psychologically for the battles that lay ahead. It also called for greater discipline and establishing a reporting system that would give the CMC and CCP Central Committee more information on what was occurring in the field and more control.[47]

In conjunction with political education and mobilization, military training and preparations to resume combat were also carried out. The large influx of new personnel into units made this especially important. Meetings were held to discuss battlefield experiences and seriously examine artillery-infantry coordination, antitank tactics, methods for attacking bunkers, and ways to counter gas attacks. Small training exercises were conducted. All the while, digging approach trenches and lateral trenches continued. So, too, did reconnaissance and planning for an all-out attack on Du Yuming's force.[48]

Du Yuming's Preparations to Break Out

On 29 December the skies over Chenguanzhuang and Nanjing cleared and the airdrop of supplies to Du Yuming's army group resumed. The good weather also allowed Shu Shicun and Dong Mingde to finally take the breakout plan to Nanjing. Shu also carried with him Du's letter, written 10 days earlier, asking Jiang Jieshi to order a breakout only as a last resort.

Jiang did not respond directly to Du's letter, but the following day he sent a message to Du expressing concern for his health and offering to send an airplane to bring him back to Nanjing for treatment. Du replied that his chronic ailments were making it more difficult to get around but that he would not abandon tens of thousands of loyal officers and men. Once more he appealed to Jiang, "Please your excellency, adopt my first alternative [concentrating forces for a decisive battle]. As long as I still have breath I will serve you faithfully."[49]

On 1 January Jiang Jieshi issued a statement calling for Nationalist-Communist negotiations to bring about a peaceful end to the civil war. Just maybe, Du thought, this might be the opening to political developments that could save his armies from destruction.[50] However, on 3 January Jiang directed him to prepare for a breakout operation. The operation was supposed to be launched following three full days of airdrops that were to begin on 5 January. Du asked for a delay because his troops were still hungry and lacked sufficient ammunition. Jiang agreed to airdrop supplies for one extra day but told Du that after that he absolutely had to execute the operation.[51]

Destroying Du Yuming's Army Group

As discussed earlier, halting the ECFA's armed attacks against Du Yuming's army group and moving to a political offensive against his force served three purposes. First, it contributed to the strategic deception effort that supported the Ping Jin Campaign. Second, it gave the ECFA and CPFA a much-needed opportunity to rest, reorganize, and replenish. Third, it added impetus to the internal disintegration of Du's armies. Regarding this last point, the political offensive was a way to keep psychological pressure on the enemy even while it rested. The results it produced were significant enough to cause the CMC, as its message of 28 December indicates, to think that the political offensive might just be sufficient to eliminate Du's force.

The political offensive, however, took time; its progress could not be accurately measured; and there was no way to know when, or even if, it would actually reach its ultimate objective. As a result, once the need to not shock the Nationalists so hard that Jiang Jieshi would order Fu Zuoyi to abandon Beiping and move south had passed, and the army was well on the way to finishing its rest and reorganization, field commanders began to press for a return to direct military action against Du. On 26 December, with the NECFA in position to block Fu Zuoyi's route to the sea and the NCFA and NECFA having recently combined to defeat large Nationalist forces along his possible routes of withdrawal from Beijing toward the northwest, Su Yu proposed to the CMC that the ECFA prepare to attack Du Yuming on 5 January.[52] The CMC's response was its message on 28 December asking him to give the political offensive a chance for 10 more days to see what would happen.[53] However, in that message the CMC may have been exposing its own doubts about what the political offensive would produce when, in laying out the possible ways by which Du's force would be eliminated, it placed "a strong attack" by the ECFA at the top of its list.[54]

Nationalist airdrops resumed into the Chenguanzhuang pocket on 29 December, stimulating Su Yu to once again propose to the CMC that he be allowed to attack Du. He felt that after a 10-day interruption in airdrops Du's army group was especially weak and it would be good to attack before more food and ammunition could be delivered.[55] On 31 December he sent a proposed plan of attack, complete with troop dispositions and objectives, to the CMC.[56] His concept was to put pressure on Second Army positions on the western side of the pocket while columns on the northern, eastern, and southern sides pushed into the pocket. His first objectives were to separate the weaker Thirteenth Army from the stronger Second Army and cut the Thirteenth Army in two. This would establish the conditions for destroying the Thirteenth Army. Once that goal was achieved, he would move immediately to attack the Second Army.

At 0200, 2 January the CMC approved Su Yu's proposal.[57] At 2400 the same day ECFA Headquarters issued its order for a general attack. The time set for the start of the attack was 1600, 6 January.[58] In case of overcast and rainy weather, the time would be moved up to 1300 the same day.[59]

For the attack Su Yu organized the 10 columns around the pocket into three groups, the eastern, southern, and northern groups. The eastern group consisted of the 3d, 4th, 10th, and Bohai Columns under command of 10th Column commander Song Shilun and his political commissar, Liu Peishan. The southern group contained the 2d, 8th, and 11th Columns and three military district regiments under command of Wei Luoqing, with Ji Luo as political commissar. The northern group consisted of the 1st, 9th, and 12th Columns and two military district regiments under command of Tan Zhenlin, with Wang Jianan as political commissar.[60] The ST Column's 105mm howitzer batteries were divided into four units and allocated to support these three groups.[61]

Behind these front-line columns several more columns were deployed in a second ring around the pocket.[62] The XXXV Corps was in the north attached to Tan Zhenlin's command.[63] Interestingly, as another example of the ECFA's organizational agility and command flexibil-

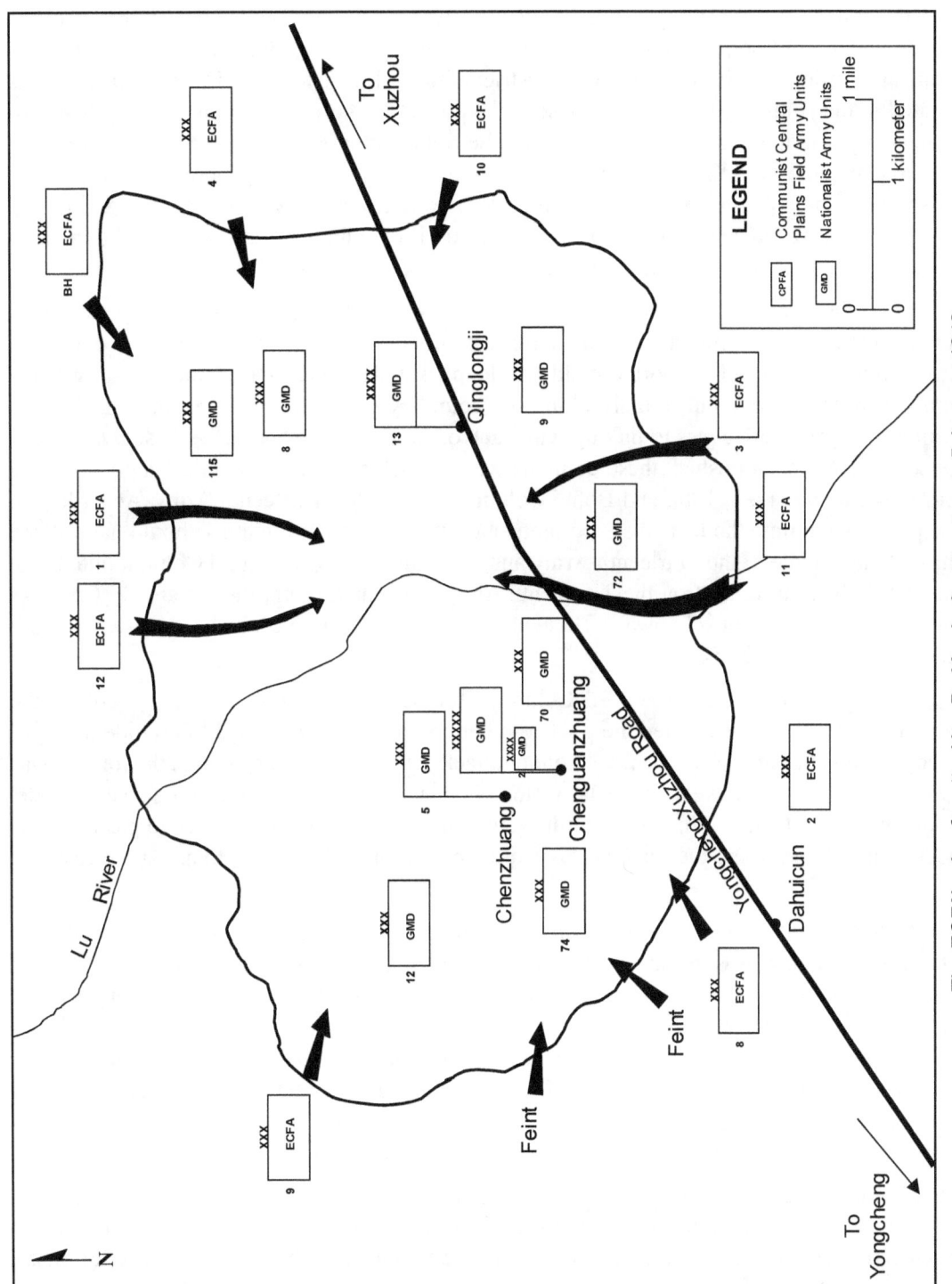

The ECFA's plan for attacking Du Yuming's army group, 5 January 1948.

259

ity that was characteristic at this time, the XXXV Corps artillery was attached to the eastern group's Bohai Column.[64] The Luzhongnan Column, which had a Yu-Wan-Su Military District division and the ECFA cavalry regiment attached, was in the Yongcheng area southwest of the pocket under Wei Luoqing's command.[65] The Liangguang Column, with the ECFA guard regiment and a militia unit from the Third subdistrict of the Ji-Lu-Yu Military District attached, was located in the Huitinglou-Xiayi area west of the pocket.[66] The 13th Column was southwest of Yongcheng behind the Luzhongnan Column, the Sixth Column was in the Suixikou area, and the 7th Column was in Xiaoxian.[67] All of the columns in the second ring were to maintain close liaison with the columns in front of them so they were aware of what the enemy was doing. Their mission was to be prepared to respond quickly if Du Yuming's forces attempted to break out and coordinate with the front-line columns to block and destroy them.

At the heart of Su Yu's concept of operations for the initial attack was the 3d Column's thrust to the north-northwest from the southeastern side of the pocket and the 1st Column's thrust to the south from the northern side of the pocket. The lines upon which these two columns were to advance ran roughly along the boundary between the Thirteenth and Second Armies. Their objective was to link up with each other and thereby separate these two armies. Once that was accomplished, these columns would block any efforts by Qiu Qingquan to aid Li Mi and help the 4th, 10th, and Bohai Columns destroy the Thirteenth Army. According to the plan, by the time the 1st and 3d Columns met, the three other columns should have sliced through the middle of the Thirteenth Army and reached the 1st Column/3d Column line. If not needed in the fight to destroy the Thirteenth Army, after linking up, the 1st and 3d Columns were to turn west and attack toward Chenguanzhuang, the location of the headquarters of both the army group and the Second Army.[68]

To help maintain the 1st and 3d Columns' forward momentum after they breached the Nationalist front and penetrated the pocket, other columns were assigned to provide flank security against possible Second Army counterattacks. The northern group's 12th Column was to penetrate the pocket west of the 1st Column's penetration and advance on a route parallel to that of the 1st Column. In the south, the southern group's 11th Column was to push into the pocket in the area where the Lu River exited the pocket and advance north along the east side of the river.[69]

As for the rest of the front-line columns, the 2d Column's main body, which was to the left of the 11th Column, was to stay in place to defend against a breakout to the southwest. On the 2d Column's left, the 8th Column's main body was to attack toward Chenguanzhuang while a portion of the column coordinated with part of the western group's 9th Column to conduct a feint toward certain LXXIV Corps positions west of Chenguanzhuang. The 9th Column's main body was to attack villages northwest of Chenguanzhuang. These attacks and feints against the portion of the pocket's perimeter that Second Army units manned were shaping operations in support of the main effort, the attacks against the Thirteenth Army.[70]

In addition to designing a plan that had columns supporting columns as a way to build and maintain momentum in decisive areas, Su Yu also presented a way for columns to develop momentum within their own attacks. He used infiltration to support penetration. The following excerpt from his order shows his vision of how infiltration would increase operational tempo, thereby not only aiding a column's penetration but also magnifying its effects. Infiltration thus became a way to introduce a Sunzian *qi* (maneuver) force into the close confines of the Chenguanzhuang pocket. Like Sunzi, Su Yu saw that by disrupting the enemy rear a *qi* force would accelerate the advance to victory:

> In order to swiftly insert forces deep into the enemy rear to create confusion and cut communication links between enemy positions, while at the same time keeping its main body focused on its assault, each column should select and organize a group of well-trained, highly competent soldiers (a battalion or regiment carrying ample ammunition and two days of prepared food) who, at the very time that the attack begins, will search out gaps in the defenses and then boldly advance into the enemy rear. There they will establish control over key strongpoints and resolutely block and wipe out enemy units coming from all directions, no matter whether they are drawing back in disarray, counterattacking, or moving somewhere as reinforcements. This will also make it easy for them to join with the main body in quickly rounding up and annihilating the enemy.[71]

The general attack began on schedule at 1600, 6 January following a one-half-hour artillery barrage. That night 13 villages around the pocket perimeter were taken, and conditions were set for strong attacks the next day. On 7 January, in the face of the 3d and 10th Columns' advances, Li Mi abandoned his headquarters at Qinglongji and fled west with his staff into the Second Army sector. By the end of the day more than 20 villages had been taken and what remained of the Thirteenth Army was in disarray. Heavy losses had also been inflicted on the Second Army's LXXII Corps, which had been positioned east of the Lu River on the south side of the pocket. What was left of that corps was also withdrawing to the west. In less than two days Su Yu's force had achieved what he had estimated would take three to seven days.[72]

The Thirteenth Army's rapid collapse was also a surprise to Du Yuming. It ruined his defensive structure and exposed the Second Army's entire eastern flank. This meant the Second Army's ability to respond to attacks against the northwest, west, and southwest sides of the pocket was greatly reduced. Furthermore, Du's ability to exercise command and control and re-establish a coherent defense was diminishing by the hour. Du did not know the location of units that were withdrawing under pressure, and his communications system was breaking down.

On 8 January the compression of the pocket had progressed so that the east side of the pocket no longer had room for all four columns of the eastern group to operate. Because of this and because there were indications that the Nationalists were going to try to break out to the west, Su Yu decided to shift the Bohai Column from the east side of the pocket to the west side. It was placed under southern group command and sent into the line between the 8th and 9th Columns.[73]

Despite Nationalist efforts to aid Du Yuming by increasing bombing and strafing sorties, on 9 January ECFA advances continued. By nightfall the 3d, 4th, and 10th Columns were all nearing the heart of the Nationalist command, the villages of Chenguanzhuang and Chenzhuang. Chenguanzhuang was the site of army group and Second Army headquarters. Chenzhuang, a village near Chenguanzhuang to the northwest, was the location of the Second Army's V Corps headquarters. During the evening of 9 January Du Yuming and Qiu Qingquan abandoned Chenguanzhuang and went to Chenzhuang to meet with Li Mi and V Corps commander Xiong

Xiaosan. Due to the rapidly deteriorating situation, Qiu, Li, and Xiong advocated that Du immediately order a breakout. Du wanted to have the breakout operation begin in the morning when the air force could provide air support, but after a heated argument with his subordinates, he agreed to their request.[74] The units that could be reached were ordered to break out to the west, and Du sent the following message to Jiang Jieshi: "All units are disorganized. It is impossible to hold out until tomorrow. Our only option is to break out separately this evening."[75]

The Nationalist attempt to break out was a complete failure. A few officers and soldiers, for example, Li Mi, did make it through the surrounding net and eventually found their way to Nationalist lines in the south. However, for practical purposes, one can say the entire force was either killed, like Qiu Qingquan, or captured, like Du Yuming. Behind them, that part of Du Yuming's army group that had not received the order to break out met the same fate. Before dawn on 10 January the 10th Column entered Chenguanzhuang and the 4th Column entered Chenzhuang. During the next several hours these two columns and those attacking from other directions swept across what remained of the pocket. By 1000 the fighting was basically over with only a few scattered Nationalist units still offering resistance.[76] By 1600 these remnants had been wiped out and the battle to destroy Du Yuming's army group was officially over.[77] The Huai Hai Campaign had ended.

Notes

1. Du Yuming, "*Huaihai zhanyi shimo*" [The Huai Hai Campaign From Beginning to End], in *Huaihai zhanyi qinli ji* [A Record of Personal Experiences During the Huaihai Campaign], Zhongguo renmin zhengzhi xieshang huiyi quanguo weiyuanhui wenshi ziliao yanjiu weiyuanhui [The Historical Materials Research Committee of the National Committee of the Chinese People's Political Consultative Conference], eds. (Beijing: Wenshi ziliao chubanshe, 1983), hereafter cited as *QLJ*, 41.

2. Wen Qiang, "*Xuzhou 'jiaozong' zhihuibu de hunluan*" [The Confusion in the Xuzhou 'Bandit Suppression Headquarters' Command Post], *QLJ*, 99.

3. Du Yuming, *QLJ*, 41.

4. Ibid.

5. Ibid.

6. Ibid.

7. Ibid.

8. Ibid.

9. Ibid.

10. Qiu Weida, "*Di qishisi jun de zaici beijian*" [The Second Destruction of the LXXIV Corps], *QLJ*, 402.

11. Ibid., 403.

12. Ibid.

13. Ibid.

14. Ibid.

15. Ibid., 402.

16. Du Yuming, *QLJ*, 42.

17. "*Guanyu Pingjin diqu de xingshi ji bushu*" [Concerning the Situation in the Ping Jin Area and Troop Deployments There], in *Mao Zedong junshi wenji* [A Collection of Mao Zedong's Military Documents (Beijing: Junshi kexue chubanshe, 1993), vol. 5, 358, hereafter cited as *MZDMD*.

18. Ibid.

19. "*Guanyu Pingjin zhanyi de zuozhan fangzhen*" [Concerning the Concept of Operations for the Ping Jin Campaign], *MZDMD*, 362.

20. "*Weijian Du Yuming Qiu Qingquan Li Mi de gezong zhi zuo fangyu bu zuo gongji*" [Every Column Engaged in Surrounding and Wiping Out Du Yuming, Qiu Qingquan, and Li Mi Will Only Defend, Not Attack], *MZDMD*, 401.

21. "*Xiang Du Yuming Qiu Qingquan Li Mi bu lianxu jinxing zhengzhi gongshi*" [Continuously Carry Out a Political Offensive Against the Forces of Du Yuming, Qiu Qingquan, and Li Mi], *MZDMD*, 410.

22. "*Dui jinhou zuozhan fangzhen de yijian*" [Thoughts on Future Operational Concepts], *MZDMD*, 382-83.

23. He Xiaohuan, Fu Jijun, and Shi Zhengxian, *Huaihai zhanyi shi* [A History of the Huai Hai Campaign] (Shanghai: Renmin chubanshe, 1983), 181, hereafter cited as *HHZYS*.

24. Ibid., 182.

25. Ibid.

26. Mao Zedong, "The Present Situation and Our Tasks," *Selected Works of Mao Tse-tung* (Peking: Foreign Languages Press, 1967), vol. 4, 162, hereafter cited as *SWM*. See also "Strategy for the Second Year of the War of Liberation," *SWM*, vol. 4, 145.

27. "*Duncu Du Yuming deng touxiang shu*" [Message Urging Du Yuming and Others to Surrender], in *Huaihai zhanyi* [The Huai Hai Campaign], Zhonggong zhongyang dangshi ziliao zhengji weiyuanhui [Chinese Communist Party Central Committee's Committee for the Collection of Party Historical Material], eds. (Beijing: Zhonggong dangshi ziliao chubanshe, 1988), vol. 1, 239-40, hereafter cited as *HHZY*.

28. "*Huadong yezhanjun zhengzhibu guanyu zhuajin shiji dali kaizhan zhengzhi gongshi de zhishi*"["Directive From the ECFA Political Department Concerning Seizing This Opportune Moment and Vigorously Developing a Political Offensive], *HHZY*, vol. 1, 250-51.

29. Ibid., 250.

30. Ibid.

31. Ibid., 249.

32. Wen Qiang, *QLJ*, 98.

33. Ibid.

34. Du Yuming, *QLJ*, 44.

35. Wen Qiang, *QLJ*, 99.

36. Ibid., 98

37. "*Zhongyang junwei guanyu ying dali kaizhan zhengzhi gongshi zhi Su Yu, Tan Zhenlin de dianbao*" [Telegram From the CMC to Su Yu and Tan Zhenlin Saying They Should Vigorously Expand the Political Offensive], *HHZY*, vol. 1, 252.

38. *Zhongguo renmin jiefangjun quanguo jiefang zhanjeng shi* [The History of the Chinese PLA's War to Liberate the Entire Country], Wang Miaosheng, ed. (Beijing: Junshi kexue chubanshe, 1997), vol. 4, 347, hereafter cited as *QJZS*.

39. Ibid., 351.

40. Ibid., 347.

41. Ibid.

42. Ibid., 348.

43. Ibid.

44. Ibid.

45. Ibid.

46. Ibid.

47. Ibid., 349-50.

48. Ibid., 350-51.

49. Du Yuming, *QLJ*, 45.

50. Ibid., 46.

51. Ibid., 47.

52. "*Zhongyang junwei guanyu ying dali kaizhan zhengzhi gongshi zhi Su Yu, Tan Zhenlin de dianbao*" [Telegram From the CMC to Su Yu and Tan Zhenlin Saying They Should Vigorously Expand the Political Offensive], *HHZY*, vol. 1, 252.

53. Ibid.

54. Ibid.

55. *QJZS*, vol. 4, 357.

56. Ibid.

57. Ibid.

58. Ibid.

59. "*Huadong yezhanjun quanjian Du Yuming jituan de mingling*" [Order for the ECFA to Completely Annihilate Du Yuming's Army Group], *HHZY*, vol. 1, 255-56.

60. Ibid., 254-55.

61. *QJZS*, vol. 4, 359.

62. For the listing of these units and their placement, see *QJZS*, vol. 4, 359.

63. "*Huadong yezhanjun quanjian Du Yuming jituan de mingling*" [Order for the ECFA to Completely Annihilate Du Yuming's Army Group], *HHZY*, vol. 1, 254. The XXXV Corps' appearance in the ECFA order of battle deserves an explanation. Nationalist units that revolted (voluntarily defected) intact had their Nationalist unit designations changed, but their original organizational structure did not change. The XXXV Corps was the former Nationalist XCVI Corps that had defected intact under command of Wu Huawen on 19 September during the ECFA campaign to take Jinan. Wu was still the commander of this corps at this time.

64. Ibid.

65. Ibid., 255.

66. *HHZYS*, 206.

67. Ibid.

68. *QJZS*, vol. 4, 358.

69. Ibid., 358-59.

70. Ibid.

71. "*Huadong yezhanjun quanjian Du Yuming jituan de mingling*" [Order for the ECFA to Completely Annihilate Du Yuming's Army Group], *HHZY*, vol. 1, 256.

72. *QJZS*, vol. 4, 360.

73. Ibid.

74. Ibid.

75. Du Yuming, *QLJ*, 44.

76. "*Huadong yezhanjun silingbu guanyu Huaihai zhanyi jingguo gaishu*" [The ECFA Headquarters' General Description of What Happened During the Huai Hai Campaign], *HHZY*, vol. 1, 309.

77. Ibid.

Conclusion

As water conforms to the shape of the ground in setting its flow, an army
follows the form of the enemy to establish its victory. In war there is no
constant situation or unchanging form. The commander who has the ability to stay
in step with every change the enemy makes and gain victory can be called divine.

—Sunzi, *The Art of War*

Epilogue

Victory in the Huai Hai Campaign was followed days later by victory in the Ping Jin Campaign. On 14 January Northeast China Field Army (NECFA) units attacked Tianjin, and the next day the 130,000 Nationalist troops defending the city surrendered. On 21 January Fu Zuoyi, well aware of Du Yuming's fate, agreed to surrender the 200,000 soldiers he still commanded in and around Beiping. This marked the elimination of the last major Nationalist force north of the Yangzi River. The next Communist step would be to cross that river and take the war to Nationalist-controlled southern China.

On 21 April the Second Field Army (new designation for the Central Plains Field Army) and the Third Field Army (new designation for the East China Field Army) crossed the Yangzi on a 500-km front centered about 100 km west of Nanjing. By the end of the day Communist forces were on the south bank in force and were moving toward key cities. Nanjing was taken on 23 April, Hangzhou on 3 May, and Shanghai on 27 May. In early May part of the Fourth Field Army (new designation for the NECFA) opened a new front in the Wuhan area. During the next several months the Communist armies continued to advance against little opposition, and on 1 October 1949, with most of China under Communist control, Mao Zedong proclaimed the establishment of the People's Republic of China. By the end of the year the Nationalist government had fled to Taiwan, and the civil war on the mainland was basically over.

The Huai Hai Campaign's contribution to this rapid turn of events was immense. By destroying five armies and killing or capturing 550,000 troops during the campaign, the Communist forces made it impossible for the Nationalists to offer more than sporadic and ineffectual resistance when Communist armies crossed the Yangzi and pushed into southern China. When Su Yu had proposed expanding the Huai Hai Campaign to destroy the Nationalist armies in the central plains, he had done so with the idea of making the Yangzi River crossing operation and the advance into southern China easier. Events proved that his assessment had been correct. Victory in the Huai Hai Campaign had produced the military conditions that made those subsequent operations so successful. It was the decisive campaign in the Communists' drive to gain their ultimate strategic goal—political power.

During the first decade of Communist rule in China, the members of the Huai Hai Campaign Front Committee—Chen Yi, Liu Bocheng, Deng Xiaoping, Su Yu, and Tan Zhenlin—all received major responsibilities. For Su Yu and Liu Bocheng, their work was primarily in national defense. Deng Xiaoping rose higher in the Chinese Communist Party (CCP) bureaucracy. Tan Zhenlin held the post of Jiangsu Provincial Governor for several years and then became a leader in promoting agricultural collectivization. Chen Yi went from being mayor of Shanghai to being China's Foreign Minister. Later these men's careers had their ups and some serious downs, but those events lie beyond the scope of this study.

As for the fate of Du Yuming and Huang Wei, after their capture they were tried as war criminals and sentenced to long prison terms. Because of family connections, Du was released in 1959 after 10 years of confinement. Huang Wei would not be released from prison until 1975. After their release from prison, both men were appointed to positions in the Chinese People's Political Consultative Conference, a united front organization the CCP led. There they encouraged the reunification of Taiwan with mainland China and conducted research on Nationalist history. Du died in Beijing in May 1981 at the age of 76. Huang died in Beijing in March 1989 at the age of 85.

The Huai Hai Campaign as Operational Art

The introduction of this study discussed the increasing attention being given to the operational level of war and the practice of operational art in U.S. Army doctrinal literature. In that literature, operational art is described as a way to ensure that military actions take place in the best sequence, use resources effectively, and achieve objectives with the least possible loss and risk. It is portrayed as a way to link the planning and execution of campaigns, major operations, and battles to produce synergistic effects. By encouraging operational-level commanders to look deeper in space and time, operational art is supposed to help them develop visions and shape events to their advantage. These many benefits have made operational art an increasingly important doctrinal concept.

One of the purposes of this study is to examine the Huai Hai Campaign as an example of operational art. Its intent is to provide information that illustrates what operational art means and shows how it can contribute to conducting war at the operational level. This campaign, because of its large scale, complexity, length, and strategic significance clearly represents operational-level warfare. That having been said, the People's Liberation Army (PLA) commanders who directed the campaign were, by definition, practitioners of operational art. This study discusses what those commanders did as such practitioners. It describes how they evaluated current situations, developed visions for the future, designed plans to create and seize opportunities, and commanded operations in the pursuit of desired objectives. The extensive quotes from messages between the commanders in the field and between those commanders and their superiors at the strategic level are presented to help readers better understand the careful thought and analysis that lay behind the operational art that Su Yu, Liu Bocheng, and their fellow commanders displayed. Those messages bring us as close as we can get to the heart of operational art—the invisible process of creative thought that occurs within a commander's mind as his instincts, intuition, knowledge, and experience interact to form responses to the challenges he faces.

The Huai Hai Campaign and Sunzi's *The Art of War*

In addition to looking at the practice of operational art during the Huai Hai Campaign, this study also examines the campaign from the perspective of the ideas and concepts contained in Sunzi's *The Art of War*. The result confirms both *The Art of War*'s continuing influence on Chinese military thought and Sunzi's position as an advocate of operational art. As noted in the introduction, the expression "moving the enemy" that is part of the title of this work is taken from Sunzi's statement, "The expert in battle moves the enemy and is not moved by him."* This sentence captures the essence of what operational art seeks to achieve. It implies the ability to look ahead, to visualize the possibilities inherent in the flow of events, to shape events so possibilities become opportunities, and to grasp those opportunities for one's benefit. This is what Su Yu, Liu Bocheng, and others did as they fashioned a series of battles that produced a great victory. Looking into the future, they saw what could be accomplished by isolating enemy armies and forcing the Nationalists to move. By seizing and maintaining the initiative, they turned their visions into reality.

This study presents many instances in which the operational concepts PLA commanders developed and their actions during the campaign are similar to the thought contained in *The Art of War*. Su Yu's original concept of operations for the Huai Hai Campaign, his plan for extending ECFA operations east of Xuzhou, and Liu Bocheng's plan for encircling the Twelfth Army all emphasized leveraging the *shi* (energy/momentum) existing in a situation and using a combination of *zheng* (fixing/holding) and *qi* (maneuver/surprise) forces to keep an enemy off balance. Both Sunzi and the PLA commanders of 1948 placed great importance on information, knowledge, deception, speed, timing, logistics, and numerical superiority at the time and place of attack. They dealt extensively with human psychology and how to motivate and manipulate others. The PLA commanders certainly followed Sunzi's advice to capture soldiers and use them in their own armies. That was not only PLA practice, it was also PLA doctrine.

To a real extent, then, the Huai Hai Campaign can be viewed as the product of *The Art of War* meeting "operational art." It was operational art with Sunzian qualities or, some might say, operational art with Chinese characteristics. This raises an interesting issue because, given the completely Chinese origin of *The Art of* War, some might argue that the Sunzian operational art that Su Yu and Liu Bocheng displayed represents a Chinese way of war. Perhaps it does. But the more important point to be raised is the high standard for executing operational art that Su Yu, Liu Bocheng, and their fellow commanders set. The quote at the beginning of the conclusion expresses Sunzi's view that in war the only constant is change. It refers to the difficulty of staying in step with the enemy. As this study has shown, Su Yu, Liu Bocheng, and their fellow commanders not only did an excellent job of staying in step with the enemy, but they also were usually a step or two ahead of the enemy. They accomplished this by practicing operational art at the highest level. They accomplished this by being extremely competent professionally. This is another lesson to be learned from the Huai Hai Campaign, especially as the U.S. Army pursues engagement with the PLA.

*Sunzi, *The Art of War*, Roger T. Ames, trans. (New York: Ballantine Books, 1993), 123.

Dr. Gary J. Bjorge is a historian in the Department of Military History, U.S. Army Command and General Staff College (USACGSC), Fort Leavenworth, Kansas. A graduate of the University of Minnesota—Twin Cities with a B.A. in international relations, he earned M.A. degrees in Chinese, political science, and library science and a Ph.D. in Chinese language and literature from the University of Wisconsin—Madison. He served for several years as an officer with the U.S. Navy in the Far East, worked as the East Asian bibliographer at the University of Wisconsin—Madison and the University of Kansas, and also taught at the University of Kansas. He is the author of numerous articles and reviews on military history topics and the monograph *Merrill's Marauders: Combined Operations in Northern Burma in 1944.* Several of his English translations of Chinese short stories have appeared in anthologies of modern Chinese literature. Dr. Bjorge has been on the USACGSC faculty since September 1984.

Synopsis of *Leavenworth Paper 22*

The Chinese civil war was the third largest war of the 20th century and the most significant war since the end of World War II. Within this war the Huai Hai Campaign was the largest and most decisive campaign that Communist forces conducted. Communist victory in this campaign, which began on 6 November 1948 and ended on 10 January 1949, determined the outcome of the war. By destroying five Nationalist armies and killing or capturing more than 500,000 Nationalist soldiers during the course of the campaign the Communists made it impossible for the Nationalists to keep them from moving across the Yangzi River and occupying southern China.

This study examines the Huai Hai Campaign as an example of operational-level warfare as described in the 2001 version of U.S. Army Field Manual 3-0, *Operations*. It also examines the campaign from the perspective of the military thought contained in the ancient Chinese military classic, *The Art of War*, and the Communist operational doctrine in effect at the time of the campaign. What emerges is a picture of what operational art can contribute to warfare. Communist commanders consistently maintained an awareness of the war situation as a whole and continually ensured that the objectives of their military operations were linked to strategic goals. The study shows that Su Yu, the acting commander of the East China Field Army, was an excellent practitioner of operational art and a general who was willing to speak out against military operations that would not contribute to achieving political, social, or economic goals.

The study contains background material on the Communist military forces that fought the campaign and the commanders who led them in the field. Using messages sent between various Communist headquarters, the study describes and analyzes the operational decisions that were made. Much of this material has not appeared before in English. This enables readers to gain a fresh appreciation for the professional competence of military men who were among the founding generation of the People's Liberation Army and later played significant roles in building the military strength of the People's Republic of China.

www.ingramcontent.com/pod-product-compliance
Lightning Source LLC
Chambersburg PA
CBHW082109230426
43671CB00015B/2646